The publisher gratefully acknowledges the generous contribution to this book provided by Sukey and Gil Garcetti, Michael P. Roth, and the Roth Family Foundation.

# What Is This Thing Called Jazz?

**MUSIC OF THE AFRICAN DIASPORA**

Edited by Samuel A. Floyd Jr.

# What Is This Thing Called Jazz?

African American Musicians as
Artists, Critics, and Activists

**ERIC PORTER**

UNIVERSITY OF CALIFORNIA PRESS

BERKELEY    LOS ANGELES    LONDON

University of California Press
Berkeley and Los Angeles, California

University of California Press, Ltd.
London, England

© 2002 by the Regents of the University of California

Part of chapter 2 was first published as "'Dizzy Atmosphere': The Challenge of Bebop," in *American Music* 17,
no. 4 (Winter 1999): 422–446.

For acknowledgments of permissions, please see page xi.


Library of Congress Cataloging-in-Publication Data

Porter, Eric (Eric C.)
    What is this thing called jazz? : African American
musicians as artists, critics, and activists / Eric Porter.
        p.    cm.— (Music of the African diaspora ; 6)
    Includes bibliographical references and index.
    Contents: A marvel of paradox : jazz and African
American modernity—Dizzy atmosphere : the challenge of bebop—Passions of a man : the poetics and
politics of Charles Mingus—Straight ahead : Abbey
Lincoln and the challenge of jazz singing—Practicing
"creative music" : the black arts imperative in the jazz
community—Writing "creative music" : theorizing
the art and politics of improvisation—The majesty
of the blues : Wynton Marsalis's jazz canon.
    ISBN 0-520-21872-8 (cloth : alk. paper)—
ISBN 0-520-23296-8 (pbk. : alk. paper)
    1. Jazz—History and criticism.   2. African
American jazz musicians.   I. Title.   II. Series.
ML3508 .P67   2002
781.65'089'96073—dc21                    2001044408
                                         CIP

Manufactured in the United States of America

11   10   09   08   07   06   05   04   03   02   01
10   9   8   7   6   5   4   3   2   1

The paper used in this publication meets the minimum
requirements of ANSI/NISO Z39.48-1992 (R 1997)
(*Permanence of Paper*).♾

For Cat and my parents

# Contents

# Acknowledgments

OVER THE PAST SEVEN YEARS, as this study has made the journey from idea to dissertation and now, finally, to book, I have benefited from the insights, encouragement, and assistance of many people.

I first would like to acknowledge the musicians for bringing a particular kind of beauty into this world and for helping to sustain African American people throughout our history. And I thank the subjects of this study for making their voices heard and for demanding that their ideas be treated seriously. Their intellectual work provided much of the inspiration for my work on this topic. I am grateful to Abbey Lincoln, Wadada Leo Smith, and Reggie Workman for generously giving their time and agreeing to be interviewed for this project. Ms. Lincoln also contributed to the project by allowing me to quote from her songs.

I would never have undertaken this project without the guidance of Robin D. G. Kelley, who was my dissertation advisor at the University of Michigan. Robin helped me refine an array of inchoate ideas into a workable thesis and since then has kept me energized about the project with his enthusiasm, generosity, and knowledge of the subject. The other members of my dissertation committee—Richard Crawford, Earl Lewis, and Jimmie Reeves—also provided invaluable advice, encouragement, and careful readings of this work. The dissertation was supported financially at Michigan by a Rackham Merit Fellowship, a Rackham Dean's Dissertation Fellowship, and a travel grant from the Center for Afroamerican and African studies–Ford Foundation project "From Margin to Center: Towards a New Black Scholarship."

A President's Postdoctoral Fellowship in the Department of History at the University of California at Berkeley provided the time and resources to accomplish most of the transition from dissertation to book. While at Berkeley I benefited from the mentoring of Waldo Martin, who also gave insightful readings of new material. I completed the book at the University of New Mexico, and I thank my colleagues there for their support. Monica McCormick, of the University of California Press, was enthusiastic about the project from the beginning and was immensely helpful in securing resources and helping me to negotiate the myriad obstacles that suddenly emerged as I prepared the final product. I was also aided at the end of the process by the editorial work of Rachel Berchten and Mary Renaud. Not only did series editor Samuel Floyd Jr. help me by agreeing to include my book in his series, he also provided careful readings of earlier drafts of the manuscript. I was greatly assisted by readings of drafts of the manuscript by John Gennari and an anonymous reader at the University of California Press.

I have many debts to scholars and friends who have provided inspiration and engaged me in conversation about music, African American history and culture, and a variety of other subjects. Although it would be impossible to name everyone from whose wisdom I have benefited, some individuals deserve special mention because they read drafts of chapters, let me read their own work, commented on presentations, or helped me refine my thinking by sharing their thoughts about the subject of this book. Thanks to Austin Booth, Daphne Brooks, Dennis Dworkin, Philip Elwood, Herman Gray, Farah Jasmine Griffin, James Hall, Patrick Hill, Josh Kun, George Lewis, Anthony Macías, Ingrid Monson, Donna Murch, Michelle Risdon, Nichole Rustin, Guthrie Ramsey, Salim Washington, and two anonymous readers at *American Music.* I am also grateful to Robert Teigrob, who helped me with last-minute research and fact checking. In addition to providing moral support, colleagues at the University of Michigan, the University of Nevada, the University of New Mexico, and the University of California at Berkeley listened to and raised questions about presentations of this work. I also obtained valuable feedback from audiences at annual meetings of the College Language Association and the American Studies Association.

The following librarians and archivists provided invaluable assistance as I conducted the research for the book: Esther Smith and Don Luck of the Institute of Jazz Studies; Lloyd Pinchback at the Music Division of the Library of Congress; and the staffs at the Schomburg Center for Research in Black Culture and the Bancroft Library at the University of California. I am also grateful to Sue Mingus for granting me permission to quote from the unpublished version of *Beneath the Underdog.*

Finally, I would like to thank my family and friends. My parents, Scipio and Barbara Porter, and my brother, Scott Porter, provided their love for me and their support for this project, even when none of us had much of an idea about where it was going. So did my grandmother, Alma Sherry, who unfortunately did not live to see this work make it into print. I have also benefited from the good feelings and helpful distraction of my extended family, in-laws, and friends in the Bay Area, Los Angeles, Ann Arbor, Reno, Albuquerque, and elsewhere.

Finally, I want to thank my wife, Catherine Ramírez, for all of her love and encouragement. She has helped me struggle through this book in many different ways. She has listened to my ideas, given insightful readings of all of these chapters, and, most important, she has helped me see the significance of the project and has reminded me that there is life beyond this book.

## Acknowledgments of Permissions

"Afro Blue," by Mongo Santamaria. Copyright © 1990 MONGO MUSIC (BMI)(administered by BUG MUSIC). All rights reserved. Used by permission.

Excerpts from the original manuscript of *Beneath the Underdog* reprinted with the permission of Sue Mingus.

"In the Red," by Abbey Lincoln, Chips Bayen, and Max Roach. Copyright © Milma Publishing. Permission to use lyric granted by Abbey Lincoln. All rights reserved.

Lyric excerpt of "Retribution," by Julian Priester and Abbey Lincoln. Copyright © 1961 Second Floor Music (administered by R&H Music). International copyright secured. All rights reserved. Reprinted by permission.

Lyric excerpt of "Straight Ahead," by Mal Waldron and Abbey Lincoln. Copyright © 1963 Second Floor Music (administered by R&H Music). International copyright secured. All rights reserved. Reprinted by permission.

"Strong Man," by Oscar Brown Jr. Copyright © Bootblack Publishing. All rights reserved. Used by permission.

# Introduction

**WHAT IS THIS THING CALLED JAZZ?** is an intellectual history focused on African American musicians who have made names for themselves as jazz players. Although members of this community have devoted much of their intellectual energy to the creation and performance of the music itself, this study brings to the foreground the often-ignored *ideas* of musicians. It analyzes musicians' writings and commentary in light of their personal and musical histories, as well as in relation to prevailing debates about jazz and broader currents in African American thought. The book also highlights the contradictory social positions of African American jazz musicians as intellectuals working both within and outside culture-producing institutions.

Some might argue that what these musicians have had to say about jazz in words is less important than what they have had to say through their music. My response is that musicians' commentary is both interesting and important in its own right and that it adds to our understanding of the changing meaning of jazz in American culture. At a basic level, the ways musicians have interrogated the word "jazz" and wondered about its relevance to their projects provide a guide for rethinking the idea of a coherent jazz tradition. Beyond that, a focus on musicians' ideas and identities as thinkers gives us greater insight into how they have assisted in the development of this music, the discourses surrounding it, and its role in American and African American life and letters.

Social theorist Antonio Gramsci argues that almost everyone is to some extent engaged in intellectual activity, though only a few have the social status of intellectuals. He also describes how intellectuals participate in the creation and dismantling of social hierarchies.[1] Gramsci's expansive definition of intellectual life, his attention to power, and his distinction between the everyday intellectual work of individuals and an intellectualism that is commonly recognized are all useful here. This study is concerned first with analyzing a group of people whose ideas are seldom acknowledged because they do not have the formal status of intellectuals. Unfortunately, African American intellectualism is still often seen as oxymoronic; and jazz, as many of the musicians cited here point out, is commonly seen as a product of emotion or instinct rather than as self-conscious activity. The book also explores how these musicians have been cast in intellectual roles and how they have embraced intellectual identities themselves. Even if musicians' social status as intellectuals has seldom been acknowledged and has been contradictory, it is important to recognize that in their efforts to articulate their aesthetic visions and publicly address issues relevant to their lives, they have functioned as arbiters of cultural tastes and cultural politics and have had a significant impact on the meanings circulating around jazz.

Beyond merely recognizing that musicians have participated in and helped to shape the jazz discourse, this study charts some of the particulars of this conversation. A fundamental challenge for musicians has been that jazz is, in Thomas Carmichael's words, "a field of both achievement and restraint."[2] Generally, this predicament has been rooted in the racial meanings associated with jazz and in the economic relationships that structure the music industry. Some African American musicians have celebrated jazz as a symbol of black accomplishment and have derived great pleasure and satisfaction from its status as such. At times, they have welcomed and benefited from the ways jazz has been written about and marketed as a mode of black virtuosity. Yet others have rejected the term "jazz," in part because it has represented both limitations on their artistry and restrictions on their lives as African Americans. Some musicians have even tried to replace the word "jazz" with terms such as "creative music," "new world music," "African American improvised music," or simply "music."

Like other African American intellectuals and artists, jazz musicians have tried to cast off the burden of race while nevertheless celebrating aspects of African American life and culture. At times, invoking jazz as a culturally, spiritually, or militantly black expression has seemed a personally redeeming or politically and economically expedient course of action. Yet at other times, claims of racial authenticity have come into conflict with the dictates of the marketplace, the opinions of others, and musicians' own aesthetic and social visions. One manifestation of this dilemma has been the tension between black nationalism and universalism evident in musicians' thoughts. Some musicians have celebrated jazz as a racially or culturally defined black music, but many of these same figures have for various philosophical or strategic reasons also seen it as an articulation of a broader human community and consciousness.

Musicians have also negotiated the fields of jazz and classical music, sometimes reifying the distinctions between them and at other times seeking to dismantle the boundaries that separate them. Their efforts have been rooted in their own aesthetic projects as well as in the politics of the music world. For musicians and commentators alike, jazz and classical music have symbolized separate spheres of African American and European (or white) artistic accomplishment. Many jazz musicians have been trained as classical players but have seen their ambitions in the realm of concert music stymied by racial discrimination. They have also been aware of jazz's "second-class" status in relation to classical music. For some of these musicians, seeking to dismantle the divisions between the fields or defining their music as an alternative "classical" tradition has been a means of legitimating their own artistic projects. Yet for others, emphasizing the distinctions between jazz and classical music has been a more affirming vision. A corollary to this discussion of jazz and classical music has been the conversation about improvisation and composition. Both improvisation and composition (traditional notation, alternative forms of writing out music, or "head" arrangements) are integral to jazz, but they have frequently been seen as discrete modes of artistic expression that correspond to the division between jazz and classical music as separate realms of black and white artistic achievement.

Developing alongside these tensions between jazz and classical music have been those between jazz and popular music. On the one hand, creating music with popular appeal has represented the possibility of earning a good living as a musician. And for some players who at various moments have wanted to reach the masses (and particularly a black mass audience) for ideological reasons, playing popular music has been integral to the activist identities these musicians have embraced. On the other hand, popular music has sometimes been seen as a threat, on economic and artistic grounds, to those committed to creating art music. For many jazz musicians, popular music has come to represent a lack of musician-ship, the intrusion of market values into the arena of artistic production, or both.

Another important theme involves the way musicians have understood creativity and their roles as artists through the lens of gender and, in par-ticular, a kind of masculine Romanticism. Most jazz musicians have been male, and it has generally been men (primarily black men and white men) who have defined the jazz discourse. African American male musicians, who receive much of the attention in this book, have often expressed their own masculinity, as well as a belief in the patrilineal development of the jazz tradition, when defining their artistic projects. In order to un-derstand the contours of the intellectual history of jazz, this study tries to come to terms with the centrality of masculinity in the formulations and interpretations of jazz artistry. Chapter 4, however, additionally ex-plores the "womanist" implications of jazz singing.

Musicians have also pondered the aesthetic components of their work from their vantage points as laborers. Most notably, they have protested the conditions under which they have had to perform and the accom-panying low wages. They have been attuned to the way that racism in-forms the operations of the music business. African American musicians have challenged what they have seen as appropriation, and sometimes theft, by white artists as well as the greater economic rewards and criti-cal acclaim reaped by some white jazz players. Black musicians have re-sponded to charges of reverse discrimination when white critics and mu-sicians have argued that they were receiving an inordinate amount of critical attention or economic support.

Making sense of the political dimensions of this music is another im-portant aspect of the intellectual life of the jazz community. While keep-ing in mind that commentators sometimes exaggerate the political mean-ing of jazz, the following chapters show how musicians have theorized the relationship between jazz and its social context. Indeed, the second half of the book focuses primarily on musicians who have defined ac-tivist roles for themselves and their music. Some have restricted such en-deavors to the personally therapeutic dimensions of music, while others have seen their music as ushering in broader social changes. Musicians also describe their role in social change in terms of spirituality. Although jazz has largely developed in a secular context, the spiritual dimensions of the music—how it can serve to express musicians' spirituality or how it might create spiritual bonds between musicians and audiences—have been a concern of many.

In addition to charting the specifics of this intellectual history, *What Is This Thing Called Jazz?* intervenes in several scholarly discussions. First, I intend this book to be a corrective to scholars' tendencies across disciplines either to ignore the self-conscious aspects of black cultural production or to pay lip service to this self-consciousness without taking it seriously enough to analyze what the producers of black cultural texts think about these texts. This oversight is not surprising, given the often simplistic and sometimes racist academic practices brought to bear on black culture. But even astute, politically committed scholars working in African American or black intellectual and cultural history, some of whom describe black music as an intellectual activity, seldom devote much attention to musicians' ideas, even when analyzing the meaning and significance of their music. By presenting an account of the ways African American musicians have made sense of the idea of jazz at a variety of historical junctures, this study illuminates a seldom-explored component of twentieth-century African American history and tries to expand our definitions of what constitutes African American intellectual life as a terrain and as a practice.

This book also enters discussions in jazz studies. The past few decades have seen a flowering of scholarship on jazz: musicologists, ethnomusicologists, historians, literary theorists, American studies and cultural studies scholars, and others have written a number of insightful monographs and essays that analyze jazz in its social context and contribute to our understanding of the music and its place in American society. To this may be added a growing number of provocative collections of commentary about jazz, compiled by academics and nonacademics alike, which provide access to primary sources that reveal how musicians and others have conceptualized jazz at various historical moments.

This multidisciplinary body of work has moved beyond the aesthetic concerns of traditional musicology and the biographical focus of much journalistic writing. We are now well aware that jazz is a hybrid cultural practice, with African, European, Latin American, and North American cultural roots; that it has been a vehicle for identity formation and self-actualization for members of disparate cultural communities; that its development has been structured by race relations, migration patterns, capitalist development, technological innovations, and the rise and decline of urban areas; and that the reception of jazz and its place in American society are fundamentally informed by beliefs about race, gender, class, sexuality, culture, commerce, and other issues. When this scholarship turns its attention to the experiences of musicians themselves, it shows how they have drawn from a variety of musical and cultural influences as they labored under conditions that often restricted their creativity. And some of the most interesting recent work explores the multiple ways in which jazz has a profound resonance in American intellectual life.

Despite the value of this scholarship, there is still a need for sustained, historical discussions of what African American musicians have said publicly about their music, their positions as artists, the "jazz tradition" in general, and the broader social and cultural implications of this music. Most studies that address the public dialogue about jazz tend to focus on commentary by white critics and other nonmusicians and pay scant attention to the ways that African American musicians have participated in the discourse and helped to create the mythology about jazz.

Over the course of writing this book, however, I have been buoyed by the publication of several studies that are fundamentally concerned with how musicians understand their music and what they have to say about it. Paul Berliner's *Thinking in Jazz* and Ingrid Monson's *Saying Something* are pathbreaking ethnomusicological studies of the contemporary jazz community that explore the thought behind the art of improvisation and describe its broader cultural implications. And Ronald Radano's *New Musical Figurations,* Scott DeVeaux's *The Birth of Bebop,* Sherrie Tucker's *Swing Shift,* and Graham Lock's *Blutopia* fuse musical, cultural, and historical analyses as a means of understanding distinct musical movements and the work of individual musicians in their larger cultural and historical contexts.[3]

*What Is This Thing Called Jazz?* builds upon the insights of this work by charting the public face of the conversation in the musicians' community over the course of the twentieth century. I believe it is possible to write jazz history that addresses sociological *and* aesthetic concerns, as well as continuity *and* historical particularity, and in doing so places the ideas of African American musicians at its center. Paying attention to musicians' ideas provides a more complicated understanding of the relationship between jazz and its historical context, allowing us to understand jazz creativity as more than just a sonic epiphenomenon of social processes. By acknowledging the self-conscious aspects of African American musical production, this approach also challenges and complicates familiar narratives that ascribe a singular meaning or purpose to the history of jazz, whether it is seen as a struggle of competing class-based ideologies, a consistently oppositional black cultural statement, an expression of the human condition, or the realization of the possibilities of participatory democracy in the United States.

## A Note on Method and Organization

Any broadly conceived intellectual or cultural history is, by definition, an exercise in exclusion. A number of musicians who appear only briefly in this study could have easily been the subjects of their own chapters, and indeed some of them already have one or more books devoted to them. Mary Lou Williams, George Russell, Ornette Coleman, Miles Davis, John Coltrane, Muhal Richard Abrams, John Lewis, and Randy Weston are only a few of the musicians whose art and ideas call for further work. Then there are the great many musicians who have discussed important and interesting ideas in venues that are not accessible to scholarly research. I chose the subjects of this book, in part, because their ideas seemed important or influential and because sources about them were readily available. But the common themes and concerns expressed by the musicians in this study tell me that their ideas are emblematic of those of a much larger community.

Concerning sources, the fact that the subjects of this study are or were professional musicians and, with a few exceptions, not professional writers and scholars has required me to employ a variety of sources, only some of which are typically used to write intellectual histories. Certainly intellectual historians commonly employ autobiographies, analytical books and essays, correspondence, and interviews, as I have done here, but I have also had to search for fragments of musicians' ideas in brief quotations in magazine or newspaper articles, course syllabi, promotional materials, liner notes, and other unconventional sources.

One can argue that almost any text reflects the ideas or expectations of individuals (such as editors, publishers, interviewers, or anticipated readers) other than the person given credit for authorship. But reading the unconventional texts just described demands a special recognition that musicians' commentary has been used and at times manipulated to serve the needs of jazz critics, record companies, and others. When using such sources, I have tried to remain aware of the possibility that musicians' ideas have been distorted, and my analysis is based upon an understanding that many of these texts were collectively created. My general standard for determining whether a particular source provides a more or less accurate reflection of what a musician thought about an issue has been to look for consistency across a range of sources concerning that musician and, in some situations, to search for consistency in the ideas of similarly placed members of the musicians' community. There are also instances in which more "traditional" sources were clearly influenced by people other than the musician authors—ghostwriters, business partners, spouses, lovers, and editors, for example. In such cases, I draw attention to these instances in the text or notes; again, my basis for using such sources is to look for consistency or to confirm in other scholars' assessments of these sources that they do justice to what the musician was thinking.

Chapter 1 explores the comments of African American musicians who attempted to make sense of jazz in the 1910s, 1920s, and 1930s and situates their ideas in broader currents of African American thought. Chapter 2 examines both the bebop movement of the 1940s and musicians' embrace or rejection of the term "bebop" as products of a collective, worldly African American intellectual orientation I term "critical ecumenicalism." Chapters 3 and 4 focus on the music and words of Charles Mingus and Abbey Lincoln, respectively, two musicians who have regarded their art as a vehicle for personal transformation and who have also negotiated the political and gendered meanings of jazz. Chapter 5 extends the treatment of Mingus's and Lincoln's political concerns by exploring how a Black Arts imperative—what Larry Neal described as a duty to "speak to the spiritual and cultural needs of black people"—developed in the jazz community in the 1960s and 1970s. Chapter 6 engages the self-published writings of Yusef Lateef, Marion Brown, Wadada Leo Smith, and Anthony Braxton and shows how each explored his own aesthetic philosophy and engaged in acts of critical intervention by creating an extramusical discourse on his own terms. Chapter 7 completes the study by discussing some of the broader implications of Wynton Marsalis's attempt to define a jazz canon from the 1980s to the present.

## A Note on the Word "Jazz"

I use the term "jazz" in this book with some trepidation because many musicians, including most of the people discussed here, have expressed some ambivalence about the word or have rejected it outright. As suggested earlier, some musicians have seen "jazz" as an inadequate label for describing the variety of styles and complicated artistic projects categorized under its rubric. Others have objected to its derogatory connotations, arguing that it demeans the music by linking it to the brothels and gin houses of New Orleans, where legend says it originated. However, the terms musicians have offered instead—such as "creative music," "new world music," or "African American improvised music"—speak to a larger community of musicians and a broader set of musical practices. I appreciate fully musicians' attempts to use such terms, precisely in response to the compartmentalization of black music by critics and record companies; yet, for all its problems, the word "jazz" remains a useful shorthand for referring to this music, and, more important, it denotes a particular process by which music and musicians have been discursively and economically positioned. And some musicians do continue to embrace the term "jazz." Thus I retain the use of "jazz" and "jazz musician" as a reference to the way each has been situated in society, and the title of the book refers to a history of musicians' critical engagement with the array of ideas and issues that have been invoked by the term. I try to make it clear when the subjects of this study are speaking about their music as something other than jazz.

# "A Marvel of Paradox"
Jazz and African American Modernity

**WRITING IN *DOWN BEAT* MAGAZINE IN 1939,** Duke Ellington defined his musical project in response to critical discussions that differentiated the "authentic" vernacular art of "jazz" from its commercial offshoot "swing": "Our aim has always been the development of an authentic Negro music, of which swing is only one element. We are not interested primarily in the playing of jazz or swing music, but in producing a genuine contribution from our race. Our music is always intended to be definitely and purely racial. We try to complete a cycle." Critics had recently taken Ellington to task for forsaking his "folk" roots and pursuing a watered-down, commercial music. Recognizing the impact that such viewpoints could have on his career, Ellington tried to undermine categories such as jazz or swing by defining his music as part of something larger. His expressed goal of creating an "authentic Negro music" that was "a genuine contribution from our race" also indicates that Ellington's musical project was consistent with some of the fundamental goals of the diasporic, black cultural renaissance of the early twentieth century. Like other artists and intellectuals of the period, he believed that the production and reception of black music would have an effect on the social standing of African Americans. In other words, Ellington tried to define a socially relevant black aesthetic under conditions that limited black creativity.[1]

Ellington was among the most prominent African American musicians in the 1930s. A familiar figure in motion pictures and radio and the subject of articles in music trade journals, the mainstream press, and black newspapers, he used his position to intervene in the nascent field of jazz criticism, which by the late 1930s was shaped by race, gender, and class relations; by modernist ideas about art, culture, and commerce; and by New Deal and Popular Front ideologies. Ellington gave his own meanings to an African American and American art form that was both an increasingly popular commodity and an object of growing debate. He described the self-consciousness of his approach at a time when many critics saw African American popular music as a product of instinct. He also passed judgment on a music industry in which commercially oriented white bands profited while most black bands remained marginal. And Ellington did so while engaging ideas of concern to white jazz critics and African American intellectuals, with a specificity rooted in his position as a musician laboring in the music industry.

Ellington's comments came at the end of two decades of public commentary about jazz by African American musicians, some of whom embraced the art form and some of whom did not. These discussions resonated with issues pertaining to the performance of this music and the state of African American society in the early twentieth century. Musicians understood that jazz had become a site for African American artistic achievement but that it was also symbolic of the restrictions that American society placed on their lives as artists and human beings. This chapter begins by sketching the social, cultural, and ideological context out of which jazz emerged in the first half of the twentieth century. It then discusses some of the reactions to this music by African American intellectuals, before launching into an analysis of what musicians themselves had to say about jazz. For James Reese Europe, W. C. Handy, Louis Armstrong, Dave Peyton, Duke Ellington, and others, jazz marked the contradictory position of black culture and black people in modern American life and anticipated numerous discussions about the music that continue today.

## "A Marvel of Paradox"

"Jazz is a marvel of paradox: too fundamentally human, at least as modern humanity goes, to be typically racial, too international to be characteristically national, too much abroad in the world to have a special home. And yet jazz in spite of it all is one part American and three parts American Negro, and was originally the nobody's child of the levee and the city slum."[2] Thus began Joel A. Rogers's "Jazz at Home," the only essay in Alain Locke's 1925 collection *The New Negro* to focus specifically on this music. This characterization, in which Rogers sought to plot jazz along the axes of geography and genotype, addressed a dilemma facing black intellectuals who were seeking to claim jazz as an African American creative force while making sense of its widespread appeal to non-black musicians and audiences. The question of whether jazz was an African American birthright was just one of the paradoxes black intellectuals pondered. Was it folk culture, high culture, or a product of the rapidly blooming culture industry? And what was its ultimate social impact? Could it be used to highlight black contributions to American society? Or did it merely play into white stereotypes about black culture and behavior, beliefs that had been shaped by pseudoscientific racism, generations of minstrelsy, and other pernicious representations of black life?

In the second half of the nineteenth century, black and nonblack observers alike increasingly considered black musical accomplishment, both in the realm of European concert music and in the development of vernacular forms, as a means of improving the social position of African Americans. Thus the stage was set for a twentieth-century cultural politics through which black intellectuals and musicians tried to challenge social and cultural hierarchies, "vindicate" African American society, and dismantle notions of irreducible racial difference by demonstrating, in Jon Michael Spencer's words, a "two-tiered mastery" of European "form and technique" and Negro "mood and spirit."[3]

One early-twentieth-century example of this cultural politics was W. E. B. Du Bois's discussion of spirituals in his 1903 book *The Souls of Black Folk*. Du Bois's treatment of this form of music anticipated future debates by situating music at the nexus of race and nation, by emphasizing the realm of spirit as a site of black achievement, and by simultaneously theorizing black musical culture as a gift to American society and as a vehicle for African American liberation. In the face of racist thought, social segregation, and racial violence directed toward African Americans, Du Bois challenged the exclusion of "black folk" from U.S. society and defined them as equal citizens by writing them into the center of the country's history and its spiritual and cultural life. During an age when social hierarchies were justified and perpetuated by marking black people as primarily irrational, emotional, and physical beings, Du Bois adhered to the logic of this discourse but inverted its hierarchical assumptions by validating the spiritual and the emotional over the material and rational. Similarly, he held on to the idea of a hereditary, racial community, while seeking to subvert some elements of biological essentialism. By virtue of innate racial characteristics *and* historical circumstance, he argued, African Americans had made a unique artistic and cultural contribution to American society. This contribution spoke of universal human values and stood in contrast and as antidote to the crass materialism of the age. While "the human spirit in this new world has expressed itself in vigor and ingenuity rather than in beauty, . . ." he wrote, "so by fateful chance the Negro folk-song . . . stands to-day not simply as the sole American music, but as the most beautiful expression of human experience born this side the seas. . . . [I]t still remains as the singular spiritual heritage of the nation and the greatest gift of the Negro people."[4]

Du Bois's discussion of spirituals is also significant because he addressed issues of authenticity and hybridity, as he lauded the music's aesthetic beauty and transformative potential. Du Bois recognized that African American folk musicians drew from multiple musical antecedents and that for decades white audiences had consumed black music and white musicians had performed it. The roots of spirituals lay in Africa, but their development in America involved African Americans' synthesis of "Negro" and "Caucasian" elements into a musical hybrid that remained "distinctively Negro." Du Bois knew that if spirituals were to be considered a "gift" to America, then, clearly, whites would consume them. Yet he differentiated between appropriate and inappropriate uses of this cultural material, the latter occurring when a white-controlled music industry transformed the meanings (or spirit) of these folk materials and disrupted their liberatory potential. Although Du Bois celebrated the impact of "Negro" songs and melodies on American popular music, he decried "debasements and imitations" such as "'minstrel' songs, many of the 'gospel' hymns, and some of the contemporary 'coon' songs,—a mass of music in which the novice may easily lose himself and never find the real Negro melodies."[5] When Du Bois distinguished the authentic from the inauthentic in black musical culture, the distinction was based less on African American uses of European forms than on white appropriation and marketing of black forms. Du Bois thus anticipated another significant question in twentieth-century discussions about music: how does one come to terms with the role of black music in African American communities—the variety of functions the music performs and the array of meanings it contains—while also making sense of it in relation to its broader audience and the institutions and business interests that control its production?

During the 1910s and 1920s, elite "New Negro" intellectuals and artists raised similar questions about secular musical forms that seemed at once part of the black vernacular and the mainstream of American musical culture. Deeming themselves free of the "myth" of the "old Negro" and attuned to the "new spirit . . . awake in the masses," participants in the Harlem Renaissance and others sought to define the parameters of black expression, uncover an African American cultural past, and determine how black culture could be used as a tool for social change.[6] As before, intellectuals and artists negotiated entrenched social hierarchies and racist discourses. But in the wake of World War I, the Great Migration of African Americans from the South to the cities of the North, and the growth of pan-Africanist and black nationalist sentiment throughout the globe, they tapped into the energies of an increasingly urbane and militant black community as well.

African Americans' discussion of culture in the 1910s and 1920s resonated with some fundamental tensions in modernist thought and some specific questions about how black culture should be understood in relation to its social and political context, its cultural antecedents, its audience, and its position in the marketplace. Should one emphasize the characteristics that distinguished African American culture from European or Euro-American forms, or did that merely play into the logic of racism and segregation? Were rural African Americans the creators of the most important expressions, or did that honor belong to urbanites working in commercial entertainment? Should expressive culture serve as propaganda, or should aesthetics be the primary concern of artists and critics? If culture was a weapon, should the focus be black community building, gaining entry into the larger American society, or both? What was the impact of the market on the production of black cultural forms? Did it somehow dilute racial or folk expressions? And what should one make of the growing attention that white consumers and cultural gatekeepers were paying to black culture? Would it reproduce stereotypes, or might it actually help to bury the stereotypical images from the minstrel stage, increase employment for black artists, and improve the position of African Americans in the process?

When the discussion turned to jazz, artists and intellectuals responded to the paradoxical position of this music. Jazz was indeed a complicated phenomenon by the 1920s. In Ted Gioia's words, it came out of the "dynamic interaction, the clash and fusion—of African and European, composition and improvisation, spontaneity and deliberation, the popular and the serious, high and low."[7] As the growing body of historical writing on jazz illustrates, this idiom emerged in the first few decades of the twentieth century as a result of the choices musicians made in the context of the profound transformations affecting American society as a whole and African American society in particular. Urbanization; migration; race, gender, and class relations; communications technologies; and the growth of mass culture—all had an impact on the growth of jazz and the way people received it. In addition to being music, jazz was a business enterprise and a set of institutional relationships, a focal point for political and social debate, a vehicle for individual and communal identity formation, and, eventually, an idea.[8]

Jazz emerged when black musicians and other African Americans became immersed in modern life at the end of the nineteenth century and the beginning of the twentieth. A series of domestic migrations brought rural African Americans to urban areas and southerners to the North. In urban areas throughout the country, musicians of different social backgrounds encountered one another in formal and informal educational networks, where they built upon existing vernacular forms and transformed them with the tools of Western music.[9] By the early twentieth century, black musicians had developed a dizzying array of secular, instrumental, and vocal musical styles. Ragtime piano players, brass bands, string bands, popular tunesmiths, "serious" composers, performers in minstrel and vaudeville shows, and members of large orchestras and dance bands created music that included elements of syncopation, improvisation, blues harmony and melodic figures, and a variety of tonal effects (growls, melismas, and so forth). All these elements helped to distinguish this music from other popular and concert music. Although "jazz" initially signified an approach to interpreting a musical score or playing one's instrument, by the late 1910s musicians and observers alike increasingly saw it as a style of syncopated, instrumental dance music in and of itself, which was performed by barroom piano players, small combos in nightclubs, and larger "syncopated" orchestras holding forth in dance halls, theaters, and, occasionally, the concert hall.[10]

As jazz became part of the American "culture industry"—that is, the commodified conglomeration of leisure practices and entertainments developing alongside the Fordist system of mass industrial production in the United States—it was soon vested with a variety of often-contradictory meanings.[11] In African American urban society, this hybrid art form served as a vehicle for community building and cultural identification. The growth of black entertainment districts in urban centers and the booming markets for player pianos, sheet music, records, and then radio expanded jazz's communal function in black communities and augmented its capital as a symbol of racial solidarity. During the 1920s, one of the traditional proletarian functions of black secular music was extended to middle-class audiences, when working-class and middle-class African Americans forged a sense of collective identity as they gathered in nightclubs, theaters, and dance halls (as well as at rent parties in private homes) to reclaim their bodies as instruments of pleasure after a day's labor and affirm communal bonds in the face of a racist society.[12]

The marketing of cultural commodities to black consumers augmented such feelings of racial community. By the early 1920s, both white and black entrepreneurs appealed to racial pride and authenticity as they marketed sheet music and phonograph records to black consumers. This was quite evident in the advertising and popularity of "race records," a phenomenon that began in 1920 with Mamie Smith's recording of "Crazy Blues" and "It's Right Here for You" and by 1923 included instrumental dance music.[13] The ability of the music to inspire racial solidarity was not lost on black nationalist political organizations. During the 1920s, the leftist African Blood Brotherhood (ABB) and Marcus Garvey's United Negro Improvement Association (UNIA) sponsored jazz and blues performances as a means of galvanizing support for their causes. Yet, in spite of its ability to draw people together, jazz could also serve as a vehicle for class distinction. Urban reformers, religious-minded folk, and certain members of the African American middle class frowned upon jazz and blues in general; others appreciated the tony dance music of a Duke Ellington or Fletcher Henderson but eschewed the frenetic polyphony and blues tonalities of a small combo from New Orleans.[14]

Further complicating jazz's organic function in black communities was the fact that it was only one of a variety of musical products being marketed to these communities. In newspapers with working-class and middle-class readerships, advertisements for music shops, record companies, and sheet music suggest that African American consumers maintained a diverse musical sensibility in the early 1920s. People in Harlem and Chicago increasingly listened to jazz and blues after the advent of race records, but they also still enjoyed everything from Tin Pan Alley novelties to spirituals to light classical and operatic numbers to comedic minstrel tunes to marches.[15] Urban black folk at large listened to an array of popular music, reflecting an interest in their vernacular music as well as their entry into a rapidly expanding American popular culture. Jazz and blues appealed to at least some working-class and middle-class people and were viewed as symbols of black achievement, as the appeal to racial pride in record company advertisements and newspaper coverage makes clear. Yet many urban African Americans also wanted the right to participate in American culture on their own terms, which could mean listening to music outside these genres. In a context where, as William Kenney notes, the production and marketing of race records were directly related to stereotypes about black behaviors and musical tastes, musical "authenticity" also symbolized the restrictions that segregation and racism had imposed on African American life.[16]

Perhaps most important in making jazz a "paradox," at least in the eyes of African American intellectuals, was the impact of white consumers and white musicians on the development and reception of this music. Not only was jazz clearly a hybrid art form in terms of its musical components, but it soon inhabited a complicated position vis-à-vis its multiple audiences and practitioners. Although rooted in African American society, jazz quickly found itself at the center of American popular music and the subject of a volatile debate. Whites had long viewed African American secular music with a combination of fear and fascination, and this continued in their reactions to jazz, which they celebrated and condemned for similar reasons.

According to Lawrence Levine, jazz developed during a period when Americans were redefining their ideas about "culture." Jazz was "almost completely out of phase" with a late-nineteenth-century concept of culture that was synonymous with "refinement." The participatory qualities of the music and the exchange between performer and audience, as well as the blurring of the distinction between composer and interpreter, threatened the aura of a "highbrow" musical culture based in European concert practices. The threat was also rooted in race. Levine points out that the very ideas of "highbrow" and "lowbrow," which entered common parlance at the turn of the century, originated in nineteenth-century phrenology. Highbrow culture, then, was often coded or explicitly defined as white or Anglo-Saxon.[17]

Jazz received a fair amount of negative press in the late 1910s and then became the object of a moral panic during the 1920s. Some whites feared jazz because it was rooted in black culture, because it played a role in facilitating interracial contact, and because it symbolized, in racially coded terms, the intrusion of popular tastes into the national culture. Such responses to the music should be understood both in the cultural context discussed by Levine and in relation to the rapid changes in American life in the wake of World War I. Not only were African Americans becoming more visible members of American urban society, as a result of the Great Migration, but they were becoming more vocal in their political demands as well. Moreover, the success of Jews and other white ethnics in the genre made it symbolic of the influx of immigrants into WASP communities. Jazz rhythms also seemed to represent an unwelcome mechanization or speeding up of modern life, along with accompanying alienation and neuroses.[18]

Much of the outcry over jazz had to do with sex. The rhythmic qualities of jazz, the participatory elements of its performance, and the physical aspects of the dancing associated with it spoke of unrestrained sexual energies, which had long been projected onto black bodies by Europeans and white Americans. At a moment when many young people (and young women in particular) were throwing off the constraints of Victorian sexual mores, anxieties over white juvenile sexuality dovetailed with fears of black sexuality and, especially, of the impact black culture might have on the sexual behavior of young whites. Nevertheless, many whites embraced jazz as they sought refuge from Victorian restrictions, a manifestation of the way jazz quickly became a vehicle for challenging cultural norms.

Even if the majority of cultural gatekeepers condemned or were ambivalent about jazz in the 1920s, some whites, whether they simply liked the music or were influenced by Freudian ideas about repressed libidos or a liberal egalitarianism, embraced African American music as they rejected the constraints of Victorian culture and challenged an elitist Anglo-Saxonism. Many of the most enthusiastic responses to jazz and blues were colored by a primitivist belief that black people possessed a vital quality that was missing from rational, "civilized" European American culture and society. Still other observers saw in jazz, and in African American vernacular music in general, the potential for a homegrown American musical expression that might challenge the supposed superiority of European music. Whatever their reasons, white fans bought race records, flocked to black Broadway productions such as *Shuffle Along*, and explored black entertainment districts in various urban areas for a taste of "authentic" expression. Jazz also became the basis of a white youth subculture, in which fans and musicians alike rebelled against the banality of their Babbittish, middle-class backgrounds or against the provincialism of their immigrant parents by developing an affinity for black music and musicians.[19]

The popularity of jazz with white audiences validated the work of African American musicians and aestheticians and eventually called into question the distance between elite and popular culture. Yet this visibility was a mixed blessing. White audiences often insisted that black music conform to their primitivist and stereotypical demands, as the common references to plantation life and African jungles in nightclub names, costumes, staging, and composition titles make clear. The culture industry played a contradictory role by sometimes making jazz visible as a black cultural form, while at other moments erasing black contributions to the genre. The music industry, in particular, did a much better job producing music performed by white musicians. In the 1920s, race records aside, many white fans probably knew jazz only through the work of white musicians. The Original Dixieland Jazz Band (ODJB), for example, a white ensemble from New Orleans, made the first jazz recordings in 1917 and soon inspired an array of imitators, many of whom emphasized the humorous potential of the new music in novelty tunes. Among the biggest acts in the early 1920s were Ted Lewis, Paul Whiteman, Eddie Cantor, and Sophie Tucker.[20] Some white musicians took it upon themselves to distance jazz from its African American origins as a means of popularizing the music or securing more prestige for it. Bandleader Paul Whiteman, for example, the self-professed "King of Jazz," attempted to make jazz more respectable by constraining its syncopated rhythms and tonal embellishments and fusing it with popular song and classical music. He presented what was billed as the first jazz concert at Aeolian Hall in New York on February 12, 1924. He traced the development of jazz from the ODJB's "Livery Stable Blues" through George Gershwin's "Rhapsody in Blue" (he actually ended the concert with a version of "Pomp and Circumstance") in an attempt to demonstrate the music's development from its humble roots to its concert hall possibilities. Whiteman paid scant attention to the role of African Americans in the development of jazz, describing the music in a press release for the concert as an art form "which sprang into existence about ten years ago from nowhere in particular."[21]

## Jazz and New Negroes

In the late 1910s and 1920s, African American intellectuals tried to make sense of the liberating power of jazz, its role in black communities, and its position as a commodity in a broader American society. Although references to jazz and blues abound in Harlem Renaissance fiction and visual art, critical commentary on the music is relatively sparse. Some have argued that the dearth of celebratory, critical writings on jazz and blues reflects the elite class and educational backgrounds of New Negro intellectuals, as well as their inability to speak to the African American working class.[22] Thinkers such as Du Bois and Alain Locke, at least in the 1920s, turned more of their attention to spirituals and especially to the "elevation" of this music to the concert stage. Even those who did write about jazz and blues often maintained a belief in a "two-tiered mastery," viewing jazz and blues as stepping stones to more sophisticated expressions.

Although the highbrow cultural tastes of many of the leading lights in the African American community must be recognized—even Marcus Garvey was said to prefer classical music—this dearth of writing and the ambivalent attitudes about jazz were at least in part a product of the paradoxical position of this music in American society. Some black intellectuals embraced an early-century modernist aesthetic sensibility, which, influenced by Boasian cultural relativism, diminished the distance between "fine art" and "folk art" but positioned both as superior to mass-produced culture.[23] Thus the disdain for jazz was sometimes less a rejection of working-class culture per se than of the music's status as a commodity. Additionally, as discussed earlier, the culture industry tended to erase the accomplishments of black musicians or to reproduce racist stereotypes when marketing their work. In other words, jazz was simply difficult to celebrate as an important African American cultural expression for much of the 1920s because of its status as a popular music. Not only was it seen as less artistically "authentic" than spirituals, but it was also clear that whites controlled the music industry, were highly visible as practitioners, and as an audience demanded that black artists conform to their expectations. Similar tensions are evident in those writers who celebrated jazz and other commercial forms of music. And it is their work that raised a number of important questions regarding the paradoxical position of jazz in African American and American society as well as some of the contradictions inherent in a cultural politics that sought to promote a commodified black expression in order to prove African American worth in a society structured by racism.

Author, composer, diplomat, and field secretary of the National Association for the Advancement of Colored People (NAACP), James Weldon Johnson devoted much of his energy during the 1910s and 1920s to promoting black culture. Like Du Bois, he attempted to subvert racist thinking and social exclusion by placing black people and black folk art at the center of American life and culture. In the preface to his 1922 collection *The Book of American Negro Poetry,* Johnson argued that racist ideology could be challenged through intellectual and artistic work: "The status of the Negro in the United States is more a question of national mental attitude toward the race than of actual conditions. And nothing will do more to change that mental attitude and raise his status than a demonstration of intellectual parity by the Negro through the production of literature and art." African Americans could succeed in this enterprise because they possessed, in his words, "the emotional endowment, the originality and artistic conception, and, what is more important, the power of creating that which has universal appeal and influence."[24]

Johnson's primary concern was the cultivation of African American poetry, but he believed music already displayed this "power of creating."

Johnson did not mention the term "jazz" in his preface, but he did discuss spirituals, dancing, ragtime, and the blues as African American achievements. Adhering to the logic of primitivism, he described ragtime as a black contribution to American life that "jes' grew" out of "natural musical instinct and talent" and "the Negro's extraordinary sense of rhythm." The latest wave of "jes' grew" music was the blues: an expression of a national spirit, an object with "universal appeal," and a product of African Americans' "remarkable racial gift of adaptability" and of the "transfusive quality" of their art.[25]

Johnson's analysis of African American music took into account its status as a product of the culture industry. On the one hand, its popularization might extend its impact and become a vehicle for legitimation. Ragtime's popularity proved that it "possesses the vital spark, the power to appeal universally, without which any artistic production, no matter how approved its form may be, is dead." On the other hand, Johnson realized the market could constrain black cultural production as well as enable it. He mentioned with some derision that whites had profited from misrepresentations of black folk music, and he was also aware that the culture industry placed black artists in an uncomfortable "artistic niche" by catering to whites' stereotypes. "When [the African American] is thought of artistically," he argued, "it is as a happy-go-lucky, singing, shuffling, banjo-picking being or as a more or less pathetic figure." Hoping to move away from the "specter of minstrelsy," Johnson looked forward to the creation of "higher forms" that maintained the "power" of the vernacular while demonstrating a mastery of classical music.[26]

Johnson's discomfort with the representations of blackness in popular culture may have been a product of his elitism, but it also reflected a fundamental conundrum facing black aestheticians during the mid-1920s. Even as they celebrated a racially defined art, they were aware of the constraints of race as a socially determined identity expressed through culture. One might celebrate black cultural distinctiveness as a means of subverting segregation or biologically based ideas of black inferiority, but one still faced a situation in which the idea of distinct black characteristics (whether biological or cultural) was central to the logic of early-century racist propaganda directed against African Americans. When the culture industry's role in the production and appropriation of black music was added to this picture, it raised additional questions regarding white audience expectations, the perpetuation of stereotypes, and control over the representations of this art.[27]

Later in the decade, New Negro intellectuals discussed jazz as a distinct genre in ways that demonstrated divergent assessments of the intersection among music, identity, and cultural politics. In the preface to his 1925 *The Book of American Negro Spirituals,* for example, Johnson spoke briefly about jazz, noting its rhythmic basis and how its growing popularity in the mid-1920s was evidence of the centrality of black rhythmic sensibilities to the national musical culture. Johnson saw in the dance rhythms of jazz a mark of black distinctiveness and, in its growing popularity with a white audience, the power to legitimate black culture. But his ironic use of the noun "swing" in quotation marks, when describing a white audience's difficulties with the rhythmic aspects of black music (they cannot get the "'swing' of it"), may well have signified, as Brent Edwards suggests, that Johnson saw some "danger" in the appropriation of the genre and the transformation of "swing" from an African American cultural practice to a fixed object of white fascination.[28]

While Johnson viewed black achievement in music as a means of proving black worth in American society, Langston Hughes, a member of a younger generation of writers, employed music as a vehicle for distinguishing black culture from the national body. Hughes celebrated jazz and blues in his early poetry and used the music to evoke the pleasure and hardships of black working-class life. In his 1926 essay "The Negro Artist and the Racial Mountain," Hughes discussed the music's function in black communities and figured it as an articulation of black working-class consciousness. "Jazz to me is one of the inherent expressions of Negro life in America; the eternal tom-tom beating in the Negro soul—the tom-tom of revolt against weariness in a white world, a world of subway trains, and work, work, work; the tom-tom of joy and laughter, and pain swallowed in a smile."[29]

Not only did Hughes's essay speak to the way jazz had come to symbolize the bonds of community, but it also demonstrated how African American and nonblack intellectuals employed the blues and jazz to mark the boundaries of racial authenticity in art and letters. In a well-known passage, Hughes castigated his colleague Countee Cullen (although he did not name him specifically) for refusing the label "Negro poet." And he ridiculed an African American clubwoman who preferred a concert of Andalusian songs to a Mamie Smith performance. Hughes feared that the impulse to assimilation—"the desire to pour racial individuality into the mold of American standardization"—was "the mountain standing in the way of any true Negro art in America." Working-class black people were not afraid of blues or jazz, he argued, and they could serve as models for black artists and intellectuals. "Let the blare of Negro jazz bands and the bellowing voice of Bessie Smith singing Blues penetrate the closed ears of the colored near-intellectuals until they listen and perhaps understand. . . . We younger Negro artists who create now intend to express our individual dark-skinned selves without fear or shame."[30]

Intellectuals also engaged the role of music in the creation of individualized racial identities. In her 1928 essay "How It Feels to Be Colored Me," Zora Neale Hurston said that one of the moments when she felt most "colored" was when she attended a jazz performance in the company of a white friend. Employing the primitivist language that marked some of her early assessments of black art and culture, Hurston described her physical reaction to a jazz band's rhythmic and harmonic execution. "This orchestra grows rambunctious, rears on its hind legs and attacks the tonal veil with primitive fury, rending it, clawing it until it breaks through to the jungle beyond. I follow those heathen—follow them exultingly. I dance wildly inside myself." After she "creep[s] back slowly to the veneer we call civilization with the last tone," she encounters her white friend, who "has only heard what I felt. . . . He is so pale with his whiteness then and I am *so* colored."[31] Whether Hurston intended her language, which so neatly conforms to racist interpretations of black culture, to be ironic or not is unclear.[32] In any case, her description of jazz as a catalyst for the creation of racial consciousness that distanced her from white society marks her recognition that this music functioned as a constituent of racial identity at the level of emotional reaction.

As Hughes and Hurston sought to locate specifically black meanings and functions in jazz, they were not oblivious to the prescriptive aspects of race or the range of issues that arose when one chose to celebrate jazz. Hughes recognized the primitivistic restrictions of the "present vogue in things Negro," but he claimed that any harm was mitigated by the increased respect for vernacular culture generated within black communities as a result of attention by outsiders. Still, even as he demanded that jazz and blues be taken on their own terms, Hughes, like Johnson, saw them as building blocks for future developments unencumbered by the restrictions placed on black artistry. "Our folk music," he wrote, "having achieved world-wide fame, offers itself to the genius of the great individual American composer who is to come."[33] And Hurston, despite her primitivistic language, explored racelessness as well as blackness in her essay. Although her consumption of jazz marked her blackness, at other moments she had "no race." Ultimately, she demanded the right to assume several identities ("colored," "feminine," "American," and so on) and saw universal links between human beings, who were like so many different colored paper bags holding similar collections of colored glass. Several years later, in her essay "Characteristics of Negro Expression," Hurston balanced commentary about the distinctiveness of African American cultural expressions with an acknowledgment of the hybridity of black music and its immersion in American popular culture. Putting a hopeful spin on this exchange, she wrote: "In so many words, Paul Whiteman is giving an imitation of a Negro orchestra making use of white-invented musical instruments in a Negro way. Thus has arisen a new art in the civilized world, and thus has our so-called civilization come. The exchange and re-exchange of ideas between groups."[34]

When Joel Rogers described jazz as a "marvel of paradox" in Alain Locke's 1925 *The New Negro,* he sought to define both its specifically African American elements and its place in a larger culture and society that had yet to fulfill its democratic promise. Rogers struggled to reconcile a belief in the transformative potential of black artistic accomplishment with the reality that jazz had become part of the broader fabric of American popular culture. He situated jazz as a product of specifically racial and cosmopolitan pasts, presents, and futures. Jazz was "atavistically African" but also related to folk music from throughout the globe. But jazz was not merely folk music; it was a thoroughly modern expression. "Jazz time," Rogers argued, "is faster and more complex than African music. . . . It is a thing of the jungles—modern man-made jungles." And, as a modern expression, it was both an African American and an American art form. Jazz was "thoroughly American Negro," he argued, and as such represented the movement of African Americans into modern urban life. However, "once achieved, it is common property, and jazz has absorbed the national spirit, that tremendous spirit of go, the nervousness, lack of conventionality and boisterous good-nature characteristic of the American, white or black, as compared with the more rigid formal natures of the English-man or German."[35]

But even if jazz had become "common property," Rogers was still invested in showing that African Americans had proprietary claims on the art form. He saw some validation in the appropriation of the art form by Paul Whiteman, and he was even more enthusiastic about the attention that European concert musicians were paying to the music. But Rogers also emphasized that black musicians such as W. C. Handy and the mythical Jasbo Brown played a central role in consolidating the idiom, and he stressed the importance of "Negro rhythm" and a cultural predilection for spontaneity to the success of the genre. Performers such as Ethel Waters, Florence Mills, Abbie Mitchell, Eubie Blake, Bill Robinson, Buddy Gilmore, and the blues singers Clara, Mamie, and Bessie Smith were "inimitable artists, with an inventive, improvising skill that defies imitation," and it would be left to bandleaders such as Will Marion Cook, Noble Sissle, and Eubie Blake to take jazz into the future.[36]

Although he displayed a somewhat elitist view toward the working class, Rogers recognized that jazz played a socially and emotionally affirming role in African American communities, with the potential for transforming American society as a whole; it was a "balm for modern ennui," he wrote, "and has become a safety valve for modern machine-ridden and convention-bound society." Yet in white society's interest in the music he saw both a means for jazz to fulfill America's democratic potential and the risk that black contributions might be erased. As of the mid-1920s, the biggest names in jazz were white Americans. Rogers believed that "cheap imitations" were pervasive and that important black pioneers such as Cook had been superseded by white orchestras because of "the difficulties of financial backing." So, like Johnson, he looked forward to an expression that might better validate black artistry and transcend the controversy surrounding the music. "Where at present it vulgarizes," he wrote, "with more wholesome growth in the future, it may on the contrary truly democratize. At all events, jazz is rejuvenation, a recharging of the batteries of civilization with primitive new vigor. It has come to stay, and they are wise, who instead of protesting against it, try to lift and divert it into nobler channels."[37]

Taken as a whole, the discussions of jazz and blues by African American intellectuals in the early and mid-1920s raised a number of vexing questions about the characteristics and ultimate importance of African American musical expression. Seeking to embrace music as a reflection of black spirit, experience, emotion, biology, or all of these elements, African American intellectuals addressed the appropriation, popularization, and primitivization of the art form. Making sense of jazz often involved a struggle, for various political and ideological reasons, to elevate the music as a black expression in spite of, or in response to, its precarious place in American life. These debates about music were also a pointed commentary about the liberating and constraining aspects of racial thinking in a segregated, racist society. By recognizing the complex place of jazz in American culture and sometimes portraying it as a symbol of African American achievement and a potential vehicle for personal or collective liberation, New Negro discussions about jazz opened up the discursive terrain for subsequent interpretations of the idiom.

## African American Musicians and the Challenge of Jazz

As secular black music was institutionalized, commodified, and consumed by African American and nonblack audiences, professional African American musicians began to analyze their changing legacy. Many musicians were undoubtedly more concerned with sonic developments than with the broader social or ideological implications of their music. Moreover, there were relatively few public venues in which early practitioners could articulate their ideas. Yet others, recognizing the changes happening in black music, the entertainment industry, and the world around them, sought to express their views in public forums.

Most of the African American musicians who managed to find a voice in the early discourse about jazz were, by virtue of training, education, or class background, relatively privileged individuals whose aesthetic sensibilities were similar to those of New Negro intellectuals. Like their counterparts, these musicians often envisioned vindication in the concert hall. As musicologist Samuel Floyd Jr. notes, the "spirit" of the "Negro Renaissance" in Harlem was anticipated by the efforts of early-twentieth-century black composers such as Scott Joplin, Will Marion Cook, and Harry T. Burleigh to develop vernacular black art into extended musical forms.[38] Yet musicians' insightful commentary about this "marvel of paradox" was distinguished by their concerns over their treatment as laborers in the music industry. Musicians also paid more attention to the creative process that lay behind the music, which further distinguished them from both white commentators and New Negro aestheticians.

One of the earliest public comments about jazz by an African American musician was an interview given by James Reese Europe shortly before his death in 1919. Europe had founded the Clef Club in 1910 as a musicians' association and "clearing house" for employment. He had also been instrumental in the drive to integrate American Federation of Musicians (AFM) Local 310 in New York. Musically, Europe had recorded ragtime numbers with small bands and was a major figure in the symphonic jazz movement of the 1910s. Some critics have suggested that the Carnegie Hall performances of the Clef Club Symphony Orchestra between 1912 and 1915 were the first jazz concerts. Europe had also made a name for himself by teaming up with the dance team of Vernon and Irene Castle, beginning in 1914, and through his position as leader of the U.S. Army's 369th Infantry band, which took jazz overseas during World War I and returned to a hero's welcome in Harlem in 1918.[39]

Europe described the origins of the term "jazz" as a "corruption" of "Razz's Band," a mysterious, rhythmically inclined group of improvisers who purportedly gained prominence in New Orleans before moving to New York.[40] Europe's reference to corruption suggests a point of origin for musicians' long-held suspicions about the ability of the term "jazz" to describe the music it supposedly signifies. Yet, as Gerald Early notes, Europe also saw jazz as a site of racial accomplishment: one that was at home in respectable venues. Europe found some characteristics of "jazz" distinctly "racial." "The negro loves anything that is peculiar in music," he said, "and this 'jazzing' appeals to him strongly." "Jazzing," among other things, involved the tonal effects produced on brass and wind instruments by using mutes and manipulating breath and embouchure. It also described a "Negro" approach to interpreting musical scores, in which musicians accentuated certain notes. "It is natural for us to do this; it is, indeed, a racial musical characteristic. I have to call a daily rehearsal of my band to prevent the musicians from adding to their music more than I wish them to. . . . I have to be continually on the lookout to cut out the results of my musicians' originality."[41]

Although rooted in a biological racial essentialism, Europe's rhetoric sought to legitimate his and others' music to those who doubted the legitimacy of black vernacular art. Europe's Carnegie Hall concerts had featured his own work as well as that of black composers such as Will Marion Cook, Harry T. Burleigh, and Samuel Coleridge-Taylor. But the validity of such explorations of folk forms had been challenged by white and black commentators alike who thought that black musical accomplishment might be better proved through mastering the work of European composers. In 1914, Europe responded to such criticisms by arguing that his particular expressions of racial feeling were worthy artistic endeavors. He justified both the instrumentation of his symphony—which included mandolins and banjos—as well as the compositions themselves as "the product of our souls."[42]

In the 1919 interview, Europe conceded that this expression of "soul" needed policing by attentive bandleaders, but he still described jazz as a way of expressing both racial feeling and artistic originality. After discussing the warm reception his group received in France—an early description of that country as a more sympathetic home for jazz and black jazz musicians—Europe said he had returned home "more firmly convinced than ever that negroes should write negro music. We have our own racial feeling and if we try to copy whites we will make bad copies." Composers such as Cook, Burleigh, and Coleridge-Taylor were "truly themselves in the music which expresses their race."[43] While Europe approached jazz more as a group of techniques than as a genre in itself, he demonstrated how musicians were beginning to look at jazz as a musical practice, a symbol of racial pride, and a vehicle for expressing individual artistry and social legitimacy.

Some of the most interesting commentary about jazz in the 1920s is found in W. C. Handy's 1926 *Blues: An Anthology.* Handy, the son of a minister, at various times made a living as a bandleader, educator, composer, and music publisher. For the previous two decades, he had sought to synthesize vernacular black music with established popular and concert forms as a means of appealing to both black and white audiences. Handy recognized that both the popular music industry and the concert music world practiced discrimination and perpetuated racial stereotypes. He saw that many talented musicians were forced into minstrelsy because they were denied opportunities in concert music.[44] Yet Handy also recognized that the expectations of diverse audiences facilitated the emergence of hybrid black musics, created the opportunity to make a living, and presented a way out of the web of minstrel representations.

Handy's recollection, in his 1941 autobiography, *Father of the Blues,* of how and why he integrated the blues into his repertoire is a fascinating account of how an African American artist was motivated by racial pride, validated by white definitions of black authenticity, and educated about the financial gains to be made by promoting an identifiably black expression. Handy said he heard the blues performed in the town of Tutwilex, Mississippi, in 1903, by a singer accompanying himself on slide guitar. He was initially resistant to this music, but he incorporated it into his compositions after an incident at a performance for a white audience in Cleveland, Mississippi. That evening, Handy's restrained dance music received a tepid response from the audience, who subsequently requested that a local band entertain them. Handy was surprised to see a string trio (guitar, mandolin, and bass) take the stage and play an earthy, rough music that he doubted would appeal to "anybody besides small town rounders." He was astonished when the group was showered with silver dollars tossed onto the stage, at which point he experienced a musical awakening.

> Then I saw the beauty of primitive music. They had the stuff the people wanted. It touched the spot. Their music contained the essence. Folks would pay money for it. . . . That night a composer was born, an *American* composer. These country black boys at Cleveland had taught me something that could not possibly have been gained from books, something that would, however, cause books to be written. Art, in the highbrow sense, was not in my mind. My idea of what constitutes music was changed by the sight of that silver money cascading around the splay feet of a Mississippi string band.[45]

Thus, during the same year that Du Bois's *Souls of Black Folk* was published, Handy embraced black folk music, which suggested to him, as a working bandleader and songwriter, the possibility of greater riches and the creation of a defiantly "American" art rooted in African American culture.

Handy quickly made the blues integral to his compositions and performances. He wrote arrangements of local folk songs and created popular original compositions such as "Memphis Blues" and "St. Louis Blues." Although his decision to embrace the blues was inspired by the expectations of a white audience, his African American public also influenced him. Handy incorporated a bit of "tango" rhythm into "St. Louis Blues" after his black audiences at Dixie Park in Memphis "convinced [him] that there was something racial in their response to this rhythm." His use of flatted thirds and sevenths (suggesting the microtonal variations and slurs that characterize blues singing and playing), his incorporation of "Negro phraseology and dialect" in song lyrics, and his creation of compositions that left room for vocal improvisation were all devices intended to replicate black folk expression and reach a black audience.[46]

After moving to New York in 1917, Handy ran a briefly successful sheet music business—an enterprise inspired by growth in the music publishing business and his ire at having been cheated out of the royalties to "Memphis Blues." He also explored the possibility of extending the blues into more elaborate musical forms. A January 1919 article on Handy in ABB founder Cyril Briggs's magazine *Crusader* described Handy's attempt to make the blues a concert music: "Mr. Handy intends making use of the tercentenary [of the African presence in British North America], to show that these BLUES can be woven into beautiful symphonies and a truly higher art." This issue also featured an advertisement for sheet music for "Afro-American Hymn," a Handy composition meant to trace African American experience from 1619 to 1919: "To those who are interested in such songs as the above which *reflect our progress and outline our aspirations* we especially recommend this *Afro-American Hymn,* which was written and set to beautiful music by W. C. Handy, and is especially adapted to the needs of Negro schools, choirs and singing societies." During the 1920s, Handy continued to invoke racial pride and artistic respectability, as he marketed sheet music for popular blues songs.[47]

*Blues: An Anthology* is a collection of lyrics and music for blues songs, with a lengthy introduction by Abbe Niles, a white Wall Street lawyer and music aficionado. This book project came together after Niles approached Handy for a series of interviews in 1925. Handy recalled that they "worked up so much material that I concluded to assemble and edit an anthology embracing not only my own work but examples of the folk songs that preceded and influenced it and the later compositions of both Negroes and whites representing the blues influence." Niles's emphasis on Handy's central role in the development and popularization of the idiom suggests that this version of blues history came in large part from the musician's own memory. (Handy would later provide a similar version of events in his autobiography.) The anthology, which allowed Handy, in his words, "to keep the record straight" about black popular music, is an early example of a white writer serving as amanuensis for a black musician.[48]

The volume describes the development of the idiom and its position in American society. The introduction notes the origins of the blues among marginalized African Americans in the South. With its simple harmonic structure (based primarily on the tonic, subdominant, and dominant chords) and three-line lyric over the typical twelve-bar chorus, the blues form facilitated melodic, lyrical, and rhythmic improvisation and thus became a "vehicle for expressing the individual's mood of the moment." The "possibilities" of this music were appreciated by none other than W. C. Handy, who is credited with bringing this folk form to the wider public through his compositions and publishing company.[49] The collection of songs begins with fourteen Handy arrangements of "traditional" work songs, spirituals, dance numbers, and country blues songs. "Friendless Blues," with words by Mercedes Gilbert and music by Handy, marks the transition to "the modern Negroid development of the blues." As one might expect, Handy is prominently represented in this section, through compositions such as "Loveless Love," "St. Louis Blues," and "Aunt Hagar's Children." The last section presents the "white viewpoint," with pieces penned by songwriters such as Irving Berlin, Anne Caldwell, Jerome Kern, and George and Ira Gershwin. The collection concludes with George Gershwin's "Rhapsody in Blue" and "Concerto in F."

The anthology suggests that Handy wanted people to understand his work and the development of the blues as a self-conscious enterprise involving artifice as well as instinct. Although Handy and Niles presented the blues as an organic folk expression in its origins, Handy appears to have realized that the primitivist attention to black music as folk expression generally denied the intent and autonomy of the artist.[50] In contrast to Johnson's assessment of the creative impetus behind the blues,

Niles describes Handy as "a colored musician with creative as well as analytical powers." This suggests a difference between the act of expressing one's mood through performance and the more reflective acts of composition and musical archaeology. Just as Handy did later in his autobiography, Niles tells the story of the composer's use of flatted thirds and sevenths (blue notes) and the habañera rhythm (for example, in "St. Louis Blues") as self-conscious efforts to represent a racial idiom.[51]

*Blues: An Anthology* also interprets the relationship of blues to the burgeoning jazz idiom in a way that highlights Handy's contributions while seeking to understand the development of jazz as a product of both racial expression and self-conscious artistic exploration. Handy and Niles define the improvised vocal or instrumental passages during the musical "breaks" in blues songs as "jazz." Although the origins of jazz lie in folk blues, the book argues that it took Handy to make jazz into "a very powerful racial impulse." The improvisational statements of the folk blues as an individual expression spoke strongly of "the common human instinct to fill in the gap," but the "racial impulse" was not fully realized until musicians could engage in the "competitive artistic effort" of "a single voice trying to distinguish itself among the rest." According to the story told by Handy and Niles, Handy had first noticed this impulse in African American church vocal music, and he claimed that it reemerged in his own band's performances of "Mr. Crump," the musical antecedent to "Memphis Blues":

> But with the first performances by a capable Negro orchestra of "Mr. Crump," something new and unheard-of took place; at a certain point in the third and final air, one musician went wild. He deviated from his score and put in some licks on his own account; he licentiously patted his feet. Up to then this, like every other dance orchestra, had played as best it could what was set before it in black and white; this fellow, indeed, had made himself subject to fine on two counts. But discipline, this time, sat an uneasy saddle, fell, and when encores came, one musician and another would put in his call before the fascinating "break," to fill it, if he could, more ingeniously than his colleagues; to assert his individuality,—just as had his forebears at the baptisin's.[52]

Jazz, then, was based on an improvisational spirit: a "racial impulse" that had a distant connection to folk blues and church music, but which received its fullest expression when individual musicians asserted their own voices by riffing off of Handy's composition. Jazz marked the culmination of two movements: black musicians extending the folk forms of their musical past through the use of composition, while simultaneously escaping the confines of the written score by reaching into the vernacular.

This characterization of the "origins" of jazz speaks to a synthetic ethos held by Handy and other black composers working in the early twentieth century. Like his colleagues inside and outside music, Handy adhered to a vision of "two-tiered mastery" as a means of promoting African American musical genius. This formulation also reflects an orientation that was firmly established in the jazz community by the 1920s. As historian Burton Peretti notes, the collision of African American and European American musical cultures created within black musicians' circles a sense of collective artistic endeavor and an embrace of art as individual expression, much like that of European Romantic artists and writers. Early jazz players were focused on developing their individual voice and innovative approaches to their music.[53] Giving voice to this self-conscious ethos of creativity also challenged, albeit incompletely, primitivist assumptions about innate, untutored black musicality.

Handy's and Niles's balancing of self-conscious artifice and "racial impulse" was also a response to the workings of the marketplace. They recognized both the benefits and the dangers of the popularization of jazz. Whether they embraced or denied the black roots of jazz, white bands reaped most of the profits from its performance. And the popularization of jazz and blues, the spate of novelty songs sold under the rubric of these labels, and the controversies that accompanied the genres made the position of African American musicians precarious. The response of Handy and Niles to this dilemma was to reclaim black music, while remaining indebted to those white musicians who might validate it without competing with black musicians. They praised Gershwin for taking jazz into the symphony hall and for demonstrating how the blues could have "an influence still of undiminished vitality and suggestiveness" while escaping the potentially "monotonous" effect that jazz as commodified dance music imposed on its listeners. Although critical of the "white man's impression of the musical Negro" (suggesting a continuing legacy of minstrelsy in jazz), they saw both Handy and Gershwin working against "imitation" in their distinct (black versus white) cultural universes. By sticking to his "native language," each composer had succeeded in making the blues (and jazz) into an important artistic statement.[54]

## Gender and Jazz

If Handy and Niles created their blues canon in response to the racial discourse and economic relationships that structured the music world, their celebration of this music also reflected the masculinist ethos in American musical culture. In other words, Handy's subsequent embrace of the title "father of the blues" symbolized not only a claim as originator but also a certain patriarchal authority as a "race man." The anthology's introduction briefly mentions Ma Rainey and various blueswomen with the surname Smith—including Bessie Smith, who is described as "the Empress, who makes up her own words before the unforgiving jaws of the recording machine." Handy's collection also contains songs that speak of women's losses in love relationships. Yet this text features only a few songs composed by women and largely ignores songs that resonate with the feminist messages and explicit sexual imagery that characterized much of the repertoire of the "classic" blues singers. *Blues: An Anthology* thus speaks to the convergence between gender relations in the music world and gendered ideas about art and culture. These connections are critical for understanding the development of the intellectual history of jazz (both within the musicians' community and without), in which manhood was often a crucial element in a discussion of aesthetics, culture, race, economics, national identity, and other issues.

As Hazel Carby and Angela Davis have shown, the song lyrics of Bessie Smith, Ma Rainey, and other singers were a running commentary on issues of interest to working-class African Americans (especially women) during this period. Blues songs spoke of migration and urbanization, natural disasters, work, crime, racial and economic exploitation, freedom, and other relevant issues. Women's blues of the 1920s also critiqued patriarchal gender relations, male violence, and the restrictions of the domestic sphere. Blueswomen told of leaving violent, unfaithful, or inadequate male lovers; boasted of their own sexual prowess and conquests; and affirmed lesbian relationships as healthy alternatives to the confines of heterosexuality. As Carby notes, these representations were "a struggle that [was] directed against the objectification of female sexuality within a patriarchal order but which also tried to reclaim women's bodies as the sexual and sensuous subjects of women's song."[55]

Sexual innuendo is evident in some of Handy's song lyrics. For example, "St. Louis Blues," a song Bessie Smith recorded, features a reference to the ubiquitous "jelly roll." Looking back on the 1920s, however, Handy was rather prudish about popular blues records and saw them as a threat to the respectability of the blues as he envisioned them. In Handy's mind, their sexual imagery spoke more to a base white audience than to respectable black folk. In his autobiography he remembered: "A flock of low-down dirty blues appeared on records, not witty double entendre but just plain smut. These got a play in college fraternities, speakeasies and rowdy spots. Their appeal was largely to whites, though they were labeled 'race records.'"[56]

Hazel Carby's and Kevin Gaines's work on black intellectual life in the early twentieth century demonstrates that the racial uplift and black nationalist ideologies of the day were saturated with masculinism; indeed, the very idea of black intellectualism was frequently coded as male.[57] As a "race man," Handy's strategy for racial and musical uplift seemed invested in controlling a "feminine" sphere of popular music while presenting himself as an intellectual and extolling the folk and concert dimensions of black musical expression. Thus his blues vision provides a starting point for exploring the ways that jazz was seen as a masculine expression, which has been critical to the meanings associated with the music for its entire history.

The origins of this ethos might be traced to pan-cultural, deep-seated beliefs about genius and the human body. Men have generally been viewed as purveyors of intellect and creativity, stemming from the assumption that women, by virtue of their reproductive capacities, are closer to "nature" while men are more attuned to "culture."[58] In African, European, and American societies, such beliefs were manifested in prejudices about women's artistic capabilities. In addition, men were thought to possess physical qualities that made them better suited for the music business. Members of the American jazz community believed that women did not have the strength to excel on horns and drums or in certain styles (stride, for instance) on the often-feminized piano. They believed, too, that success in music depended on the ability to negotiate continued absence from home and family responsibilities and the means to survive dangerous performance spaces without damage to one's body or reputation. And since working as a jazz musician, as Linda Dahl argues, "came to represent both symbolic and concrete proof" of African American manhood, black women received heavy pressure not to compete for these jobs. From the beginning, then, bands, musicians' organizations and unions, and the jazz education system were generally organized along the lines of patriarchal authority and "male fraternity."[59]

This masculinist ethos within the musicians' community was also a product of the contradictory class politics of black music and the hybrid world musicians inhabited. It derived from the music's unsteady location at the margins of high art, folk expression, and commodified mass culture as well as from the collision between working-class and bourgeois orientations and African American and European American musical cultures. The masculinist sense of jazz artistry was established in part during the first decades of the twentieth century, as musicians shared entertainment spaces with people involved in the underground economies of drug dealing, pimping and prostitution, and gambling. Musicians encountered prostitutes, dancers, and other women whose vocations made them "commodified sex objects" in an economy in which black men sought to reclaim their own sense of masculinity by partaking of the "sporting life." A handful of musicians participated in this economy themselves. Ferdinand "Jelly Roll" Morton, for example, claimed to have worked as a pimp in the 1910s and 1920s; and a few others boasted of having done the same in the post–World War II era, to supplement the meager income provided by performing. Whether one was a participant or an observer, the "sporting life" affirmed male power and devalued female creativity by placing women in roles associated with sex.[60]

The "sporting life," as Patrick Hill demonstrates in a study of Chicago during the Great Migration, provided more than mere material rewards. Directly participating in this hypermasculine culture, or even developing an affinity with it, offered access to alternative, expressive capital that challenged American society's denial of the status and rights of manhood to African American men. In a world where most working-class black men had few opportunities to safely challenge existing social relations, verbal performances (urban toasts, the dozens, and so forth), sexual play, and "spectacular" sartorial display composed a "masculinist politics of style" that articulated a new urban identity, demanded respect, and critiqued race relations while affirming a gendered hierarchy. The valorization of "bravado" and "brilliance" that was part of this subculture fed into the improvisational ethos in jazz and ultimately helped to validate black male genius in a society that denied it.[61]

Even the more innocuous, heterosocial world of dating contributed to the development of the masculinist ethos in the jazz community. As many male musicians have testified, an important impetus for becoming a professional musician was to meet women. In his autobiography, Duke Ellington recalled the attention he received from female admirers at one of his first public performances: "From then on, I was invited to many parties, where I learned that when you were playing piano there was always a pretty girl standing down at the bass clef end of the piano."[62] Although jazz musicians and other popular performers might have been shunned by some of the more conservative members of the community, the life of a well-dressed musician who was an object of female desire was appealing to young musicians, whose other option was often menial labor. The better one's musical reputation, the more appealing one was to a female audience, and the more surely one could derive a heightened sense of one's own heterosexual masculinity.

To the extent that jazz intersected with the "sporting life" and the amusements of working-class (or middle-class) young people, its existence stood in opposition to the uplift strategies and Victorian morality of middle-class clubwomen and other female reformers. These women kept a wary eye on the vices of the tenderloin and the underregulated interactions between young men and women in dance halls and nightclubs. When Langston Hughes criticized the clubwoman's preference for Andalusian song, he demonstrated how jazz's function and status as a popular expression was often created in contradistinction to notions of African American female respectability.[63]

The masculinist ethos in the jazz community was also influenced by gendered ideas about creativity and genius that were entrenched in Western musical cultures. As Susan McClary argues, music in the West has long reflected gender relations and has been a site where "various models of gender organization . . . are asserted, adopted, contested, and negotiated." Classical music in particular reflected strong cultural biases about the male's supposed superiority in the realm of intellect and creativity. Moreover, as a result of musicians and music aficionados having been branded "effeminate" because of music's association with the body and sensuous pleasure, "male musicians have retaliated in a number of ways: by defining music as the most ideal (that is, the least physical) of the arts; by insisting emphatically on its 'rational' dimension; by laying claim to such presumably masculine virtues as objectivity, universality, and transcendence; by prohibiting actual female participation altogether."[64] Ironically, the creation of a masculine artistic ethos often involved the embrace of supposed feminine attributes. During the Romantic period, musical and literary genius was attained by incorporating "'feminine' imagination with masculine reason." In classical music, certain compositional elements used to portray female subjects or femininity (such as "excessive ornamentation and chromaticism") have also been seen as indicative of genius. As musical and literary high culture developed in nineteenth-century Europe and America in the wake of Romanticism, these elements were figured as male in contrast to a more "feminine" mass culture.[65]

Jazz musicians drew upon this Romantic ethos with its masculine implications as they developed an aesthetic sensibility that favored originality, creativity, and emotional expression. McClary stresses that the gendered meanings in music are not timeless, yet it is clear that Romantic ideals continue to influence our understanding of music and musicians' ideas about themselves.[66] Although only a handful of early-twentieth-century African American musicians had anything approaching full access to musical high culture, the ideological framework set in place during the early nineteenth century permeated institutional and informal musical discourse and education and affected the way some jazz musicians understood the arts of improvisation and composition.

Moreover, the emergence of Romanticism as a set of aesthetic principles was rooted in economic relationships of the late eighteenth and early nineteenth centuries. Threatened by the ascendant power of the scientist and the capitalist, Romantic poets embraced masculine metaphor and competition while seeking to craft a "pure vision" that allowed them some influence in a world increasingly dominated by market relations and technological innovation.[67] Similarly, African American musicians in the early twentieth century—who were entrenched in the economics of the music industry, the technologies of the mass media, and their attendant discourse—embraced artistic ideals such as originality, spontaneity, and emotional expression as a way of generating self-respect. These ideals also provided financial reward if those who held the purse strings in the culture industry recognized the artistry of these musicians. The cultivation of originality and the embrace of art as an expression of one's emotional core provided a means to power in a system that exploited black musicians and erased black genius. Black musicians knew they were producing a commodity. Unlike some of their white peers in classical music, they did not have the luxury of rejecting a mass audience. Yet the artistic ethos of Romanticism, including the ideal of not "selling out," existed side by side with the desire to gain remuneration and respectability through popularity.

When Handy and Niles gave short shrift to the legacy of female blues performers, they articulated a Romantic ethos that esteemed male artistry. They presented the movement of the blues from its folk roots to jazz's entry into the concert hall, but they conveniently elided women's blues. Classic blues songs appear to have been threatening to Handy's vision because they smacked of sexuality and popular entertainment and thus were difficult to reconcile with his project of making the blues a legitimate art. The importance of the blues instead lay in the reconstitution of a "racial impulse" through Handy's compositional skills and the instrumental virtuosity of his band. Ultimately, racial genius, as presented in the anthology, was also male genius; it was attained through written music and instrumental innovation and stood in juxtaposition to the feminized world of popular blues songs.

Scholars have noted the irony of the recorded legacy of the masculine world of instrumental jazz developing out of women's blues music in the early 1920s. Record companies at first had little interest in recording instrumental jazz until its practitioners established their reputations by accompanying female blues singers.[68] But since then, the jazz world has been a male-dominated sphere of activity. Beginning in the early years of the twentieth century, there developed a homosocial jazz community, whose ethos of male camaraderie provided refuge from the outside world, a model for behavior on the bandstand, and an ethos for artistic growth in a friendly yet competitive atmosphere. The jazz world mirrored gender inequalities in the broader society, the labor force, and the arts in general. This community was in part forged out of subaltern aesthetic and professional responses to dominant structures of race and class as well as the incorporation of dominant, gendered aesthetic ideals into its members' artistic visions. Both of these moves were rooted in the economic relationships in which musicians found themselves. This is not to say that the early jazz community was uniformly misogynist—although sometimes individuals were—or that women were always excluded from musical circles. Male musicians often spoke warmly of their female colleagues; and women instrumentalists, singers, and, occasionally, bandleaders challenged prejudice and made their own mark on the genre. But such interventions did not fundamentally alter an ethos predicated on the marginalization of women in musicians' circles and the cultivation of the idea that one's artistry was linked to one's manhood.

## The Trouble with Jazz

The second half of the 1920s witnessed transformations in jazz music, the music industry, and perceptions of jazz as an art form. New recording technologies facilitated changes in the music. The shift in 1924 from acoustical recording (where large horns funneled sound vibrations to a cutting stylus) to electrical recording with microphones allowed engineers to increase the range of recorded frequencies. Lower tones could now be reproduced more effectively, allowing bassists and drummers to take a more prominent role on records. And because they did not have to play so loudly, musicians could moderate their tones and explore greater musical dynamics.[69] Improved technologies helped to showcase the talents of African American artists who transformed the genre. Sidney Bechet and especially Louis Armstrong began to change the conception of the jazz solo in the mid-1920s. As evident on his Hot Five and Hot Seven recordings beginning in 1925, Armstrong developed a large tone and a variety of complex rhythmic ideas as he shifted the focus of small group performance away from collective improvisation toward swinging solo improvisations. Jazz groups began to develop more rhythmically sophisticated ensemble playing as well. Fletcher Henderson and Duke Ellington developed big band arrangements with intricate, call-and-response passages between brass and reed sections, the showcasing of individual soloists, and an effusive rhythmic propulsion that appealed to dancers.[70]

New technologies and the innovations by these and other artists highlighted African Americans' role in the development of jazz as an art form and raised the level of professionalism in their community. Phonographs and radios spread musical innovations and served as educational devices for young musicians. The effect of these media was to increase the level of knowledge about jazz and its possibilities as an art form, while encouraging standardization in the genre. Moreover, the rise of big bands increased the number of literate musicians and accelerated the reliance on written scores, as musicians came to see reading as a necessary step to full employment and bandleaders viewed musical literacy as a vehicle for creative growth.[71]

Despite these developments, jazz still presented restrictions to professional African American musicians. Some became jazz players because it was clear that segregation and racism would limit their aspirations in art music. Those working in the jazz business—often under the employ of gangsters—found the wages low, the conditions difficult, and unions of little help. Moreover, musicians faced a fickle and contradictory marketplace. Black musicians knew that white musicians usually gained greater respect and remuneration from jazz performance. To the extent that African American jazz remained visible in American society, black musicians often had to negotiate the primitivist demands of white patrons, who flocked in increasing numbers to places like New York's Cotton Club and Savoy Ballroom (which opened in 1922 and 1926, respectively).

Chicago-based bandleader, union delegate, and newspaperman Dave Peyton displayed a good deal of ambivalence about jazz. In his weekly column for the *Chicago Defender,* which ran from 1925 to 1929, Peyton provided news of the local and national African American musicians' community, promoted codes of professional behavior, and chastised those musicians who did not adhere to his standards. Peyton has been seen as emblematic of an "assimilationist" or "middle-class" perspective on music. He celebrated the virtues of classical music, often denigrated jazz as a "low" form of music, and worried that jazz players were musical ignoramuses whose lack of professionalism threatened the status and livelihoods of more respectable artists and their ability to "uplift" their communities.[72]

But Peyton was sometimes willing to take jazz seriously when it could be viewed as a symbol of African American innovation and achievement. Although he generally looked down at the collectively improvised "gut-bucket" music of New Orleans, he regularly praised Louis Armstrong, who was at the time developing a unique solo style. In one column, Peyton wrote that the trumpeter was in a "class by himself," celebrating that Armstrong so impressed white musicians that they followed him to night-clubs to try to figure out his "weird jazz figures."[73] Peyton was even fonder of the urbane, arranged big band music and the skills its musicians displayed. In a 1928 column, he presented a brief history of jazz, noting its roots in ragtime and New Orleans communal music making. Although he frowned on the collectively improvised music of New Orleans, he believed that "this crude style of jazz playing has developed into the world-famous artistic jazz music. . . . The beautiful melodies garnished with difficult eccentric figures and propelled by artful rhythms, hold grip on the world today, replacing the mushy, discordant jazz music."[74]

Peyton vacillated in his assessments of whether jazz was just a passing fad or an art form that was now entrenched in American society. His sometimes schizophrenic attitude toward jazz was in part a product of his concerns about the employment opportunities available to African American musicians and the artistic limitations the music industry placed on these performers. Peyton recognized that African American musicians, regardless of their contribution to the field, were vulnerable to the vicissitudes of the market and the competition for resources. In one column, he decried bandleader Noble Sissle's retirement from the stage because jazz had been "usurped" by white musicians. In another, he noted that members of Chicago's white musicians' local were actively trying to keep black players out of certain venues. He also asserted that black musicians had been pigeonholed into playing certain popular forms. Peyton wrote: "In the past the big recording companies have confined our musicians to one style of recording. This style of recording they consider our orchestras are perfected in. They confine us to low jazz and blues. They have an idea that our orchestras cannot play real music for recordings, but they never were so wrong."[75] Typically, his advice to musicians was to remain versatile in both jazz and classical music as a means of keeping their options open. In a 1928 column, he praised the piano playing of James P. Johnson, Lillian Armstrong, Fats Waller, Clarence

Williams, Earl Hines, and Eubie Blake and implied that their music exceeded that of classically oriented performers. Yet Peyton still thought the "jazz craze" was on the wane, so he counseled musicians to "save their money" and "use their leisure time in studying real music."[76]

Another musician Peyton discussed in his column was Duke Ellington, the Washington, D.C., native who moved to New York in 1923, made a name for himself locally, and then became nationally and internationally famous after obtaining his long-running engagement at Harlem's Cotton Club. This gig lasted from late 1927 until 1931 and was broadcast live at times by NBC. During the same period, Ellington recorded with increasing frequency, releasing 180 sides between December 1927 and February 1931.[77] Ellington developed a distinctive sound that he applied to a variety of musical expressions, including dance tunes, popular songs, production numbers, "mood" pieces, and instrumental jazz compositions. Using his band as an "instrument," Ellington's intricate horn arrangements showcased a range of instrumental voices and tonal effects and provided a framework for the improvisational skills of his band members.

In the late 1920s and early 1930s, Ellington received growing attention from the press, where he occupied a contradictory position. In a series of articles in *Phonograph Monthly,* music critic R. D. Darrell characterized Ellington's recordings as serious artistic accomplishments on a par with classical music. Praising Ellington's 1931 Victor recordings of "Limehouse Blues" and "Echoes of the Jungle," he wrote: "The elaborate texture and diabolically ingenious arrangements will astound even the student of such modern orchestrators as Ravel and Strawinski." Others merely viewed Ellington as the purveyor of "jungle jazz," a label that signified both Ellington's unique explorations of the tonal qualities of jazz and the primitivistic expectations of white audiences. Some early accounts of his Cotton Club performances spent as much time celebrating the venue's light-skinned chorines as they did his music.[78] Yet such consideration, despite its unevenness, gave Ellington the opportunity to express his aesthetic vision and to strategically challenge the restrictions black musicians faced in the music industry.

During these years, Ellington maintained a coherent aesthetic politics consistent with the goals of the Harlem Renaissance. Ellington had developed this perspective in Washington, D.C., where as Mark Tucker notes, his "dignified manner and cultivated persona, his social consciousness, his use of vernacular sources as the basis for original compositions, and his deep pride in the Afro-American heritage" were rooted. Ellington was influenced by a community interest in black history and by local professional black musicians such as Henry Lee Grant, who viewed popular music as a serious enterprise. In New York, Ellington encountered or drew from the work of Will Marion Cook, James Reese Europe, and Ford Dabney, all of whom championed black musical traditions and drew upon vernacular idioms for original compositions. Ellington adopted their public personae, which commanded respect out of dignity and decorum; and, like them, he rejected generic labels, while believing strongly in the ability of music to express a "racial" feeling.[79]

In an interview with Janet Mabie of the *Christian Science Monitor,* Ellington articulated, in Tucker's words, "two concerns that would stay with him for a lifetime: his aversion to the word 'jazz' and his commitment to the ideals of 'Negro music.'" When asked about jazz, Ellington said the term confused him. He described his music instead as a project of recuperation and uplift: "I am just getting a chance to work out some of my own ideas of Negro music. I stick to that. We as a race have a good deal to pay our way with in a white world. The tragedy is that so few records have been kept of the Negro music of the past. It has to be pieced together so slowly. But it pleases me to have a chance to work at it." Ellington's New Negro musical vision depended upon access to multiple forms of musical knowledge. Speaking of the necessity of his early training, Ellington said: "I had a kind of harmony inside me, which is part of my race, but I needed the kind of harmony which has no race at all but is universal." These comments suggest not so much a capitulation to "white" or European standards as a desire to have all possible musical tools at his disposal while developing an African American form. And, as Graham Lock notes, such commentary rejected the narrow prescription of "jungle jazz," when that term had come to signify audience expectations more than Ellington's own aesthetic vision.[80]

Ellington also sought to understand his music as a "popular" art. In another interview from 1930, he expressed the belief that his music could break down the divisions between high and low culture, folk and popular expression, and American and European music. In this vision, the music's legitimacy would be determined by its mass appeal: "You have only to watch a dance floor full of dancing couples to realize that music is the most vital thing in swaying the emotions of a multitude." Ellington identified a new kind of American music that had popular appeal and black folk artistry at its center:

> I am not playing jazz. I am trying to play the natural feelings of
> a people. I believe that music, popular music of the day, is the real
> reflector of the nation's feelings. Some of the music which has been
> written will always be beautiful and immortal. Beethoven, Wagner
> and Bach are geniuses; no one can rob their work of the merit that
> is due it, but these men have not portrayed the people who are about
> us today, and the interpretation of these people is our future music. . . .
> The Negro is the blues. Blues is the rage in popular music. And popu-
> lar music is the good music of tomorrow![81]

New Negro intellectuals crafted such a vision as they sought to prove black worth in American society. Ellington appears to have adhered to this vision for reasons of racial uplift and as a means of validating his role and the roles of other professional black musicians in American society.

Ellington expanded upon the themes of racial contribution and popular appeal in a 1931 essay he contributed to *Rhythm,* a British magazine directed to dance band musicians. Noting that rhythm was fundamental to the success of dance music and to human existence itself, Ellington still recognized that an emphasis on a dance-friendly beat could create a monotonous sound. Many bands were stagnating because of the "soulless nature of this continual churning out of four-in-a-bar rhythm." The way out of this predicament was artistic originality. His band refused to use "printed orchestrations," instead relying on his own arrangements, which left room for his players to contribute to the rhythmic conception of the piece.[82]

Like Handy, Ellington defined his originality as a racial expression that stood in opposition to the standardization the music industry encouraged in dance bands:

> The numbers I write are never, I think you will agree, of the 'corn-
> fed' type. Always I try to be original in my harmonies and rhythms.
> I am not trying to suggest that my tunes are superior to those of other
> writers. Because I think that the music of my race is something which

is going to live, something which posterity will honour in a higher
sense than merely that of the music of the ballroom to-day, I put my
best musical thoughts forward into my tunes, and not hackneyed
harmonies and rhythms which are almost too banal to publish.

Ellington was not trying to chart a vision in which legitimacy was based
on his music's distance from the forces of the market. He clearly realized
that as a dance band leader he had "to consider the financial side" of music and appeal to a mass audience. Yet he wanted to move outside the
thirty-two-bar popular songs done with a "strict tempo." He celebrated
the work of black concert hall performers such as Paul Robeson, Roland
Hayes, and Samuel Coleridge-Taylor; and, like James Weldon Johnson
and others, he looked forward to the day when "from the welter of Negro dance musicians now before the public will come something lasting
and noble."[83]

Ellington's similarity to New Negro thinkers is also evident in his view
of black musical culture as a means of exploring the past. He defined
African American dance music as a product of the history of black people
in America. The music's origins lay in the transplanting of Africans to
American soil and their experiences of slavery. Music provided a way of
articulating "what we could not say openly" and was a "timeless" means
of expressing black personality. Yet this sonic expression was thoroughly
modern as well, expressing the optimism of urban black America and
the cultural renaissance it produced: "In Harlem we have what is prac-
tically our own city; we have our own newspapers and social services,
and although not segregated, we have almost achieved our own civilisa-
tion. The history of my people is one of great achievements over fearful
odds; it is a history of a people hindered, handicapped and sorely oppressed, and what is being done by Countee Cullen and others in literature is overdue in our music."[84]

Ellington described his own desire to create an extended composition
that would move outside the limitations of dance music (while maintaining a connection to his audience) and thematically explore African
American experience. He said he was in the process of writing a composition consisting of four or five movements that would be an "authentic
record of my race written *by a member of it.*" As Graham Lock points
out, Ellington may well have been influenced by concert representations

of black life and history by W. C. Handy, James P. Johnson, William Grant Still, and others. The extended composition he described in this essay was most likely his "Symphony in Black" (1934), a four-part, nine-minute composition that used elements from earlier pieces while exploring the themes of labor, romance, religion, and urban life. Part One, "The Laborers," maintains a slow blues feeling and employs the hammer-fall punctuation of a work song. Part Two, "A Triangle," depicts a romantic love triangle through an up-tempo dance number and the vocal blues lament of a spurned lover. The third part, "A Hymn of Sorrow," explores the sonorities of a mournful spiritual. The work concludes with "Harlem Rhythm," a fast-paced, intricately arranged section that portrays the complexity of black urban life. The composition anticipates Ellington's symphonic-length depiction of African American experience, *Black, Brown and Beige,* which premiered at Carnegie Hall in 1943, and other extended interpretations of black themes.[85]

Ellington was a unique individual in many respects, yet his artistic project and aesthetic vision, informed by the parameters of the music industry and the ongoing jazz discourses, bore similarities to those of other musicians. He embraced the ideal of black artistry while moving beyond limitations imposed on African Americans by race. Striking a balance between race consciousness and universalism would be a defining characteristic of Ellington's work throughout his lifetime, and it was a challenge to which future generations of musicians returned again and again, as they did to his ideal of creating a music that challenged the supposed supremacy of European concert music and that drew its legitimacy from its popular appeal.

## "Swing That Music"

When scholars and critics discuss the "swing era" in musical terms, they generally refer to the ascendancy of the big bands in the 1930s, their continued popularity through World War II, and the musical changes they brought about. "Swing" in this sense refers to the shift from two-beat to 4/4 time, the replacement of small groups with larger ensembles, a move away from collectively improvised ensemble playing to multisectional written arrangements supporting solo improvisations, and the development of a propulsive rhythm conducive to dancing. Although large dance bands were growing in popularity in the late twenties and early thirties, as Ellington's success makes clear, the Great Depression and the rising popularity of radio and films helped to keep people away from dance halls and clubs and caused a drop in record sales in 1932. Yet big band jazz soon made its way to the center of American popular music. Record sales slowly began to rebound and then exploded in the late 1930s, and the repeal of Prohibition in 1933 brought masses of people into dance halls. Swing as a popular movement was facilitated by a growing capital investment in the culture industry and the increasing proliferation of mass communications technologies. Jazz historians generally point to the highly acclaimed, nationwide broadcast of Benny Goodman's August 21, 1935, performance at Los Angeles's Palomar Ballroom as the symbolic beginning of the "swing era."

This musical movement was part and parcel of related cultural phenomena. Recent historical treatments of swing view it as emblematic of a democratizing ethos in American society and a more inclusive ideology of American exceptionalism that emanated from the New Deal and the antifascist Popular Front. David Stowe, Lewis Erenberg, and Michael Denning have described swing's ascension as the result of changes in American thinking about race, class, cultural hierarchies, and other issues in the 1930s. During this decade, Boasian cultural relativism, New Deal liberalism, antifascist activism, and radical internationalism all challenged the most blatant aspects of racist thought. Although some moral panic erupted over jazz in the 1930s, changing ideas about race helped to make it relatively subdued compared to the furor of the 1920s. Swing was a product of a decade that witnessed a new ideology of "Americanism," which balanced nationalism and faith in American institutions with a veneration of working people and their culture and a growing commitment to ethnic pluralism.[86]

This democratizing ethos in American society and the cultural fusion taking place were facilitated by the culture industry. As the mass media served the needs of business, they also helped to promote cultural synthesis. "The emergence of this new commercial culture," Denning writes, "had several major consequences. . . . Forms which had had a local base traveled far and wide; the 'classics,' once owned and preserved by the cultured and leisured classes, were now cheaply available, and the working-class entertainments of black and ethnic neighborhoods were available to the educated classes." And when Popular Front activists and artists entered institutions in the culture industry, they played a direct role in reshaping American culture. Members of the left figured prominently in the network of critics, collectors, record shops, and independent labels that supported jazz; and individuals such as John Hammond and Norman Granz actively fought segregation and discrimination in the music industry in the late 1930s and 1940s.[87]

The possibilities of high and low cultural synthesis and racial egalitarianism were perhaps nowhere clearer in the swing world than in jazz concerts and integrated dance halls. Stowe points out that Benny Goodman's 1938 presentation of jazz at Carnegie Hall and various "battle[s] of the bands" at the Savoy Ballroom in Harlem challenged racial and cultural boundaries. Integrated audiences attended both venues, a rare occurrence before 1930, and increasing numbers of black and white musicians were performing together live and on records. On the evening of May 11, 1937, the four thousand patrons lucky enough to gain admission to the Savoy witnessed local hero Chick Webb take on Benny Goodman, the ostensible "King of Swing." Much of the audience crowded around the bandstand to evaluate the performances of the groups. Goodman received an enthusiastic response, but when "Chick gave them the first beat of the bass drum, the crowd went absolutely mad and screamed their applause." Webb's band drew upon its status in the Harlem community to wrest away Goodman's title, at least in the eyes of its fans.[88] By dancing to, listening to, and cheering on Webb and his band, Harlemites joined people from downtown in celebrating the art form that brought them together, while simultaneously building upon a collective identity in which self-worth and black cultural excellence were affirmed by Webb's "victory" over Goodman.

The seriousness with which people listened and danced to these groups was indicative of the loosening of cultural boundaries. Active listeners were important to the growing popularity of jazz concerts during the 1930s. Part of the impetus for this growth came from a mass audience who would gather around radios and bandstands, paying close attention to the music, and, in a more direct manner, from record collectors and members of "hot clubs," who sought to institutionalize musicians' jam sessions as public events, where jazz in its "purest" form could be appreciated by a paying audience. Jazz concerts promoted a greater focus on listening and demanded of the audience that performers be "accorded the kind of respect due concert artists."[89] In contrast to the 1920s, when musicians transformed jazz in order to make it appropriate for the concert hall, audiences of the 1930s brought a concert hall reverence to hot, commercially oriented dance music.

That many jazz concerts were benefits for leftist causes makes them even more emblematic of changes in American society during the 1930s. Although some members of left organizations disdained black popular music, instead favoring "authentic" folk or high cultural expression, others immediately saw value in jazz or eventually overcame their aversion to commercialized music. In Harlem, this newfound respect for jazz went hand in hand with the Communist Party's institutional support for black arts, a component of the party's broader attempt to gain favor in African American communities. Black artists and intellectuals by no means universally welcomed the party's cultural politics during the Popular Front, but left-wing sponsorship encouraged politically minded musicians to lend their names and talents to progressive causes. Duke Ellington made one of the earliest such appearances at a Harlem Communist dance in 1930, and near the end of the decade black musicians participated in several concerts to raise money for the Republican cause during the Spanish civil war.[90] The validation of black popular culture by the left during the late 1930s may well have influenced more centrist institutions such as the NAACP, whose leadership had historically frowned upon jazz. By the end of the 1930s, the NAACP, clubs, and churches sponsored performances of jazz and blues and used the services of Ellington and others at organizational benefits.[91]

As much as swing culture promised them, however, African American musicians still found themselves facing discrimination and exploitation. Although the culture industry might have promoted aesthetic egalitarianism, it did not necessarily treat black workers fairly. The integration of Benny Goodman's small group and big band—Teddy Wilson joined the Goodman trio in 1935—may have been a symbol of changing times, but segregation and discrimination still ran rampant in the music industry. Managers, booking agents, and record companies seldom paid a fair wage, and radio actively discriminated against black bands. A few of the major black artists—Ellington, Armstrong, and

Basie—benefited from the growing popularity of swing, but they were the exceptions. Even as record sales exploded in 1938, African American musicians increasingly found themselves in financial distress. Moreover, changing racial and cultural mores, which made black jazz music more appealing to a wide audience, also threatened to displace these performers. In the early 1930s, black bands had more or less a "monopoly" on "hot" dance band music, with whites dominating the slower, less kinetic realm of "sweet" music. As hot music became more acceptable, the black monopoly on the genre was destroyed, as bands like those headed by Goodman and the Dorsey brothers reaped most of the benefits.[92] "Swing," like jazz, became a symbol of the dilemmas facing African American musicians. Some claimed the label as a means of self-promotion or celebrated it as an affirmation of African American success. Others saw swing as a dilution of black aesthetics and a marker of the restrictions the music industry enforced against them.

One of the earliest recorded commentaries on swing by a black musician was Louis Armstrong's 1936 autobiography, *Swing That Music*. This was one of the first published "biographies" of a jazz musician, and it was also one of the earliest attempts to record jazz history. Interspersed with a discussion of the aesthetics of swing were details of Armstrong's life and his role in music making in New Orleans, Chicago, and New York. Armstrong's input in the creation of this largely ghostwritten volume is somewhat unclear. William Kenney suggests that Armstrong's "authentic" voice is most clearly heard in the narration of actual events in his life, while the "didactic" commentary on swing is likely the voice of the ghostwriter. Thomas Brothers, however, argues that a "great deal" of Armstrong's own insights come through in the text.[93] I believe Armstrong's voice may be heard in the commentary on swing—especially when the description of the genre extols black creativity while validating the role of African American musicians in the development of the music.

Armstrong differentiated "trashy, popular jazz [from] fine swing music." Jazz, in his mind, had been corrupted by the market; it had lost its vitality by being "written down and recorded." Swing, in contrast, represented both the artistic possibilities of jazz and the contributions of African American musicians. Armstrong described swing in Romantic terms as the expression of musicians' feelings. He compared "hot," or swing, musicians to "the greatest writers" who "liked best to write just the way they felt." A "sweet" musician (or commercial jazz player) was like "a writer who writes stories for some popular magazines." Just as in other art forms, a popular audience may not recognize the contributions of a great swing musician, and the market may not reward him. Thus, Buddy Bolden remained unknown outside a small circle of musicians and fans; and Armstrong recognized that, but for a few lucky breaks, he might have remained unknown himself. The genre's current popularity, however, offered greater possibilities to those musicians (black and white alike) who kept the spirit of early New Orleans musicianship alive.[94]

Armstrong asserted that swing was "growing into a finer and broader and richer [and] truly American" music through the incorporation of "classical influences." Although Armstrong argued that jazz had been corrupted by "writing it down," he also recognized the importance of knowing how to "play to score." One merely had to remember that to access the "true spirit of swing" one had to "originate and not just imitate." Yet the artistry of swing and its ability to express feeling were rooted in "free improvisation," which "was at the core of jazz when it started back there in New Orleans thirty years ago." He described early New Orleans musicians: "They were composers *and* players, all in one, and they composed as they played and held what they had done only in their musical memory." This invocation of the "mental" compositions of early innovators hinted at an argument that would often be used by musicians and commentators alike: that the art of improvisation was a spontaneous kind of composition. This suggestion implicitly challenged the hierarchical assumptions separating improvised jazz and classical music and championed an African-derived approach to making music, which Armstrong further supported by figuring New Orleans in the first decade of the twentieth century as a black musical environment. As Handy had before him, Armstrong was careful to emphasize that black achievement in the genre was the product of both instinct and hard work.[95]

Armstrong's comments, however influenced they might have been by the ghostwriter, were a subtle yet significant attempt to validate black artists in the face of commercial forces that had the potential to erase black musicianship in the dance music world. Armstrong's aesthetic formulation, while bearing some similarities to those expressed by earlier black artists and aestheticians, directly addressed "swing," a concept that was part of the lingua franca of the jazz community and which was also a generic label gaining currency with the music industry and a mass audience. He positioned himself as a practitioner of swing and put his name to a narrative that suggested that the popularity of "hot" dance music would validate jazz artistry and black musicians' contributions.

The year 1936 also witnessed the publication of Alain Locke's *The Negro and His Music,* a book-length treatise on the history and aesthetics of African American music. The Howard University professor had been writing about music since the 1910s, and in this text he expanded upon the New Negro principle of "two-tiered mastery." Locke recognized the changing face of jazz music and its position in American society in the mid-1930s. Having witnessed the innovations of contemporary jazz artists, Locke was deeply moved by their work. He described Armstrong as the best of the jazz players and Ellington as the preeminent jazz composer, who was one of the people most likely to create the "classical jazz" to which artists and intellectuals had looked forward. Locke cited *Swing That Music* several times. He quoted at length a passage in which Armstrong described the basis of swing as the art of improvisation, as he attempted to show that jazz was a legitimate art form. Recognizing that the term "classic" was a device that created musical hierarchies, Locke drew upon Armstrong's assertion that "good" and "bad" were more important criteria for evaluating a piece of music, regardless of its high cultural legitimacy. Musical developments in jazz in the 1930s and the critical reception of the idiom suggested to Locke a kind of aesthetic leveling wherein individual and racial expression and technical virtuosity could be as important a standard of legitimacy as an adherence to high cultural forms. In his view, an Ethel Waters performance of "Stormy Weather" or Duke Ellington's rendition of "It Don't Mean a Thing (If It Ain't Got That Swing)" could easily outshine Tin Pan Alley versions of the same compositions as well as "a mediocre attempt in the classical forms."[96]

Yet Locke's celebration of jazz went only so far. While he celebrated jazz artistry and the accomplishments of jazz musicians, he considered the form something of an artistic dead end. Locke defined "jazz classics" as music in the "limited dance and song-ballad forms" that "achieve[d] creative musical excellence." "Classical jazz" represented "more sophisticated and traditional musical forms" that drew from "jazz idioms." These forms illustrated the possibilities of black music, but they would "never become great music nor representative national music over the least common denominator of popular jazz or popular ballads that are in common circulation today. Even 'classical jazz,' promising as it is, is perhaps only a transitional form. Eventually the art-music and the folk-music must be fused in a vital but superior product."[97]

Why did Locke stop short of a complete validation of black accomplishment in jazz? The answer seems to lie both in his continued investment in high culture and in a recognition of the restrictions facing black musicians working in the idiom. Although the Harvard-trained philosopher was by background and training something of a cultural elitist, who favored the common ground of universalism over an ethnically particular pluralism, scholars recognize that Locke's take on black music was also strategic: to him, it seemed the best way to challenge Eurocentric ideas about art and racist representations of black people.[98] Locke's take on jazz was also based on the premise that "one of the handicaps of Negro music today is that it is too popular." Not only were classically oriented musicians forced into popular music by discrimination and need, but popularity imposed limitations on jazz as well. On the one hand, Locke believed that the swing music vogue had "rejuvenated" black artists such as Ellington and Armstrong. The popularity of hot music and the institutional support it received from swing clubs and critics encouraged these musicians to return to their musical roots and to reject the diluted sweet music the market had previously encouraged. But, on the other hand, Locke's optimism was tempered by a recognition that the popularity of jazz threatened the integrity of the music as a black expression. A musician operating in this idiom always had to negotiate white tastes. Moreover, the critical discourse presented impediments to musicians' livelihoods. Generic categories (that is, hot, classical, or swing) were ultimately of more interest to critics and white musicians. "What to the white musicians are different schools and contrasted techniques of jazz are to the Negro musicians, and a few whites thoroughly saturated in the tradition, interchangeable varieties of style." In the end, the investment in categories by the combined forces of the music industry and the jazz writers was predisposed to benefit white musicians to the detriment of African Americans.[99]

Locke saw greater hope for black vindication through classical forms. But more than that, he called for a diasporic aesthetic orientation. He encouraged musicians to study black folk music from the West Indies, Central America, and Africa. These idioms, he argued, "are more strongly racial and are free of the cultural distortion of the plantation tradition; that is, they have no minstrel taint. A healthier primitivism and a more dignified tradition are valuable today when we are trying to develop the deeper possibilities of our music." Although he recognized that explorations of African music and dance were often guided by "sentimental admiration for its effects" rather than "scientific study," he suggested that the latter could be achieved. One of the most important recent explorations of black musical culture, he argued, was Asadata Dafora's African dance opera *Kykunkor,* which had played in New York in 1934.[100]

Locke recognized the expanding artistic possibilities of jazz, while understanding the specific limitations that the industry presented to black musicians. His book extended the New Negro discussion of music into the early swing era and provided a link between the discussion about jazz in the 1920s and 1930s and that of future generations of intellectuals and musicians. His turn to a diasporic vision as a means of countering the restrictions facing jazz players anticipated the struggles of future generations of musicians, and his suspicion of both the jazz economy and the critical discourse about jazz was a perspective that musicians were adopting and articulating with increasing frequency.

## Musicians and Critics

One of the outgrowths of the popularity of jazz in the 1930s was the consolidation of jazz criticism in new trade publications such as *Down Beat* and *Metronome,* small journals for record collectors, and left-wing organs such as *New Masses.* This jazz discourse, by and large created by whites for a white readership, recycled some of the same primitivist ideas put forth by writers in the 1920s. The 1930s dialogue, however, reflected, in complex and often contradictory ways, changing ideas about American society. These discussions anticipated debates about the music that would occur in later years and set the stage for how future musical movements would be received. Jazz criticism also provided musicians with a limited voice for expressing their ideas about their music and life in the music industry. Most musicians generally cared little for the opinions of critics, and the terms of the debate were seldom of their own choosing. Yet the critical discourse held the potential to validate their artistic projects, and its consolidation helped to establish a larger role for musicians in the public dialogue about the music. As musicians helped to define the place of jazz in American life, however, jazz criticism itself presented its own set of restrictions.

When critics debated the merits of "hot" and "sweet" music, big bands and small groups, and jazz and swing in the late 1930s, they addressed intersecting ideas about art, culture, commerce, nation, race, gender, class, and politics. In other words, their comments reflected modernist aesthetic dilemmas as well as broader issues in American society.[101] Many of the young men writing about jazz either had direct connections to the left or were more generally invested in left-liberal politics. Jazz and swing became, in their eyes, emblematic of the pluralistic and democratic America they idealized. Critics increasingly celebrated jazz as an African American expression—although many continued to focus on white artists—and by and large the major jazz publications approved of integration in the music industry.[102]

Yet jazz critics' attention to African American musicians was a mixed blessing. Overlaying the attention to politics were questions of cultural legitimacy. Was African American jazz to be considered a folk form, high art, popular entertainment, or some combination of these categories? Some critics lauded the growing popularity of swing music and saw it as an expression of a thoroughly modern American democracy or a technologically advanced consumer society. Others saw its commercial viability as a mark of illegitimacy, because they preferred either an unadulterated expression of the folk form or a "serious" art form that might challenge the supremacy of classical music. These issues were manifest in the numerous attempts by critics to define jazz styles through the lens of race. Such accounts showcased African American accomplishment in the music industry, but they often defined in narrow terms what was acceptably black expression. Paul Eduard Miller, for example, emphasized the African American roots of jazz in ripostes to commentators who claimed jazz and swing had white roots. Miller, however, was also invested in a primitivist concept of black art, as he distinguished the "truly rich and wholesome jungle jazz of Duke Ellington" from "swing" music, which in his mind included syncopated versions of popular songs and fusions of jazz and classical music. When critics responded that such views reproduced the logic of Jim Crow and offered instead a color-blind theory of jazz accomplishment, they challenged the inherent racism of such statements but also encouraged practices that marginalized black musicians.[103]

Despite the efforts of activist critics like Hammond to fight discrimination in the music industry, jazz criticism could have a detrimental effect on black musicians. Any attempt to define what was legitimate jazz expression or to set up generic boundaries—whether cast in racial terms or not—had the potential to affect the livelihoods of African American musicians at a moment when many were struggling financially. This precarious situation was compounded by the fact that some working critics—including Hammond—had financial interests in the artists they championed in print. Other writers simply knew little about jazz and were careless with their remarks. One of the striking aspects of jazz criticism in the late 1930s, however, is that it almost immediately began to interrogate its own methods. In this climate, jazz writers began to turn to black musicians in order to authenticate their own perspectives and raise questions about the assumptions of their peers.[104]

As musicians helped to shape the discussion about jazz, they expressed their own concerns. In a 1937 *Metronome* article entitled "Do Critics Really Know What It's All About?" saxophonist Benny Carter described the need for critical standards. Carter understood that the capricious tastes of the "commercial ickies" (swing fans) from the daily papers, as well as those of the Ivy League dilettantes who wrote for jazz journals, had a real effect on the lives of working musicians. He called for a "more objective viewpoint in the criticism of dance music" that took seriously what musicians were trying to accomplish rather than merely imposing a critic's own personal taste on a performance or recording.[105]

In three 1939 essays in *Down Beat,* Duke Ellington once again articulated his New Negro concept of musical artistry and took on issues relating to jazz criticism as well. He recognized that critical assessments of jazz seldom addressed the relative merits of the music but instead reflected the ideological prejudices and financial interests of jazz critics. Such criticism not only placed restrictions on what was acceptable jazz performance; it also facilitated a system from which commercial white bands were profiting more than black bands.

In the first essay, Ellington explored the development of jazz and swing. Jazz, he suggested, was an "original and authentic form" that was moving "toward legitimate acceptance, in proportion to its own merits." Swing, however, had been transformed from a verb (that is, an approach to playing music) to a noun (a genre).[106] The consolidation of swing began innocently enough when enthusiastic supporters in Europe and the United States "combin[ed] their efforts to popularize jazz music" and in so doing expanded its audience and "seemed to afford musicians the moral courage and incentive necessary to the open adoption of swing as a style of playing." Yet swing began to stagnate when "writers, faddists, band managers, night club proprietors, entertainers and newspapermen entered the field with a vengeance." Ellington was careful to note that even commercial swing "demand[ed] superior musicianship," but, as art became a commodity, the problem was that "genuine values became distorted and false ones set up in their places."[107]

The blame, Ellington argued, lay in part with critics who had not adequately educated fans about the more artistically inclined bands. Instead, audiences were patronizing the more banal purveyors of the current craze. The promotion of the most popular bands hurt African American groups whom he considered the greatest purveyors of the art form. In the last essay in the series, Ellington made subtle reference to the process by which white groups profited from music with African American roots. Although his tone was diplomatic, he described how black bandleaders such as Fletcher Henderson, Don Redman, and Jimmie Lunceford had not received adequate attention or had seen their innovations appropriated. While Ellington voiced praise and respect for Benny Goodman and some white bandleaders, he gently chastised others for profiting from "musical-simplification to the 'nth' degree" and "reach[ing] a pleasing musical middle." Regarding Bob Crosby, Ellington implied that his "blues influence" was borrowed: "We feel that here the tan has attained a very luxurious luster, perhaps through absorption."[108]

Ellington also chastised critics for imposing unfair standards on bands. He did not think jazz was beyond criticism; but, like Benny Carter, he believed a problem arose when critics used "personal standards" of judgment without understanding what musicians were trying to achieve. He named several prominent critics who had been guilty of misrepresentation. Ellington reserved his strongest comments for John Hammond, whose judgment, he claimed, was influenced by his financial interest in certain artists and his role as an "ardent propagandist" with connections to the Communist Party—a charge he would retract a month later. Ellington was not an anticommunist, as his support for Popular Front causes in the 1930s and 1940s attests, but he was involved in a feud with Hammond. A few years earlier, Hammond had written a blistering review of Ellington's twelve-minute composition "Reminiscing in Tempo," in which he charged that Ellington's music "is losing the distinctive flavor it once had, both because of the fact that he has added slick, un-negroid musicians to his band and because he himself is aping Tin Pan Alley composers for commercial reasons." But, he wrote, the "real trouble" with Ellington was his lack of social conscience. Hammond chastised Ellington for not speaking out about the Scottsboro case—in which nine young African American men were falsely accused of raping two white women in Alabama—or the general conditions facing black working-class and poor people. He asserted that Ellington's lack of political commitment led him to perform music that was "formless and shallow" and divorced from its social context.[109]

While critics who supported more commercially successful white bands could negate the contributions of African American bands, such progressively minded assumptions as Hammond's about proper performances of black music and black identities could be just as limiting. Hammond, as Stowe notes, had by 1938 positioned himself as "the arbiter of African American musical authenticity." He thought Ellington's musicianship, extended compositions, and commercial appeal had moved him too far from his folk roots. Instead, Hammond championed blues players, gospel singers, and New Orleans jazz musicians whose expression was not yet diluted by musical training or the marketplace as well as those commercially successful artists—such as Count Basie, Billie Holiday, Fletcher Henderson, and Benny Goodman—in whom he had a financial stake.[110]

Ellington's way out of this quandary was to hold true to his New Negro ideals and the aesthetic principles of his music. After predicting that swing's entry into the concert hall might lessen its banality, Ellington said that his band members were unconcerned with the conditions in the swing industry. In fact, what they were involved in was larger than jazz or swing. Their "aim has always been the development of an authentic

Negro music" that was "a genuine contribution from our race." His band drew strength from itself and its community. "As a group of musicians we understand each other well. We have identical feelings and beliefs in music. Our inspiration is derived from our lives, and the lives of those about us, and those that went before us." By situating himself in a lineage of musicians immersed in an African American community, Ellington claimed another kind of authenticity: one that carried with it political and cultural meanings as a means of subverting the strictures of the market and the critical discourse. He described a vision that carried with it some of the goals of the Harlem Renaissance and directly addressed the position of African American artists in the music industry.[111]

## Coda

Jazz was indeed "a marvel of paradox." It consisted of elements of African and European musical cultures and had developed at the intersection of African American and American society, art and popular music, and high and low culture. In existence for only a few decades, it became imbued with a variety of equally paradoxical meanings by its fans, its detractors, and the people who created it. Like Europe, Handy, Peyton, Armstrong, and a number of "traditional" intellectuals, Ellington responded to the brief history of the meanings associated with jazz and helped to chart its future.

The questions remained, however, and would continue to echo. Should one reclaim the music as an African American expression, or did such a move merely reproduce the logic of racist thinking and social segregation? Was it possible to reconcile a belief that jazz was an important African American expression with its larger place in American culture and the vast numbers of white musicians who were contributing to the idiom? Would it make more sense to describe it as an expression of a national identity or as a universal human impulse? Did musicians benefit from critical definitions of jazz as a product of intuitive, natural genius, or was it important to stress the hard work and self-consciousness that went into the production of the music? Could this music implement broader social transformations? How did one come to terms with the music's popularity, when popularity represented both the people from whom the artists drew sustenance as well as the machinations of the jazz industry and the conditions under which musicians labored? Would casting jazz in the image of classical music be better? And what were the gendered implications of defining jazz in relation to high culture and popular culture?

As the discourse about the music evolved in different social contexts and around new ways of playing jazz, musicians found themselves and their music celebrated and disparaged in changing ways. Musicians who chose to express their ideas in public would come to terms with the idea of the "jazz tradition" and its formal and ideological components. They spoke also of their own musical projects and expressed ideas consistent with their identities as artists, human beings, racialized subjects, and men and women. And black musicians continued to address concerns about their marginalization in the music industry. The following chapter takes this analysis into the 1940s, exploring changes in the jazz community during those years and the challenge that bebop as an emergent art form and a discursive field presented to musicians.

**"Dizzy Atmosphere"**

The Challenge of Bebop

**EXAMINING THE DEVELOPMENT OF BEBOP** in the 1940s is crucial to understanding jazz as we know it. A product of jam sessions, big bands, small combos, and countless hours of woodshedding, the musical language of bebop included rapid tempos, dissonant chords and melodic lines, tritone and other chordal substitutions, extensive chromaticism, offbeat piano accompaniment (comping), walking bass lines, polyrhythmic drumming, and, perhaps most important, a focus on extended, improvised soloing on the front-line instruments. Swing-era heavyweights such as Coleman Hawkins, Lester Young, Roy Eldridge, Art Tatum, Duke Ellington, Jimmy Blanton, and Walter Page had previously explored aspects of this language in the 1930s, but all the elements came together in spectacular fashion in the work of Charlie Parker, John Birks "Dizzy" Gillespie, and Thelonious Monk, to name only a handful of bebop's best-known practitioners.[1]

Bebop continues to be a core element of the language of jazz. It informs the work of most contemporary players, and many stylistic and technical innovations created in the 1940s remain integral parts of jazz education. Bebop marked the ascendance of the small combo as the basic performing unit of jazz (which is still the case today), and its production and reception transformed the meanings associated with jazz and its place in American culture. Coming to prominence at the end of World War II, amid rising African American political demands and increasingly visible American youth cultures, bebop garnered new capital for jazz as a music that spoke to observers of social and cultural resistance. At the same time, bebop also gave jazz unprecedented capital as art music and signified its move into its current, albeit precarious, position at the intersection of high art and popular culture.

Bebop was also a product of a 1940s African American social, cultural, and intellectual milieu. Building on recent scholarship on bebop that has sought to understand, as well as complicate, the relationship between bebop and its historical context, this chapter reconsiders the place of this music in African American life. Rather than viewing the music as an explicitly political, class-specific, or aesthetically uniform project, my aim is to understand bebop in its social context in somewhat different terms. It is precisely in its varying musical expressions and in musicians' differing interpretations of its meanings that bebop speaks of a collective orientation rooted in transformations in African American life during the 1940s. Not only did the development of the music itself reflect the forward-looking, worldly perspectives of many of its practitioners, but their public responses to the idea of bebop (whether they embraced or rejected the term) also spoke of a rejection of artistic and social boundaries, which inspired their music. Ultimately, bebop marked a crucial juncture in African American musicians' critical conversation about jazz, as it ushered in new identities for them and transformed the jazz discourse.

## "The World Was Swinging with Change"

In recent years, bebop has become a test case for rethinking jazz history. Much writing about jazz, as Scott DeVeaux suggests, presents the music as a self-contained progression of styles that are divorced from their social context. Consequently, some write about bebop as if it is merely another chapter in the aesthetic development of the idiom. Others pay closer attention to social context and, in so doing, describe bebop as a cohesive aesthetic movement with a seamlessness between the formal qualities of the genre and the ideological orientations and social positions of musicians and their audience. Such narratives explain how bebop mirrored transformations in black life, attitudes, and politics in the crucible of urban America during World War II. By creating a new music, adopting a renegade style, asserting their intelligence, and demanding to be treated as artists, young African American musicians forged a cultural politics that challenged all at once the banality of popular swing music, the complacency of older musicians, and a system of economic exploitation and cultural expropriation by whites in the music business. In doing so, they helped to forge a subculture that distanced itself from and confronted the mainstream. We see this approach in Amiri Baraka's *Blues People,* where the author argues that bebop music and styles represented an "anti-assimilationist" rejection of black middle-class and white society, and more recently in Eric Lott's description of how bebop's "aesthetic of speed and displacement" reflected, albeit indirectly, the militant aspirations of its youthful, working-class audience and the political demands of the "Double-V" campaign (victory in the war overseas and victory in the fight against racial prejudice at home).[2]

Still other studies challenge both types of narratives. Reexamining bebop's place in the artistic development of jazz and interrogating assumptions about its political significance are staples of recent work. Bernard Gendron suggests that the construction of bebop in high cultural terms and as political expression was facilitated less by any inherent meanings in the music than by a preexisting modernist discursive field surrounding it. David Stowe argues that the perceived schism between swing and bebop is a product of the political meanings imposed on the music rather than a radical departure by the musicians themselves. Taking on Baraka's analysis, Stowe rejects the notion that bebop was a significant expression of black militancy. Bebop's interracial audience was more threatening to white society than the music's role as a symbol of race pride, Stowe contends, and the political activism of many swing-era musicians was more explicit than that of any of the beboppers. According to Stowe, it was the cultural style of bebop that shaped the perspective of later commentators, who read the politics of bebop's reception into the music itself.[3]

DeVeaux challenges the assessments of bebop by both Baraka and Lott in his own recent book on the topic. He welcomes Baraka's attention to history and is convinced by his insistence that bebop must be understood in the context of "the sense of resentment" that African Americans felt during World War II, when they encountered unyielding racism at a moment that offered promise for change. Similarly, he agrees with Lott's assertion that "militancy and music were undergirded by the same social facts." "But what, exactly," DeVeaux asks, "constitutes the 'intimate if indirect relationship' of music to politics?" He characterizes the relationship of bebop musicians to politics as "oblique at best" and problematizes their relationship to a black mass audience, which at the height of bebop's popularity turned its attention toward rhythm and blues. Ultimately, DeVeaux argues, the emergence of bebop stemmed less from the political orientation of its practitioners and audience than from a series of aesthetic and career decisions made by young, professionalized, primarily African American musicians, who were inspired by a variety of artistic challenges and frustrated by a music industry that provided some opportunities but was also rife with discrimination. Eventually, this led a number of musicians to forego the restrictive atmospheres of the swing big bands in favor of the relative artistic and social freedoms that small combo jazz afforded.[4]

This recent work by DeVeaux, Gendron, and Stowe complicates some of the claims other scholars have made about the political significance of bebop, which ultimately say as much about observers' interpretations of the music as they do about the orientations of musicians. Yet there is room for exploring further the "social facts" of African American life in the 1940s and their relationship to the emergence of bebop and the meanings later ascribed to it. Even if bebop should not be read as a direct expression of black militancy, we can understand it as a product of a worldly intellectual orientation and an experimental aesthetic sensibility I term "critical ecumenicalism." The music may not have represented a particular, class-specific ideological stance, but it did reflect changing orientations and perspectives among working-class and middle-class African Americans, especially black youth and young adults.

Most considerations of bebop touch upon Minton's Playhouse as one of its points of origin. Located on 118th Street in Harlem and owned by AFM Local 802 delegate Henry Minton, the nightclub was the site of lengthy jam sessions where many of the musicians instrumental to the consolidation of bebop developed their techniques and musical ideas. Minton's club catered to African American musicians, although others patronized the establishment as well. Pianist Teddy Hill took control of the club's music policy in 1940, hiring a house band and making jam sessions a prominent part of the club's operations. The Monday night buffet dinners, given in honor of whomever was performing at the Apollo Theater, brought together musicians from all over the country.[5]

Looking back on these Monday night dinners and the jam sessions that followed them during the early war years, Ralph Ellison evoked an atmosphere that resonated with expectancy, camaraderie, and an element of the unknown:

> They were gathered here from all parts of America and they broke bread together and there was a sense of good feeling and promise, but what shape the fulfilled promise would take they did not know, and few except the more restless of the younger musicians even questioned. Yet it was an exceptional moment and the world was swinging with change. . . . For they were caught up in events which made that time exceptionally and uniquely *then*, and which brought, among the other changes which have reshaped the world, a momentous modulation into a new key of musical sensibility; in brief, a revolution in culture.[6]

What can we make of such memories? On one level, the ambiguity of Ellison's comments suggests that the atmosphere at Minton's, and by extension the emergence of bebop, did not simply reflect the political and social struggles of the war years. Indeed, later in the passage Ellison carefully distinguished artists' concerns from those of sociologists and historians, as he maintained that musicians and fans alike went to Minton's to seek sanctuary from the war and the social tensions around them. But what, then, do we make of the "needs of feeling" that brought people to the club, the "promise" that society held out to them, musicians' kindred spirits of exploration, and a "world swinging with change"? And just how did these elements relate to this "revolution in culture"?

Musicians who participated in the movement have similarly resisted making direct connections between bebop and political activism. Drummer Kenny Clarke expressed an ambiguous account of the relationship of bebop to its moment. Asked if he was making a statement about the world around him, Clarke responded: "Yeah, in a way. The idea was to wake up, look around you, there's something to do. And this was just a part of it, an integral part of our cultural aspect." If there was a message to African Americans, Clarke continued, it was this: "Whatever you go into, go into it *intelligently*. As simple as that."[7] Dizzy Gillespie also made it clear that he saw no direct connection between music and politics: "We didn't go out and make speeches or say, 'Let's play eight bars of protest.' We just played our music and let it go at that. The music proclaimed our identity; it made every statement we truly wanted to make." Yet Gille-

spie thought that he and other beboppers were in the "vanguard of social change." What he remembered was a collective will to artistic excellence and a sense of African American pride joined with a rejection
of social, creative, and even national boundaries. Speaking to charges that
beboppers expressed unpatriotic attitudes, Gillespie remarked: "We
never wished to be restricted to just an American context, for we were
creators in an art form which grew from universal roots and which had
proved it possessed universal appeal. Damn right! We refused to accept
racism, poverty, or economic exploitation, nor would we live out uncreative humdrum lives merely for the sake of survival."[8]

Bebop emerged at a crucial moment in African American life. The
1940s witnessed an acceleration of trends that had begun earlier in the
century: migration, proletarianization, urbanization, and immersion in
mass culture. The war economy and the political climate attending the
conflict also contributed to changing cultural tastes and shifts in class,
gender, and race relations. The ideological war against the white supremacist Nazi regime made the enduring racism in American society
all the more glaring. African Americans' sense of group identity was augmented by a widespread belief that the expanding wartime economy, and
an anticipated democratization of American society, would lead to
greater access to jobs, housing, and education. This collective sense of
expectancy translated into the overt political demands of A. Philip Ran-
dolph's March on Washington movement, which promised a June 1941
march on the nation's capital if discrimination in defense industries did
not end. The march never materialized, but the threat was enough to
pressure President Franklin Roosevelt into issuing Executive Order 8802,
forbidding discrimination by the government and defense industries and
subsequently establishing the Fair Employment Practices Committee
(FEPC) to enforce the order. The hopes of black Americans during World
War II were also evident in the *Pittsburgh Courier*'s December 1941 call
for a "double victory" campaign "to declare war on Japan and against
racial prejudice in our country"; in early civil rights lawsuits; in the growth
of union participation by black workers; in struggles against housing discrimination; and in the subtle, individual struggles for respect and equal
treatment in public spaces like street corners and buses. When social freedoms did not materialize, or when acts of resistance were met either with
government intransigence (for example, the FEPC ultimately did little

to end discriminatory practices) or with violent responses by the state or unruly white mobs, African American solidarity was fused with anger and growing militancy.[9]

Reconfigured racial affiliations and identities in flux accompanied the climate of militancy and expectancy in urban centers. For our purposes, the relationship of this growing, politicized, African American consciousness to black culture and intellectual life is critical. Writing in 1943 about New York, Roi Ottley discussed the development of African American solidarity and what might be called a popular culture of black nationalism. This collective feeling cut across class lines; it could be found in the thoughts of Garveyites, highbrow cultural critics, religious leaders, historians, and journalists. "Black nationalism," Ottley wrote, "torn from its circus aspects, and made more palatable to a wider section of the Negro population, permeated every phase of Negro life." This orientation was also a product of pan-Africanist sentiment and the developing feelings of kinship with other people of color both within the United States and throughout the globe. African Americans expressed internationalist affinities in their support for Ethiopia during the Italo-Ethiopian war from 1935 to 1941; and, as Penny Von Eschen has shown, such sentiments were evident in the internationalist orientation of African American politics and popular culture in the 1940s as well as in the treatment of African affairs by the African American press. Moreover, as George Lipsitz argues, racist propaganda directed toward Japan and the internment of Japanese Americans helped to generate domestic interethnic affiliations among people of color.[10]

As Von Eschen illustrates, the pan-Africanist popular discourse of the 1940s was based not on biology but on a historical awareness of divergent yet shared experiences under European and Euro-American domination. Such historical knowledge helped to forge a widespread understanding of the "constructed nature of race," which was paralleled among African American intellectuals by a growing, publicly stated distrust of a biologically determined, undifferentiated concept of race as a marker of cultural identity and basis for political affiliation. Among the texts that interrogated the idea of a static "Negro" identity in the early 1940s were W. E. B. Du Bois's autobiography *Dusk of Dawn* (1940), Zora Neale Hurston's autobiography *Dust Tracks on a Road* (1942), and Alain Locke's essay "Who and What Is 'Negro'?" (1942).[11]

At the same time, a collective sense of African American pride during the war facilitated cultural sharing across class boundaries. Although the structural aspects of class stratification in African American communities were significant, this period saw a loosening of cultural distinctions. Class lines had been broached in the 1920s, and they were further challenged in the 1940s as a result of the economic dislocation brought by the Great Depression, the cultural leveling of the New Deal, the impact of left-wing political ideas, and the rapid growth of African American urban society. Ottley identified the emergence of a "Cafe au Lait Society," a professional and intellectual middle class with liberal political beliefs and fewer social pretensions than the "traditional" black bourgeoisie. The existence of this group and its consumption of popular entertainment (including jazz) were symbolic of the cultural sharing between distinct groups of African Americans.[12]

Rising black awareness and militancy, combined with shifting class relations, an internationalist perspective, and a dissatisfaction with the limitations of racial identities, fostered a certain kind of oppositional consciousness among African Americans from different social backgrounds.[13] On the musical front, this often translated into a critical ecumenicalism, with many artists maintaining a strong sense of identity as African Americans while embracing a cosmopolitan approach to life and art. Musicians bristled at the primitivist stereotypes to which they were expected to conform. They also resisted the imposition of cultural boundaries, whether based on highbrow "legitimacy," race, or national identity; often rejected the generic categories that separated jazz from other kinds of music; and, at times, refused to accept the political meanings ascribed to their craft. Ellison's evocation of a community based on "feeling," and his attempt to celebrate the artistry of bebop while rejecting the militant intent ascribed to the music, may be read as a description of a cultural expression that spoke of group affirmation and demand yet resisted the confines of blackness as a racial category. Gillespie's rejection of creative and social boundaries also resonates with this ethos, as does Clarke's description of bebop as a call to "wake up" and approach the world "intelligently."

## "Now's the Time"

As chapter 1 described, jazz developed through institutional channels that facilitated cultural interactions among African Americans of different social backgrounds. By the 1930s, jazz was often incorporated into the curricula of both public schools and private instructors in black communities and elsewhere. As jazz was institutionalized in community educational networks, it reflected general patterns of aesthetic leveling in New Deal America and provided the tools for moving the music in new directions and transforming artistic identities. Jazz education networks perpetuated professionalism and the ethos of "progress" DeVeaux identifies in the jazz community of the 1920s and 1930s, which stressed, among other things, an interest in musical exploration, developing one's individual technique, and a focus on synthesizing traditional forms with new musical elements.[14] In the 1930s, a new generation of musicians of middle-class and working-class backgrounds built upon this ethos, as they moved effortlessly between idioms and increasingly envisioned the creation of a serious music that might incorporate a variety of musical elements.

The well-documented role that music teachers versed in jazz and other idioms played in the development of modern jazz in Los Angeles provides a useful example of how the music education circles in different areas of the country affected the emergence of modern jazz and dovetailed with the worldly orientations of young musicians. These prototypical jazz educators had a profound influence on the development of the artistic sensibilities of young musicians. Sam Browne held master's degrees in music and education from the University of Southern California and headed the music department at Jefferson High School, where he established special courses and methods of instruction. Browne offered a broad-ranging musical education, which provided a strong background in theory and explored a variety of musical styles. Among Browne's many prominent students was saxophonist Elvira "Vi" Redd, whose great-aunt, Alma Hightower, ran a music education program at a playground. Through this program, funded by the New Deal's Works Progress Administration (WPA), she taught theory and harmony and put together a youth big band—Miss Hightower and the Melodic Dots—which performed at the local YMCA and made appearances at the California state fair in 1939 and 1940.[15]

Also playing a significant role as an educator in Los Angeles's circle of black musicians was Lloyd Reese, who ran a conservatory out of his house on McKinley Avenue. A saxophonist and trumpeter, Reese had studied music at Whittier College, was a prominent member of the Les Hite band, and was among a handful of African American musicians to get work in Hollywood studios. Reese augmented his basic curriculum with innovative ways of thinking about harmony. He also ran a Sunday rehearsal band at the black musicians' union hall, where his students and other musicians worked out their ideas. In addition to teaching the mechanics of music, Reese encouraged in his students a sense of themselves as artists and an expansive vision. One of his students, saxophonist Dexter Gordon, recalls that Reese "gave us a broader picture and an appreciation of music. He made us more aware. He was teaching us musical philosophy."[16]

Formal and informal educational networks helped to instill in musicians a serious-minded approach to their craft and an artistic orientation that linked creativity, originality, respectability, and a willingness to go beyond musical boundaries. With roots earlier in the century and consolidation in the 1930s, these shared networks imparted a theoretical grounding, an expansive vision, and a collective purpose that allowed musicians to take pleasure in artistic accomplishment and to break new ground in the music world. The musical ethos and artistic agenda they developed would be instrumental in the transformation of music and artistic identities in the 1940s, as they tapped into the critical ecumenicalism of the moment.

Of course, one subject that musical veterans of the 1940s have seldom been ambiguous about is economics—more specifically, the financial position of African American musicians in the music industry. The swing craze of the 1930s offered a certain amount of monetary promise to African American musicians, particularly to a younger generation of instrumentalists who were buoyed by the popularity of virtuosos such as Coleman Hawkins and Lester Young. But when the popularity of swing declined after 1939, black musicians were marginalized in the music business, as the recording business went into decline, venues that had featured black groups hired white bands instead, and radio networks and hotels continued their policies of discrimination.[17]

As mentioned earlier, DeVeaux carefully documents how the "birth of bebop" was in part a function of the simultaneous freedom and restriction the wartime music industry presented to young African American musicians. Events during the war hurt black musicians in several ways.

In urban areas, entertainment taxes, frequent blackouts, and curfews dampened social life and musical performances. Gasoline and rubber rationing restricted travel, as did the Transportation Edict of 1942, which limited the use of buses and rail cars for civilian purposes. This edict was especially hard on black bands—who depended on travel for their livelihoods—and became the focus of activism by Cab Calloway, the NAACP, and booking agents Moe Gale and Joe Glaser. Black bands that were able to travel often did so in the Jim Crow South, where insult and physical danger continually loomed large. A recording ban began in June 1942, when AFM president James Petrillo announced a strike in an attempt to get recording and jukebox companies to pay royalties to musicians. This action was not completely resolved until the last of the major record companies came to terms in November of 1944. Adding to the impact of the ban was shellac rationing, which made recording possible only when recycled shellac was available to replace the amount used by the record industry. Like transportation restrictions, the ban disproportionately hurt black musicians, who tended to make a greater proportion of their income from recordings because of discrimination in radio and hotel jobs. And the military draft put a good number of musicians' careers on hold and was sometimes personally disastrous—as it was for Lester Young, who was excluded from the band at the base where he was stationed and served ten months in army detention barracks for drug possession.[18]

While wartime rationing, the recording ban, and the draft presented major hardships for African American musicians, the social forces of the war and a climate of racial hostility in the music industry drew black artists together and provided an impetus for musical change. Although urban uprisings and fears over miscegenation led to the temporary closing of the Savoy Ballroom as well as to police crackdowns on Central Avenue in Los Angeles and Fifty-second Street in New York, there remained a hungry audience of urban jazz fans, who needed to relieve the tensions of life during the conflict and who might have pocketfuls of spending money from defense jobs. The big bands that could find work became "incubators" for new styles, and the difficulties these bands faced because of travel restrictions, gasoline rationing, and higher taxes on dancing promoted the emergence of the small, soloist-centered combo as the primary vehicle for modern jazz. The recording ban, which cut off a source of income for musicians, ultimately led to the emergence of independent record labels that, though sometimes unscrupulous in their dealings with musicians, were initially more open to new jazz styles and helped to create an audience for this innovative music. Although the military was rife with discrimination, some musicians found that they could develop their craft and be exposed to new musical ideas in military bands. After their service was complete, musicians took advantage of the GI Bill to pay for further musical education.[19]

The wartime economy and the rhetoric of democracy that accompanied the war against Hitler also held out some promise to African American musicians, even before the United States entered the conflict. Some musicians believed that conditions outside and inside the music world would improve. One of the "restless," "younger musicians" who performed at Minton's was pianist Herbie Nichols, who had a short stint as a columnist with the *New York Age,* before he was drafted in September 1941 at the age of twenty-one. In a series of columns entitled "The Jazz Life," Nichols voiced his opinions about jazz artistry and the state of the music industry. His comments illustrate how financial and professional concerns and a broader artistic vision might intersect. Nichols was sanguine about the economic realities of the music business. Club owners seldom confused ends and means; nightclubs existed primarily to make a profit, not to showcase good music. He recognized that the business aspects of jazz often required black musicians to spend extended periods on the road and demanded a quick turnover in money and personnel. Musicians also had to contend with the regulation of nightclubs by the state through cabaret, liquor, and cigarette sales licenses, as well as through inspections by the fire, health, and police departments. As Nichols asserted, "The jazz life is ninety percent sham and front."[20]

Yet there was reason to be optimistic. Anticipating U.S. participation in the current conflict and recognizing that World War I had been an important period for black activism and the growth of Harlem's culture industry, Nichols explained that "war is a boom time for song writers." Moreover, white audiences maintained an appetite for "primitive entertainment" that could not be sated outside of jazz. The challenge for black musicians, then, was to recognize the limitations in the jazz business while taking advantage of the opportunities it presented. The "jazz racket" provided a "financial foothold" in life, and as long as musicians recognized that the business was a "means to an end" rather than "an end in itself," they could survive economically and pursue serious artistic projects as well. Nichols looked to Art Tatum as someone who had some success in the jazz business while exemplifying artistic originality and musical genius.[21]

After returning from the war in 1943, Nichols contributed several pieces to the short-lived, black-run music journal *The Music Dial,* whose editors saw possibilities for democratic change in the music industry and the musicians union, even as they voiced a withering critique of these institutions. The publication expressed a "Double-V" and, at times, left-internationalist perspective, as it linked the struggles against segregation and discrimination in the music industry to those against racism, fascism, imperialism, and class inequalities. The magazine's "prospectus" clearly articulated the goals of its editors: "To carry on a militant fight to eliminate job discrimination, locally and nationally. To protect the interest of musicians who are in the armed services and defense plants. To create a general agency where talent can be secured. To aid those forces that are waging a fight to raise the economic level of the Common people."[22]

In a series of 1944 articles on the "Jazz Purist," Nichols bemoaned an industry that marginalized African American musicians financially and cared little about quality music. One solution to this dilemma was state sponsorship, he argued in one article. Yet his focus in these pieces was on a "purist" devotion to one's art as a means of countering the difficulties and furthering the development of modern jazz. Stressing that "intelligence in jazz" was a rare quality, he also saw the articulation of new, innovative, and imaginative musical ideas as a way to improve the position of jazz and provide fulfillment to artists. He believed such qualities could spread throughout the musicians' community. As "top jazzmen find it possible to put forth their own ideas through their own public lens," he wrote, "jazz purism will not be the rarity that it happens to be during 1944."[23]

Pursuing the life of a jazz purist, however, was often easier said than done. Nichols's homecoming was also marked by disillusionment, as he struggled to find work playing his own music—or any modern jazz styles, for that matter. Even when the bebop market opened up after the war, Nichols still could not earn a living playing his music; he was forced to support himself by teaching piano and playing for Dixieland bands.[24]

Other musicians were able to make it as practitioners of new forms of jazz, as they negotiated the transformations within and outside the music industry during and after World War II. These artists forged a new style, as they balanced their aesthetic objectives with the need to make a living in the jazz industry. These goals influenced musicians' stylistic developments as well as their recording projects, band personnel decisions, and compositional strategies. Musicians resisted the artistic restrictions and rampant racial discrimination of the music industry, while tapping into a climate of critical ecumenicalism that linked them to a broader African American community during the 1940s. In doing so, they developed bebop as an idiom that was initially unnamed.

The music first came together publicly in the big bands of Billy Eckstine, Earl Hines, and Coleman Hawkins and at jam sessions at Minton's and Monroe's Uptown Club in New York. Musicians also gathered privately, in places like Mary Lou Williams's Harlem apartment, to work out musical ideas outside the glare of the spotlight. The music came to prominence in a small group format when Dizzy Gillespie and Oscar Pettiford parlayed their status as winners of an *Esquire Magazine* jazz poll into an engagement at the Onyx Club on Fifty-second Street at the end of 1943 and early 1944. Their changing personnel featured George Wallington on piano, Don Byas on tenor saxophone, and Max Roach on drums. Roach remembers that the musicians got "so high off the music" that they had to go downstairs and calm down between sets. "Everything seemed absolutely fresh, absolutely new. A new music was rising out of a dead body of cliches. The stale shit was over." Soon Charlie Parker and others were performing on Fifty-second Street, and before long the movement found its way into the public imagination. By the end of 1944, the word "bebop" was being used by hipster fans as an onomatopoeic description of the two-note phrases that seemed characteristic of the music. With the lifting of the recording ban, which for two years had kept many fans ignorant of what the modern players were developing, "bebop," in pianist Billy Taylor's words, "seemed to burst on the scene from nowhere."[25]

Taylor also recalls how the young "modernists" inspired musicians throughout the country, even before their music had a name. He met Gillespie and Parker when they came through Washington, D.C., with Earl Hines's band in 1943. Taylor saw similarities between what these musicians and his idol Art Tatum were doing harmonically. He soon moved to New York, took an apartment a block from Minton's, and worked to combine Tatum's complex harmonies and florid embellishments, based in stride and swing rhythms, with the dissonant melodic phrasing and complicated rhythmic conception of Parker and Gillespie. After sitting in with Parker and Gillespie in the Billy Eckstine band, on the group's 1944 swing through the Midwest, Miles Davis decided to forego an education at Fisk University and instead go to New York for musical training at Juilliard and in Fifty-second Street nightclubs. In the military, musicians exposed one another to new musical ideas by sharing early recordings by bebop pioneers and through their interactions with musicians versed in new harmonic and rhythmic elements. Saxophonist Jackie Kelso, for example, encountered trumpeter and fellow Angeleno Ernie Royal in a Navy band at St. Mary's College in the San Francisco Bay Area during the early war years. Royal had gone to New York with Lionel Hampton's band a few years earlier, where he had been exposed to the emergent bebop idiom in New York; and he fused elements of Gillespie's style and harmonic knowledge with ideas from his own classical training.[26]

During the years 1944 to 1946, as DeVeaux documents, major bebop figures such as Gillespie and Parker moved back and forth between small combo work and big bands. They explored Fifty-second Street clubs, the concert stage, and southern black dance halls, as they searched for monetary reward and artistic fulfillment. By 1945, Parker and Gillespie had largely escaped an earlier model of the black entertainer's role (although Gillespie, as he later admitted, engaged in his own brand of "Tomming" during the bebop era) while achieving some measure of commercial success. With their Guild recordings "Shaw 'Nuff" and "Hot House," they had completed the process of consolidating the new genre by fusing virtuoso soloing with intricate and "asymmetrical" thematic statements in original compositions.[27]

Turning to ideological motivations for the development of bebop, DeVeaux offers an interesting discussion of beboppers' vexed relationship with the blues. Although some of Parker's earliest recorded musical accomplishments—for example, his 1944 work on Tiny Grimes's "Red Cross" and "Tiny's Tempo"—stemmed from his ability to fuse "bluesy 'rice and beans' gestures" with the "esoteric arabesques of the improvising virtuoso," many beboppers saw the blues as a symbol of the limitations placed on them as musicians and as African Americans. Not only was the harmonic structure of most blues tunes fairly simple compared to original modern jazz compositions, but in addition the blues had come to symbolize both the primitivist expectations of a white audience and the demands of a culture industry that wanted to pigeonhole black music. Blues music also represented a rural cultural past with which "upwardly mobile professional musicians" no longer wanted to be associated. Drawing in part from a passage in Gillespie's autobiography, DeVeaux argues that many beboppers were "ashamed" of the blues, as were many members of the African American cultural and political elite. The musical limitations were rather easily overcome, but the social implications of the blues were harder to change. Musicians knew they had an obligation to a black audience that demanded the blues, and they often found these performances inspiring. Yet they also saw the blues less as a cultural essence or birthright than as a "point of exchange, between artist and audience." In keeping with a "progressive" ethos that linked musical experimentation and racial uplift, musicians often looked to bebop as a way out of the blues, and they tried to "educate their audiences" in the process.[28]

DeVeaux is correct in describing the blues as a symbol of social and musical restrictions for young African American musicians. In addition, however, this response to the blues and the bebop movement in general can be situated in the African American cultural and intellectual context sketched out earlier. One can read the passage from Gillespie's autobiography as evidence of both the anxiety and the affirmation that came from interclass cultural sharing. A few lines later, he discusses how he defended his own explorations of the blues to other musicians: "Man, that's my music, that's my heritage," he told them, adding that Charlie Parker was a "real blueser" as well. Ultimately, the young musicians in DeVeaux's analysis in some ways remain rooted more in an early-century, Washingtonian doctrine of racial uplift than in a more fluid, forward-looking ethos and an acute awareness of identity stemming from the cultural and intellectual ferment of the 1940s. This view does not negate the professionalism of these musicians, the middle-class orientation of some, or the legacy of uplift ideology. Rather, it emphasizes that beboppers' rejection of the blues may also be understood as a product of a collective ethos involving exploration, mental acuity, group pride, an aversion to categories, and an understanding that racial boundaries and assumptions can be called into question. Speaking in 1948, Dizzy Gillespie's arranger Gil Fuller suggested that earlier forms of music were simply no longer relevant as African Americans moved into the future: "Modern life is fast and complicated. . . . We're tired of that old New Orleans beat-beat, I got the blues pap."[29]

The politics of bebop's style reflected this broader ethos, as intellectual practice and sartorial display coincided for musicians and their audiences. Although Eric Lott's assessment of bebop essentially describes a cohesive and rather narrowly defined cultural and aesthetic politics, his description of bebop's "style" calls attention to the way musicians and fans alike engaged in serious mental endeavors that responded to the world around them. "Bebop," he writes, "was about making disciplined imagination alive and answerable to the social change of its time," and the style "was where social responsiveness became individual expression, where the pleasures of shared identity met an intolerance for racist jive." Beboppers and their fans even adopted the personae of intellectuals; goatees, berets, and horned-rimmed glasses became the uniform of the subculture.[30] The adoption of this regalia of the intelligentsia not only distanced musicians from the mainstream but also challenged racist ideologies that were based in part on a belief in African American mental inferiority. We may also understand bebop style as a signifier of musicians' collective search for a better understanding of music theory and the world around them.

Beyond style, the artistic projects, activities, and ideas of African American musicians provide insight into their critical ecumenicalism. Musicians involved with bebop during and after the war pursued their creative goals and their professional careers while negotiating the growing, albeit precarious, popularity of the genre and, occasionally, its discourse. The World War II period witnessed a new stage in the development of jazz's contradictory status as both a serious art form and the music of youthful rebellion. By the late 1940s, bebop had come to symbolize, among other things, social deviance, black militancy, masculine assertion, serious artistic expression, intellectualism, and a threat to the very existence of jazz.

For a brief moment, bebop seemed to be a vehicle for making serious black jazz artistry respectable and remunerative, for winning legitimacy based on its potential to smoothly enter the realm of high culture or perhaps on its oppositional capital as avant-garde expression—or perhaps on both characteristics. Yet bebop was never quite able to escape its association with social deviance. As bebop became institutionalized as black creative expression and intellectual work in these contradictory ways, musicians were able to a certain degree to voice their aesthetic visions and their concerns about their lives in the music industry. The artistic projects and the words of African American musicians show that bebop was not a unified ideological and aesthetic movement. Rather, it was an artistic challenge that was understood in a variety of ways in its social, cultural, intellectual, and creative context. Musicians' comments illustrate how an ethos of critical ecumenicalism helped to fuel the development of the idiom and eventually caused some musicians to reject bebop as an inadequate description of a broader musical and intellectual endeavor. As during the swing era, musicians' ability to make their ideas known was restricted by the extent to which they agreed with or could successfully influence writers. Yet there was some consistency between musicians' views and those of the people who controlled the press. Although the space for commentary was limited, musicians nevertheless raised critical issues that future generations would address more fully.

When Gil Fuller described bebop to the *New Yorker* as a "fast and complicated" music linked to "modern life," he voiced an artistic orientation that was presentist and forward-looking, seeking to escape the stereotypes and audience expectations of the past. Fuller rejected both the blues and the music of the Dixieland revival. Likening Dixieland and bebop, he argued, was like comparing "a horse and buggy with a jet plane." As Dizzy Gillespie discussed the genesis of bebop, he dismissed older jazz forms as well: "That old stuff was like Mother Goose Rhymes. . . . It was all right for its time, but it was a childish time. We couldn't really blow on our jobs—not the way we wanted to."[31] In a conversation published in the *Baltimore Afro-American,* swing star Lionel Hampton was less dismissive of early forms, but he too saw bebop as relevant to the social context of the 1940s in a way earlier styles were not. Blues, spirituals, and New Orleans–style jazz were all relevant to their particular moments; but the new music, he noted, was the product of a youthful group of musicians who had benefited from better training and were "now capable of expressing their basic feelings and ideas in a new and more relevant idiom."[32]

The *New Yorker's* Richard Boyer perceptively noted that beboppers rejected the labels of "critics who referred to them, with the most complimentary intent, as modern primitives playing an almost instinctual music." Similarly, an article in the African American publication *Our World* described how musicians often explained the development of bebop as a psychological response to conditions and as "a revolt by Negro musicians against the old-time jazz which, they felt, white people expected them to play." They refused the "Uncle Tom" roles and the "so-called compliments of critics who called jazz an art form imported from Africa." Although a number of musicians did have some interest in African music and culture, this particular rejection of African roots should be understood as a response to the primitivist language that many jazz critics, particularly those who championed the Dixieland revival, used to describe the music. Ralph Ellison later wrote: "By rejecting Armstrong [beboppers] sought to rid themselves of the entertainer's role. And by getting rid of the role they demanded, in the name of their racial identity, a purity of status which by definition is impossible for the performing artist."[33] But we should keep in mind that, like Ellington before them, some musicians were in fact rejecting an essentialist and racist discourse about music and attempting to redefine jazz and African American artistry in terms that they thought responded to their historical moment.

This intellectual orientation and its ethos of exploration were critical to the development of the small combo extensions of popular song and blues forms that have come to represent bebop. Well-known recordings by major figures in the movement—such as "Now's the Time" and "Koko" from Charlie Parker's November 1945 Savoy date—reflect the disdain of category and a self-conscious worldliness that demanded access to a variety of cultural referents. Parker extended the language of the blues on "Now's the Time," a medium-tempo blues, on which Dizzy Gillespie provides piano accompaniment with Thelonious Monk–like dissonant chords and jarring comping. Parker and Miles Davis each provide solos, although Parker's is more complicated, as he weaves together chromatic runs and dissonant intervals with soulful blues licks. "Koko" gives a sense of the radical approach to the popular song form that many of the beboppers embraced. Based on the chords of Ray Noble's "Cherokee,"

Parker and his quintet dramatically transform Noble's sixty-four-bar tune. Played at a blistering pace, "Koko" begins with a thirty-two-bar section of new material in which Gillespie and Parker perform an introductory theme in unison. Then Gillespie and Parker state their own improvised material as a call and response, with the two horns coming together to restate the introductory theme. The main section of "Koko" consists of two choruses over which Parker solos. The extended harmonies and substitutions by bass, piano, and saxophone dramatically alter the original tune in the complex interplay of spontaneous composition. Parker also employs the familiar bebop practice of calling generic boundaries into question by quoting from the existing jazz, classical music, and popular song repertoire—in this instance, a clarinet part from the New Orleans march "High Society." The performance ends with a drum solo by Max Roach and a restatement of the introductory theme.[34]

On the West Coast, the heterogeneous responses of young Angeleno musicians to East Coast players and their recordings are illustrative of their ecumenical visions. When bebop recordings became available, and later when East Coast–based musicians visited Los Angeles, California musicians were exposed to a fully articulated genre. Howard McGhee relocated to Los Angeles in early 1945, Parker and Gillespie played an engagement at Billy Berg's in Hollywood in late 1945 and early 1946, and ex-Angeleno Dexter Gordon returned home in 1946 fully versed in the new style. Although the Billy Berg gig was something of a financial disaster (and a personal disaster for Parker, who ended up in a mental institution), the visit of Parker and Gillespie had an effect on many young players. After his release from the hospital, Parker stayed in Los Angeles for several months and took on a mentoring role in the musicians' community, as did Howard McGhee. For some musicians, moving fully into the bebop idiom was a logical extension of the harmonic and rhythmic ideas and the expansive ethos already circulating in the Los Angeles musicians' community. Cecil McNeely and Sonny Criss formed a "progressive" band during their last year of high school. They were initially influenced by older musicians such as Lester Young, Don Byas, and Coleman Hawkins; but bebop quickly drew their attention. As McNeely put it, "When we first heard this stuff, man, it was just incredible and we really enjoyed it and we got right into it." Others drew upon the bebop idiom while maintaining a broad musical vision. Buddy Collette never fully immersed himself in bebop, but his exposure to Parker and others inspired him to incorporate bebop phrasing into his own playing. Charles Mingus thought of himself first and foremost as a serious composer and wrote music that was grounded in both the jazz and the classical music idioms, yet he too eventually adopted bebop phrases and harmonic ideas.[35]

We see this critical ecumenicalism in other attempts to move into areas of musical and extramusical study that called into question racial, national, and creative boundaries. The recording of Gillespie's September 29, 1947, concert at Carnegie Hall is an important artifact from the history of the genre.[36] The concert, which symbolized bebop's growing, albeit contradictory, cultural legitimacy, provides a window into the wide range of artistic visions and stylistic influences maintained by musicians associated with the bebop movement. In the first set, Gillespie's quintet (featuring Parker) performed several bebop "standards," including "Koko," "A Night in Tunisia," and a version of "Dizzy Atmosphere" taken at an incredible tempo. On these numbers, one can hear respectful applause by the Carnegie audience as well as raucous cheers of encouragement from some of its members, demonstrating that even in the concert hall the music had not lost its ability to inspire interactions between performers and their loyal audience. A set by Ella Fitzgerald and the Gillespie big band followed the quintet. Fitzgerald and Sarah Vaughan were among a handful of female vocalists who had incorporated bop intervals and chromatic melodic figures into their vocal lines and had helped to move jazz singing in new directions. The big band's performance of Babs Gonzales's "Oop-Pop-A-Da" shows how musicians could weave together novelty song and serious musical statement.

The Gillespie big band's instrumental performances reveal an even wider range of expressions and a variety of approaches to incorporating bebop language into compositions and arrangements. "Cubano-Be, Cubano-Bop" is representative of Gillespie's strong affinity for Afro-Cuban music. Both Parker and Gillespie, in fact, were interested in Afro-Cuban rhythmic concepts; Gillespie in particular was influenced by associations with trumpeter Mario Bauza, vocalist and conguero Chano Pozo, and bandleader Machito. We can also hear this ethos in Gillespie's 1947 Afro-Cuban–influenced big band hit "Manteca," his other recordings with Chano Pozo, and in Parker's 1948 and 1949 recordings with

Machito's Afro-Cuban group. Pianist and composer George Russell cowrote the multisectional "Cubano-Be, Cubano-Bop." Russell built upon the theme that Gillespie had sketched out for the first part, adding a modal introduction. Russell wrote the second part himself and added a section in which Pozo improvised passages on percussion and vocals. The piece contained a variety of influences, but the main goal was to synthesize elements of Afro-Cuban and "traditional" jazz rhythms. As Russell put it, "We were striving for exactly that kind of world grasp, a kind of universality." Russell spent the next several years rethinking the harmonic relationships in Western music and devising a new theoretical system for improvisation. He eventually consolidated his ideas as *The Lydian Chromatic Concept of Tonal Organization for Improvisation* (completed in 1953), the first widely acknowledged work in music theory written by a jazz musician. Gillespie's band also performed pianist John Lewis's "Toccata for Trumpet and Orchestra," a composition that anticipated Lewis's attempts to fuse the language of classical music and jazz in the work of the Modern Jazz Quartet.[37]

Parker's own well-known interest in contemporary classical music was also emblematic of many beboppers' aversion to musical boundaries. Parker quoted classical motifs in his solos, discussed the work of Stravinsky and other composers in interviews, and hoped to take lessons in composition from Edgard Varèse. In a 1948 *Metronome* "Blindfold Test," he rejected the divisions between musical genres and said that as far as he was concerned there was "no such thing" as jazz. "You can't classify music in words—jazz, swing, Dixieland, et cetera; it's just forms of music; people have different conceptions and different ways of presenting things. Personally, I just like to call it music, and music is what I like."[38] In a 1949 interview with *Down Beat,* Parker again expressed this forward-looking orientation. Although he rejected the bebop label in other interviews, at this particular moment he viewed bebop as an entity distinct from jazz or classical music. As a rhythmically complicated idiom, where front-line instruments had more of an impact on the rhythmic accents of a performance, bebop provided more flexibility than earlier forms of jazz, in which musicians were constrained by the steady beat. Parker thought bebop succeeded best in a small group format, yet he also saw it as the first step in a broader musical expression. He saw possibilities in an orchestral context where one could explore a "variety of coloration" and looked forward to the development of music that would combine harmonic structures from modern classical music with the emotion and dynamism of the jazz idiom. "Music is your own experience," Parker argued, "your thoughts, your wisdom. If you don't live it, it won't come out of your horn." And this personal expression should not be encumbered by category: "They teach you there's a boundary line to music. . . . But, man, there's no boundary line to art."[39]

Parker tried to move in new musical directions with his 1949 and 1950 recordings with symphonic strings, a project that was consistent with his interest in classical music but that also suffered from substandard arrangements Parker had contracted out to others.[40] A more successful and dramatic attempt to use bebop harmony and rhythms as a basis for a classically oriented musical statement was pianist and composer Mary Lou Williams's "Zodiac Suite," a twelve-part, extended composition inspired by the astrological signs and, more important, the friends, fellow musicians, and other entertainers who had been born under them. "Libra," for example, was dedicated to her "great friends" Gillespie, Art Tatum, Bud Powell, and Thelonious Monk. Williams introduced the suite early in 1945 on her Sunday radio program on WNEW, recorded it on solo piano and with a trio in June, and performed it at the end of the year at Town Hall with an eighteen-piece orchestra, consisting of a small combo featuring Ben Webster and a complement of symphony players. In 1946 she performed three movements of the composition at Carnegie Hall as part of a Carnegie Pops Concert Series.[41]

In a 1947 article entitled "Music and Progress," Williams articulated the goals of this musical project while offering insight into how the celebration of bebop was often tempered by a recognition of its controversial reputation.[42] Williams challenged the discourse linking bebop with juvenile delinquency by arguing that the problems facing young people in the 1940s were no different from those she had encountered as a young woman in the early 1930s. As long as one used "good judgment, clear reasoning and unbiased thinking," there was little to worry about. Advocating a rudimentary kind of goal orientation and open-mindedness as a means of succeeding in society, she then applied the same philosophy to modern jazz: "If we are to make progress in modern music, or, if you prefer *jazz*, we must be willing and able to open our minds to new ideas and developments." New ideas must be developed to perfection and will then become the old ideas upon which new ones are built: "This is not only progress in music, for the same is true for all forms of art including painting, sculpture, architecture, and even the theatre." Bebop, which was the "newest invasion into the field of modern music," was the most important development to hit the jazz world in years. "I believe that all musicians should open their minds to it in order to understand what it means to them and to their music. Those who have already accepted Be-bop have found the inspiration and feeling they have been looking for."[43]

Williams's comments about young people and her vision of "progress" rejected the idea that jazz (and bebop in particular) was a site of social deviance or a threat to the musicians' community or society in general. For African American women immersed in the idiom, charges that bebop was socially deviant resonated in particular ways. Not only did a woman have to affirm her legitimacy in the male-dominated jazz world, but her reputation both as a woman and as a musician could be damaged by the sexual connotations of the "bebop" label. Williams's call for "acceptance" of the genre in almost religious terms sought to win widespread recognition for the art form and make it part of the everyday language of jazz.

By embracing bebop and seizing this notion of progress, Williams also validated her own aesthetic vision and demonstrated discomfort with the constraints that generic categories placed on music and musicians. Jazz could be celebrated as black musical culture, but it signified the primitivist expectations of its audience as well. Jazz also symbolized the limitations on where black musicians could perform. In a 1944 interview, Williams asserted that many of the best black musicians performed on Fifty-second Street because symphony orchestras would not hire them. In 1947 her desire to situate bebop as part of "modern music" rather than "jazz" illustrates a common dissatisfaction with the stereotyped images and entertainer's role, while optimistically looking forward to musical and social transformations. In Williams's opinion, bebop provided a means of moving beyond the formalistic and spatial constraints of jazz. Noting her performance of "Zodiac Suite" with a seventy-piece "'Pops' Symphony orchestra" at Carnegie Hall earlier that year, she announced plans to perform with Syracuse University's symphony orchestra in the near future. Williams celebrated the scholarly attention to modern jazz and saw it as a means of moving outside the economy that produced it: "I have discovered that a good many University people are musically up-to-date and I try my best to cooperate with them when they suggest new ways of getting music across to the public." With this attention, she hoped to realize her ambition of presenting more of her work with the New York Philharmonic or the Boston Symphony Orchestra.[44]

Beboppers even explored African music and culture and, at times, did so in ways that challenged primitivist ideas about the continent. Parker's and Gillespie's affinity for Afro-Cuban music was developed in part through performances with African and Cuban drummers and dancer Asadata Dafora at benefit concerts at the Diplomat Hotel for the African Academy of Arts and Research. Williams and Dafora performed at a two-day Carnegie Hall "festival" in April 1945. This show took a serious look at the relationship between African dancing and music and their counterparts in the West.[45] Drummer Art Blakey took interest in Africa in another direction in 1948, when he spent a year on the continent. Although he later claimed that his intent was not to study music but to immerse himself in Islamic philosophy and religion, Norman Weinstein points out that Blakey's 1953 recording "Message from Kenya," his later African-themed albums, and his intricate cross-rhythms, use of space, and manipulation of pitch suggest he was profoundly influenced by African drummers.[46]

Blakey was one of a growing number of African American musicians turning to Islam in the 1940s. Although reports of "Mohammedism" in the jazz community were often exaggerated and sometimes used to discredit the bebop movement, a small cohort of New York–based musicians did become practicing Muslims. In 1948 Gillespie noted that many musicians had turned to Islam in response to the injuries that society inflicted upon them. Blakey, who at times used the Arabic name Abdullah ibn Buhaina, became a Muslim after he was almost beaten to death by a white policeman in Albany, Louisiana, for failing to address the man as "Sir." "After that experience," he remembered, "I started searching for a philosophy, a better way of life." Beginning in 1947, he and Barrymore Rainey ran a Muslim mission out of Blakey's apartment, before moving to a mosque on Thirtieth Street in New York.[47]

Although musicians gave a variety of reasons for becoming Muslims, the desire to find spiritual purpose and social dignity was a common denominator. Many turned to Islam at least in part to oppose the stigma attached to race in American society. Some claimed they were attracted to the religion because it recognized no color line, while others used their new religious status to challenge segregation. A number of Muslim musicians said they claimed an identity that was something other than "Negro" American; as citizens of a community that transcended the social mores of Jim Crow, they demanded to be served in restaurants and hotels while on tour in the South. The popularity of Islam in the musicians' community reflected the overall growth of Islam in African American communities in the postwar era, but it was also a product of the will to defy social categories that fueled the imaginations of many musicians. Thus a broad-minded approach to both life and art could serve as a weapon in the struggle against the absurdities of race in American society.[48]

Mary Lou Williams's comments notwithstanding, it must be noted that this broad-minded approach to art and life was generally articulated by men and did little to challenge gender prescriptions in the jazz community. The bebop movement further consolidated the notion that jazz was a masculine expression, and beboppers quickly became seen by black and nonblack observers alike as symbols of a serious, politicized, and sometimes pathological black male creativity. This marks the emergence of the figure of the modern black jazzman as a defiant, alternative, and often exotic symbol of masculinity, an image that is common in postwar American arts and letters. Often such a view had as much to do with the needs and desires of male and female observers themselves as with anything else, but the fact remains that only a handful of women participated as musical equals in the bebop community, whose self-conception also tended to be masculine in orientation.[49]

Understanding the African American social, cultural, and intellectual context of bebop demands attention to both shifts and continuities in ideas about gender in the wake of some of the contradictory gains black women made during World War II. In her recent book on the "all-girl" bands of the 1940s, Sherrie Tucker links the experiences and perceptions of women in jazz during the war and the postwar years to broader patterns in women's experiences in the military and on the home front. As Tucker and a number of labor historians and scholars of African American history document, the wartime economy provided some opportunities for black women to leave low-paid and often demeaning domestic service and agricultural work for more lucrative jobs in the defense industry or in other industrial employment. These gains, of course, were limited. Like other women, African American women were often expected to give up higher-paying jobs when men returned from war, and government agencies and private employers made an effort to push black women back into domestic service once the conflict ended. Moreover, the gains women made during the war did little to change their overall position in the work force; in defense work, African American women still faced the double bind of sexism and racism, as they had difficulty securing these jobs, were often the first to be fired during slowdowns, and generally found themselves doing the lowest-paid work. Yet, even as wartime events fueled feelings of anger and frustration, they also raised questions about prescribed gender roles and helped create a climate of possibility for African American women, who moved in great numbers from the South to the North, joined the industrial labor force and trade unions, participated in nascent civil rights struggles, and went to college in increasing numbers.[50]

In the jazz world, the opportunities of the war years provided black women with a basis for rethinking racial, gender, and creative identities. During World War II, despite many roadblocks, female musicians made small advances in the jazz industry. Employment opportunities surfaced when male musicians joined the military or devoted their time to defense work, and ideas about the proper role of women's work in general expanded. Tucker shows how African American or primarily African American all-women's bands such as the Prairie View Co-Eds, the International Sweethearts of Rhythm, and the Darlings of Rhythm achieved significant prestige among jazz fans. Meanwhile, some women instrumentalists were able to secure employment in male-dominated bands. In doing so, women musicians began to challenge gendered conceptions of jazz artistry.[51]

Tucker also describes how the ideas and activities of these female band members were at times consistent with the ethos of critical ecumenicalism that permeated the African American jazz community at large. She uncovers the various kinds of subterfuge that members of integrated black bands used to avoid harassment, violence, and prosecution from local authorities for challenging de facto and de jure segregation while traveling in the segregated South. Tucker argues that such "survival strategies" not only affirmed the multiracial membership of these bands but also "challenged the philosophy and institutions of white supremacy"; they should be considered, she continues, "alongside other wartime civil rights actions of African Americans in the 1940s." Moreover, the International Sweethearts of Rhythm, a primarily African American band with an ethnically diverse membership, projected an image of black and brown solidarity that was consistent with the alliances forged during the 1940s between African Americans and people of color throughout the globe. The group's embrace of "internationalism" also challenged the narrow and demeaning definitions of blackness imposed by the white supremacist social order in the United States.[52]

Despite the ways that women musicians participated in the expansive intellectual orientation of the jazz community of the 1940s, however, members of all-women's bands and women in men's bands still faced many obstacles in their struggle for full acceptance by musicians and fans. They struggled with entrenched stereotypes about women's artistry in the jazz community and in society at large. Just as women's gains in the labor force in general were impermanent and restricted to certain spheres, women musicians often had to play the role of "glamour girls" and sex objects and were expected to (and often did) give up their positions in the music industry when men returned from war.

And it was at this moment, at the end of a war effort that had legitimized male aggression and promised men a return to their "rightful" place in society, that bebop emerged as a significant musical and cultural phenomenon. A broader cultural veneration of manhood reinforced the masculinist ethos in the jazz community. In addition, beboppers tapped into an androcentric artistic modernism as they constructed themselves as "serious artists." As in earlier decades, musicians' ideas about their own artistry went hand in hand with economic relationships with women. Dizzy Gillespie suggests that the economic patronage of white women played an important role in the development of bebop. Although some of these relationships were sexual, he remembered, "often, they were supportive friendships that the musicians and their patrons enjoyed."[53] Whatever the case, Gillespie's reminiscence calls attention to the way such patronage systems reinforced the construction of jazz as a site of male artistic accomplishment during and after the war. Such relationships fed into a particular manifestation of the Romantic artistic ideal, in which some musicians might be threatened by the competition of women's creativity yet were willing to be supported by their wages. This ideal bore similarities to the practices of the male hipster subculture entrenched in urban centers during World War II, wherein resistance to the wage economy sometimes took the form of parasitical relationships with black and white women. Indeed, as Robin D. G. Kelley notes, some song lyrics boasted about living off women, as did some musicians in accounts of their lives during the 1940s.[54]

Some relationships between male and female musicians, rooted in respect but based nonetheless on prescribed gender roles and an expectation that women should provide economic and emotional support, paralleled the patronage system described by Gillespie. Even for well-respected players in the jazz community such as Melba Liston and Mary Lou Williams, participation and acceptance in jazz circles sometimes depended upon their ability to double in a "maternal" role. According to Valerie Wilmer, Williams's Harlem apartment was a place where musicians gathered for "appreciation, help and understanding" as well as the exchange of musical ideas. Melba Liston is said to have kept a pot on the stove for hungry musicians, some of whom used her apartment as a mailing address.[55] A reminiscence by Liston about her reception when she joined Dizzy Gillespie's big band in 1947 illustrates the ideas that some men had about female creativity, as well as the roles that women had to play to gain respect:

> The first thing, all the guys in the band said, "Goddamn, Birks, you sent all the way to California for a *bitch*?" Dizzy said, "That's right." He said, "Did you bring the music that I told you to write?" I said, "Yes, sir." He said, "Pass it out to these muthafuckas and let me see what a bitch you are." He said, "Play the music, and I don't want to hear no fuckups." And of course they got about two measures and fell out and got all confused and stuff. And Dizzy said, "Now who's the bitch!" Dizzy was really something. So after that I was everybody's sister, mama, auntie. I was sewin' buttons, cuttin' hair and all the rest. Then I was a woman again.[56]

Although Gillespie's inclusion of Liston in his band may well have indicated that he was willing to rethink gender as well as racial categories, the response by his male band members and the roles that Liston adopted speak to the fact that, in general, gender roles changed little in a bebop community that venerated male creativity.

## The Problem with Bebop

Despite the social and creative freedoms that bebop promised, many African American musicians eventually concluded that it too had become symbolic of the creative and social restrictions facing them. By the end of the 1940s, bebop represented both the challenges to and the constraints of jazz as an art form and commodity. As African American musicians discussed bebop in the press, their comments demonstrated a complicated understanding of the connections between the music's status as art, the racial politics of the jazz world, their own livelihoods, and the possibilities for social change at this historical juncture. This was particularly the case at the very end of the decade when the jazz industry went into decline and its ill fortunes led to a strong backlash against bebop.[57]

Before exploring musicians' ambivalent responses to bebop, then, it is necessary to consider in more detail the broader reception of this music, for the complicated critical response to bebop not only created a space for musicians to articulate their aesthetic visions, it also presented a discursive field that was sometimes at odds with them. Moreover, the reception of this music fundamentally altered the way jazz has been understood by musicians and commentators alike since the 1940s.

Early in 1945, the African American and jazz press began paying attention to the new music and its practitioners, although they seldom identified it as bebop or saw it as a cohesive movement. By the end of the year, some commentators were hailing Parker, Monk, and especially Gillespie as the innovators of a unique and even "revolutionary" genre that was sometimes given the status of art music.[58] But bebop soon became the object of pejorative scrutiny by the media. As Bernard Gendron describes, bebop entered the popular imagination in 1946 amid a controversy stemming from Los Angeles radio station KMPC's decision to ban bebop from its play list because of its lascivious lyrics and alleged propensity for causing juvenile delinquency. KMPC was primarily concerned with novelty vocal numbers by the likes of Harry "The Hipster" Gordon and "Slim" Gaillard—whose repertoire included songs like "Cement Mixer" and "Who Put the Benzedrine in Mrs. Murphy's Ovaltine?"—but because Gaillard and Gordon had recently shared the bill with Gillespie and Parker at Billy Berg's nightclub in Hollywood, the instrumental bebop styles were seen as part of the same movement. This Southern California response to bebop stemmed from fears over a youth zoot subculture, whose members' clothes had become a metonym for brown and black juvenile delinquency, especially in Los Angeles.[59] Yet the larger, contradictory reception of bebop during the war years and the immediate postwar period was also the product of the music itself, changes in the jazz industry and the jazz community, and the broader social transformations occurring in America.

Bebop soon came to symbolize a larger movement of black assertiveness and political demands. Events on the domestic front during the war were instrumental in determining the way musicians, fans, and critics alike made sense of the bebop movement and musicians' social roles. In addition to fostering African American militancy and group identity, the war reminded whites about black demands at home. Commenting on the racial rhetoric accompanying the war against Japan, John Dower notes: "For white Americans, 'color' was a blunt reminder that the upheaval in Asia coincided with rising bitterness, impatience, anger, and militance among blacks at home."[60] Some whites were sympathetic to black demands, but others were increasingly fearful of this assertiveness and viewed it less as a call for a full extension of democracy than as the breakdown of civil society.

The activism of the jazz community in general may well have been one reason some believed bebop was a militant expression. Although few beboppers were actively involved in political struggle, bebop emerged during a period when other musicians and observers increasingly saw jazz as a vehicle for African American political activism. The federal government's enlistment of black musicians to perform at USO shows, make V-disc recordings for troops, and appear in jazz-themed films with patriotic messages afforded these musicians and their supporters the opportunity to engage in Double-V activism, in which they linked support for the war with a demand for African American rights within and outside the music industry. Black newspapers covered the struggle waged by musicians, the NAACP, and John Hammond to integrate radio house bands in 1942. In an editorial challenging the AFM's discriminatory practices, Hammond pointed out the contradiction posed by continued American racism at a time when the United States was at war with a white supremacist power.[61]

Musicians themselves became more outspoken about their treatment in the music industry, as the commentary in *The Music Dial* illustrates. Fletcher Henderson and Teddy Wilson were among the musicians who spoke out against Jim Crow in the music business in a 1944 *Esquire* "Jazz Symposium." Don Redman's band refused to tour the South in 1944 because of Jim Crow, and in April 1945 Earl Hines announced that he would no longer play engagements for segregated audiences. The existence of Jim Crow within the patriotic entertainment system itself made the contradictory aspects of American race relations all the more clear and gave African American musicians opportunities to make emphatic statements about racism in the United States. The USO, for example, remained largely segregated through the war, and prominent African American bandleaders (including Ellington and Calloway) were not invited to perform overseas. Lena Horne cut short a visit to Camp Robinson, Arkansas, and complained to the local NAACP when she learned that Nazi prisoners of war could attend her show but African American soldiers could not.[62]

Duke Ellington incorporated a Double-V ethos into his music. In a 1941 speech to a Los Angeles Methodist church, Ellington invoked Langston Hughes's phrase "I, Too, Sing America," as he described African American contributions to American culture and society. He concluded by asserting that black people had "recreated in America the desire for true democracy, freedom for all, the brotherhood of man, principles on which this country had been founded." That July, Ellington premiered his musical revue *Jump for Joy* in Los Angeles. He hoped the show would "give an American audience entertainment without compromising the dignity of the Negro people." Ellington followed with his lengthy compositions *Black, Brown and Beige* and *New World A-Coming,* thematic explorations of African American life that he intended to be vehicles for social change. Both works premiered at Carnegie Hall in 1943.[63]

When black musicians performed wartime benefits for African American or left causes, regardless of how strongly they believed in these causes, they expanded the political meanings of jazz. Luckey Roberts brought his International Symphonic Syncopated Orchestra to New York's Town Hall on May 28, 1941, to play a benefit for the Urban League and Bethune-Cookman College. In 1942 Earl Hines played a benefit for the Southern Negro Youth Congress at the Royal Windsor Ballroom in New York, while an April 1943 Carnegie Hall concert entitled "From Swing to Shostakovitch" featured Albert Ammons and Hazel Scott performing a benefit for the Soviet Union. A 1944 "Freedom Rally" at Madison Square Garden, sponsored by the Negro Labor Victory Committee, featured a performance of Ellington's *New World A-Coming.* On the West Coast, Norman Granz's first Jazz at the Philharmonic concert at Los Angeles's Philharmonic Auditorium in 1944 was a benefit for eleven Mexican-American youths and one white youth wrongly imprisoned in the Sleepy Lagoon case. Granz's concert series also challenged racism by bringing integrated audiences into previously segregated Los Angeles venues.[64]

Presenting some of these explicitly political expressions in a "concert" setting helped to create a climate in which observers linked jazz's increasing political currency to its growing capital as serious artistic expression. The growth of jazz concerts, and the public jam session in particular, affirmed black musicians' desires to create an art music and played a critical role in the construction of modern jazz as both sophisticated art and avant-garde "insurgent" expression. Jazz concerts accomplished this by presenting the spectacle of musicians playing "for their own artistic fulfillment" rather than giving the impression that they were there to please the audience—however artificial that distinction might be.[65]

Moreover, the war years revealed a continuation of the modernist discourses about the music that had characterized the emergence of jazz criticism during the 1930s. As Bernard Gendron argues, the critical debates between proponents of swing and New Orleans revivalists ("moldy figs") during the early 1940s prefigured later debates about bebop and played a crucial role "in preparing the way for the emergence and acceptance of an avant-garde jazz" by making it "possible" and "very natural" to refer to jazz as "an art music." And because these discussions were "laced with the idioms of commerce, politics, gender, and race," ideas about the political dimensions of the music often went hand in hand with ideas about its artistic legitimacy.[66] Although such discussions were largely produced by white critics, they were not always inconsistent with the visions of African American artists. In fact, this criticism helped to generate a subsequent understanding of black avant-garde music as an articulation of political assertiveness and cultural resistance.

Jazz concerts also illustrated that the music world of the 1940s was a place where ideas about respectability were highly charged and up for grabs. A 1946 *Ebony* article pointed out that the jazz concert audience reflected the new music, as "top hats and tails gave way to zoot suits and extreme porkpie hats."[67] These comments suggest that the high cultural trappings of the concert hall, if not those of formal men's wear, were relevant to a youthful, modern, and forward-looking population of working-class and middle-class young people. Concerts also provided a springboard from which musicians moved in a multiplicity of directions. This serious orientation and demand for musical respectability guided endeavors by modern jazz musicians in the years to come.

Changing ideas about sex and gender, as well as gendered conflicts, inflected the racial and political climate in wartime America, and this too affected the reception of bebop. The war itself, with its climate of violence, increased and legitimated male aggression; and, as George Lipsitz observes, "fights between men of different races often involved competition for power over women or over access to them. . . . On the home front and overseas battles between black and white war workers, service personnel, and civilians stemmed from struggles over sex—over rumors of rape, competition for dates, and symbolic and real violations of the privileges of white masculinity." At the same time, the limited inroads made by women in war industries and the military were seen as a threat to family life and men's economic position, while women's independence led to fears of female sexuality. In the case of black women, race compounded the economic and sexual threat of greater female participation in the labor force, as their proximity on the job and in public spaces unnerved white men and women and black men. Anxieties about working mothers and a destabilized social structure fostered widespread concern about juvenile delinquency. Urban uprisings, such as the 1943 Detroit Riot, the Harlem Riot, and the Zoot Suit Riots in Los Angeles, increased these fears, especially in regard to black and Latino youth.[68]

The jazz world refracted such anxieties in a variety of ways. The real and alleged drug use among musicians contributed to the construction of jazz as deviant expression, as did its association with out-of-control youth being led astray by a music with African American roots that fostered multiethnic interactions. As at other historical moments, fears about black militancy and criminality merged with fears about black sexuality, but the Harlem of the 1940s was considered by outsiders as far more physically dangerous than the Harlem of the 1920s. The interactions between black and white men and women in the entertainment districts of major cities added to the perception of jazz and black entertainment as deviant. The Savoy Ballroom in Harlem was closed for six months beginning in the spring of 1943. Ostensibly the club was shut down to protect white servicemen from venereal disease spread by prostitutes working Savoy dances; however, some African Americans believed the action stemmed from the interracial dating between black men and white women that these dances fostered.[69]

Whether based on sex, love, friendship, or patronage, relationships between black male musicians and white women were usually perceived in sexual terms, and this perception led to trouble. Gillespie recalls an incident on a New York street, where he and Oscar Pettiford were accosted by three southern white sailors for talking to a "white woman," who, unbeknownst to the sailors, was the entertainer Bricktop, an African American woman with a light complexion. The resulting brawl spilled into the subway station and ended with Gillespie hiding on a subway catwalk until the military police dragged the sailors away. In Los Angeles, the city's police department continually harassed trumpeter Howard McGhee and his wife, Dorothy, a blonde former model.[70]

When bebop came into greater visibility in 1945 and 1946, its popularity grew as independent record labels disseminated the music to legions of young fans. During this period, coverage of the music in the black press, national news and lifestyle publications, and jazz magazines fluctuated between celebration and condemnation. As Gendron demonstrates, the uneven reception of bebop in the jazz press from 1946 to 1948 was conditioned by the perceived fortunes of the music industry. As the popularity and profitability of swing declined—the result of postwar inflation and other economic factors, the presence of pop vocalists such as Bing Crosby and Frank Sinatra, and emergent hybrid music such as urban blues, jump, Latin, and polka—critics paid close attention to bebop, wondering whether it might prove a worthy and profitable successor to the fading swing genre or whether it might threaten the footholds the industry and established musicians had made with the public. Thus when bebop's fortunes rose (the music reached the height of its popularity in 1948 and early 1949), the major jazz trade publications and other media began to celebrate bebop more consistently on the grounds of its artistic legitimacy.[71]

Beyond the general parameters of acceptance and condemnation, writers for jazz magazines, black newspapers, the mainstream press, and the "little magazines" of the left infused bebop with additional meanings rooted in the social context in which it emerged. Even as commentators discussed bebop as a legitimate art form, they often understood it as a music of revolt. Some saw this revolt largely confined to the realm of music. Entrepreneur and critic Ross Russell called bebop a "reexamination of the basic problems of polyrhythms, collective improvisation, and jazz intonation" and of the harmonic principles of swing arranging. But ultimately, he wrote, "bebop is music of revolt: a revolt against big bands, arrangers, vertical harmonies, soggy rhythms, non-playing orchestra leaders, Tin Pan Alley—against commercialized music in general."[72] Others saw bebop in explicitly political terms, which sometimes reached exaggerated extremes. In 1947 *Saturday Review* tried to categorize some available jazz recordings according to ideological orientation. The "right wing" was represented by Louis Armstrong and his Hot Five, the "left wing" by bebop and Lennie Tristano, and the "center" was occupied by Billie Holiday, the King Cole Trio, and Benny Goodman.[73]

Other writers grounded bebop in the historical context of the 1940s while more carefully connecting aesthetics to social transformations. In a 1948 article in *Down Beat,* Dave Banks called jazz a "social art." In order to adequately understand bebop, he asserted, one must examine the "creative musician's psychological response toward the war," which had "forced the musical imagination further into the infinite reaches of its expression producing a revolutionary approach to music." Banks found antecedents of musicians' wartime attitudes in the "strong sense of anti-discrimination" in Kansas City, where Charlie Parker was born and where transitional figures Coleman Hawkins and Lester Young received much of their musical education: "Having heard the creative peak of improvisation that backgrounded his early life, it was only natural that Bird should seek a radical expression." Writing in 1950, Marshall Stearns wondered whether the perception of bebop as "revolt" might "obscure [the] radical experimentation in the music itself," but he also situated bebop's emergence "in an atmosphere of restless rebellion, [when] a great migration to the North was taking place and time itself seemed to be speeded up."[74]

Although only a few African American intellectuals paid attention to bebop in the late 1940s, those who did also ascribed social meanings to it. Writing in *Phylon* about a 1949 Dizzy Gillespie performance, African American scholar L. D. Reddick criticized those who tried to find explicit philosophical or political meanings in bebop. The music was not, he argued, about existentialism or communism. But Reddick did see bebop as a product of its historical context: "Bop is essentially modern and urban. It is unconventional. It is the music of sophisticated and modernized individuals and groups. Beyond that any careful critic would refuse to go." Reddick was also interested in the race and class dynamics at Gillespie's show, noting that the atypically integrated audience was populated by African American and white youth as well as whites from the "Persian-lamb-mink-coat-gang." "Respectable" members of Atlanta's black bourgeoisie were noticeably absent, leading him to conclude that they were even more pretentious than their white counterparts.[75] In a 1949 "Simple" column in the *Chicago Defender,* Langston Hughes identified bebop as a fading genre but also as a response to police brutality. Differentiating "Be-Bop" ("the real thing like the colored boys play") from "Re-Bop" ("an imitation like most of the white boys play"), Hughes's working-class savant, Jesse B. Semple, explained the relationship: "Every time a cop hits a Negro with his Billy club, that old club says, 'BOP! BOP! . . . BE-BOP! . . . MOP! . . BOP!' . . . That's what Bop is. Them young colored kids who started it, they know what bop is."[76]

If bebop could express its social context, then it might be a vehicle for expressing social justice as well. In a 1949 article in *Down Beat,* Amy Lee argued that bebop was illustrative of a collective African American search for musical and social freedom and also a black-generated vehicle for breaking down segregation in the world of concert music. In his 1950 *Harper's* article, Stearns hoped that if bebop were to be recognized as an art of the moment, it might encourage white observers to recognize African American demands for full citizenship: "This music is the sharply outlined reflection of the musicians who play it and, especially, of the environment in which it is played. Born in protest, both social and artistic, and cradled in contradiction, Bop mirrors the pace, complexity, and confusion of the times—frequently with too much accuracy for comfort."[77]

Lee's and Stearns's arguments resonated with ideas put forth by radical cultural critic Sidney Finkelstein in his 1948 book-length history, *Jazz: A People's Music.* Steeped in Popular Front egalitarianism, Finkelstein saw bebop as a complex and contradictory form that proved that blacks and whites had the same potential in both jazz and classical music. However, he also recognized that the institutions in which musicians labored were rife with inequality. Rejecting the boundary between jazz and European concert music, Finkelstein sketched a program for the advancement of jazz, arguing that its current state was artistically limiting and reflected the music industry's rampant discrimination against black musicians. Jazz, he argued, would not reach its fullest expression until a "democratic change" in American musical culture allowed musicians to incorporate jazz elements into orchestral compositions and create a more universal expression.[78]

In addition to ideas about art and politics, a crucial element of the discourse concerning bebop was the way it constructed musicians as intellectuals. Some considerations of bebop as a product of intellectual thought were tongue in cheek, but the musicians' obvious skill, their seriousness of purpose, and their bohemian accouterments influenced other observers. And arguing that the music was the product of intellectual enterprise helped to legitimize it as art and countered some of the stigma attached to black creativity.[79] A concern for bebop's origins led commentators to cast musicians as organic scholars, as well as inventors, of their art form. Charlie Parker was the object of this sort of attention, as was pianist Thelonious Monk, whose eccentric manners and jarring yet euphonic compositions appealed to some critics. A 1947 *Down Beat* profile by Bill Gottlieb described Monk as the "genius of bop," and these sentiments were repeated in the magazine a year later in a feature about the pianist that coincided with the release of some of his Blue Note sides. The *New Yorker* described Monk as a "somber, scholarly" man who liked Ravel, Stravinsky, Debussy, Prokofiev, and Schoenberg and was "intensely interested in basic principles of life."[80]

The validation of bebop musicians as intellectuals was uneven, however. Even as the practitioners of bebop were cast as artists and intellectuals, they could still be objects of the primitivist fascination that had long characterized the jazz discourse. The perception of musicians as social deviants was by no means inconsistent with the construction of jazz as avant-garde expression. Ingrid Monson observes that "the historically close association between madness, pathology, and racial difference made the image of the jazz avant-garde artist especially prone to appropriation by primitivist racial ideologies." Similarly, Ronald Radano discusses the development of a "primitive/intellectual homology" used to comprehend the character of black jazz musicians in the postwar United States. White observers frequently saw "contrasting images of respectability and degeneracy, of noble romanticism and black bestiality" as they sought to understand the jazz artist. Although some observers compared jazz musicians to European masters, "more often, musicians struck a balance between the intellectual artist and the exotic Other, seemingly based on the casting of Charlie Parker as the drug-crazed creative genius victimized by the urban jungle." And Andrew Ross argues that many observers saw in postwar black musicians a kind of "outsider knowledge." With roots in the 1940s, such assessments would culminate in the writings of some of the Beats, who saw jazzmen as "untutored, natural geniuses."[81] As Robin D. G. Kelley points out, the "iconography of Monk" (that is, the representation of Monk in photographs and on album covers) reflected the development of this primitive/intellectual homology. Whereas early representations of Monk often showed him bespectacled and studious at the piano, he was represented in increasingly eccentric terms on his Riverside and Columbia album covers in the 1950s and 1960s.[82]

Musicians were also constructed as gendered intellectuals. Writers in the 1940s continued the practice, established in earlier decades, of celebrating jazz artistry largely as the province of men. But during the later decade, their reading of male jazz artistry was informed both by the nononsense stage presence of musicians and by general anxieties about black assertiveness, which was sometimes understood through the modality of gender, that is, as black male assertiveness. As Steven Elworth argues, "the rise of a generation of young African American beboppers created an image of masculinity and creativity difficult to sell to white society." As a result, some jazz critics cobbled together artistic legitimacy with constructions of white masculinity in their glorification of figures such as Stan Kenton.[83] Yet this response was not universal among white critics and intellectuals. Indeed, the validation of black male assertiveness was part of the discourse that developed around bebop and has remained a constant in jazz criticism ever since.

In the end, bebop's status remained precarious, in large part because of the state of the jazz industry and concerns about race and African American political demands during and after World War II. The black press generally avoided the moral panic about bebop, once the music reached a certain level of legitimacy and was stripped of its association with juvenile delinquency; but the jazz press became increasingly critical of the genre at the end of 1949 and in 1950. The enthusiasm of many jazz critics for white musicians only increased when the popularity of bebop and jazz in general declined in 1949, and writers in the mainstream press often followed suit. As Gendron demonstrates, some critics were increasingly more interested in "'great white hopes'—white modernists, like [Lennie] Tristano and Kenton, with whom a mostly white readership would feel more at home." He surmises that "a racial code" may have been "operating in the white critics' expressed desire for a more cerebral and European modern jazz, as well as a jazz purified of any association with life-styles, argots, or dress."[84]

Despite such conflicts and misconceptions, some musicians continued to put their faith in bebop at the end of the decade. Pianist and future jazz educator Billy Taylor published a small musical instruction volume entitled *Basic Be-Bop Instruction for Piano* in 1949. Taylor was already crafting a persona for himself as a champion of jazz. The following year he told *Down Beat:* "My objective is to do all I can to call attention to the fact that jazz, like any other art form, can and should be presented in an artistic manner."[85] In the first lesson of his volume, "What Is Be-Bop?" Taylor linked bebop to a particular creative context, arguing that it had emerged as the result of experimentation by young musicians who were not content to play in the "stereotyped" styles of the 1930s. Taylor emphasized how bebop "enlarged the scope of jazz" through the "ingenuity" of its practitioners. He identified a central component of the artistry of bebop in the "alteration" of existing compositions to the extent that new compositions were created during performance. The music's complexity, however, did not remove it from the jazz tradition. Taylor placed the music firmly within a jazz canon; bebop was merely the "most recent and most revolutionary development." No matter how "intricate" a particular passage, "it *must swing* or it is *not* good be-bop."[86] Taylor also provided lessons in bebop rhythm, melody, and harmony, with a concluding section on how one could improvise all these elements when revising a popular tune.

Taylor's little book linked the ideas of New Negro intellectuals, an earlier generation of musicians, and later considerations of jazz. Taylor situated bebop firmly in an American context, arguing that jazz was both the "most truly American music" and "an art form, originated and used as a medium of expression by the American Negro."[87] Like James Weldon Johnson, W. C. Handy, Duke Ellington (although Ellington usually rejected the term "jazz"), and others before him, Taylor presented jazz as an important American artistic form that was rooted in black creativity but had universal appeal. Bebop was a further extension of this history of achievement. Taylor's analysis paralleled the formulation of black experience put forth by Ralph Ellison in *Invisible Man* (1952), which defined an African American birthright by placing black people at the symbolic center of American life and history. His comments anticipated Ellison's later essays on music and the work of Ellison's intellectual descendants Albert Murray, Stanley Crouch, and Wynton Marsalis, who have more recently figured jazz as simultaneously a product of American exceptionalism and black cultural achievement. In the context of the jazz community of 1949, Taylor's celebration of bebop as both American and African American art seemed geared toward validating black creativity, challenging the derogatory articles about bebop in the press, and perhaps improving the economic situation of its practitioners by demystifying it through jazz education.

But at various points during America's love-hate affair with bebop during the late forties, musicians often saw it as a loaded term that obscured as much as it illuminated and might even threaten their livelihoods. As Ralph Ellison later wrote about the label, "A word which throws up its hands in clownish self-deprecation before all the complexity of sound and rhythm and self-assertive passion which it pretends to name; a mask word for the charged ambiguities of the new sound, hiding the face of art." Similarly, some musicians reacted to the often-absurd meanings that were ascribed to the music. Signifying on critics' sometimes overzealous desire to find a social context for artistic expression, Dizzy Gillespie once explained that his late 1940s big band arrangement of "Things to Come" represented the conflict between Slettibus and Molotov during the formation of the United Nations; another time he claimed that it symbolized the struggle between good and evil during a nuclear war. The term "bebop" was especially troubling during periods when the music was the object of hostile attention. Speaking to *Metronome* in 1947, Charlie Parker said, "Let's not call it bebop. Let's call it music. People get so used to hearing jazz for so many years, finally somebody said 'Let's have something different' and some new ideas began to evolve. Then people brand it 'bebop' and try to crush it. If it should ever become completely accepted, people should remember it's in just the same position jazz was. It's just another style." And in the 1949 interview discussed earlier, in which Parker described bebop as a step toward a more expansive musical statement, his comment "I've been accused of having been one of the pioneers" speaks of the baggage that accompanied the label.[88]

In a 1948 article for *Record Changer,* pianist and composer Tadd Dameron trivialized various labels while championing the music itself: "Call it be-bop, rebop, progressive, or modern; whatever you call it (and whatever you think of it) it's the only kind of music I've ever wanted to play." Charting the development of a progressive aesthetic in the jazz community, he celebrated the flexibility that the new music gave to composers and interpreters alike. "Modern music seems to me to have a much greater freedom. We can improvise on both structure and melody and we aren't hampered by a strict dependence on the beat the way the old jazz is." In his mind, the "high spot in our work so far" was Gillespie's Carnegie Hall concert, for which he had done much of the arranging. Dameron also saw possibilities in work with nontraditional jazz instrumentation; he mentioned strings and French horns specifically. Yet "modern music" as a movement was incomplete. "We're just beginning; we've only been at it a few years; this is still a crude music." The present state of modern music was just a step along the way to future developments, which musicians would create while educating audiences along the way. Fats Navarro expressed a similar perspective in a conversation with *Metronome.* He too employed the term "modern music" to describe an artistic expression, rooted in complicated chord progressions, that was yet to reach full fruition.[89]

And then there was money. Ultimately, the idea of bebop was inextricably linked to the marketing of the music. As bebop became popular, the market created a certain expectation for a product that might not have been consistent with musicians' own aesthetic visions. Although a Romantic notion of the African American bebop musician as artist, working against and outside the restrictions of the market, has been an overused staple of critical interpretations of the idiom, the question of "selling out" was an issue for musicians.[90] This is not to say that bebop musicians were unconcerned about making a living. As professionals, they were clearly interested in getting paid and worried about not getting paid by unscrupulous booking agents and record companies. Some musicians were, however, concerned with musical standards or projects that were at odds with the expectations of the marketplace.

When Dameron spoke about the need to educate an audience about the new music, he noted that musicians might have to simplify it somewhat so that the public would understand it. He suggested that Gillespie might have been responsible for some of the hostility toward the music because he refused to "compromise" his speed and technique. He thought that Gillespie's music might be too complicated for the public and suggested that musicians bring their audience along slowly, "giving them just so much at a time." He characterized this as "commercializing it a bit," a process with which he seemed somewhat uncomfortable but apparently thought was necessary. Parker, in contrast, said in 1949 that Gillespie had become too commercial. He criticized Gillespie's stage antics and dress, as well as the selling of bebop in general. By catering to the tastes of a dancing audience, Gillespie and others had stymied their own musical development. "Diz has an awful lot of ideas when he wants to, but if he stays with the big band he'll forget everything he ever played." Yet Parker did recognize the need to balance one's survival in the music industry with one's creative output. He looked to France, where he spent part of 1949 and 1950, as a place where he could relax, study, and write music. Ideally, he said, his yearly schedule would include six months in France and six months in the United States: "You've got to be here for the commercial things and in France for relaxing facilities."[91]

The economic reasons for rejecting "bebop" as a label became more obvious when the music's popularity began to decline. During the second half of 1949 and into 1950, bebop's status degenerated as the jazz industry as a whole continued to suffer the effects of postwar inflation and economic readjustment, as well as competition from other musical forms such as popular vocal music, country and western, urban blues, and rhythm and blues. Dance halls and nightclubs went out of business or cut back their hours. Even black middle-class audiences began paying more attention to urban blues and rhythm and blues. A 1949 *Ebony* article explored the music of Louis Jordan. A 1950 feature on the blues celebrated the popularity of Dinah Washington, Jimmy Rushing, T-Bone Walker, Chippie Hill, and others, while noting the centrality of the blues idiom in the creation of jazz. Soon writers in the jazz press began to see bebop as the cause of the industry's decline, and musicians themselves began to question their commitment to the genre.[92]

In a December 1949 *New York Age* article, vocalist Babs Gonzales traced the development of bebop. He said that in 1945 "so-called 'bop'" had been an important musical movement that involved "about 20 progressive musicians," but by 1947 the label "bebop" had become a marketing tool used to describe an array of musical styles, only some of which maintained the spirit of the early experiments. The music, he argued, had suffered from unscrupulous disc jockeys and promoters showcasing inferior products, as well as from hostile reactions from older musicians, whose lack of education and musical training prevented them from understanding some of the intricacies of the new music. Gonzales thought bebop's interracial audience was one cause of the unfavorable reaction by the press, and he recognized that "bebopper" had become a synonym for juvenile delinquent. In the end, Gonzales championed the music itself and encouraged young musicians to devote themselves to composition, orchestration, and arranging, while learning from established figures such as John Lewis, Walter Fuller, Miles Davis, and Mary Lou Williams. Yet he also claimed that the meanings associated with the word "bebop" exacerbated the "unemployment situation" facing musicians. Commenting on *Down Beat*'s contest to find a new word for "jazz" at this moment of crisis, he suggested that Dan Burley and the *New York Age* do the same for "bebop."[93]

Dizzy Gillespie's career and his comments in 1949 and 1950 offer insight into his own attempts to balance artistic goals, professionalism, and popularity as the bebop idiom fell out of favor. For several years, Gillespie and his management worked hard to promote his image as a bebop innovator, yet during this period the trumpeter also worked hard to maintain his connection to a dancing audience. Although his 1945 big band ran into trouble with the "unreconstructed blues lovers in the south," he achieved a measure of success in the concert and dance halls when he launched his second big band in 1946. But even this band faced the dilemma of whether bebop was made for dancing or listening. And when dancers began looking elsewhere for entertainment, the band's existence became increasingly precarious.[94]

In a 1949 response to Parker's *Down Beat* comments, Gillespie emphasized that, contrary to the saxophonist's remarks, bebop was part of the jazz idiom. And as part of that tradition, it was crucial that it kept its steady beat. "Bop is part of jazz, and jazz music is to dance to. The trouble with bop as it's played now is that people can't dance to it. They don't hear those four beats. We'll never get bop across to a side audience until they can dance to it. They're not particular about whether you're playing a flatted fifth or a ruptured 129th as long as they can dance." In an effort to recapture the audience that was slipping away, Gillespie announced his intention to change his repertoire to make his band more dance-friendly. As a big band, his group could not support itself (or even fit into) small nightclubs, so they were forced to play larger auditoriums. But they could not depend on a loyal cadre of bop fans to fill these halls consistently and needed the support of a larger, dancing audience.[95]

Despite his efforts, Gillespie was forced to break up his band in 1950. In a *Down Beat* interview that September, he lamented the lack of work that led to the decision. He claimed that bebop might have reached the end of its road, as he found himself displaced by the "dance music" (probably rhythm and blues) that he considered inferior. His comments also suggest that part of the failure had to do with his continued association with the "bebop" label and the contradictory meanings associated with it. Gillespie believed that the cool pose adopted by some of the modernists, whom he claimed were not committed to entertaining their audiences, contributed to the economic hardships for black jazz musicians. For Gillespie, bebop meant artistic seriousness, but it also meant playing the role of the entertainer. Chastising fellow musicians, he said, "They think it would be a drag if people were to think they like what they're doing. They think it's enough if they just blow. . . . If you've got enough money and can afford to play for yourself, you can play anyway you want to. But if you want to make a living at music, you've got to sell it."[96]

Two months later *Down Beat* columnist Ralph Gleason lamented Gillespie's predicament, suggesting that the problem lay with Gillespie's management continuing to market him as a "bebopper." Gleason wrote: "He's so much more than the best connotation of that twisted word that it's a mortal shame." Shortly thereafter, in response to a *Milwaukee Sentinel* article that linked bebop to juvenile delinquency, *Down Beat* opined: "Perhaps it's all for the best. When people all begin thinking that be-bop is a swear word, or a noun to be connected only with shoplifters, drunks, or users of narcotics, then they'll forget its origin. And then the music can go on being played with no stigma attached. It'll all be jazz again. And maybe the whole music business will be a lot healthier."[97] Many musicians seemed to follow this lead, for in the context of the economics of the industry and the racial discourse surrounding the music, the label had the power to fix a complicated series of musical innovations in a particular time and place and make them irrelevant. Gillespie recalled that Ellington warned him about the problems with categories: "Duke Ellington once told me: 'Dizzy, the biggest mistake you made was to let them name your music be-bop, because from the time they name something, it is dated.'"[98]

## Coda

Bebop did not disappear when the market bottomed out. It continues to be a core element of the language of jazz. Although many of its major African American figures experienced hard times in the late 1940s and early 1950s, at least some of them had resurgences in popularity during the 1950s and beyond, even as their music, the market, and its categories changed. Bebop was critical not only for determining the direction of jazz history but also for influencing the way it was understood. Just as bebop changed the sonic language of jazz, the response to bebop institutionalized a variety of meanings that have characterized jazz and jazz musicians up to the present.

Bebop also marked the emergence of a particular aesthetic and critical orientation in the African American musicians' community. African

American musicians changed the direction of jazz as an art form by rising to the artistic challenges presented by existing music, drawing from
their own experiences and from a broader social, cultural, and intellectual milieu. Musicians expressed a keen sense of African American identity, while calling into question narrowly defined racial categories and
embracing a forward-looking worldliness. Their disparate aesthetic
projects reflected this emergent consciousness, as did their embrace of
the idea of bebop. And when they recognized the limitations of bebop
as both genre and idea, their rejection of the term similarly spoke of this
orientation, as well as of the constraints placed on them by the economics of the jazz business.

# 3  "Passions of a Man"

## The Poetics and Politics of Charles Mingus

**BASSIST AND COMPOSER CHARLES MINGUS** was among the musicians who developed their craft in the intellectual and cultural climate that produced bebop. Born in Nogales, Arizona, in 1922 and raised in Watts, Mingus was a member of the community of young modernists working in and around Los Angeles during the 1940s. Like other musicians who came out of the educational and performance networks in Los Angeles, Mingus maintained a catholic approach to music. Although he was never fully immersed in the bebop idiom and was initially ambivalent about this music, in the late 1940s he drew upon the beboppers' harmonic and rhythmic innovations while incorporating influences ranging from the blues to Ellington to composers of classical music. After moving to New York in the fall of 1951, he eventually developed important working relationships with Charlie Parker, Max Roach, and other architects of the idiom.

Beyond its musical influence, bebop at various times symbolized for Mingus both the possibilities and the limitations of jazz. The music and personae of Charlie Parker and other artists represented black musical genius, a community committed to artistic exploration and fulfillment, and an assault on musical convention. Yet bebop, and the tragic lives of some of its practitioners, also signified the mistreatment of black artists by the music industry and the limitations that generic categorization and marketing placed on art. Contemplating the legacy of bebop was but one element of Mingus's intellectual project, which sought, among other things, to make sense of his own music, the position of improvised and composed music in mid-twentieth-century America, the experiences of African American musicians in the jazz business, and the future of American society.

Beginning with a letter written by Mingus to jazz critic Ralph Glea-

son, which appeared in the June 1951 issue of *Down Beat*, and concluding with a discussion of the published and unpublished versions of Mingus's autobiography, *Beneath the Underdog*, which takes us into the 1960s,
this chapter explores the connections between Mingus's personal musical history, his aesthetic visions, and the social and cultural climate of
the civil rights movement. During these years, Mingus articulated a shifting aesthetic philosophy that was a product of a continual struggle to
reconcile his music, his identity, and his position in the society in which
he lived. He was keenly aware of how racism and economic exploitation
operated in the music industry, and his critique of industry practices was
linked to a broader perspective on race and African American experience.
Mingus interpreted these issues through the lens of gender as well. This
is most obvious in the sexual politics of *Beneath the Underdog*, but it also
emerges subtly in his earlier comments in the jazz press, which articulate a Romantic approach to art and creativity. In both cases, his ideas
about artistry were intertwined with a masculinist response to the material conditions and the racial politics of the jazz community.

## "All Music Is One"

*Down Beat* columnist Ralph Gleason wrote an article for the June 1, 1951,
issue of the magazine in which he reproduced passages from a letter
penned by Mingus, who was at the time an up-and-coming musician
still based on the West Coast. Mingus offered this letter to supplement
an interview Gleason had conducted with him while he was appearing
with the Red Norvo trio at the Blackhawk in San Francisco a few months
earlier. Aware of the difficulty of getting one's point across when someone else was asking the questions, Mingus used the letter to establish his
own agenda for a conversation about music.

Mingus addressed the challenges he faced as an African American practitioner of jazz in the early 1950s, while articulating several of the often-
contradictory opinions he would express in public over the course of his
career.[1] He described jazz in Romantic terms, as an important artistic
expression that was the product of one's spirit and emotions and that often existed in opposition to the values of the marketplace. But rather than
evade commodification, the jazz artist had a duty to create an audience

for his or her music by working within commercial enterprises to reach out and educate listeners whose attentions lay elsewhere. Even as he celebrated jazz as a distinct art form, Mingus tried to dismantle the boundaries between jazz and classical music. This erasure of generic boundary not only affirmed musical projects (like his own) that incorporated elements from both fields but also sought to give jazz a cultural legitimacy equal to that of classical music—an act of aesthetic leveling. Moreover, these claims of musical universality also responded directly to the way jazz symbolized social and artistic restrictions on the lives of African American musicians. In Mingus's view, jazz was a site of black accomplishment, but it was also a term to be rejected because of its association with the limitations imposed by race.

Mingus told Gleason that jazz, like any other art, was "the individual's means of expressing his deepest and innermost feelings and emotions"; but he also described the difficulties of remaining true to this vision. Writing during the decline of bebop's popularity, Mingus saw how some musicians were caught between an audience for classical music, which disdained jazz as a popular expression, and a popular audience, which preferred the exuberance of jump and rhythm and blues over the cerebral textures of modern jazz. Recognizing that "every individual musician must seek his own individual solution to the problem of making a living," he noted that many musicians had given up their artistic pursuit or had turned to drugs or alcohol as a result of this crisis. Yet he encouraged others to maintain their artistic goals and personal integrity as they waited for their talents to be recognized.

Mingus's own solution to this "problem of making a living" was to remain true to his ideals and to argue for a blurring of the boundaries between jazz and classical music. Invoking Charlie Parker and his recent recordings with strings, Mingus argued that "all music is one." Challenging those who claimed that these recordings showed an incommensurability between jazz and symphonic instruments, Mingus explained that the problem was that the strings were playing straight eighth notes while Parker was improvising with a swing feeling. With proper writing, Mingus asserted, classically trained musicians could play jazz, and "violins will swing for the first time in history." Then, while interrogating the idea that composition is the principle that separates classical music from jazz, he wrote: "Charlie Parker is in his own way creating complete, clearly thought-out compositions of melodic line every time he plays a solo, as surely as one was ever written down by Brahms or Chopin or Tchaikovsky." Ultimately, Mingus hoped, "those who have always separated the two into jazz and classical will finally see that it's all one music we're playing and what they've been buying is just the confusion out of the separation of the two."

Mingus's belief in the universality of musical expression was, on one level, a product of the aesthetic philosophy he developed as a young musician in Los Angeles. Mingus often called attention to the diverse influences on his development as a musician during his youth, influences that ranged from concert music to Duke Ellington to the music he heard in the sanctified church. Mingus was also energized by the educational networks in Los Angeles, and he was trained in both jazz and classical idioms. Having begun his studies on the trombone at the age of about eight, he soon switched to cello, which he played briefly with the Los Angeles Junior Philharmonic. Although he took up the bass at fourteen and started playing jazz, he continued to play a wide range of music, as did many young African American musicians in Los Angeles. Major influences on Mingus's bass playing included the classically trained jazz player Red Callender, from whom the young Mingus took lessons, and Ellington's bass player, Jimmy Blanton, who approached the instrument with a high level of harmonic and rhythmic sophistication and helped bring it to the foreground of jazz ensembles. Later, Mingus studied privately for five years with Herman Rheinschagen, who played bass at one time with the New York Philharmonic.

Beyond the instrument itself, Mingus was interested in modern harmony and composition. He took classical music courses at Los Angeles City College and studied composition and theory with Lloyd Reese. Early classical music influences included Debussy, Ravel, and Richard Strauss. He was also inspired by pianist Art Tatum's harmonic substitutions and, of course, by Ellington's sophisticated arrangements of dance music and his blurring of the lines between jazz and classical music in his longer compositions. Mingus further honed his composing and arranging skills by working for about a year as an assistant to Hollywood film composer Dmitri Tiomkin.[2] Later, Mingus was influenced by the harmonic and rhythmic developments of bebop, also perhaps acquiring Parker's aversion to musical category.

During the 1940s, Mingus developed a musical vision that emphasized composition, experimentation, and challenges to musical boundaries. Although he made ends meet through jobs such as arranging for Dinah Washington and working as a sideman with artists such as Louis Armstrong, Kid Ory, and Lionel Hampton, Mingus thought of himself first and foremost as a serious composer and wrote music grounded in both jazz and classical music. He was convinced that the lines between classical music and jazz were not immutable, and he saw composition as a means of moving outside the marketing categories imposed upon jazz. Early orchestral tone poems such as "Half-Mast Inhibition," "The Chill of Death," and "God's Portrait" were products of this vision,[3] as was his involvement in the short-lived experimental group The Stars of Swing, which included Buddy Collette, Lucky Thompson, Britt Woodman, Spaulding Givens, and John Anderson. This vision is also reflected in the pieces Mingus wrote and recorded with big bands and small combos in the mid- and late 1940s, which maintained strong roots in the swing tradition, incorporated bebop elements, and emphasized composition and arranging as much as improvising. This can be heard on "Mingus Fingers," recorded with Lionel Hampton's band in 1947, and on the eight sides Mingus recorded in 1949 for Hal Fenton's "Fentone" label—four with a twenty-two-piece big band and four with a quintet. One of the pieces from this session, "He's Gone," features Mingus on cello and a written flute part performed by the San Francisco Symphony Orchestra's Dante Profumato.[4]

Mingus also maintained a Romantic aesthetic philosophy, viewing musical performance and composition as idealized expressions of one's imagination, emotions, and spirituality. "The Chill of Death," for example, includes lyrics that touch on philosophical themes and mysticism. In 1946 or 1947, he recorded this composition for Columbia with a spoken-word part. Although the recording was not released, the performance reflected Mingus's desire to link composition to other forms of artistic expression. These compositional ideals were, in part, a product of Mingus's wide-ranging intellectual interests, which paralleled his preference for fluid musical forms. Mingus often referred to his autodidacticism, claiming to have dabbled in Freudian theory, theosophy, and other subjects. He was also deeply influenced by the San Francisco Bay Area artist Farwell Taylor, whom he had met on a trip to San Francisco the summer before he graduated from high school. In addition to becoming Mingus's confidant and sounding board, Taylor introduced him to Vedanta Hindu beliefs and encouraged him to stick to his desire to be a composer.[5]

Mingus's insistence that "all music is one" and his Romantic approach to artistic integrity were also products of his experiences as an African American musician. Mingus pursued his hybrid musical vision within institutions and social spaces structured by racism. He and other black Angelenos recognized that musical categories and tastes were forms of distinction that went hand in hand with the logic of racism and segregation, as well as with class divisions within the black community. By drawing upon a variety of musical influences, including those considered elite or serious, young black musicians took pleasure in artistic accomplishment and symbolically challenged the social order. Experimenting with convention subtly resisted the oppressive aspects of playing or composing distinct, racialized musical genres, while still maintaining an allegiance to an African American tradition.

But engaging in such cultural politics did not necessarily translate into substantive material changes. At the time he wrote the letter to *Down Beat,* Mingus had labored for more than a decade in California nightclubs. Although he had some successes, his career, like those of many black musicians, had suffered from the combined effects of segregation and a fickle marketplace during the late 1940s. Jazz musicians had to endure increased federal taxes on ballrooms and nightclubs, the shifting fortunes of the jazz industry during the late 1940s, and the growing popularity of pop vocalists and emergent musical forms such as urban blues, jump, and Latin dance music. African American musicians in California had to contend with segregated unions in Los Angeles and San Francisco, which often limited their employment options to small clubs and after-hours joints and effectively kept them out of symphonies, radio orchestras, Hollywood studio work, and better-paying nightclub gigs. Mingus's experience in the late 1940s of being mistakenly admitted to the white union in San Francisco (a bandleader "passed" him off as Latino) and subsequently turned in by a fearful black union delegate gave him particular insight into the absurdity of segregated social spaces and cultural categories. Although bebop and the modern jazz movement on the East Coast provided greater opportunities for black musicians who challenged generic categories, opportunities on the West Coast remained lim-

ited. Mingus found few critical or financial successes with his own music during the 1940s, and his work as a sideman proved unfulfilling. When
he was hired by Norvo in the summer of 1950, he was not on the rolls
of dues-paying members of the black musicians' local in either San Francisco or Los Angeles and was apparently working at the post office.[6]

By supporting the dismantling of the boundaries between jazz and classical music in his *Down Beat* letter, Mingus demonstrated an understanding of both the cultural politics and the material realities of the music industry. He recognized that categories such as "jazz" and "classical"
were constructs informed by racialized ideas about virtuosity and genius
that in turn contributed to inequality in the music business. He sought
to undermine these categories while holding on to the idea that jazz was
an arena of African American musical accomplishment. Even as Mingus
found much to cherish in the improvisational tradition, he recognized
the limitations of "jazz" as a category. At its best, as in the work of Parker,
jazz could be the expression of the artist's "inner self"; but jazz was also
a commodity created by the music industry to conform to its idea of the
tastes of a mass audience. Ultimately, Mingus saw jazz genres, as defined
by critics and the music industry, as dead ends. "What will live on past
the arrested development of boogie-woogie, Dixieland, and bop," he
wondered, "remains to be seen." Making reference to Lionel Hampton
as an artist who was compromised by the marketplace, Mingus looked
forward to the day when "it will no longer be necessary for a musician
to jump up and down on a drum or to dance on a bandstand to receive
recognition of his talent."[7]

By claiming that music was a unitary enterprise, Mingus suggested that
notions of distinct traditions were artificial and limiting for jazz and classical musicians alike. Describing Parker's improvisations as compositions
enabled Mingus to redefine jazz and Western classical music as part of a
universal tradition by finding parallels, as Armstrong did in *Swing That
Music,* between written composition and the spontaneous composition
that occurs when jazz soloists improvise on preexisting melodic, harmonic, and rhythmic structures. Mingus imagined a world free of racial
restrictions and generic categories. With words similar to the rhetoric of
the burgeoning civil rights movement, he called for greater integration
in the music world. "Today," he argued, "musicians in all races are proving that no race is endowed with special abilities for any profession and

that every musician has an equal chance if given the proper start and study needed for playing correctly."

Mingus's comment about the need for a "proper start and study" was probably in part self-referential. Throughout his life, he complained that despite his wide-ranging musical training in the black community, there were shortcomings in his education as a result of discrimination. Mingus pointed to problems other musicians faced as well, contending that once their talent was recognized, skilled musicians such as Buddy Collette, Milt Hinton, and Bill Douglass would find their places in symphonies from which they were currently barred because of "color." He asked: "Can we send a potential Ravel, Debussy, or Stravinsky to his grave without affording him the chance to prove that music has advanced many steps and that many composers as great as any of the old are being forced to write background music for the slipping of Mabel's girdle, rather than the true emotions of his inner self?" Although his comments about Parker indicate a desire to acknowledge jazz as an expression of black genius, Mingus recognized that racially based ideas about artistry lay behind the systematic discrimination black musicians faced in classical music and elsewhere. So who better to bring into the discussion than white bandleader Stan Kenton, who actively sought to remove jazz from its African American roots? If the boundaries between jazz and classical were dismantled, Mingus reasoned, "then Kenton can play Carnegie, not just as the representative of 'jazz,' but as a modern composer of American music."

Mingus's comments may also have referred to the struggle by African American musicians to desegregate the American Federation of Musicians local in Los Angeles. In the late 1940s, Collette, Douglass, and other black members of segregated Musicians Local 767 put their aesthetic philosophies into practice as they began a fight for amalgamation with Local 47, whose members were white or Latino. The successful merging of the union locals in 1953 launched a nationwide movement to eliminate segregated AFM locals. One weapon in the Los Angeles struggle was the sixty-five-piece Community Symphony Orchestra, through which black, white, and Latino musicians, classical and jazz players alike, presented public rehearsals of music to promote the cause of integration. They began with Monday evening classical performances and then added Sunday afternoon jazz jam sessions. The orchestra challenged both musical divisions between jazz and classical and social divisions between black and white, which in Los Angeles's music world meant discrimination against black musicians. Mingus did not participate in the orchestra or in the political maneuverings that preceded amalgamation of the union locals. Collette recalls that Mingus was reluctant to join the orchestra because he wanted to concentrate on his own music, and he was in New York during the most active part of the union struggle. Collette and others, however, give Mingus credit for spurring on the movement because he was so vocal about segregation in the Los Angeles music world of the 1940s; and they recall that he participated in early conversations about amalgamation.[8]

Mingus's aesthetic vision had a gendered element as well. Mingus suggested that careful study and a firm belief in one's artistic vision would help musicians work through the restrictions they faced. A devotion to the "true expression of the self" provided an ontological and spiritual challenge to the material structures of the music industry. Just as male Romantic poets and aestheticians of the nineteenth century venerated individual emotional expression and artistic originality as ways of countering the alienation that Enlightenment rationality and technological transformations had wrought, Mingus's emphasis on music as an expression of the emotional self served as an act of reclaiming a masculine— as well as racial—self threatened by the material and discursive strictures of the jazz world. Thus, in the 1951 letter to Gleason, we find antecedents to Mingus's appeal to "true" artistry that would later be expressed in the sexual politics of *Beneath the Underdog*.

Mingus recognized the power of jazz journalism and its effect on the ability of jazz musicians to earn a living. This was particularly true for black West Coast musicians, who suffered from a lack of critical attention throughout the 1940s. In response, he tried to create a climate in which these musicians would have the creative freedom and material resources to pursue their art. By writing to Gleason and expressing ideas consistent with those of the critic, Mingus carved out a space in the jazz discourse from which to articulate his aesthetic vision and voice a critique of inequality in the music business.

As discussed in chapter 2, jazz criticism at the end of the 1940s was a field rife with contradictions and clashing opinions. In the early 1950s, jazz became the object of increased scholarly attention, and debate raged over just what jazz was and what it said about American culture. Over the course of the decade, faith in the idea of an identifiable "jazz tradition" strengthened, but the contours of jazz criticism often mirrored the unsuccessful struggle to develop a consensus about a complex musical form and the social context it purportedly reflected.

One of the many conflicts involved the question of whether jazz was an entity unto itself or whether it was best understood in relation to other forms of music. Another critical issue was race. During this period of ascendant American nationalism and Cold War consensus ideology, the jazz discourse often erased the artistic contributions and economic struggles of African American musicians. Ronald Radano argues that through a process of "reinventing the music's past in the image of the European classical tradition," a "doctrine of progress" was created during the 1950s, wherein jazz was seen as a collection of folk forms that grew into "complex patterns of greatness." Jazz, he continues, was often removed from its African American cultural referent and defined in deracinated terms as a respectable expression of American democracy.[9] Yet this discourse sometimes validated black accomplishment and called attention to the predicaments musicians faced. As John Gennari demonstrates, many of the critics who adhered to the liberal consensus paid some attention to the sociology of the music industry and embraced the ideal of racial equality. Leonard Feather, for example, viewed jazz in America as an expression of freedom and saw its ultimate success as dependent upon the dismantling of segregation in the jazz world and the cessation of the economic exploitation of African American musicians. Marshall Stearns also took a progressive stand on race relations. He sought out the ideas of black intellectuals such as Ralph Ellison, Langston Hughes, and Sterling Brown as he formulated ideas about jazz that mirrored liberal ideologies of the period.[10]

The conversation about jazz as a legitimate national musical expression no doubt marginalized the contributions of African American musicians and elided the material struggles they faced in the music industry. So too did the embrace of jazz as a symbol of a "color-blind" society.[11] Yet because the jazz discourse was infused with ideas about race, culture, citizenship, civil and economic rights, and black genius, it also provided the opportunity for African American musicians to express their own artistic beliefs and to challenge the practices of the music industry. Mingus's ideas were published in *Down Beat* because he found a sympathetic supporter in Gleason, who championed equal opportunity in the jazz business and was invested in breaking down barriers between jazz and classical music as a means of legitimating the homegrown art form. Gleason had written glowingly of Mingus in a 1949 *Down Beat* article and was now convinced that Mingus's experimental music, skills as a bass player, and ideas about the false dichotomy of jazz and classical music would soon make him "one of the most important musicians that jazz has produced." Presenting Mingus as a "thinking musician" gave jazz further legitimacy by showing that musicians were self-consciously producing their art.[12] By presenting himself as a "thinking musician," Mingus brought his own agenda into this conversation.

## "The Latest and Greatest in Jazz"

In September 1951, a few months after the publication of the *Down Beat* piece, Mingus left Norvo's trio in New York. One explanation describes a falling out with the leader, who had replaced Mingus for an upcoming television appearance because of pressure from network officials who were worried about how a "mixed" band would play to their sponsors and a southern audience. Another version holds that Mingus was removed from the gig because he was not a member of Local 802 in New York, which actively tried to restrict New York television work to its members. In any case, Mingus remained in New York after this incident and made it his new base of operations. There, he found work with East Coast–based African American musicians who influenced the direction of his art, career, and ideas. Mingus performed intermittently with Charlie Parker for the next three years, during which time the saxophonist had a growing impact on him. Max Roach quickly became a musical collaborator and an associate in Mingus's critique of music industry practices. Mingus also encountered like-minded white experimentalists who were interested in extending jazz forms through composition and were invested in the idea of legitimizing and developing jazz through education. Pianist Lennie Tristano shaped Mingus's musical ideas during his early years in New York, and both Mingus and Max Roach taught briefly at Tristano's jazz school. Also influential was pianist and theorist John

Mehegan, with whom Mingus recorded a 1952 album entitled *From Barrelhouse to Bop: A History of Jazz Piano.*[13]

Mingus also entered the production end of the music business. With his wife, Celia, and Roach, he established an independent record company, Debut Records, and a publishing company, Chazz-Mar, Inc., in the spring of 1952. These businesses were the first incarnations of a series of independent recording and publishing ventures that Mingus operated over the years, and Debut was one of several musician-run labels to emerge in the early 1950s.[14] Although the company existed on paper into the 1960s, it recorded only between 1952 and 1957. Operating under the motto "the latest and greatest in jazz," Debut recorded some well-known artists and attempted to bring to the public the work of musicians who had not received attention from other companies. In addition to sessions led by Roach and Mingus, the company recorded popular vocal groups; straight-ahead jazz combos led by Miles Davis, Thad Jones, and Kenny Dorham; and several ensembles that walked the line between jazz and classical music. Debut's best-known releases were three LPs from a 1953 Toronto concert featuring Mingus, Roach, and bebop pioneers Parker, Gillespie, and Bud Powell.

The Minguses and Roach quickly found that running a record company was not easy. Major labels, for example, often demanded loyalty from their distributors, which made it difficult for independent labels to get their products on the market.[15] Debut thus provided Mingus with another education about perfidy in the music business. Moreover, because of Mingus's and Roach's performance schedules, much of Debut's creative work ended up falling on the shoulders of Celia Mingus, who started out as secretary and bookkeeper but eventually conceptualized and organized recording sessions, edited tapes, and designed album covers.[16] Yet Debut nevertheless offered Mingus a vehicle for putting his aesthetic ideals from the 1951 letter into practice while negotiating the business aspects of the music industry and trying to create a more receptive environment for his music and modern jazz in general.

The earliest of Mingus's own Debut sides and his attempts to promote them provide insight into the coalescence of his personal aesthetic vision, his assessment of the state of jazz music, and his company's marketing strategies. In April 1952, Mingus recorded four of his original compositions—"Portrait," "Extrasensory Perception," "Precognition," and "I've Lost My Love"—with vocalists Bob Benton and Jackie Paris and a quintet consisting of bass, cello, drums, piano, and alto saxophone.[17] These recordings reflect the catholic approach to music that Mingus had developed in Los Angeles and was now nurturing in New York. These sides not only breached the wall between jazz and classical music by emphasizing the use of written composition in jazz performance but also expressed the aesthetic Romanticism and the heartfelt attention to romance that often infused Mingus's writing.[18]

"Portrait" is a fusion of popular song, chamber music, and jazz. A slow-tempo piece, it is marked by the lush, moody textures that Mingus wrote for George Koutzen's cello and Lee Konitz's alto saxophone. Mingus originally composed "Portrait" as an orchestral piece and later recorded it as "God's Portrait" for Fentone in 1949 with a twenty-two-piece big band featuring himself on cello. According to Nat Hentoff, a dejected Mingus wrote the composition after the breakup of his first marriage, with lyrics that represented the feelings of a misanthropic man's affinity for nature.[19] "Portrait" is also a description of Mingus's self-conscious attempt to portray the natural world through music, as the lyrics describe a composer "painting" a landscape with musical notes. Mingus uses specific musical devices to represent the images of the lyrics, as when Phyllis Pinkerton plays swirling, arpeggiated chords on the piano to accentuate Jackie Paris's vocalized description of a rainstorm.

"Extrasensory Perception" and "Precognition," in contrast, are clearly influenced by bebop rhythms and phrasing. But Mingus took bebop in the direction charted by John Lewis, Miles Davis, Gil Evans, Lee Konitz, and other participants in the "Birth of the Cool" sessions of 1949 and 1950, who had experimented with complicated written passages and orchestral instruments. "Extrasensory Perception" is in thirty-two-bar form and employs the common bebop practice of presenting a chorus of thematic material and then showcasing individual soloists (Konitz, Mingus, and pianist Phyllis Pinkerton) on succeeding choruses. Yet Mingus wrote out all the musicians' parts, including Konitz's solo, and added a cello part that provided a layer of counterpoint to the main theme and heightened the melodic and rhythmic tension of the piece. The session also shows the influence of Lennie Tristano, who was the sound engineer on the date as well as mentor to Konitz, Pinkerton, and drummer Al Levitt. Tristano's approach to modern jazz at the time emphasized the rhythmic and melodic tensions created by the lines of the front-line instruments rather than complicated rhythm section work.[20]

During the early days of Debut's existence, Charles and Celia Mingus actively sought to get their records on the market by cultivating relationships with jazz writers, disc jockeys, and distributors. They wrote to well-known critics whose views on music seemed consistent with those of Mingus. They also initiated contact with like-minded disc jockeys across the country after reading letters the disc jockeys had written to the editors of jazz magazines. This correspondence demonstrates that Mingus saw Debut as a means of developing a broad and attentive audience for modern jazz and as a way "to record and play exactly the way I want."[21] These letters also offer insight into his motivations for writing, arranging, and recording these early compositions and document his view of himself as an heir to the musical legacy of Parker and Gillespie.

Shortly after the release of Mingus's early Debut sides, he sent copies of the records to Barry Ulanov and included a letter explaining what he was trying to accomplish with them. Mingus did not know the writer personally, but Fats Navarro, shortly before his death, had told Mingus that Ulanov was one of the few jazz critics who understood musicians. Although Mingus acknowledged that he was better known as a bassist, he told Ulanov that his "real ambition has always been in writing." Music, he said, was "a kind of international language and through it one can express his feelings about life, the world and conditions in it—the bad with the good." (He also noted that his view of the world at the moment included interests in psychiatry, the relationship between mind and body, and extrasensory perception.) Although he acknowledged that this music was far from "perfect," Mingus believed that his use of a classical cellist on these recordings proved his contention that "music can be *written* so that it swings itself just by being read correctly." He saw this approach as an extension of Charlie Parker's modern experimentation, which should have heralded "a new beginning in Jazz and not a suspended ending for everyone else to go copying from."[22]

Mingus wrote a similar letter to French critic Charles Delauney a month later, in which he again described bebop as an important artistic movement that had become stagnant. He saw his Debut sides as "something new and different in progressive music [that] should at least be received as a welcome departure from the now played-out, worn-out clichés that were originally and wonderfully introduced by such wonderful artists as Charlie Parker and Dizzy Gillespie and that have since become the prey of other imitative and uncreative musicians." Mingus described "Portrait" and "Precognition" as compositions of "equal musical merit" that established "different mood[s]" and illustrated the "variety" of modes of jazz composition. And once again he expressed his belief "that it is possible to write jazz so that when read correctly by a classically trained musician, the music would naturally swing itself."[23]

Elsewhere Mingus explained that the juxtaposition of these performances on record also had a strategic purpose. He wrote a letter to a California disc jockey who had suggested in *Down Beat* that a more appreciative audience for jazz could be established by interspersing "good jazz records" with "the commercial stuff most people want to hear." Mingus agreed, stating he had "always felt that if Jazz is ever to make any headway with the unhip public it will have to be done by a slow process of gradually building up their interest and confidence." Mingus reported that he was trying to take a similar tack with his own music and record company. "I have already backed 'Precognition' which would appeal strictly to jazz fans with 'Portrait' which I feel will appeal to not only the jazz fans but to the general public as well. If they like 'Portrait' well enough to buy it, at some time they are bound to play the other side and who can tell to what extent it might eventually lead to arousing their interest in jazz?"[24] By walking the line between popular and art music, Mingus sought to educate and expand a jazz audience that would be receptive to his future projects.

Over the next few years, he and his partners at Debut pursued this policy by recording a wide variety of artists, including experimental musicians who sought to take jazz in new directions.[25] Mingus also followed this approach in his own musical projects. From 1952 to 1955, he played gigs or recorded with various bebop musicians, including Parker and his pre-bop idols Art Tatum and Duke Ellington.[26] But it was through a series of "workshop" ensembles that he most effectively integrated elements of classical music and jazz and explored the possibilities of incorporating intricately written passages and orchestral instruments into jazz performance.

Mingus had first encountered the idea of an enterprise in which musicians shared ideas and collectively explored new material in classical music workshops at Los Angeles City College in the early 1940s. The Stars of Swing, with Buddy Collette and Lucky Thompson, was an early attempt to create a collectively run, composition-oriented group. In the summer of 1953, Mingus and Max Roach began a series of concerts and rehearsals at the Putnam Central Club in Brooklyn, whose participants included Thelonious Monk, Art Blakey, Kenny Clarke, John Lewis, Teo Macero, and John LaPorta. Out of the Putnam Central group emerged the Jazz Composers Workshop, a loosely organized group of musicians interested in collaborative jazz composition and cooperative economics. Kenny Clarke and John Lewis were among the early participants, but they soon left to devote their energies to the Modern Jazz Quartet, which began a more rigorous concert schedule in 1954. Although the full workshop ensemble never recorded, it performed concerts in January and May of 1954; and Mingus recorded with various members of this group for Debut, Savoy, and other labels in 1954 and 1955.[27]

On October 31, 1954, Mingus led a sextet featuring Teo Macero, John LaPorta, and pianist Mal Waldron on a recording of four original compositions and two standards. These performances include an extensive use of contrapuntal melodic lines, one of Mingus's favorite compositional devices during this period and a feature of the work of other Jazz Composers Workshop members. At times the counterpoint involves musicians improvising melodies behind one another's solos, as on the Mingus original "Purple Heart." Mingus also used counterpoint in another favorite pursuit: synthesizing similar melodic figures or harmonic progressions (or both) from several existing pieces into new compositions. On the standard "Tea for Two," Mingus counterpoises the melody of this tune with lines from "Body and Soul," "Perdido," and "Prisoner of Love," which are all based on similar chord progressions.[28]

In this session, Mingus also pointed to the direction of future works. "Eulogy for Rudy Williams," a Mingus original, is a multisectional composition that features thematic material and a four-bar turnaround that Mingus would later work into "Pithecanthropus Erectus." "Gregarian Chant" and "Getting Together" are vehicles for collective, unplanned group improvisation, which Mingus apparently saw as a means of getting musicians to express their emotional selves during performance. He asserted that the success of these recordings resulted from the sensitivity of the other musicians' performance, adding that "this style of playing is actually the sincerest method of musical expression." While trying to keep the composition as "tonal" as possible for this "initial presentation," he hoped that he could move further into dissonance once this basic approach gained an audience: "If and when these present constructions are accepted, I will venture to delve a little more into the so-called dissonance of free form improvisation—which one may then label atonal."[29] These performances anticipated the less structured approach to composition Mingus would soon take, as well as the "free jazz" of Ornette Coleman and others in the late 1950s and 1960s.

## "Brubeck Doesn't Swing" (?)

Mingus's work with the Jazz Composers Workshop came at a crucial transition in his career. These recordings expressed his desire to make jazz swing by writing it down, and the project marked the apex of his public investment in an artistic identity as a composer based on the model of European classical music. Yet these groups also explored free improvisation and increasingly incorporated a stronger rhythmic drive and a greater use of blues tonalities that were critical to Mingus's subsequent development and to the "hard bop" movement of the second half of the 1950s. Over the next few years, Mingus professed a major change in his approach to composition, while also articulating a stronger critique of music industry practices. Although many elements of his musical and intellectual projects remained consistent, he seemed to find some incommensurability between an integrationist and universalist aesthetic vision and his identity as an African American laboring in the music industry. Mingus's music became, in a sense, "blacker," as he himself adopted a more outspoken and more critical public persona.

Despite his attempts to win economic reward and critical acclaim through his hybrid musical vision, Mingus did not become, in Al Young's words, the "nigger Stan Kenton."[30] His reputation as a virtuoso musician grew tremendously during the first half of the 1950s, but he never received the acclaim he desired as a composer. Despite Debut's operations, he continued to have problems making ends meet. He even returned to work at the post office briefly in late 1952 and stayed there until Charlie Parker reminded him of his "aesthetic responsibilities" and summoned him to a gig in Philadelphia.[31]

In comments reproduced in a 1953 *Down Beat* article by Nat Hentoff, with whom he had established a correspondence and who would champion his musical project through the 1950s and 1960s, Mingus vented his frustrations about his own lack of steady employment and vowed not to compromise his aesthetic ideals. He also criticized the way the jazz industry treated African American musicians who dared to experiment, voicing an even stronger critique than he had expressed in his 1951 letter. On the one hand, many promoters expected black musicians to conform to the entertainer's role. "A pure genius of jazz," he noted ironically, "is manifested when he and the rest of the orchestra run around the room while the rhythm section grimaces and dances around their instruments." On the other hand, he argued, serious jazz artistry had become the province of white "copyists," who had reaped greater critical and financial rewards than black innovators such as Charlie Parker or Jimmy Blanton.[32]

Mingus made even stronger comments in a *Down Beat* "Blindfold Test," published in the June 15, 1955, issue of the magazine.[33] These "tests" were administered by critic Leonard Feather, who asked musicians to identify, rate, and comment on unfamiliar recordings. The results were later published and gave Feather support for his "color-blind" theory of jazz, as musicians often made mistakes when they guessed the personnel on the recordings, identifying anonymous white artists as black artists and vice versa.[34] With his comments, however, Mingus put forth a "color-conscious" perspective about inequality in the jazz world.

Mingus recognized Parker's recording of "Cosmic Rays"—which was made shortly before the saxophonist's death in March of 1955—and argued against the commonly held opinion that Parker's "dissipation" had taken away his creative force:

> You know what's funny? Now I know that Bird was progressing still. The other cats were the ones that were standing still and making Bird sound old, you know? Bird isn't just playing riffs on here, the way his imitators do. You know how he used to be able to talk with his horn, the way he could tell you what chick he was thinking about. That's the way he's playing here. How many stars? FIFTY!

Mingus's validation of Parker came at the expense of prominent white jazz musicians. Whereas in 1951 Mingus had celebrated Stan Kenton's potential to transcend the limitations of jazz, in 1955 he recognized Shelly

Manne's drumming on a record and praised him for having finally "found out what jazz is" since leaving Kenton's group.

Mingus reserved his greatest criticism for Dave Brubeck. Recognizing the playing of saxophonist Lee Konitz on a piece called "Bop Goes the Leesel," Mingus lamented, "I didn't know that Lee Konitz played as dead as [Brubeck saxophonist] Paul Desmond."

> This makes me mad, because it's not jazz, and people are calling this kind of beat jazz. Dave Brubeck gets the same beat. And it's leading Lee to think this swings, because Desmond has made it like that, and they call it swing. . . . It's like five dead men, this record. No stars, man. They shouldn't ever have released it. Not release it—they shouldn't even *play* like that!
>
> I think these cats hate jazz, but for some reason they've convinced the public that this is jazz. I don't know what to do about it, unless cats like Bird and Diz—well it's too late for Bird—change their music and call it something else. 'Cause if they play jazz, I don't play jazz, and neither does [Oscar] Pettiford!

Mingus's investment in writing himself into a hermetic jazz tradition and the severity of his condemnation of Brubeck may seem odd, especially given his own aesthetic orientation that had heretofore sought to expand the parameters of the genre.[35] Although Brubeck was a controversial figure in the jazz world because many claimed he did not "swing," it would seem that Mingus's broad-minded approach would have led him to oppose writing anyone out of the jazz tradition for failing to adhere to prescribed conventions. But Brubeck's reputation was on the rise, at a moment when jazz was achieving greater social prestige and profitability. In that context, Mingus's comments represent a highly charged response to the growing popularity of white musicians from the West Coast, who were being rewarded both critically and monetarily while most African American modern jazz musicians were still struggling to make a living.

Although Brubeck was, by all accounts, a racially sensitive and ethical artist, his reception in the jazz press and the mainstream media had a pernicious effect on African American musicians. A November 8, 1954, *Time* magazine cover story on Brubeck and the "new kind of jazz age in the U.S." employed a discourse of respectability as it celebrated Brubeck and his contemporaries while marginalizing the contributions and experiences of black musicians. The article associated blackness and immorality in jazz and saw the new "mainstream" jazz as a step forward from an unhealthy past. *Time* presented Brubeck as an intellectual musician and a happily married family man who rarely drank. Unlike the heyday of the 1920s, when jazz was equated with the spirit of "Hades," the "jazz age" of the 1950s was defined by Brubeck and other white "modernists," the article claimed, whose music "evokes neither swinging hips nor hip flasks." Photographs included with the article showed Brubeck holding his wife, playing music with his children, and engaging in dialogue with Father Norman O'Connor, "one of several priests among his friends."[36]

The article's erasure of black contributions to the development of this "legitimate" modern jazz movement continued with a brief history of the music. Jazz had arisen from slave chants and the blues, moved through New Orleans and Chicago, and stopped briefly in big band swing and bebop before going on to "modern" music. This history elided the contributions of African American musicians after New Orleans, except for bebop, which it characterized as "briefly fashionable" protest music that quickly ran out of steam because of its "off-beat, spastic rhythms." Whereas six years earlier magazines like *Saturday Review* and the *New Yorker* had celebrated bebop as an intellectual art, *Time* dismissed it as a "fashion" and made it a foil for the intellectual expressions of white West Coast musicians. The new music "swings as vigorously as any of its predecessors," *Time's* correspondent wrote, "but once it starts swinging, it seems to move on to more interesting matters, such as tinkering up a little canon á la Bach or some dissonant counterpoint á la Bartok or even a thrashing crisis á la Beethoven."[37]

The omission of African American musicians from this narrative of jazz history must have been particularly galling to Mingus, who had first-hand experience with the hardships black musicians faced while pursuing their own "interesting matters."[38] Few African American experimental musicians received substantial critical support, and many modern players battled addiction and poverty. However unfair to Brubeck Mingus's comments were, his insider knowledge surely made the attention that a national publication like *Time* gave to Brubeck and the new profitability of jazz especially infuriating. As the article pointed out, 1954 had witnessed a jazz boom, created in part by the popularity of Brubeck and his colleagues and exemplified by the birth of the Newport Jazz Festival. Although major record labels had expressed only limited interest in modern jazz in the early 1950s, they were now garnering substantial profits from the music. A host of smaller labels had emerged, putting out nothing but jazz. While many African American musicians struggled to pay their rent, *Time* estimated Brubeck would make $100,000 in 1954 through his performances, shares in Fantasy Records, and other sources.

Mingus's comments in the "Blindfold Test" indicate his growing recognition that a color-blind and universalist perspective about musical genres, which had earlier appeared to be a way to counter racial inequality in the music business, was also consistent with the logic by which jazz writing and the marketplace marginalized African American musicians. Mingus demonstrated a greater investment in the construction of "jazz" as a distinct tradition with identifiable, African American innovators. Within the African American jazz community, in dialogue with politicized musicians such as Max Roach, Mingus—at times, at least—saw more clearly the value of the idea of a distinct jazz tradition, defined by black innovators. By reconstructing these boundaries, Mingus simultaneously tapped into a celebratory, self-affirming discourse from the community of black musicians and a critical discourse that sought to legitimize jazz by creating a tradition, employing them both to protest the treatment of black musicians by the jazz industry.

Mingus was soon reminded, however, that he too was vulnerable to criticism based on jazz orthodoxy. Although resources were not always allocated fairly, the jazz boom of the mid-1950s eventually created a market for other expressions besides so-called cool jazz; and some African American musicians were able to take advantage of this market. In addition, in response to the staid elements of Cold War American culture, observers of all hues saw black culture as a source of vitality missing from the mainstream. African Americans of various class backgrounds increasingly looked to vernacular culture as a site of pride and pleasure. Even as the West Coast sound rose in popularity, some devoted jazz fans and critics continued to pay attention to music that spoke more strongly of African American culture. The second half of the 1950s witnessed what is called the "hard bop" movement—an inadequate term, to be sure, given the array of music and styles considered part of it—but a signifier nonetheless of the collective effort among black musicians to find an artistic voice, economic stability, and a connection to black audiences who were leaving jazz. Musicians, fans, and producers alike increasingly embraced music that had stronger rhythmic propulsion, a more pronounced bottom end, and more identifiable blues or gospel influence in its melodic lines and harmonic structure.[39]

Among the musicians representative of this orientation was Miles Davis, whose streamlined recordings for Prestige and Blue Note were celebrated by a small but loyal following during the first half of the 1950s. More recently, Davis had successfully engineered a comeback from heroin addiction and put on a celebrated performance at the 1955 Newport Jazz Festival, which led to a recording contract with Columbia. Before recording with Columbia, however, Davis did a session with Debut in July 1955, which included Mingus on bass, Elvin Jones on drums, and Teddy Charles on vibraphone. Neither Mingus nor Davis was happy with the album, and it appears to have created some rancor between them.[40]

In a November 1955 *Down Beat* interview, Davis made explicit criticisms of Mingus's music. He compared some of the compositions Mingus and Teo Macero were writing for small groups to "tired modern paintings." Other pieces he described as simply "depressing." Using "Mingus Fingers" as an example, Davis claimed Mingus was capable of better writing than his compositions recorded with the Jazz Composers Workshop. Speaking of this work, Davis quipped: "For one thing, in his present writing, he's using the wrong instrumentation to get it over. If he had a section of low horns, for example, that would cut down on some of the dissonance, he could get it over better."[41]

In "An Open Letter to Miles Davis," published in *Down Beat* a few weeks later, Mingus apologized to Brubeck and his admirers and backed away from an exclusionary definition of jazz.[42] He gently rebuked Davis by appealing to the legacy of Parker, who supposedly loved his fellow musicians too much to engage in such petty infighting. Rather than criticize one another, musicians—and, by implication, critics—should understand the subjectivity of perception and recognize that individual artists have their own standards:

It seems so hard for some of us to grow up mentally just enough to realize that there are other persons of flesh and bone, just like us, on this great, big earth. And if they don't ever stand still, move, or "swing," they are as right as we are, even if they are as wrong as hell by our standards. Yes, Miles, I am apologizing for my stupid *Blindfold Test.* I can do it gladly because I'm learning a little something. No matter how much they try to say that Brubeck doesn't swing—or whatever else they're stewing or whoever else they're brewing—it's factually unimportant.

Mingus referred to the definition of "swing" Davis had used in his interview to chastise other musicians—"if a guy makes you pat your foot, and if you feel it down your back, etc."—when arguing that imposing such standards on the music would cause one to inaccurately exclude people from the jazz tradition. By Davis's logic, Brubeck swung as well as anybody because of the response he received from his audiences, whereas Ellington strayed from the jazz continuum on his compositions without tempo. Mingus also appeared to have come to terms with Brubeck's popularity and economic successes. Brubeck was popular, Mingus contended, "not because Dave made *Time* magazine—and a dollar— but mainly because Dave honestly thinks he's swinging. He feels a certain pulse and plays a certain pulse which gives him pleasure and a sense of exaltation because he's sincerely doing something the way he, Dave Brubeck, feels like doing it."

Recognizing the delicate position he fell into as an Ellington and Parker devotee with universalist aspirations, Mingus broadened the parameters of the jazz tradition as a response to the threat, on the grounds of both racial and stylistic orthodoxy, to his own musical credentials. Mingus found renewed importance for his long-standing ideas about music as a multidimensional expression of the self: "Just because I'm playing jazz I don't forget about *me.* I play or write *me,* the way I feel, through jazz, or whatever. . . . My music is alive and it's about the living and the dead, about good and evil. It's angry, yet it's real because it *knows* it's angry." Mingus also warned Davis to beware of the power of his words, especially in a jazz press that had the power to disrupt the careers of his fellow musicians: "Truly, Miles, I love you and want you to know you're needed here, but you're too important a person in jazz to be less than extra careful about what you say about other musicians who are *also trying* to create."

Over the rest of his career, Mingus's public comments reflected some of the fundamental tensions he expressed in the 1955 "Blindfold Test" and "An Open Letter to Miles Davis." Jazz as personified by musicians like Parker (and himself, for that matter) remained a noble artistic pursuit that expressed one's emotional and spiritual self and was ideally unencumbered by the expectations of critics, the audience, or the industry. And Mingus was increasingly invested in legitimizing jazz through elements that were intrinsic to the idiom (for example, improvisation, "swing," blues tonalities) rather than by invoking musical universality or arguing for the erasure of the boundary between jazz and classical music. Jazz, however, still remained an endeavor rife with restrictions. Not only did the jazz industry treat African American musicians unfairly, but Mingus often viewed different kinds of jazz orthodoxies as antithetical to the expansive elements of his musical project.

## The Jazz Workshop

As Mingus made these comments about Brubeck and Davis, he was in the process of consolidating a sound that placed him more firmly in the mainstream of hard-swinging African American jazz during the second half of the 1950s. Whether it was based on a fear of being marginalized by black reformulations of the idiom, the influence of Charlie Parker and other bebop architects, the expectations of record labels and audiences, the political moment, an artistic impasse, or, more likely, a combination of factors, Mingus changed his approach to composition and bandleading. He began working with original compositions that included more African American vernacular musical elements (for example, gospel and blues inflections), and he allowed musicians greater leeway in creating the melodic (if not harmonic) structure of each performance of these compositions. In the fall of 1955, he began to rehearse a new workshop, dropped the term "composers" from the name of the group, and taught the musicians his songs through oral instruction rather than through a written score.

Working without charts was nothing new for jazz ensembles; one certainly did not need them for familiar standards, blues numbers, and simple modal compositions. But what made Mingus's approach somewhat

unique was that he taught his band relatively complicated compositions that were meant to be learned by ear alone. Moreover, the contours of these orally transmitted compositions allowed his sidemen, like
Ellington's, to play an important role in the ultimate shape of each performance. Most important, Mingus himself described this change as
significant, which signaled a different way of thinking on his part.

Mingus explained his new approach in the liner notes to his 1956 Atlantic album *Pithecanthropus Erectus*. At a fundamental level, he said, "my
ideas have not changed—only my method of producing them." But he
rejected his earlier idea that jazz, if written correctly, could be performed
by either classical or jazz musicians and still retain its feeling:

> Jazz, by its very definition, cannot be held down to written parts to
> be played with a feeling that goes only with blowing free. A classical
> musician might read all the notes correctly but play them without
> the correct feeling or interpretation, and a jazz musician, although he
> might read all the notes and play them with jazz feeling, inevitably
> introduces his own *individual* expression rather than what the com-
> poser intended. It is amazing how many ways a four-bar phrase of
> four beats per measure can be interpreted.

He asserted that his approach to composition took into account both
the artistic vision of the composer and the need of the "true" jazz improviser to inflect a piece of music with the player's own meanings:

> My whole conception with my present Jazz Workshop group deals
> with nothing written. I "write" compositions—but only on mental
> score paper—then I lay out the composition part by part to the
> musicians. I play them the "framework" on piano so that they are
> all familiar with my interpretation and feeling and with the scale
> and chord progressions to be used. Each man's own particular style
> is taken into consideration, both in ensemble and in solos. . . . In
> this way, I find it possible to keep my own compositional flavor in
> the pieces and yet to allow the musicians more individual freedom
> in the creation of their group lines and solos.[43]

As Mingus rethought his ideas about composition, he held on to his idea
of artistic creation as the fulfillment of the self and continued to explore
musical ideas he had developed in earlier years. But he did so while pub-

licly stating a stronger allegiance to an improvisational ethos he considered central to the ideas and practices of the jazz community.

The Charles Mingus Jazz Workshop—featuring pianist Waldron, drummer Willie Jones, trombonist Eddie Bert, and tenor saxophonist George Barrow—first opened at New York's Cafe Bohemia in October 1955 and returned for a long engagement beginning in December. Debut Records recorded one of the group's December performances; but before the session could be released, the attention Mingus's group received led to a contract with Atlantic (his first with a major label as a leader) and the recording of *Pithecanthropus Erectus* in late January 1956.

These first Jazz Workshop recordings provide a snapshot of Mingus's transition. Some performances on the Cafe Bohemia date are clearly extensions of musical ideas that Mingus had been working on earlier. "Percussion Discussion," a moody, dissonant musical dialogue between Mingus and Max Roach (who was sitting in with the group), continues Mingus's exploration of freely improvised music. "Septemberly" and "All the Things You C#" are further examples of his practice, perfected in the Jazz Composers Workshop, of creating new compositions by juxtaposing similar harmonic structures and thematic material from existing popular standards or classical pieces. "Septemberly" explores the similar melodies and harmonic bases of "September in the Rain" and "Tenderly." "All the Things You C#" counterpoises thematic material from Rachmaninoff's Prelude in C-sharp Minor, the introduction to Parker and Gillespie's version of the Kern and Hammerstein standard "All the Things You Are," and the rhythmic basis of "Claire de Lune."[44]

"Jump Monk," however, points more clearly in new directions. Consisting of a sixty-four-bar chorus in A/A/B/A form, with three sixteen-bar A sections of introductory material, this original composition profiles Thelonious Monk's "complex personality" and provides a tribute to his music. The invocation of an African American modern jazz icon situates Mingus in a particular artistic lineage, and this piece simply swings harder than his work with the Composers Workshop. The piece also reflects Mingus's changing approach to jazz composition, which allowed him to convey his own musical vision while providing other members of the ensemble sufficient improvisational freedom to participate in the spontaneous creation of each performance.

Although Mingus gave his horn players set melodic figures for some sections, he merely provided scales for others, thereby allowing the musicians to create their own figures.[45] We can hear this in the introduction and the chorus of "Jump Monk." The introduction begins with a sixteen-bar section played by bass and drums only. Barrow comes in for the second sixteen-bar section to play a bluesy melodic figure tapering into an improvised passage. Then Bert joins him for an improvised call-and-response exchange in the third section, which is based on the main melodic idea from the second. In the chorus, the first eight bars of each A section feature Bert and Barrow playing the outline of the primary melody loosely but in unison; and the second eight bars of each A section feature their improvised interpretations of Mingus's thematic material in crescendos that suggest the collective improvisation of early New Orleans jazz. When comparing two versions of this composition that were recorded the same December 1955 evening, one can hear the degree of freedom the horn players had in interpreting both the freely improvised passages and the outlines of the set melodic figures. These interpretations set a different mood for each performance and provided fresh thematic material on which the different instrumentalists based their solos.

*Pithecanthropus Erectus* further illuminates Mingus's transformation. Replacing Bert and Barrow on this recording are alto saxophonist Jackie McLean and tenor player J. R. Monterose. On the title track, Mingus again fuses vernacular elements with experimentalism, as he intersperses blues tones, collective improvisation, and straight-ahead swing with off-beat accents, shifts in tempo and meter, and tonal manipulations for dramatic effect. As he did in other works from this period, he provides a rough framework (that is, suggested scales and melodic lines) that allows his sidemen to help "compose" each piece. The A/B/A/C structure gives the musicians additional flexibility as well. Not only are the B and C sections based on two alternating chords (I minor and $IV^7$) over which the musicians engage in modal improvisations; in addition, these sections are of indeterminate length, allowing the ensemble and the soloists the flexibility to extend or shorten a section, depending on mood or the success of an improvised passage.[46]

This composition also expressed a broader outlook on life and art, which was rooted in Mingus's Romantic aesthetic vision and which also reflected the development of an increasingly outspoken and politicized artist. In the early 1950s, Mingus had called attention to discrimination in the music industry but suggested that the artistic solution was to transcend structural inequalities by remaining true to one's artistic vision. By the mid-1950s, however, his music indicated a belief that the jazz musician had a duty to address injustice through art as well as through public comment. Mingus performed and recorded two politically oriented "folk" tunes, "Work Song" and the then-unreleased "Haitian Fight Song," at the 1955 Cafe Bohemia date—one of the first public instances of a black jazz musician using the title of a composition to make a militant political statement in the context of civil rights and anticolonialist struggles.[47]

In the liner notes to *Pithecanthropus Erectus,* Mingus called the title composition a "jazz tone poem" that told the story of the decline of modern civilization, with obvious references to its intransigence toward the freedom struggles of oppressed people. Mingus likened the arrogance of contemporary humankind to the false sense of pride that early man supposedly felt upon rising up on two legs, "pounding his chest and preaching his superiority over the animals still in a prone position." Anticipating his modern counterparts, early man's "failure to realize the inevitable emancipation of those he sought to enslave, and his greed in attempting to stand on a false security, deny him not only the right of ever being a man, but finally destroy him completely." Mingus described each successive chorus as a movement that expressed the rise and fall of humankind: "(1) evolution, (2) superiority-complex, (3) decline, and (4) destruction."[48] As the piece reaches a crescendo in the C section of the last chorus, the wailing instrumental voices are joined with human screams, "indicating the final destruction in the manner that a dying organism has one last frantic burst of motion before gasping its last breath."

Over the next several years, Mingus built upon this new approach to jazz composition as he reworked old musical ideas and developed new ones. He continued working on his written compositions, but his recordings generally followed the direction of *Pithecanthropus Erectus,* as he visited terrain that simultaneously situated him firmly in the jazz tradition and also put him on the cutting edge of jazz avant-gardism during the 1950s and 1960s. He explored the blues on thematically organized albums such as *Blues and Roots* (1959) and *Oh Yeah* (1961). Other endeavors, such as *Mingus Ah Um* (1959) and *Mingus Dynasty* (1959), on which he used large ensembles, demonstrated a wider range of musical influences. He

continued his experiments with jazz and the spoken word in collaborations with Langston Hughes, Jean Shepherd, and Melvin Stewart.[49] Mingus also explored the "Spanish tinge," as Jelly Roll Morton called the Latin
influence on jazz, on his 1957 recording *Tijuana Moods,* which evoked
memories of a trip to Mexico that Mingus and Danny Richmond had
taken earlier that year.

Mingus further positioned himself within the lineage of modern
African American jazz musicians through a series of compositions, following "Eulogy for Rudy Williams" and "Jump Monk," that paid homage to major practitioners of the idiom. "Reincarnation of a Lovebird,"
"Bird Calls," "Gunslinging Bird," "Dizzy Moods," "Open Letter to
Duke," and "Goodbye Porkpie Hat" (a tribute to Lester Young) are only
some of the pieces Mingus recorded that invoked African American musicians, either by quoting styles or musical ideas associated with them or
merely by seeking to portray his "feelings" for them. "Reincarnation of
a Lovebird," for example, a medium-tempo ballad on *The Clown,* begins
with a series of quotations from Parker's compositions or performances
and features Parker-like lines by Mingus's alto player, Shafi Hadi. But
such direct references were not the rule. "Usually when I write something about Monk or Bird," Mingus once said, "I'm not trying to write
the way they write, I just write my interpretation of my feeling for them
and their feeling for me."[50]

Mingus also continued to write and record political material, situating himself among the growing number of activist musicians—most notably Max Roach, Abbey Lincoln, Randy Weston, and Sonny Rollins—
who drew inspiration from the civil rights movement and from the
struggles of African colonies for independence.[51] "Fables of Faubus," originally recorded for *Mingus Ah Um,* lampooned the follies of Arkansas
Governor Orval Faubus, who had achieved notoriety for attempting
to stymie the court-ordered desegregation of the Little Rock public
schools.[52] Although Columbia refused to record the version with lyrics,
demonstrating the resistance of major record companies to expressions
they found too assertive, Mingus was later able to record a version with
words for Candid Records in 1960. Later that year, he followed "Faubus"
with "Prayer for Passive Resistance," inspired by the student sit-in movement of that spring.

As he worked with the Jazz Workshop in the late 1950s and early 1960s,

Mingus saw his reputation grow and his finances improve. Now he was able to benefit from the rising fortunes of the jazz industry.[53] Although some still believed his music did not adequately swing, the identifiable reassertion of African American roots in his music, combined with an equally apparent "serious approach" and the incorporation of influences ranging from Latin to spoken word, impressed like-minded experimentalists and more than a few critics. Commentary following the release of *Pithecanthropus Erectus* gave Mingus some of the attention he had long desired as a jazz composer. Ralph Gleason again described him as a "thinking" musician, this time employing the term "genius" when describing Mingus's approach to a music that seemed destined for the "concert hall."[54] Another writer described him as an heir to the legacy of bebop and wrote that he was taking jazz in a new, and serious, direction:

> A bold experimentalist, Mingus is comparable to the Gillespie or Parker of a decade ago in the sense that the music is fresh, unusual—in a phrase, "far out" for its particular time. But he is, I should say, a much more consciously "literate" composer in the sense that he understands theory, probably better than any man now working in jazz. His use of rhythms, dynamics, tone color and atonality is conscious and intelligent; he knows what he is doing and why, though he does not sacrifice spontaneity to composition![55]

Indeed, many observers celebrated Mingus as a composer who embodied both the spontaneity of modern jazz and the studied sophistication of concert music.

Yet Mingus's reputation as a jazz composer was often inseparable from his reputation as a contentious personality. Stories about his tirades directed at audiences and band members, rumors of his mental instability (enhanced, no doubt, by his brief stay at Bellevue in 1958), and a series of fist fights further imbued him with the contradictory capital of the "primitive/intellectual homology." As Mingus asserted a militant attitude, adopted a public "badman" persona, and railed against injustice within and outside the music business, critics and fans paid more attention to his music. His irrational behavior appealed to audiences at a moment when many members of American society (of whom Beat writers were emblematic) were looking to the oppositional aspects of black culture for solutions to their dissatisfaction with consumerism, conservative politics, repressed sexuality, constrictive gender roles, and other social ills.

Writing in the fall of 1956, Barry Ulanov described the Mingus "legend" growing in the "New York scene": "All sorts of things, stories, epithets will be tossed your way as you inquire about Charlie Mingus, if you inquire about Charlie Mingus. Be careful how much you believe. Only a very small percentage of what you hear will be true, and rarely in the version in which you hear it." Although Ulanov tried to deflect attention from the more audacious elements of Mingus's reputation, his column reflected the way Mingus was often presented: as a dichotomous figure, whose musical personality was an amalgamation of the rational and the irrational, the mental and the physical. Ulanov said that when he listened to Mingus's recent music he thought of "personality (jazz division), the spread thereof, and that most expansive example of all the constituent parts of personality expressed in jazz—the physical, the mental; the emotional, the intellectual; the frivolous, the fundamental— Charles Mingus."[56] Mingus's status as a thinker was often inseparable from his emotional intensity and his physical presence. Such considerations were consistent with a conception of black male genius, so common in the world of bohemian letters, in which thought was inseparable from instinct, feeling, and action. These assessments continued in the press through the 1960s.[57]

In spite of this attention, and in some ways as a result of it, Mingus was frustrated at times by his chosen path as a "jazz" artist. During these years, he maintained some interest in his earlier project of reconciling the jazz and classical music genres. In 1957 Mingus was commissioned to write a piece, "Revelations," for classical conductor David Broekman's Music in the Making concert series at Brandeis University. In May 1960 Mingus recorded the album *Pre-Bird*, which, in addition to the very contemporary "Prayer for Passive Resistance," included two Ellington pieces and several of his own early compositions performed by a twenty-five-piece ensemble and a nonet with vocalist Lorraine Cousins. And, of course, he continued to work on his unfinished, symphonic-length composition *Epitaph*, which integrated existing compositions and new material, recording part of it with a large ensemble at an unsuccessful concert at Town Hall in 1962.[58] Nevertheless, most of his recorded material followed the pattern established by his early Jazz Workshop.

Mingus remained disillusioned in some ways by the limitations jazz presented as an artistic enterprise and as an occupation. His antipathy toward both kinds of restrictions is evident in a series of drafts for the liner notes to *Blues and Roots,* which Mingus wrote in collaboration with his assistant and lover Diane Dorr-Dorynek. In the version that appeared on the album cover, Mingus said the concept of the album had been suggested to him by producer Nesuhi Ertegun, who had encouraged him to do an entire blues album in the vein of "Haitian Fight Song" because people said his music did not "swing enough." Although Mingus emphasized that the compositions on this album represented but one aspect of his varied musical project, he said he had undertaken the project to give his detractors a "barrage of soul music" while demonstrating that "blues can do more than just swing."[59]

Earlier drafts of these liner notes tell a somewhat different story. In these versions, Mingus and Dorr-Dorynek ascribed more of the responsibility for the project to Ertegun, emphasizing the disparity between a narrowly defined recorded project and Mingus's expansive creative vision. Mingus saw the blues as fundamental to the field of jazz, which he considered an expression of "life"; yet it maintained this function only as a "natural" expression of the artist. A program created by a record company ran contrary to what he viewed, in the ideal, as a full expression of the musical self: "I feel that there is great value in an artist's work being programmed according to his choice. As unrelated as my pieces often seem because I am a creative person they should be performed in the order I choose as part of the expression of me. Each piece treated as a separate entity is important and together they should form a total expression of what I'm trying to say."[60]

In the final version of these liner notes, Mingus welcomed the chance to prove to critics that his music could both swing and be interesting. In the earlier versions, however, he bristled at the impact the critics and industry employees could have on the direction of one's artistic project. Mingus believed that Ertegun's concept of the album had been influenced by critics who did not understand the full range of his musical project but were nonetheless able to affect the direction jazz was taking. And Mingus blasted a culture industry that emphasized profits over artistic integrity: "A creative person should not be influenced by what the A&R [Artists and Repertoire] man wants but should express himself as purely as possible. . . . Evolution in all forms of art is thwarted because American publics are brainwashed from hearing anything that might be beyond the control of the industries that have become nothing but profiteering organizations who want to take the easy way out."[61]

Mingus's frustrations may well have stemmed from the precarious position he occupied as a working artist, despite his recent critical and financial successes. He and other musicians had to contend with unscrupulous club owners, booking agents, and record companies for whom profit was the bottom line; dangerous gangsters involved in the New York music business; an unsupportive union; police harassment; hostile critics; and a nightclub audience that often saw jazz as background music rather than serious artistic expression.[62] Although Atlantic Records clearly did not want their album covers to contain such commentary, Mingus drew upon his artistic and intellectual capital to voice elsewhere an increasingly militant critique of music industry practices. Ironically, his volatile personal life brought him more attention, which in turn gave him more space to express his critical views. Indeed, as John Corbett argues, in discourses about black music "insanity" has functioned as a signifier for the daunting oppression musicians faced, while forming an "ec-centric margin" or a type of "radical creative space" from which black musicians could voice their ideas and critique the status quo.[63] With increasing frequency, Mingus openly criticized the profit-making aspects of the music industry and called attention to the poor conditions under which musicians were forced to labor. And he often upbraided his audience for being noisy and inattentive, a practice that, as some of his sidemen remembered, became an anticipated part of his act.[64]

Offstage, Mingus tried to influence industry practices through institutional means. Jazz Workshop, Inc., became the second incarnation of his music publishing business in the late 1950s; and as Debut's recording operation was being dismantled, Mingus released a few recordings by other musicians on the Jazz Workshop label. He also asserted that the Jazz Workshop organization was intended to protect the interests of musicians.[65] In 1959 he wrote to President Dwight Eisenhower, protesting that musicians were usually ineligible for unemployment benefits because nightclubs did not consider them employees and refused to pay their insurance. He described how he had tried to pay unemployment insurance for his sidemen in the past, only to have the offer refused by the state.

Later, an unemployment board ruled that, as a bandleader, he was in fact the employer of the musicians and ordered him to contribute to an unemployed musician's benefits. Mingus also complained to the president about police corruption and gangsters running nightclubs on Fifty-second Street. Mingus offered to come to Washington and perform for Eisenhower for free, assuring the president that the White House would not be responsible for the musicians' benefits.[66]

Mingus continued to express such dissatisfaction with the jazz industry into the 1960s, as the growing militancy of the black freedom struggle provided an inspiration for activism and a changing context for interpreting the problems facing African American musicians. Mingus said in 1961 that "the commercial people are so busy trying to sell jazz that they are strangling the original talent that's around. Jazz to them is a fashion—a product." In 1962 he threatened to leave jazz for good, stating his intent to live on the island of Majorca and dedicate his time to composing a symphony. The following year he concluded that if one is to remain a "jazz" artist, one must contend with vindictive jazz criticism, the commodification of art by an industry that was beginning to direct its resources toward rock and roll, and the decline of musician-centered institutions (for example, educational networks and big bands as keepers of the tradition). Despite this pessimism, Mingus thought musicians held the power to change the music industry and the larger society through their music. "There are rays of hope while people still have the right and the guts to protest." Although he doubted he would be the one leading people to freedom, he imagined a collective movement in which sonic ideas would join forces to create social transformation.[67]

Mingus directly challenged the practices of the music industry through various actions. In 1960 he teamed up with Max Roach, from whom he had been estranged since the dissolution of Debut Records, to organize an "alternative" jazz festival at Newport, Rhode Island. Mingus and Roach believed that jazz festivals underpaid African American artists and were no longer committed to presenting "quality" music. Performers included Mingus's quintet, free jazz proponent Ornette Coleman, and a Max Roach group with Abbey Lincoln, Roy Eldridge, Jo Jones, and Coleman Hawkins. Although attendance at their festival was initially sparse, it picked up after a "riot" by white college students forced the termination of George Wein's parent festival.[68]

Later that year, Mingus, Roach, and Jo Jones formed an organization called the Jazz Artists Guild, organized to promote economic and artistic self-sufficiency. They recorded an album for Candid called *Newport Rebels*. This group soon disbanded because of internal conflict, but in 1963 Mingus proposed an educational enterprise—the School of Arts, Music, and Gymnastics—to be housed in a loft he had rented on Third Avenue. With anticipated funding from Harlem Youth Opportunities Unlimited, Mingus, Willie Jones, Max Roach, Buddy Collette, and dancer Katherine Dunham were to be the instructors. Although these projects never got off the ground, they paralleled other attempts (discussed in chapter 5) to organize musicians around issues of economic and artistic autonomy and community education.[69]

Mingus wrote letters to union officials to protest the treatment that he and other African American musicians experienced in the nightclub and recording industries. He filed a complaint with the union, claiming that United Artists owed him more than $20,000 in unpaid expenses and royalties from his Town Hall concert. He also complained directly about the union's failure to protect black musicians' interests. As he explained in one letter: "We feel that the black heirs to this country need fear no more the fakers in high positions in musicians' unions who neglect their duty when it suits them best in regard to the black man in honest business with the white man."[70]

Mingus also contacted major record labels with whom he had previously recorded, informing them that he was going to re-release under his own name records he had made for them.

> With the advice and help of my attorneys, I have found a simple solution to the problem which has interfered with our friendship for so many years. Since you have been kind enough, for the past seven years, to use my name on your label and to press and market my records, I am going to return the favor now by marketing my music . . . on your records, in your name. . . . You paid nothing for the use of my name on your labels, and, by the same token, I owe nothing for the use of your name on mine.[71]

Although Mingus's business proposition appears to have been tongue-in-cheek, it did provide biting commentary on industry practice. On a more serious note, in 1965 Mingus launched another short-lived record company, Charles Mingus Enterprises, which was another bid to take control of the production and marketing of his work. Mingus sold recordings, including those of his 1964 concerts at Town Hall in New York and the Monterey Jazz Festival, through his own mail-order record club in an attempt to cut down on the profits going to other parties. As he had done with his Debut label, Mingus tried to appeal to a "growing audience of jazz connoisseurs" who would appreciate "quality" music.[72]

In a changing social context, however, Mingus was at times uncomfortable with the growing political capital being ascribed to black music and the way it was commodified as such. Although he released politically oriented compositions such as "Once There Was a Holding Corporation Called Old America" (1965) and "They Trespass the Land of the Sacred Sioux" (1965) on his record label, he faced the daunting prospect of finding consistency between his militant and universalist philosophies. Moreover, just as "jazz" worked for him as a symbol of black resistance and African American affirmation, it remained a signifier of racial stereotypes and the strictures that the music industry and the broader society placed on black musicians. Even as he was cultivating an activist persona within the jazz world, he was continuing to question his own relationship to the idea of "jazz." "There is no jazz," he said in 1962, "there is no classical, there is only music."[73]

Some of Mingus's anxieties about the racial politics of musical expression no doubt stemmed from his own racial ambiguity and the question of how he might relate to the growing collective sense of racial consciousness in black America during the late 1950s and 1960s. Although he was generally positioned as black by the music industry and society, his family's mixed-race background and his own relatively light skin occasionally vested him with the privilege and liminality of a "mulatto" identity. In his autobiography, Mingus related stories of being caught between the black and white communities in Los Angeles during the 1930s. He described being victimized by white racism at the same time that he experienced his family's bigotry toward other African Americans and the "color prejudice" of darker members of the community toward him.

In comments made to Nesuhi Ertegun upon the release of his 1961 recording *Oh Yeah,* Mingus invoked a universalist aesthetic philosophy that was informed by a new manifestation of his complicated relation-

ship to the ideal of "black" music, the marketplace, and his own identity. If jazz was already a signifier of black artistry and resistance in a new
political context, as well as of the limitations that racial identities imposed upon African Americans, then Mingus's relationship to the term
was bound to be complicated. Commenting on a piece called "Passions
of a Man," which features free instrumental and vocal improvisations
and allusions to the Mau Mau rebellion in Kenya, Mingus defended his
decision to move deeper into the blues. He described this music as a sin-
cere expression of his identity, yet he also expressed anxiety over whether
he would be accepted by the imagined community of black America:
"Still my identity is to be accepted by my own people as a black man.
The whole struggle, the whole truth . . . of what I think good of myself
and bad of myself is in this one record here. So if it's insincere, then I'm
not alive, because you can't live and be insincere." Even as he stated that
he originally wanted "Passions of a Man" to be called "Passions of a Black
Man," he wondered whether his musical vision was consistent with society's definition of black music.[74]

Mingus expressed these dilemmas through contradictory statements
about different jazz styles. He was critical at times of the "soul" jazz of the
Adderley brothers, fearing a music that spoke of racial pride but also of
a narrowly conceived marketing strategy. Mingus also on occasion rejected the increasingly popular practice of using African themes in jazz
performance, choosing instead to situate his art in an African American
context. In 1961 he stated: "There is a lot of talk about Africa today. But
African music belongs in Africa. American music, which is what we play,
belongs with people who have a feeling of freedom and like to play together without discrimination."[75]

Mingus's reaction to the music of Ornette Coleman and John Coltrane,
which oscillated between lukewarm support and outright hostility, was
also revealing. The hoopla over Coleman's arrival in New York in late
1959 represented a potential validation of Mingus's own "avant-garde"
project. His November 1960 pianoless quartet recording, *Charles Mingus Presents Charles Mingus,* seems to reflect Coleman's influence. And at
the end of a 1960 *Down Beat* "Blindfold Test," he linked Coleman's music to his own experimentalist approach to jazz.[76] But the music of
Coltrane and, especially, Coleman was treated with a level of seriousness
that Mingus's work never quite received. In other interviews, Mingus was

quite dismissive of both players. In 1961 comments about the "avant-garde," Mingus emphasized that previous generations had worked with modal music and extended chords and that he himself had explored "this 'Free Form' business" in the 1940s.[77] Mingus's disdain for certain avant-garde players, or at least for their reception, also suggests a reaction against the ability of the critics and the recording industry to define the avant-garde, determine its parameters, and thus influence the future direction of jazz.

## "The Black Saint and the Sinner Lady"

As Mingus was developing the workshop concept and struggling against the restrictions of the music industry, he was also working on an auto-biography. Although *Beneath the Underdog* was not published until 1971, he began writing it in the mid-1950s and was circulating a draft as early as 1960. This version of the manuscript was rambling (it was rumored to be more than one thousand pages), yet brilliant by some accounts. Over the years, a variety of friends, relatives, and associates typed, ed-ited, or rewrote sections of it. In 1962 Mingus began talking about the book in the press, and it was reported that he had received a $15,000 ad-vance from McGraw-Hill to finish it. McGraw-Hill brought in Louis Lo-max, author of *The Negro Revolt,* to whittle the manuscript down to a manageable size and eliminate some of the potentially libelous criticisms of individuals working in the music industry. Although Lomax and Min-gus reduced the length of the manuscript, the two had a falling out; and McGraw-Hill withdrew from the project, in part because of the text's fo-cus on Mingus's sexual exploits. The manuscript was subsequently con-sidered and rejected by Random House and Playboy Books before finally being published by Knopf, after Nel King completed the editorial process.[78]

The version of *Beneath the Underdog* that finally made it into print is a fantastic and egocentric, sometimes tender and quite often misogynist and homophobic coming-of-age narrative. It purports to tell Mingus's story from childhood through his early days in New York, although in a number of instances events from the late 1950s and 1960s slip into the text. Framed as a conversation with Mingus's psychiatrist, the autobiography explores Mingus's childhood experiences, musical development, sexual exploits, and career as a "pimp." Mingus's presentation of himself as a hypersexualized, mentally unstable character seems almost a parody of Beat generation conceptualizations of African American musicians, although, as Gene Santoro notes, it may also have been inspired by the "autobiographical impulses" evident in much Beat writing. As published in 1971, the text is also a testament to the increasing visibility of sexuality in American society in the late 1960s and early 1970s, the rise of the pimp as a heroic figure in the popular cultural politics of the Black Power era, and the continued fascination of nonblacks with black male sexuality.[79]

*Beneath the Underdog* can also be understood as another of Mingus's interventions in the jazz discourse, one that is firmly rooted in the late 1950s and early 1960s, when he initially produced the text. In both the published version and an extant 875-page draft that apparently was completed in the early 1960s, Mingus considers the place of jazz in American society, criticizes music industry practices, lends political and spiritual purpose to African American music, articulates militant and universalist philosophies, and ponders the parameters of race in American society.[80] He does so as he expresses his continuing frustration with the jazz profession and interrogates his own racial identity during this moment of heightened collective racial and political consciousness in black America.[81]

Moreover, *Beneath the Underdog* is crucial for demonstrating how Mingus's aesthetic sensibility, spiritual purpose, and critical perspective were channeled through codes of masculinity as well as through race, class, and artistry. By spinning tales about his sexuality and participation in the sex industry, Mingus provides insight into the cult of masculinity that emerged from the homosocial world of jazz musicians and an attendant perspective that considered genius a male province. In particular, the figurations of pimping in the book serve as symbolic alternatives to the wage economy of the music industry, the artistic compromises jazz musicians were often forced to make, and the commodification of blackness at a politically charged moment. By taking on the role of the pimp and then rejecting it, Mingus expresses the distinct ways that gender informed ideas about power and artistry in the jazz community during the post–World War II era.[82]

As he did in public statements in the 1950s and early 1960s, Mingus describes his vexed relationship with jazz as an idea and a profession. As Thomas Carmichael puts it, *Beneath the Underdog* maintains "a fundamental ambivalence about jazz as a field of both achievement and restraint." Mingus at times figures jazz as an expression of African American genius, but he also alleges that the institutions that produce jazz conspire to oppress black musicians. He relates numerous stories of how he and other musicians are treated unfairly by unions, government agencies, nightclub owners, booking agents, and jazz critics. As a result, black musicians play noisier venues, receive lower wages, suffer police harassment, and are given less attention than their white counterparts. When they do receive attention from critics and audiences, it is often at the expense of their artistic ideals. Mingus also returns to a critique he first voiced in print in his 1951 letter to *Down Beat,* as he suggests that the very notion that jazz as a site of black accomplishment is a product of racism.

Mingus expresses much of his critique of music industry practices through a series of dream-sequence dialogues with Fats Navarro, the Afro-Cuban trumpet player whom Mingus befriended when they played in Lionel Hampton's band in 1948. Navarro, who died shortly thereafter in 1950 from complications of tuberculosis and heroin addiction, is a symbolic bebopper, whose characteristics are consistent with other representations of beboppers in the 1950s. Like the popular perception of Charlie Parker, Navarro is both a devoted artist and a victim of society. Mingus describes Navarro's death as a suicide spurred on by white ownership of his body and art, and he thus represents a possible future for Mingus: a consummate artist whose dedication to his work and victimization by the music industry ultimately destroy him. Yet unlike many representations of beboppers, Navarro is presented by Mingus as a musician with a critical perspective on both music and society.[83]

Navarro educates Mingus about racial perfidy in the music business and the restrictions that jazz places on the individual artist. African American musicians are constrained by this system, whether their employers are underworld figures or "legitimate" entrepreneurs who have conspired to force black people out of the business side of music. According to Navarro, "Jazz is big business to the white man and you can't move without him. We just work-ants. He owns the magazines, agencies, record companies and all the joints that sell jazz to the public. If you won't sell out and you try to fight they won't hire you and they give a bad picture of you with that false publicity."[84] Not only are African American musicians treated unfairly by the industry, but the very idea of jazz is suspect. The Navarro dialogues figure even more prominently in the early draft of the manuscript, where Mingus uses the figure of Navarro to engage in another level of critique. The identities of black jazz musicians are produced by a music industry just as broader economic relationships shape other social identities. Navarro describes how jazz and racial identities can be sources of African American pride but are also restrictive modes of existence: equating the terms "jazz" and "Negro," he says that "acceptance of either in place of music or race by the black man separates him from economical justice."[85]

The gangsters, the "legitimate" business owners, and the state, which all conspire against African American musicians, as well as the racial politics of the jazz world, are manifestations of a capitalist American society that is corrupt to the core. Navarro again figures prominently in this discussion, but an even more explicit critique is put forth by the character of Mingus's cousin, the pimp Billy Bones, who appears in both versions of the autobiography as a reservoir of wisdom about life in the music world and power in society. Bones makes oblique references to this widespread system of corruption in the published version of the autobiography, but his comments in the earlier draft are more to the point. The existence and successes of pimps and gangsters, he argues, are the result of a system of exploitation that dates back to Columbus and the earliest English settlers. Pimps are no worse than the "legitimate" citizens who have profited from this system by exploiting (that is, pimping) poor people. Bones employs Mingus's critique from the liner notes of *Pithecanthropus Erectus,* calling into question the arrogance of Western civilization and its predilection for oppression: "It's all so ridiculous that something as primitive as the wheel and a boat with sails could cause man to think he is *the* pithecanthropus erectus of civilization's progress, that this *machine world* we see would never have been . . . if not for the religious fanatics and white slaves who thought it their idea in [their] quest for freedom and ventured to America as pilgrims."[86]

Mingus's deployment of pimping as a way to understand corruption in society is instructive. It symbolizes his emphasis on masculinity and heterosexuality as a means of personal and creative fulfillment and as a mode of social analysis. Not all of Mingus's performances of masculine identity in the book are hypermasculine and patriarchal. As Nichole Rustin observes, *Beneath the Underdog* is a complicated text, which often highlights Mingus's sensitivity and the deep emotional bonds between male musicians and which challenges, on some level, stereotypical interpretations of black masculinity projected onto musicians by white critics.[87] Yet, throughout the text, Mingus makes ample connections between black male creativity and sexual potency. And he most effectively achieves power and prestige, both within and outside the community of musicians, through his sexual conquests of black, brown, and white women. At the same time, women and family responsibilities present a threat to black male creativity, and musicians are in danger of being emasculated when they are victimized by the corruption permeating society.[88]

Mingus generally writes black artistry and resistance in masculine and heterosexual terms. Mingus and Navarro discuss how jazz players are akin to "sex slaves" because of the way they are exploited by the music industry. As Navarro contemplates his own dissipation, itself a manifestation of the emasculating restrictions on black creativity, he lashes out in heterosexist terms against white society:

> Mingus, I'm bleeding 'cause I want to bleed. I got T.B. intentionally and I'm hoping there ain't no heaven or hell like you say there is. Think how drug I'd be to get there and find the white man owns that too and it's rent-controlled in heaven and hell's the slums. I'd tell them, "Kill me, white faggot cocksucking angels, like you did down on earth, 'cause you ain't gonna get no work or rent from my soul!"[89]

An alternative to Navarro's fate is found in the life of the pimp, who is both a symbol of the corruption in society and a hypermasculine response to it.

Mingus describes his own experiences as a pimp and spends ample time agonizing over his decision to leave the profession and contemplating whether to reenter it. Many of Mingus's friends and associates have doubted that he ever worked as a pimp, and near the end of his life Mingus said such claims were a front.[90] Whether fact or fiction, the act of pimping operates at least on a symbolic level, as Michael M. J. Fischer observes, as a commentary on and alternative to victimization by the music industry: that is, musicians are pimped by the industry's economic and discursive structures and must turn to pimping to liberate themselves. Navarro tells Mingus at a certain point that in order to survive as a musician, one has to either "play for money" (conform to the desires of the market) or become a pimp. Billy Bones instructs him: "Now, Mingus, here's how to save yourself from depending on what rich punks think and critics say about jazz, true jazz, your work. By my reckoning a good jazz musician has got to turn to pimpdom in order to be free and to keep his soul straight."[91]

Pimping serves as a means for personal liberation that reflects, albeit in exaggerated terms, the gender politics of the jazz world sketched out earlier. Artistry and social relations in the jazz world had long been understood and carried out through codes of masculinity as well as race. Musicians who worked in urban entertainment centers were familiar with the underground economy of prostitution, gambling, and drug dealing that served as an alternative to the wage labor system of the jazz industry. Moreover, by the end of the 1950s, musicians and critics alike had invested black musicians with a hypermasculine aura that was rooted in the complex music, virtuosity, and perceived nonconformity of members of the bebop movement. Norman Mailer's essay "The White Negro," in which he locates a model for rebellion in the supposedly unbridled sexuality of black musicians and hipsters, is the most obvious example of this.[92] Through its discussion of pimping, Mingus's text follows the logic of Mailer's essay and other commentaries by focusing on his own sexuality and embracing the most sexually exploitive of professions as a means of charting his own rebellion. As at least a symbolic alternative to the wage labor system and the artistic compromises facing African Americans in the jazz industry, pimping in *Beneath the Underdog* is an attempt to reclaim masculinity in these spheres of activity by exercising domination over women, reaping economic rewards, and affirming the homosocial bonds of the jazz community.

Writing about pimping in Miles Davis's autobiography, Hazel Carby argues that representations of domination over sex industry workers perform this function in part by relegating women to the realm of the body and the material, while elevating male jazz performance to the realm of genius. This elides the fact that many jazz "geniuses" were dependent upon women for sustenance and support.[93]

> To see women as "bitches," to relegate them to a service role, and to treat them with violence was the way to forge the bridge of male intimacy and to protect it from the danger of being considered unmasculine in conventional terms. Both the denial of dependency upon women and the aggression toward them fostered the homosocial jazz world of creativity, just as in the wider world female labor supports and maintains the conditions for the production of male creativity.[94]

Pimping in Mingus's autobiography serves a similar function, and it is interesting to contemplate how these representations of pimping may have stemmed from Mingus's anxieties over the role that his wives and other women played in running his businesses and providing financial support and inspiration for his musical projects.

But it is in Mingus's rejection of pimping that we get the clearest sense of his gendered construction of genius. At various points in the text, Mingus voices a romantic, idealized, and more or less egalitarian notion of heterosexual love between men and women. In the unpublished manuscript, he talks at length about "metathesis," the formation of a new, creative self achieved by two people (a woman and a man) forging spiritual and intellectual connections while operating outside an economy of sexual desire.[95] Yet, with the exception of a brief mention of his third wife, Judy, near the end of the text, the women in *Beneath the Underdog* fail to live up to this spiritual and intellectual demand, and the pimp/prostitute relationship is a product of this failure. Ultimately it is the male musician who embarks on a Romantic path of spiritual creativity. In the published version, he writes: "My music is evidence of my soul's will to live beyond my sperm's grave, my metathesis or eternal soul's new encasement. Loved and lovers, oneness, love."[96]

Mingus eventually gives up pimping to concentrate on his music, turning over the business to Donna and Lee-Marie, two women with whom he has been in love relationships and who work for him as prostitutes. Mingus contrasts an idealized vision of his own artistry with what he considers the debased desires of these women, who want to continue selling their bodies. As he contemplates leaving the business, he tells Donna and Lee-Marie, "I'll have more to say musically, living with the underdogs—*beneath* the underdogs—more to write about." Later, he returns the money they had earned for him and chooses music over the sex industry. "I'm a musician, this is my pad and don't come in here with your fucking commercial plans!"[97] It is thus in the rejection of pimping, more than in his participation in the profession itself, that Mingus constructs artistic genius as a male quality, defined in contradistinction to the material world of economics and women's bodies.

But Mingus's considerations of pimping in *Beneath the Underdog* also contain another layer of meaning. His actions speak to his discomfort with the confines of jazz and race, an ongoing concern that took on new urgency in the politically charged period of the late 1950s and early 1960s. Late in the text, when Judy asks Mingus what he would do if he did not play jazz, he responds:

> I'd become a pimp, bigger and better than my cousin Billy Bones out in San Francisco. I wouldn't get involved with music or women at all, other than what they could do for me. My main motive for living would be getting money to buy my way out of a decaying society that's destroying itself while trying to figure out what to do with the new kind of "black" it produced. But I'd have nothing to do with black or white, I'd be a member of the raceless people of this earth.[98]

This passage contains a certain amount of ambiguity, as Judy believes Mingus is joking, and Mingus as narrator suggests he never would have married her if his answer to her question was truthful. But this consideration of racelessness appears time and again in both versions of the text. It speaks to Mingus's own complicated identity and his attempt to synthesize nationalist and universalist perspectives on art and society. In this effort, he stands at the intersection of the critical ecumenicalism of an earlier generation and the more militant black nationalism that informed much of African American activism in the 1960s.

Although Mingus speaks from a racial perspective when criticizing white society and white control of the music industry, he expresses concern that racially based identity politics mirror white racism. After the mother of one of his girlfriends informs him that she doesn't "want a half-breed coming around her daughter," Mingus's father suggests he inform her that one of his grandfathers was an African chieftain. Mingus opposes this, saying to his father:

Telling the Parkses your father was an African chieftain has the same
sound to me as the white man telling me I'm a nigger. Somebody—
the God of love or someone—seems to believe the world can make
it with all these races here or things wouldn't have gone this far. . . .
People who want freedom should consider the white man's weaknesses
too—his greed and wastefulness, his suicidal tendencies. He's insane! . . .
They're sick and maybe it's our duty to care for them, to be their doc-
tors and nurses and heal them—or else we might catch the same disease and infect our future and wreck our hopes of ever living in a truly
free world—and that would be more dreadful than the atomic bomb!
No, Daddy, Barbara's mother can belittle me, my body, my family, my
house, but I don't dig badges, skin colors, blood lines. I'm not using
any of the rules.[99]

Mingus also links this evasion of race to musical expression. In a scene
in the unpublished manuscript, where he relates the banter between musicians on a bandstand, Mingus chastises white critics for failing to understand what Parker and other black musicians are trying to accomplish
artistically. But he suggests that he himself is beyond racial category and
that reducing oneself to a racial identity is like calling oneself a "jazz musician."[100] Later, he links the confines of jazz specifically to the confines
of race in American society: "If you and I, Bird, or any lover of the arts
wants the music to survive then we must *denounce* the word 'jazz.'" One
must reject it the same way one must reject the words "Negro" and
"white":

> Fuck "Negro." Fuck "jazz." First I'm of the black people but in
> this country I want to be accepted as an American now with all the
> rights—or forget it and I'll show Kruschev how to guide his missiles
> due South. . . . I can write good music with a beat or without so I
> want to be called a musician—not a Negro musician or white musi-
> cian. I want my rights as the music's musician. I don't want my music
> to sell like hotcakes. I want it to sell like good music—not stopped by
> a word, "jazz."[101]

Thus Mingus links his civil rights as an American citizen to his right to
evade the constraints of race and the racialized conceptions of artistry.

The constraints of race also clashed with the spiritual purpose with
which he tried to imbue African American music. Mingus's juxtaposition of the spiritual ethos behind black music with the values of West-

ern society recall Du Bois's discussion in *The Souls of Black Folk* and parallel the ideas of some members of the jazz avant-garde of the 1960s. Although some of these musicians conceived of this spiritual duty in racially separatist terms, Mingus's vision remained deeply universalistic. Speaking in *Beneath the Underdog* of Art Tatum's music, he writes: "What can I say? There's Jesus, Buddha, Moses, Duke, Bird, Art." He charts the role that he and other African American musicians must play in a corrupt society. He tells Navarro: "Someday one of us put-down, out-cast makers of jazz music should show those church-going clock-punchers that people like Monk and Bird are dying for what they believe. That duty's supposed to be left to holy men but they're so busy building temples they haven't got time for you and me." Mingus describes Parker as a Christ-like figure, which is consistent with how he described him in his 1955 letter to Miles Davis. At the end of the autobiography, he even defines God as "Bird without wings, motherfucker! Bird."[102]

Mingus also talks at length of his readings in Eastern mysticism and his extrasensory perception. In the unpublished manuscript, which addresses spirituality much more deeply than the published version, he describes his own aesthetic and spiritual powers:

> I believe I could be of great help for us of the unconscious worlds of God. . . . I'm as old as time and my knowledge of all the worlds express an Edison, Buddha, *Christ,* or Bird, etcetera. We have likenesses in opposite spirit form that produce a Hitler, Mephistopheles, Bilbo, etcetera. . . . God Soul is slowly winning the battle of proper balance throughout the universe, beauty, love, the arts of creation good and evil.[103]

Later, he says that the message of his book is "to teach people throughout the world that they can have this earth governed just about perfect to the universal truth the way they see it together in God's mind in perfect harmony."[104]

## Coda

In 1963 Mingus recorded the album *The Black Saint and the Sinner Lady* for Impulse! Records. Although it might be a stretch to claim that the album title reflects Mingus's gendered ideas about artistry and his spiritual vision, it certainly is consistent with the discussion of both in *Beneath the Underdog*. This album is another example of Mingus reaching back into his musical past, here with the encouragement of producer Bob Thiele. "I wrote this music for dancing and listening. It is true music with much and many of my meanings. It is my living epitaph from birth til the day I first heard of Bird and Diz." Indeed, the lush textures and arrangements for eleven instruments recall Ellington more than hard bop or free jazz. Mingus employed both written and oral methods of composition, and the six tracks on *The Black Saint and the Sinner Lady* fit together as a piece of program music. In fact, Mingus originally conceived of this as a single piece of music; it was later divided up for radio play.[105]

This intermittent embrace of an earlier version of his identity as a composer is one of the concluding themes of the autobiography. Mingus reproduces in the text a letter he purports to have written to Nat Hentoff during a short stay in the psychiatric ward at Bellevue Hospital. Describing his reaction to listening to recordings of quartets written by Béla Bartók, Mingus tells Hentoff: "Hearing artists like this reminds me of my original goal but a thing called 'jazz' took me far off the path and I don't know if I'll ever get back. I am a good composer with great possibilities and I made an easy success through jazz but it wasn't really success—jazz has too many strangling qualities for a composer."[106]

For the rest of his life, Mingus attempted to reconcile his aspirations as a composer with his life in the jazz industry. His later public comments continued to contain assessments of the state of American race relations and the jazz industry as well as thoughts about creativity and spirituality. Yet Mingus's comments during the 1950s and early 1960s give particular insight into changes in his musical philosophy and shifts in the jazz discourse at this critical moment.

**"Straight Ahead"**

Abbey Lincoln and the Challenge of Jazz Singing

**IN ITS JUNE 12, 1958, ISSUE,** *Down Beat* magazine announced Abbey Lincoln's "arrival" as a jazz singer. After spending several years pursuing a career as a "supper club singer," Lincoln had made the decision to leave the glamour, lavish staging, and revealing dresses behind and reshape her approach to music. In October 1957, working with Max Roach (whom she would marry in 1962), she recorded *That's Him,* the first of three Riverside albums released under her name in the late 1950s. Although she continued to perform pop-oriented tunes in plush nightclubs, these new albums were symbolic of her embrace of jazz singing. In 1960 Lincoln appeared on Roach's landmark album *We Insist! The Freedom Now Suite,* inspired by the civil rights movement, and in 1961 followed that performance with her own album *Straight Ahead.* Although these records were controversial with critics, they established Lincoln as an important singer in the jazz idiom. Lincoln would not record again under her own name until 1973—the hiatus a product of both hostility to her politics and the ill fortunes of the jazz industry—but she remained among the most vocal of socially oriented jazz artists for much of the 1960s.

This chapter explores the various meanings Lincoln ascribed to this musical transformation, as she publicly found her voice as an artist and as an African American woman during the politically charged period of the late 1950s and 1960s. Whereas Mingus during these years often described jazz as a system of constraints on his ability to express his creativity, Lincoln's comments suggest that she embraced jazz as a means to artistic fulfillment, as a signifier of her racial and gender identity, and as a social statement. To better understand Lincoln's transformation, this chapter also addresses the ways she defined her artistic and social identity in relationship to contemporary male artists and the legacy of jazz singer Billie Holiday. Although the idealized jazz artist was usually conceived of as male, by the time of Holiday's death in 1959 she had come to represent the pinnacle of jazz vocal artistry as well as the marginalization of African Americans, women, and artists in American society. Lincoln's description of her own debt to male artists and her reading of Holiday convey a sense of how she negotiated the constellation of politics, aesthetics, and gendered concepts of artistry in the jazz community of the late 1950s and early 1960s. We also see how Lincoln's comments about gender-specific spheres of artistry stood in homologous relationship to broader social concerns about female respectability and the redemption of black men. As Lincoln became more vocal about these issues during the 1960s, she drew upon her status as a jazz artist to voice dissent around issues of race and rights and raised interesting questions about the role female vocal artists might play in the African American freedom struggle.[1]

## From Supper Club Singer to Jazz Artist

Lincoln was born Anna Marie Wooldridge in Chicago in 1930 and was raised in Michigan. She moved west in the early 1950s, working in Honolulu for nearly two years before arriving in Los Angeles in 1954. As a supper club singer, Lincoln performed under several different stage names while cultivating a persona that positioned her as an object of male desire. Her repertoire included sexually suggestive popular songs and stage antics, and she appeared as a bikini-clad "centerfold" in *Jet* in 1954. The owners of the Moulin Rouge nightclub in Los Angeles persuaded her to change her name to Gaby Wooldridge (she would change it again to Gaby Lee) because they wanted their singers to have names that sounded "French" and presumably sexier. By 1956 Lincoln was a major star on the supper club circuit, her big break coming from an engagement at Ciro's in Hollywood. She also recorded an album that year, *Affair: A Story of a Girl in Love*, for Liberty Records. Although orchestrated in part by Benny Carter, the lush arrangements and Lincoln's straightforward treatment of the material place it more in the popular category than in the jazz genre.[2]

The year 1956 also marked a critical moment in Lincoln's political awakening. She was inspired by the burgeoning civil rights movement and took the stage name Abbey Lincoln (derivative of Abraham Lincoln) at the suggestion of her manager, Bob Russell—the lyricist for Duke Ellington's "Do Nothing 'Til You Hear from Me" and "Don't Get Around Much Anymore"—who thought the name was consistent with her strong views on race relations and her independence. In 1957 she was deeply moved by her reading of E. Franklin Frazier's historical and sociological consideration of black life *The Negro in the United States,* which was published that year. She was also influenced in the late 1950s by her relationships with activist African American artists and intellectuals such as Max Roach, Maya Angelou, and Oscar Brown Jr.[3]

Despite the name change, Lincoln was still packaged as a sex object in those days. The jacket of *Affair: A Story of a Girl in Love* featured a photograph of her reclining in a seductive position. A publicity flyer from this period, Lincoln recalled, featured "a photo of me dressed in one of those Marilyn Monroe–type skin-tight dresses and superimposed over President Lincoln's face on a penny." Indeed, her management's promotional strategy seems to have relied heavily on comparisons to Monroe. In a brief appearance in the 1956 film *The Girl Can't Help It,* Lincoln performed a song while wearing a dress that Monroe had supposedly worn in the film *Gentlemen Prefer Blondes.* In 1957 Lincoln appeared on the cover of *Ebony* wearing the same dress; and, in the photo spread inside, Lincoln's image appeared side by side with Monroe's in approximations of six poses made famous by the Hollywood star. Reviews of her nightclub performances from this period indicate that the marketing strategy was successful. A writer for *Variety* called her a "sultry dish with a lissome figure," and *Time* observed that "through her pouting lips floats out her sad, sexy lyrics in a voice smoky with longing."[4]

But this image was increasingly incommensurate with the way Lincoln saw herself as a social actor. "It was the early days of the civil rights movement," Lincoln remembered, "and we were all asking the same questions. But they were questions that glamour girls weren't supposed to ask. As I toured the country, I noticed that black people everywhere were living in slums, in abject poverty. I wanted to know why." Unable to find fulfillment as an artist and a black woman in the supper clubs of Los Angeles, she turned to the jazz idiom.[5]

In a 1958 conversation with *Down Beat,* Lincoln said she became a jazz singer because jazz promised a measure of artistic freedom and an outlet for expressing emotional honesty, neither of which she was able to find in the supper clubs. Describing the difference between a "jazz singer" and "just a singer," Lincoln explained: "Well, I think if you sing in tune, sing well, imaginatively, freely, without anyone telling you what to sing . . . this is what a jazz singer is." She did not maintain a naive devotion to art over commerce, however. Like other professional musicians, she wanted to be paid. And, especially since the bebop movement of the 1940s, jazz had represented at least the possibility of making serious, socially relevant African American musical expression remunerative. Of course, this did not always work out in practice. As chapter 3 discussed, black musicians were increasingly outspoken during the late 1950s about unfair treatment by booking agents and record companies; and there were those, like Mingus, who also saw the very idea of jazz as a constraint on their own musical projects. Yet Lincoln was fairly optimistic that if she could "make it as a jazz singer," she could reclaim her artistic integrity while maintaining her income level. If not, she explained, then the personal satisfaction to be gained through jazz singing would outweigh the decrease in wages.[6]

Lincoln's optimism also appears to have been fueled by the sense that jazz singing provided a way to move outside the sexist economy of supper club singing and generate a kind of personal respectability. She spoke in the jazz and African American press of her desire to present herself and be treated as a "dignified Negro woman." As the work of Evelyn Brooks Higginbotham, Darlene Clark Hine, and others demonstrates, the concepts of "dignity" and "respectability" have been used by African American women for over a century, in a variety of social and historical contexts, to deny stereotypes about black sexual promiscuity and passion that were rooted in a history of slavery and reified in popular culture.[7] Lincoln invoked "dignity" as she extricated herself from the linked systems of representation and economics that constituted the world of supper club singing, which, she suggested, had turned her voice and body into a sexualized commodity for the pleasure of men (and particularly white men). She not only professed a desire to do away with her sexually suggestive act; she also said she was unwilling to "shun" black men and date white men as a means of advancing her career. Nor would she continue to work with a vocal instructor to remove the "Negro" intonation from her singing voice. In 1959 she stopped straightening her hair, in a self-conscious rejection of what she described as white beauty standards.[8]

This recuperation of dignity went hand in hand with Lincoln's desire to forge a deeper connection with her female audience. "I like to get them to identify with me," she told *Down Beat*. "I sing songs that tell stories women like to tell." Dignity also demanded that Lincoln respond to social movements in the United States and to anticolonial movements in the Third World. The sense of womanhood she tried to express in her music was in part based on a social and aesthetic commitment to a global black freedom struggle; it was a way of understanding her personal search for self-respect as part of a collective effort by black men and women to do the same. Jazz offered the opportunity to articulate her identity as a socially aware and responsible African American woman and to tap into the culture of the people she saw herself representing: "I'm a black woman," she told *Jet* magazine in 1959, "and I have to sing about things I feel and know about—jazz. In the supper clubs something inside me isn't content."[9] Thus, at a moment when some musicians were rejecting the idea of "jazz" because of the musical and racial restrictions it suggested, Lincoln embraced the term as a symbol of black artistic accomplishment and as a means of reclaiming her personal dignity and defining a politicized racial and gendered identity.

Lincoln's transformation, however, involved not only her move from supper club singing to jazz singing but also her development into a certain kind of jazz singer. Lincoln is such an interesting and compelling figure during this period in part because her ideas about jazz singing intersected with ideas about gender, race, civil rights, and black nationalism in complex and often contradictory ways. A reading of Lincoln's music and of her statements about her metamorphosis during the late 1950s and early 1960s requires an understanding of the racial and gender politics of African American women's song as well as those of jazz artistry in general. It demands a consideration of her comments within a tradition of African American women's thought, and it calls for a perspective on the ways that civil rights and black nationalist discourse during this period (even when articulated by women) often involved an attention to dysfunctional heterosexual or familial relationships and an emphasis on the redemption of black men.

As Lincoln tried to extricate herself from the artistic impasse she faced as a supper club singer, along with the accompanying system of stereo-types about black women's sexuality, she faced a variety of racial and gen-dered meanings associated with jazz at a politically charged moment. Ac-cording to her comments, when Lincoln remade herself as a vocalist and sought to become a "dignified Negro woman," she did so in conversa-tion with politicized male jazz instrumentalists, including her future hus-band Max Roach. She defined herself as an artist in relation to standards of jazz artistry that were generally established by men. Looking back on the period, Lincoln said it was Roach who convinced her to wear her hair in a natural and get rid of the "Marilyn Monroe dress." In the liner notes to her 1961 album *Straight Ahead,* she said that Roach helped her discover "how wonderful it is to be a black woman. . . . I learned from Max that I should always sound how I feel and that whatever I do, I should do it *definitely.* I got to know a number of other jazz musicians and from hearing them talk, I gained insight into the kind of individu-ality that *was* mine and that needed bringing out. And I decided I would not again sing anything that wasn't meaningful to me." Roach also taught her about composing, techniques for practicing, and the importance of integrating creativity in art and life. Even when Lincoln spoke of her tran-sition in the 1958 *Down Beat* article, her reverence for male instrumen-talists was obvious, as was the validation they gave her as an artist. "If I can have my own group," she said, "I'll have a chance to hear beautiful music all night. This is one of the things that decided me to be a jazz singer. I can work with men like those on my record. It would be the end to just sing and have Wynton Kelly inventing things behind me."[10]

Lincoln also positioned herself in relation to black female vocalists, es-pecially Billie Holiday, and she explored what jazz singing represented in terms of the limitations and possibilities of female artistry. It is no sur-prise that during the late 1950s, when the meaning of "jazz" itself was be-ing contested, the questions of just what constituted jazz singing and just who was a jazz singer were complicated ones. As Will Friedwald argues, defining jazz singing has long been difficult because of its close rela-tionship to popular song, the blues, folk music, and concert music. From the moment jazz was identified as a genre, it drew from and informed the development of other vocal genres—and the lengthy careers of artists as diverse as Ella Fitzgerald, Ethel Waters, Bing Crosby, Louis Armstrong, and Frank Sinatra show how arbitrary these categories could be. Questions have also arisen about the specific qualities that define the artistry of jazz singing. Is jazz singing defined by the material one chooses or by the musicians with whom one works? Is it based on an emotional quality one brings to a song or on the way a singer transforms a lyric through inflection or intonation? Is it, as many have argued, defined primarily by the singer's rhythmic conception? Or does it depend on certain "instrumental" qualities of voice that reflect a century of the mutual influence of jazz players and singers? Is a jazz singer one whose vocal timbre resembles a trumpet's? Or one who can successfully reproduce the phrasing of a bop saxophonist?[11]

In the late 1950s, at the moment when jazz was being redefined as an art form in a context of civil rights activism and high modernist aspirations, these questions resonated in specific ways. Although jazz artistry was primarily defined through the work of male instrumentalists, jazz singing was the one area in which women's contributions to the genre were widely recognized and appreciated—indeed, their work was usually deemed superior to that of their male counterparts. Yet female jazz vocalists had a limited status as artists as a result of the marginal role they had played in the community of male musicians and their fans (many saw the vocalist's turn at the microphone as something to suffer through before the band could commence playing in earnest again), the close relationship between jazz and pop singing, and the general prejudices against women in music.

There were exceptions, to be sure. Ella Fitzgerald, Dinah Washington, Sarah Vaughan, Carmen McCrae, Betty Carter, and a handful of others, through their musical accomplishments and the strength of their personalities, challenged sexist assessments of female vocalists inside and outside the musicians' community. Yet even Fitzgerald, who made "scat singing" a household term, had her jazz credentials called into question on occasion. Fitzgerald was one of the few singers who had both sufficient technical knowledge of harmony to make sense of bebop chord changes and sufficient vocal dexterity to incorporate its odd intervals into melodic statements. Her legions of loyal fans and critics were impressed by the instrumental qualities of her voice, even when they worried that she was leaving jazz when she began her series of "songbook" recordings for Verve in 1956. But some still wondered whether she might lack the intellectualism and emotional fire that were thought to drive artists such as

Thelonious Monk, Charles Mingus, and Charlie Parker. In liner notes to a collection of Decca recordings, Nat Hentoff acknowledged Fitzgerald's superior musicianship and stopped short of saying she did not "sing jazz"; but he wondered whether she had become a jazz singer "less through fierce personal conviction than through the gradual force of circumstances." He suspected she was "happier . . . in the less naturalistic pop world where she can sing popular songs and standards in a jazz-influenced style and never meet anything more forbidding than the Wizard of Oz." Like other critics, Hentoff described Fitzgerald as an "innocent," also using the term to describe the generic "pop singer," "who does not have to expose her own feelings as nakedly and urgently as the jazz singer."[12]

In the late 1950s, Billie Holiday was one female vocalist whose credentials as a jazz singer were usually beyond reproach. She convinced critics and musicians alike that she possessed a command of both the technical and emotional qualities necessary for success as a jazz singer. In a professional career that spanned three decades, Holiday gained great respect from musicians as a vocalist who brought dignity and artistry to jazz singing and who was able to integrate herself fully into jazz ensembles. Holiday possessed an excellent sense of time and a tone that made her sound, in Robert O'Meally's words, "simultaneously raw and sophisticated." She also possessed the ability to transform the meaning of even the most banal pop songs through cadence and intonation. Although heroin addiction had damaged her voice, many critics believed, as they continue to do today, that her singing had become richer and more complex by the mid-1950s. When she died in 1959, she was still being hailed as the greatest jazz singer of the era.[13]

Holiday's successes as a vocalist and her image as a "jazz singer" were also based on what audiences knew of her life and the mythology surrounding her. Holiday's composition "God Bless the Child" and her incorporation of Abel Meeropol's anti-lynching song "Strange Fruit" into her repertoire caused some to view her art as social statement. Holiday herself often embraced the title "race woman." Her well-publicized arrest and imprisonment for heroin possession in 1947, which resulted in the loss of her cabaret card, augmented her reputation as a tortured artist and victim of society. Her autobiography, *Lady Sings the Blues,* published in 1956, provided plaintive testimony about her mistreatment by state authorities, abusive men, and law enforcement officials, as well as a scathing critique of music industry practices. Although the accuracy of some parts of the book is suspect, and Holiday may have had little to do with writing it, the text cemented her image as a victim and critic of white society. Some contemporary observers believed the book put too much emphasis on the tragedy of her life without saying anything substantive about her art, but in a review of the autobiography for *Down Beat,* Nat Hentoff welcomed her criticism of the music business and thought it would "help those who want to understand how her music became what it is—the most hurt and hurting singing in jazz."[14]

Gerald Early points to Holiday's November 1956 concerts at Carnegie Hall, where her set was punctuated by *New York Times* writer Gilbert Millstein reading passages from *Lady Sings the Blues* between songs, as "the final public acceptance of jazz as an art form and of the black performer as artist." One may or may not agree with Early's assertion that Holiday's maudlin performance signaled a moment when jazz "ceased to be art while being swallowed by the weight of its artistic pretensions" and instead became "a forlorn and fashionable pulp." But his observation that Holiday's triumph was inextricably bound to her victimization (as a woman, an artist, and a black person), as well as to her public's voyeuristic appreciation for the tragedy of her life, seems right on the mark.[15]

Many observers in the 1950s believed Holiday sang the truth, whether emotional, political, or a product of the circumstances of her life. As a purveyor of jazz honesty, Holiday possessed something that other female singers and the popular music industry as a whole were thought to lack. In an obituary in *Saturday Review,* Richard Gehman wrote in anguished tones about Holiday's death and bemoaned that she did not receive as much exposure as the singers who "stole her techniques and tricks and machine tooled all the emotion out of them." But he drew comfort in the knowledge that it was Holiday who sang with the greatest veracity, even as he coupled his description with dubious assessments of other vocalists: "Her voice was harsh; it rasped at words like a tool to tell the truth, heading them to the truth as she felt it, and that may have been why she never achieved an audience that, say, the sweet voiced (and all but emotionless) Ella Fitzgerald or the pseudo-passionate (and all but tuneless) Sarah Vaughan, both had."[16]

For many commentators, the supremacy of Holiday's artistry was a function of her technique, emotion, and the baggage that accompanied her life. Holiday succeeded, where other jazz vocalists were deemed to have fallen short, by giving her audience a direct window into her life. She exceeded the realm of the popular and was perceived as a kind of Romantic artist—and a tragic one, at that. To some extent, Holiday undermined the definition of jazz artistry as a male province, through her technical mastery of the idiom, her emotional intensity, and her lyrical demand that female social experience become art. Yet Holiday's image was tempered by observers' views of her as somewhat passive and victimized, even if they recognized some measure of social agency on her part. Moreover, because she was a woman and her success lay in the feminine sphere of vocal jazz, her artistic reputation was circumscribed by the perceived limits of emotion and irrational behavior, qualities associated with the female body.[17] As commentators praised Holiday's artistry primarily for its emotional qualities, they defined it in a gender-specific way but seldom elevated it to the realm of musical "genius." Unlike Parker, Mingus, or Monk, she was not vested with the status of the intellectual, however contradictory that status might be.

As Lincoln crafted her transformation into a jazz singer, she did so in the shadow of Billie Holiday. The image of Holiday being constructed in the jazz and mainstream press was not irrelevant to Lincoln. She has described Holiday as "my teacher," remembering that she had been introduced to Holiday's music at age fourteen by a record her sister brought home. Lincoln has also defined herself as an heir apparent to Holiday and asserted that the singer represented social and emotional "truths": "I'm her spiritual relative. When I first heard Billie, she went right to my soul. She was honest. She didn't garnish anything. She sang her heart. Billie inherited from Bessie [Smith], and I inherited from Billie. . . . There were many great singers, and they were great because they were original, but Billie was the only one who was social." This social commitment was particularly evident in "Strange Fruit." "She sang 'Strange Fruit' when they were lynching the people in the South. She was the only one of her time who had the courage to defend herself." Lincoln also appreciated the "way [Holiday] sang a song. She wasn't showing off her chops; she was only telling you something through music."[18]

Yet because Holiday's music remained somewhat rooted in Tin Pan Alley love songs, and because of Holiday's experiences with men, she also represented to Lincoln some of the limitations of female jazz vocal artistry. As a member of the jazz community in the late 1950s, Lincoln knew first-hand of the abuse Holiday had suffered from the men in her life.[19] Although Lincoln at times acknowledged Holiday's ability to transform the meanings of masochistic popular songs, she increasingly found inconsistencies between Holiday's material and the image she herself wanted to embody. Thus, part of Lincoln's artistic transformation involved a partial rejection of aspects of Holiday's legacy. In a different take on Holiday, Lincoln remembered: "I saw myself in Sarah and Billie and in the song lyrics they sang, the sad songs that women sing about unrequited love. But I didn't really want that life—'My Man' and those things."[20]

Through her comments about Holiday, Lincoln positioned herself within a trajectory of African American women vocalists' commentary about love relationships and other issues. Patricia Hill Collins places such perspectives within a broadly conceived tradition of black feminist thought. This body of thought emanates both from established thinkers and from those (for example, blues and jazz singers) who do not have the status of traditional intellectuals. Black feminist ideas have emerged in various contexts in which black women have had their labor exploited, their rights denied, or their bodies, minds, and sexuality represented unfavorably. Although Collins is quick to point out that black women experience oppression in disparate ways and that no monolithic black feminist viewpoint exists, she identifies several "core themes" that define this intellectual history. These include an understanding of the relationships among race, gender, and class oppression; a recognition of the need to redefine the image of black women; a belief in activism; a sensitivity to sexual politics; and a concern for black families.[21]

Discussing Lincoln in the context of a tradition of black feminist thought requires further definition. Lincoln herself has said she is not and was not a feminist. Moreover, her attention to promoting healthy heterosexual relationships and her concern for the redemption of black manhood complicate her identity as a feminist. Indeed, Farah Jasmine Griffin, drawing on the work of Clenora Hudson-Weems, situates even Lincoln's strongest statements from the 1960s about the oppression of black women within an "Africana womanist" perspective rather than a black feminist one for these reasons.[22] Collins employs Alice Walker's definition of "womanist" to describe how some black feminists have honored the moral and epistemological perspectives of black women while also expressing concern for the health and welfare of all human beings, men and women, black and nonblack alike. Although the tension between women and men is an important theme in womanist thought, so is the "great love Black women feel for Black men." In women's music, for example, "African American women have long commented on this 'love and trouble' tradition in Black women's relationships with Black men."[23] Therefore, to consider Lincoln within the broadly defined feminist tradition defined by Collins, it is useful to understand her comments as coming from a womanist perspective, which some scholars would see as distinct from feminism and others would view as a particular trajectory of feminist thought.

Like the blues singers of the 1920s and Billie Holiday before her, Lincoln articulated in her music what Angela Davis calls "quotidian expressions of feminist consciousness."[24] She confronted unfavorable representations of black women's sexuality as she rejected the identity of a supper club singer and tried to fashion herself as a jazz artist. She also presented a frank but affirming portrayal of heterosexual love relationships. Yet Lincoln adopted a critical perspective on this vocal tradition, which she expressed in her choice of material, songwriting, and commentary. Lincoln initially addressed the "love and trouble" tradition in her work, but she eventually chose to emphasize material that spoke of wholesome relationships and broader social issues over music that spoke of heartache. This choice can be understood as a rejection of the constraints that the jazz vocal repertoire placed on female vocalists, and on Lincoln in particular as she was trying to define herself as a "dignified Negro woman." And, interestingly enough, Lincoln's rejection of aspects of the jazz repertoire apparently involved the embrace of a jazz artistry coded as male.

Lincoln's transformation must also be seen in relation to the events and rhetoric of the black freedom struggle. As she learned about and identified with that struggle—and eventually associated herself with black nationalist activism—she adopted a critical perspective on the music industry, seen through the lens of social movements. She saw in music a way to articulate her personal feelings as well as a larger concern for the mutual liberation of black men and women. Such concerns place her firmly within a womanist intellectual tradition but also within a particular discourse of the black freedom struggle of the late 1950s and early 1960s. Inspiring activism and serving as rhetorical ammunition during this period was the idea that racism and structural inequalities in American society had psychologically damaged African American men, women, and children and created pathological, matriarchal families. African American freedom, then, would be won, in part, by creating healthier relations between men and women and redeeming black manhood. Lincoln may well have been influenced by Frazier's assessment of damaged families in *The Negro in the United States,* an example of this strategic discourse.[25] Lincoln's commentary reflects engagement with this discourse, as does her representation of dysfunctional relationships and her subsequent decision to present a more optimistic view of black society.

## The Riverside Recordings

Lincoln's three Riverside recordings, *That's Him, It's Magic,* and *Abbey Is Blue*—recorded in 1957, 1958, and 1959, respectively—document her movement from supper club singer to jazz artist.[26] They also reflect her growing politicization as an African American woman. Even the representations of Lincoln that grace the covers of these albums show a striking transformation of her image. Although Riverside used Lincoln's looks to sell each of the records, a portrait of an artist emerges as the stereotypical imagery of black female sexuality is toned down on each successive album cover. *That's Him* shows an exuberant Lincoln, reclining in a low-cut, embossed white dress, with cleavage exposed and a strap falling off one shoulder. The cover of *It's Magic* moves away from the overtly sexualized imagery. Leaning over a basket, with only her head and arms visible, Lincoln wears a white sweater, an array of silver jewelry, and her hair cut short. *Abbey Is Blue* features a photograph (tinted blue) of Lincoln's face only, with her smile here suggesting she is in the midst of a performance.

Beyond these images, there is also a marked difference between the material on the first album and that on the third.[27] Most striking is the move from the romantic ballads and torch songs of *That's Him* to material with more existential or social themes that anticipate her activism of the early 1960s. Lincoln also articulates a growing sense of African American pride and a shifting perspective on how to represent hetero-sexual love relationships between black men and women. All three albums express concerns she would address more specifically as she was drawn into the public dialogue about jazz and achieved some measure of voice as an activist in the early and mid-1960s.

On *That's Him,* Lincoln expresses the "love and trouble" tradition of black women's song by juxtaposing songs praising black men and celebrating black heterosexual relationships with numbers about unrequited and abusive love. Taken together, the songs on this album suggest Lincoln was interested in representing a certain amount of realism about relationships. The most striking piece on the album, given the political context and the public statements Lincoln would make about black men, is her performance of "Strong Man." The song was written, at her suggestion, by Oscar Brown Jr., then a Chicago-based singer, songwriter, and activist.[28] This piece emphatically denies stereotypes about black men by affirming their physical attractiveness and their commitment to relationships. "I'm in love with a strong man, and he tells me he's wild about me," the song begins, "What a hard working hero is he." The lyrics also describe his physical qualities and his affection:

> Great big arms, muscled hard, dark and shining,
> He holds around me.
> Hair crisp and curly and cropped kind of close.
> Picture a lover like this.
> Lips warm and full that I love the most
> Smiling between every kiss.

Other songs on *That's Him* provide an optimistic view of love relationships and do so in racially specific ways. Lincoln does versions of "Porgy" from *Porgy and Bess* and "Happiness Is a Thing Called Joe" from *Cabin in the Sky.* Although they are not radical reassessments of gender relations (the lyrics to both define a woman's happiness as contingent on her place in the domestic sphere), these songs do celebrate black love relationships. Both the affirmation of such relationships and the veneration of black men fit the needs of this political moment, when black liberation was sometimes defined through the affirmation of individual psyches and mutually beneficial familial relationships.

*That's Him* is also remarkable because of Lincoln's invocation of Billie Holiday. Holiday's influence is suggested not only by Lincoln's vocal techniques (her tone, timing, and phrasing) but also by her choice of material. Lincoln performs four songs associated with Holiday: "My Man," "I Must Have That Man," "When a Woman Loves a Man," and "Don't Explain." These songs present a more ambiguous account of heterosexual relationships than others on the album, for all of them speak of women's undying devotion to men who cheat on them, beat them, or otherwise mistreat them.[29] We can interpret these songs in several ways. Performing songs from Holiday's repertoire was a means for Lincoln to define and legitimate herself as a jazz singer. Through Holiday's music, Lincoln may have been trying to reach her female audience. As she told *Metronome* in 1958: "Billie and I both have the same approach to lyrics, I believe. I like to sing about men and love, and so does she."[30] Read alongside "Strong Man," these songs affirm African American heterosexual love relationships, even as they implicate women in their self-destructive aspects.

There is also a question of whether Lincoln's performances of these songs might serve to point out the problems in heterosexual love relationships. Scholars note Holiday's ability to transform the meaning of even the most banal pop songs through cadence and tone. Not only was she able to drain the innocence from popular standards, but, as Angela Davis suggests, Holiday's approach to singing, whether intended or not, allowed her female listeners to hear lyrics smacking of female masochism as critiques of gender relations. In a discussion of Holiday's 1948 recording of "My Man," for example, Davis suggests that Holiday's ironic tone and phrasing "highlights the contradiction and ambiguities of women's location in love relationships and creates a space within which female subjectivity can move toward self-consciousness."[31]

Lincoln's renditions of Holiday's songs suggest that she was trying to locate something of virtue in them. Her recording of "My Man," for example, begins with a melodramatic instrumental introduction. Lincoln enters to sing of the misdeeds of her man to spare accompaniment, with the musicians answering her with subtle clusters of sound but providing no set rhythmic framework. Then, as the lyrics affirm the singer's love for her man, despite his misdeeds, the musicians come together to set the tempo for a slow but swinging ballad. The shift into swing rhythm, combined with the strength of Lincoln's voice, her enunciation of certain words, the way she stretches out lyrics that affirm the depth of her feelings, and her technique of raising the pitch of her voice and increasing the vibrato at the end of each phrase indeed construct this relationship as ambiguous. She juxtaposes the description of a "no account" man with the upbeat gestalt of a performance that affirms the singer's agency as a participant in the relationship. Thus, one can imagine how Lincoln and her female audience might have read into such performances both an affirmation of heterosexual love relationships and a critique of their constraints.

But regardless of the alternative meanings we locate in such songs, or how her audience may have interpreted them, as Lincoln herself moved toward "self-consciousness" she was increasingly dissatisfied with the limitations of the repertoire of popular standards and even with the legacy of Billie Holiday, who symbolized emotional honesty and socially conscious art—but victimization as well. As mentioned earlier, Lincoln was growing uncomfortable with songs of unrequited love, and after *That's Him* she reevaluated the content of this music. In another recollection of this period, she recalls her decision to change her material. She would continue performing standards but would try to stop doing songs about unrequited love and "no-good men who didn't know how to treat women. I discovered that you *become* what you sing. You can't repeat lyrics night after night as though they were prayer without having them come true in your life."[32] Lincoln may have understood Holiday's ability to transform the meanings of popular standards through jazz performance, but she had a growing sense that these lyrics were ultimately confining. Such songs contradicted her personal experiences with her future husband, and they implicated women as participants in unhealthy and destructive relationships. They also ran contrary to a vision of jazz singing as an art form that could transcend the medium of the romantic ballad, provide more favorable representations of black men and women, and address broader social issues. Holiday thus appears to have represented both the possibilities and the limitations of jazz singing at this time. Part of Lincoln's artistic transformation, then, involved both an embrace of Holiday and then a rejection of aspects of the singer's legacy, as Lincoln moved into more socially oriented songs and cultivated a more stylized, instrumental approach to singing.

Lincoln's reminiscences of the late 1950s highlight the influence of the male jazz community (and Max Roach in particular) as she underwent this transformation. Lincoln has been quite consistent and emphatic about these points. Male jazz artists provided another model for emotional honesty and artistic integrity that lay at the heart of jazz as an art form. Since the early part of the century, critics and musicians alike had constructed jazz in Romantic terms, against the feminized world of popular culture. When Lincoln left the supper clubs, and when aspects of Holiday's legacy seemed inconsistent with her own musical project, Lincoln drew upon this concept of jazz artistry as she moved outside the tradition of torch songs and romantic ballads. Male musicians provided a model for personal integrity in the face of social injustice as well. By defining herself through these male artists, Lincoln not only commented on the limitations she saw in the female jazz vocal tradition but perhaps compromised her ability to craft a music that spoke to other African American women.[33] Yet her discussion of Roach's influence indicates that her respect for male members of the jazz community and the sense of artistry she derived from them were critical to the way she thought of herself as a politicized jazz singer. Moreover, as some of her later comments indicate, this musical vision would coalesce with a personal and social vision that linked dignity, political purpose, and mutual liberation of black men and women.

Lincoln's material and performances on *It's Magic* largely continue the approach from *That's Him,* although the album notably lacks pieces that speak specifically about black relationships. She again balances songs that celebrate mutually beneficial relationships with those that describe unrequited or dangerous love. One exception is "Little Niles," a minor-key composition by Randy Weston, with lyrics by John Hendricks. "Little Niles" points to Lincoln's later work in several ways. First, it signals a shift in the thematic content of her recordings. Performed at a slow tempo with a lullaby feeling, it tells the story of a young boy caught between youth and adulthood. The performance also highlights the instrumental qualities of Lincoln's voice. The composition requires that she sing uncommon intervals, and she takes the role of a horn as she sings wordless vocals, trading fours with Art Farmer and Benny Golson.

*Abbey Is Blue,* as we might expect, is an exploration of blues forms and feelings. But the blues music on this album stems less from the failure of individualized romantic love than from the vicissitudes of social experience, psychological angst, and spiritual longing. "Lonely House," for example, a Langston Hughes poem set to music by Kurt Weill, speaks of intense feelings of loneliness, but it is a meditation focused on existential alienation and urban ennui rather than on an emptiness produced by failed romance. Similarly, Oscar Brown Jr.'s "Brother, Where Are You?" speaks of the social isolation of a young boy on a city street as a metaphor for human beings' alienation from one another. Even the Hammerstein-Romberg standard "Softly, As in a Morning Sunrise," a cautionary tale about the dangers of passion, is more generally about love as an emotion rather than being a first-person account of experience.

The material Lincoln performs on this record also begins to engage more directly, albeit subtly, the political context of the black freedom movement, and it anticipates her more politically explicit work in the 1960s. Duke Ellington's "Come Sunday," which Mahalia Jackson had performed on Ellington's recent recording of *Black, Brown and Beige,* is a plaintive call for God's deliverance. "Long as You're Living," another song with lyrics by Brown, is self-consciously didactic, as it calls on people to, among other things, enjoy the simple pleasures of life, strive for self-improvement, and recognize a common humanity. "Let Up," a fourteen-bar blues, for which Lincoln wrote lyrics to Roach's melody, speaks of frustrations in a general (that is, social rather than romantic) sense and wonders when life will get easier.[34]

"Afro Blue," a Mongo Santamaria composition with Brown's lyrics that opens the album, addresses the theme of love between black men and women. Done in 6/8 and arranged in an A/B/A/B/A/B form—with the sections connected by a staccato, minor instrumental figure performed by trumpet, trombone, and tenor sax—"Afro Blue" evokes Africa as both an ancestral home and a mythical land of romance.[35] "Dream of a land my soul is from," Lincoln begins, "I hear a hand stroke on a drum." The lyrics describe a beautiful African girl, two young lovers dancing with "undulating grace," and an environment conducive to passion. The lyrics fit into a long history of imagining Africa as a sexualized landscape, yet Lincoln's 1959 performance of the song also symbolizes a growing affinity with Africa among African American artists in the context of decolonization movements across the continent. Lincoln's treatment of the song's refrain—"Shades of delight, cocoa hue / Rich as the night, Afro

Blue"—so that "cocoa hue" sounds like "cocoa you," and the shift in the narrative, where "my slumbering fantasy assumes reality / Until it seems it's not a dream, the two [dancers] are you and me," define African American love through an affirmation of African culture. Lincoln refigures the blues: here, blues music speaks not of the difficulties of relationships but of a culturally based and healthy love between black men and women.

## Straight Ahead

In the summer of 1960, Lincoln appeared with Max Roach at the alternative Newport festival, and recorded with members of the Jazz Artists Guild that fall; during August and September, she performed the vocals on Roach's Candid recording *We Insist! The Freedom Now Suite.* In February 1961, Roach and his band backed Lincoln on her own Candid release, *Straight Ahead.* She joined another Roach ensemble that August on *Percussion Bittersweet* and performed on Roach's *It's Time* (both for the Impulse! label) the following year. During this period, Lincoln changed her approach to singing. She experimented with a broader array of timbre and techniques; and, thanks in part to Roach's arrangements, she began to use her voice more like a front-line instrument. She also became more outspoken about race and civil rights; and, like Roach and other musicians with whom she engaged in dialogue, she made no secret of her dissatisfaction with the treatment of black artists by the music industry. Lincoln also addressed issues of concern to women, particularly black women, eventually becoming a notable voice among black women artists expressing dissent in the early and mid-1960s.

Roach's *We Insist! The Freedom Now Suite* is perhaps the strongest political statement made by jazz musicians at the turn of the decade. Each of the five pieces on this album bears a political stamp, and together they explore three themes that were prominent in politically oriented jazz circa 1960: the African American experience with slavery, the contemporary freedom struggle, and an affinity with Africa. In addition to Lincoln, the recording featured Nigerian drummer Michael Olatunji and veteran tenor saxophonist Coleman Hawkins, who had performed with Roach at Newport that summer and had joined Roach and Mingus in the short-lived Jazz Artists Guild. *We Insist!* began as a collaboration between Roach and Oscar Brown Jr. They originally conceived it as a longer work, to be performed on the occasion of the centennial of the Emancipation Proclamation. However, the lunch counter sit-ins in Greensboro, North Carolina, and other cities in the early part of 1960 inspired Roach to use this music to express solidarity for the civil rights movement. The premier public performance of the *Freedom Now Suite,* at the Village Gate in New York in January 1961, was sponsored by the Congress of Racial Equality (CORE).[36]

"Driva' Man" and "Freedom Day" feature lyrics by Brown and melodies by Roach. "Driva' Man" opens with Lincoln, accompanied by the occasional beat of the tambourine, singing about the physical brutality of slave labor and the slavedriver's role in maintaining order on the plantation. The rest of the band enters to establish the harmonic structure and a 5/4 beat, with Roach's rim shots emulating the crack of a whip on the fifth beat of each measure. Hawkins plays a long, searching solo; and then Lincoln returns to finish the lyric with the full band's backing and a tambourine now supplying the crack of the whip. The full ensemble opens "Freedom Day," with the horns stating the main theme. Lincoln comes in over a blistering pace set by the rhythm section, with lyrics that speak of the euphoria and cautious optimism surrounding emancipation. She is followed by a series of instrumental solos on trumpet (Booker Little), tenor saxophone (Walter Benton), trombone (Julian Priester), and drums (Roach); and she returns at the end to conclude the lyrics.[37]

Lincoln's performances on these pieces represent a shift in her approach to jazz singing and technique. One critic thought the "most spectacular" change was in the "intensity of her performance."[38] Lincoln also displays a more diverse range of vocal texture, phrasing, and timing than on her Riverside releases, which she demonstrates on the 5/4 "Driva' Man" and in the rapid pace of "Freedom Day." She had been praised for her ability to mesh with the musicians on her Riverside dates, but here she exhibits a more instrumental approach, as Roach fluidly writes her into the arrangements. On both of these tracks, her voice operates as a front-line instrument. On "Driva' Man," she sets the theme and the emotional tone of the performance, to which Hawkins responds in his solo. On "Freedom Day," the horns establish the theme, and Lincoln's first vocal chorus follows it closely. In the second chorus, her phrasing and melodic line reinterpret the theme, as would an instrumental soloist. The other musicians in turn address her melodic ideas as they construct their own solos.

Lincoln explores the instrumental qualities of her voice in even greater detail on "Triptych: Prayer/Protest/Peace," a duet with Roach that the drummer had originally composed as a ballet and had previously performed with the Ruth Walton Dancers. The piece begins with Lincoln demonstrating the range of her voice as she projects a wordless spiritual over Roach's accompaniment. "Protest" is a frenetic section, with Roach complementing Lincoln's primal screams with furious drum rolls, bombs, and crashing cymbals. According to Nat Hentoff's liner notes, the section is a release of "rage and anger" that demands "catharsis" and is meant to represent "all forms of protest, certainly including violence." The piece concludes with Lincoln's lilting vocal line over a steady rhythmic pulse, conveying, as Roach put it, "the feeling of relaxed exhaustion after you've done everything you can to assert yourself. You can rest now because you've worked to be free."[39]

"All Africa" begins with Lincoln invoking "the beat" as a signifier of the continuity of black history and culture throughout the diaspora. The composition moves into a steady polyrhythmic groove, facilitated by Olatunji's conga drums and the playing of Afro-Cuban percussionists Ray Mantilla and Tomas Duvail, whose presence provides both a musical and symbolic expression of pan-Africanism. The lyric consists of Lincoln calling out the names of various African peoples, with Olatunji, singing mainly in Yoruban, offering an antiphonal statement about freedom particular to each ethnic group. Roach wanted "Tears for Johannesburg" to evoke the 1960 massacre by South African police in the black township of Sharpeville but ultimately to express an affirming vision of freedom. Unlike many invocations of Africa in African American art from this period, this piece speaks directly of contemporary political struggle on the continent. The tune has a steady ostinato bass figure and polyrhythmic percussion underneath contrapuntal horn lines. Lincoln states the theme in a mournful, wordless vocal line before it fades out in an ethereal falsetto. As on "Driva' Man" and "Freedom Day," she sets the tone for the other instrumentalists' solos.[40]

Lincoln's contribution to Roach's *Percussion Bittersweet* is limited, as she appears on only two tracks. Yet her participation contributed to her reputation as a politically motivated and instrumentally inspired vocalist. Roach wrote "Garvey's Ghost" as an homage to the black national-ist Marcus Garvey. The drummer had been inspired by his impression that "many of Marcus Garvey's dreams and ambitions are currently reach-ing fruition in the new independent nations of Africa."[41] The piece be-gins with a 6/8 polyrhythmic groove performed by Roach, Carlos Valdez, and Carlos Eugenio on drum kit, conga, and cowbell, respectively. Then Lincoln (singing wordless notes) and the horns (trumpet, trombone, and saxophones) enter to state the theme in unison. After a series of solos, including a lengthy one by Roach, Lincoln and the horns return to re-state the theme before the piece ends. On perhaps no other recording from this period does Lincoln's voice operate so thoroughly as a horn, as she joins the brass and reeds in setting up the harmonic basis and feel-ing of the composition. On "Mendacity," written by Roach and Chips Bayen, Lincoln again takes the role of an instrumentalist in establishing the tone of the piece. This composition points out the hypocrisy of the American political system. Commenting, for example, on the issue of voting rights for African Americans, Lincoln sings of the mortal danger facing those in certain Southern states who try to exercise those rights.[42]

February 1961's *Straight Ahead* gives a broader picture of Abbey Lin-coln as singer, vocal instrumentalist, and composer. Joining her on this recording is a large ensemble led by Roach.[43] The personnel and the over-all musical feeling are similar to *We Insist!* and *Percussion Bittersweet,* but here the emphasis is on the ballad. Yet these are no ordinary ballads; none of them are popular standards. Instead, the material consists of straight-ahead jazz compositions, pieces influenced by free jazz, blues numbers, and ballads that by virtue of form and subject matter fall outside the pop genre. Lincoln demonstrates a wide range of vocal textures and emotion, working in concert with the band and playing the part of front-line in-strument as well (although on these performances her emphasis is on the lyrics rather than on assuming the role of a horn). Her choice of mate-rial and her own compositions also establish her social agenda.

Thematically, several interesting things happen on this record. Two songs reference major figures in modern jazz and position Lincoln as an artist who is drawing from both male and female antecedents. With Thelonious Monk's blessing, Lincoln created a set of lyrics to his compo-sition "Blue Monk." The group performs the piece at a slower tempo than many versions of the original composition, with the horn section and the singer's voice providing a polyphonic statement of the melody. Like Mingus before her, Lincoln pays homage to Monk, here casting him as an iconic bluesman and consummate jazz instrumentalist. Using the term "Monkery" to describe Monk's unique personality and wisdom transformed into art, she portrays the pianist and composer as a man who has experienced hardship yet perseveres through his music.

Complementing this piece is "Left Alone," a composition that had been written by Billie Holiday and Mal Waldron on a 1959 plane flight from New York to San Francisco shortly before the singer died. Waldron finally had the chance to record the song on *Straight Ahead* and supplied the arrangement as well as the piano accompaniment.[44] This piece is vintage, melancholic Holiday in its subject matter, as it tells the story of a woman perpetually frustrated in her search for love. Brief passages by the brass at the beginning of the piece and between sections establish a sorrowful mood, as do Art Davis's bowed bass line at the beginning of each section and Coleman Hawkins's tenor solo at the end of the first chorus. But though this song speaks of emotional injury, it does not sanction abuse. Moreover, with Lincoln's studied attempt to emulate Holiday's intonation and emotional intensity, the performance seems less a commentary on relationships than an homage to an important predecessor.

Also complementing one another are two upbeat numbers on the album based on poems written by African Americans. "When Malindy Sings" is an Oscar Brown Jr. composition that takes four stanzas of Paul Laurence Dunbar's 1895 poem, eliminates the exaggerated dialect while maintaining some elements of black vernacular syntax, and sets the poetry to music. Performed as a swinging blues, the lyrics speak of the majesty of vernacular black song. "African Lady," Randy Weston's musical rendition of a recent Langston Hughes poem, features a polyrhythmic mix over which Lincoln sings uncommon intervals and chromatic figures in dialogue with the dissonant punctuation of the horns. The lyrics describe the beauty of an African woman as the product of the natural world but also look optimistically to her centrality in the future of the continent. Taken together, these compositions explore the African American cultural past, invoke an imagined Edenlike Africa, and affirm black womanhood.

The three additional compositions for which Lincoln wrote lyrics address her personal experiences and link them to social issues. The title track is a slow, dark ballad, on which Lincoln balances lilting vocal lines with reprimanding statement. These lyrics, which Lincoln cowrote with Earl Baker, describe her own hardships after finishing an exhausting run in the theatrical production *Jamaica* and connect them to difficulties in contemporary American society.[45] Using "the road" as a metaphor for social experience, she describes in general terms the difficulties that life presents and then moves into a subtle, yet forceful, social critique. "For some, this road is smooth and easy / Traveling high without a care / But if you've got to use the back roads / Straight ahead can lead nowhere." The final verse laments the slow pace of the struggle against injustice: "On this road you've got a problem / Getting where you want to go / Speed limits almost down to nothing / Straight ahead, but awful slow." Contributing to the mood of the piece is a solemn horn arrangement, with Coleman Hawkins adding a poignant tenor solo.

"In the Red" appears to have been influenced by the free jazz movement and modern concert music. Lacking a steady pulse or tempo, the performance is carried forward by a conversation between Lincoln and the rest of the band that is punctuated by instrumental crescendos. Lincoln sings the lyrics with a calculated dissonance, and the effect of her voice and the voices of the other instruments is one of tension and expectancy. The lyrics describe the financial difficulties she and Roach were experiencing while performing the *Freedom Now Suite* and relate their troubles to larger social inequalities: "Rich folks say to keep on smiling / But poor folks pay the dues." Taken in its social and political context, the song concludes with a simultaneously ominous and upbeat promise for social change that is accompanied by a harmonious horn passage. "There won't be no peace of mind," Lincoln sings, " 'til I see better days." Lincoln articulates a clearer political demand on "Retribution." Sung with boppish intervals over a rolling twelve-bar blues in 5/4, this song takes the voice of a person who has known no privilege but asks for no assistance, save that the "retribution" will "match the contribution, baby."[46]

Taken together, Lincoln's performances on these three albums redefined her as a jazz singer, as she adopted a more instrumental approach to singing, positioned herself as a jazz artist whose work exceeded the romantic ballad and torch song, and defined herself as a socially committed artist. Responding to the political moment, Lincoln presented in her music an updated, radicalized version of the dignity she sought when she underwent her transformation from supper club singer to jazz artist. Her changing approach to singing seemed bound up in how she perceived herself. She recalled that the primal scream on *We Insist!* "freed me up. It deepened my voice and made it more melodious." These albums also improved her reputation among established members of the jazz community. "When Max first introduced me to them," she remembered, "I was still singing 'Love for Sale.' They thought that was kind of nice, but it wasn't until I started with the original music and new compositions that they saw me in a different light—as a serious artist." Lincoln continued to invoke Holiday as an influence, but she also drew on an ethos of artistic integrity, which she located in the male jazz community, to move beyond the romantic ballad. In 1961, Lincoln told the *Pittsburgh Courier* that she was fortunate to be of a different generation than Billie Holiday. Unconstrained by the limitations of the romantic ballad, jazz could now represent African American history, respond to the political present, and portray African American women in a new light. In the early 1960s, she and Roach performed benefit concerts for Malcolm X, the Black Muslims, CORE, the NAACP, and other organizations. Outside of music, she led an organization called the Cultural Association for Women of African Heritage, whose purpose was to present more favorable and accurate representations of African American women. The group's activities ran the gamut from fashion shows promoting "African hair styles" to a 1961 demonstration at the United Nations to protest the assassination of Patrice Lumumba.[47]

## The Challenge of Musical Activism

In a 1961 conversation with *Down Beat,* Lincoln affirmed her identity as a black nationalist. Although she agreed that people could take the philosophy too far in the direction of an unhealthy, self-aggrandizing, or hateful separatism, she saw great value in taking increased pride in black culture and history. "We are taught to be nationalistic about America. We are proud of being Americans, and we point with pride to our accomplishments. Actually, this is the same with the true black nationalist. And it is such a wonderful feeling to suddenly become aware of the fact that my people were kings and queens."[48]

Over the following several years, Lincoln made a series of comments that demonstrated the "wonderful feeling" she derived from a political and aesthetic devotion to black people and black culture. She also articulated some of the complications that attended her adoption of black nationalism: the way her political stance appears to have negatively affected her career, as well as the way her investment in a black nationalist focus on the redemption of black men tempered the womanist aspects of her project. Again, comments about Billie Holiday and male musicians, particularly Max Roach, figured prominently in her assessments.

The combined effect of Lincoln's politics and musical approach bolstered her reputation among some observers. After *We Insist!* was released, Lincoln remembered, "some people decided I was a great singer, critics who never thought I was part of the music until this album." Other jazz critics were hostile to her. This animosity was shared by record companies, who considered her "too hot to handle," and Lincoln did not record again until 1973. Although she continued to sing throughout the 1960s, she turned some of her attention to television and appeared in films such as *Nothing But a Man* (1964) and *For the Love of Ivy* (1968). As difficult as this period was for her, however, Lincoln found solace in her decision to leave the supper clubs behind. "The word was out on me, and I was in plenty of trouble. But at least it was trouble of my own choosing. Before, encouraged to portray a woman of easy virtue, I was on the road to loneliness and despair."[49]

When critics evaluated *Straight Ahead*, they sometimes did so through comparisons with Billie Holiday, who after her death remained a litmus test of female jazz vocal artistry. John S. Wilson, for example, began a 1961 review of Lincoln's album with an homage to Holiday and lamented the current state of jazz singing. Since Holiday's death, he wrote, the definition of "jazz singer" had been "badly out of focus." The term had been applied "indiscriminately to vocalists, invariably female, whose relationship to jazz was often tenuous." The best of "these girls," he continued, were better identified by the term "torch singing." Holiday had succeeded, he thought, in part because she was so fully enmeshed in the jazz idiom; she was neither a pop singer nor a blues singer. But even as a prototypical jazz singer she stood alone. Many tried to imitate her, "but none could project the inner fire that was her special quality." Wilson saw in the Lincoln of *Straight Ahead* some of the qualities he celebrated in Holiday. Although he was critical of Lincoln's Riverside recordings, considering them somewhat derivative of Holiday, he thought her most recent album was an achievement. *Straight Ahead* succeeded not because Lincoln sounded like Holiday but because she shared her personal involvement with the music and maintained a "searing intensity that burn[ed] through her singing." He also praised her songwriting. "In place of this rather bland girl," he wrote, "we now hear a woman, assured, positively directed and glowing with conviction."[50]

*Down Beat's* Ira Gitler, in contrast, castigated Lincoln for failing to live up to Holiday's standards. Although he liked Lincoln's renditions of "Blue Monk" and "When Malindy Sings," he largely dismissed the rest of her project. Gitler began his review by voicing his opinions about art and propaganda and the merits of Holiday's "Strange Fruit":

> It is usually beyond the reviewer's province to discuss anything but the music, but here the sociological aspects are too interwoven with the material to be ignored. I dislike propaganda in art when it is a device. Billy [*sic*] Holiday's *Strange Fruit* had a social message, but it was art first. It was a song that echoed the particular time in which it was done, but it was poetry of a lasting nature, too. *Straight Ahead,* the title song, fits the '60s, true, and I am in agreement with its sentiments—but its validity does not make it good art.

Later Gitler invoked Holiday in order to make more specific criticisms of Lincoln's singing. He accused her of singing out of tune on "African Lady" and called her lyrics to "Retribution" "banal." As to Lincoln's tone and inflection: "The reference I made to Billie Holiday was not accidental. Miss Lincoln has adopted some of Miss Holiday's mannerisms, and on her they don't sound quite the same. The effect is caricature."[51]

Despite disclaimers that his evaluation was primarily concerned with the quality of Lincoln's music, Gitler's criticisms exhibited a profound discomfort with Lincoln's politics and with what he considered a calculated performance of identity. He wrote off Lincoln's attempt to express her racial pride as a gimmick, accusing her of becoming a "professional Negro." Like many white jazz critics writing during this period, he was uncomfortable with music that hinted at militancy and black nationalism. He called her politics exclusionary; at one point, he compared her beliefs to those of Elijah Muhammad—an ironic claim, as the songs on the album made no obvious reference to race and defined social struggles largely in terms of economics. Gitler also commented on a passage in the liner notes, where Hentoff quoted Lincoln exclaiming, as she looked around the recording studio, "In a way, all these tunes are about Billie . . . they're about all of us." Gitler concluded: "All the musicians on the date are Negro. Therefore, the 'all of us' seems to exclude whites. The irony here is that the main audiences for her segregated singing will most probably be white, as the greater part of the general jazz audience is white." He charged Lincoln with being politically "naive" as well, noting her leadership of the Cultural Association for Women of African Heritage. He referred her to an article in a recent issue of the *New Yorker* that described the antipathy of certain Africans toward African Americans. He concluded his review by stating: "Now that Abbey Lincoln has found herself as a Negro, I hope she can find herself as a militant but less one-sided *American* Negro. It could help her performance."[52]

These disparate reviews of *Straight Ahead* again call attention to the gendered construction of jazz singing as an art form during these years. Wilson's characterization of Lincoln's transformation from "bland girl" to "woman" describes jazz as a place where "girl" singers leave the realm of the popular to become women and serious artists. Yet jazz singing continued to be a genre defined in somewhat limiting fashion as the product of personal experience and emotional intensity. For some, jazz singing remained but a footnote to the larger and more important project of instrumental music. Although instrumental jazz was sometimes defined as a product of the emotional, it was also considered a product of male intellect and genius. In Gitler's mind, Lincoln did not do justice to Holiday's legacy. He thought that her singing did not do justice to the skills of her male accompanists either.

Shortly after *Down Beat* published Gitler's hostile review, the magazine responded to letters written by Lincoln and others by organizing a panel discussion with Gitler, Lincoln, Roach, trumpeter Don Ellis, Argentinean composer Lalo Schifrin, *Down Beat* editors Bill Coss and Don De Micheal, and Nat Hentoff, the jazz writer and the producer of Roach's and Lincoln's Candid albums. *Down Beat* sponsored the discussion to address the "growth of ill feeling—based on racial differences—between Negro and white jazzmen," which some feared would tear the jazz community apart. Gitler's review of Lincoln's album seemed an apt vehicle for creating a discussion based on these issues.[53]

Although much of the anxiety white jazz critics felt about racial issues during this period stemmed from their discomfort with the real and imagined militancy of African American musicians, substantive economic issues underlay these tensions. As the jazz industry felt the financial effects of the popularity of both rhythm and blues and rock and roll, competition increased among a growing population of musicians for a declining number of jobs and recording contracts. Many black musicians voiced their anger—in increasingly political tones—over white control of the music industry and what they perceived as the preferential treatment of white musicians. One line of defense was the argument that black players were superior jazz musicians, whether by nature or by culture. Conversely, some white musicians thought that black bandleaders discriminated against them by closing ranks and hiring them in lesser numbers. As a result, the "Crow Jim" debate of the early 1950s was revived, although in the early 1960s the focus was less on the tastes of white jazz critics than on acts of "discrimination" by black musicians. *Time* magazine described the emergence of a "regrettable kind of reverse segregation known as Crow Jim—a feeling that the white man has no civil rights when it comes to jazz."[54]

Within this context, much of the *Down Beat* panel discussion covered predictable terrain. The participants addressed the working conditions musicians faced in nightclubs, the merits of integration, African Americans' supposed cultural proclivity for jazz excellence, and the question of whether Lincoln's politics constituted black separatism. Accompanying these issues was an interesting update of the debate about the qualifications for jazz writing; a dialogue about the relationship of art to propaganda; a consideration of whether black artists had the right and duty to identify themselves as such; and a discussion about the political implications of popular song lyrics.

The published version of the discussion began with an interrogation of Gitler's characterization of Lincoln as a "professional Negro." Gitler affirmed his criticism, arguing that Lincoln was using her identity "to exploit a career." In response, Lincoln asked: "How can I sing as a black woman, as a Negro, if I don't exploit the fact that I'm a Negro?" Other panelists supported Lincoln's position using several lines of reasoning.

Roach argued that in a culture industry where white people had historically marketed blackness in many different forms, black people should be able to control these representations and perhaps benefit from them as well. "If anybody has the right to exploit the Negro, it's the Negro. Everybody else up until this point has been exploiting the Negro. And the minute the Negro begins to exploit himself, even if this was so, here comes somebody who says they shouldn't exploit themselves. But who *should* exploit the Negro? Here's the point: she has a perfect right to exploit the Negro."[55]

Hentoff and Schifrin challenged Gitler's resistance to the political dimensions of jazz, arguing that "the art of today" came out of a particular political context and should not be devalued for reflecting it. Art was not beyond ideology, Hentoff argued; even the "evasion" of politics reflected a certain "attitude."[56] Roach and Lincoln took the argument even further, as they questioned whether white critics had a sufficient understanding of black experience to write intelligently about jazz and its social context. Whereas Mingus and other musicians had often criticized jazz critics for their lack of musical knowledge, Roach and Lincoln were part of a wave of politically engaged musicians who believed that at this moment, when many African Americans were producing art that spoke more directly of its social context, jazz criticism demanded a kind of black cultural literacy. Their brief comments updated the calls of New Negro intellectuals for a black-produced literary criticism and anticipated Amiri Baraka's 1963 essay "Jazz and the White Critic" and the efforts of others to establish black, culturally based aesthetic criteria for evaluating African American art and culture.[57]

As the panelists debated whether Lincoln was a separatist (she said she was not) and whether Gitler had given the musical aspects of *Straight Ahead* a fair evaluation (he said he had), the conversation took an interesting turn. If Gitler did not like Lincoln's singing, Roach asked, then whom did he consider a good singer? When Gitler answered, "Billie Holiday," Lincoln accused him of a kind of double standard:

> Tell me, why is it that you never censured her for being an obvious masochist? Everything Billie Holiday sang was about unrequited love, nearly. Now, why is it nobody got after her about her subject matter? She sang about what was most important to her. And I, Abbey Lincoln,

sing about what is most important to me. And what is most important to me is being free of the shackles that chain me in every walk of life that I live. If this were not so, I would still be a supper-club singer.

When Gitler responded that he had never had a chance to review Holiday's records, Lincoln retorted: "Well, then why do you like her so much, because she was really one-sided. Billie sang about 'My Man Don't Love Me' and 'My Man's a Drag.' My Man, My Man, My Man. . . ."[58]

In her comments, Lincoln displayed the ambivalent attitude toward Holiday's material that is evident in the progression of her recordings in the late 1950s and early 1960s. While affirming Holiday's right to choose songs that made sense to her personally, Lincoln was uncomfortable with Holiday's "masochism," which, she suggested, was inconsistent with her own current experience. Lincoln wanted to sing songs that reflected her own political orientation and a more optimistic view of relations between black men and women—a perspective that went hand in hand with her transition from supper club singer to jazz singer. In fact, if there had been any moment when she actually was a "professional Negro," Lincoln continued, it was when she played the supper clubs: "There was a time when I was *really* a professional Negro. I was capitalizing on the fact that I was a Negro, and I looked the way Western people expect you to look. I wore ridiculous dresses, and I sang the songs that were expected. I was a professional Negro. I was not an artist. I had nothing to say. I used inane, stupid material on the stage." In Lincoln's mind, then, a "professional Negro" was not the woman who had taken control of her art and career and tried to fashion herself into a responsible and socially committed jazz artist. Rather, it was a woman who remained trapped by the subject matter of popular standards and catered to a white audience's assumptions about black women's sexuality.[59]

Yet Lincoln had not given up on Holiday. Even if her songbook contradicted Lincoln's personal and political vision, Holiday still represented the possibility of jazz singing that spoke to women. Later in the conversation, Lincoln acknowledged the particularity of Holiday's message for black women. Speaking to the issue of whether certain forms of music spoke more directly to blacks than to whites, Lincoln said:

> I always go back to Billie Holiday, because she's an example of a lot of things to me. Billie Holiday sang to women—more than to men—

a woman who is in her same circumstance, who had a man and she was frustrated. It was more profound to that woman than it would be to anybody else. . . . Negro women are in a class to themselves, too. Women really have a problem. But the black woman has another problem because her man has another problem. She's a part of her man.

Holiday remained important, in part because she articulated issues that were relevant to black women. In Lincoln's view, black men and women were struggling through a difficult time together, and Holiday was able to express the frustrations they faced.[60]

Lincoln's comments indicate the direction in which her ideas about music and society were moving. Over the next several years, she worked as a jazz singer, but did not record in the United States. She performed at community events and benefits for black causes and spoke out on a variety of social issues, yet her comments about her music show that she was trying to strike a balance between being a socially committed artist, being true to herself, and catering to the expectations of the audience that supported her financially. She also made a series of statements in the press, in which she linked the fortunes of black men and women.

In a June 1962 article, the African American newspaper *Amsterdam News* quoted Lincoln as saying she was feeling the effects of the controversy surrounding *We Insist!* and *Straight Ahead*. She now described the representation of her as a "nationalist" as inaccurate. Although she stressed her goal of deriving dignity from her work, she deemphasized her role as a protest singer and stressed that her upcoming shows at the Village Vanguard would mark a "return to a melodic blend of jazz and popular tunes." In a conversation with the *Herald Tribune* a short time later, she was more forthcoming about her politics but justified her exploration of a full range of material as an attempt to portray a full "awareness of who I am as a human, as a woman, as a black woman, as an artist and as an entertainer. All these things together are me. They make me unique."[61] She also, in the *Amsterdam News*, characterized her own attempt to represent her true feelings and her respect for black men by once again invoking Holiday's legacy: "Billie Holiday used to sing, in her day, of 'my man who treats me mean,' and that kind of material, . . . but I don't see Negro men that way. I prefer to sing 'Strong Man.' I am a black woman and a married woman [she had married Roach earlier that year]. I no longer see trite songs as an expression of our social existence."[62]

Lincoln made one of her strongest statements about black manhood, and about her man in particular, in "Black Man in Japan," a 1964 article that she and Roach cowrote for *Liberator.* Roach provided commentary about their experiences while on tour in Japan. He was astonished to find himself treated as a legitimate artist and as a human being, which was a marked improvement over life on the road in the United States and which reminded him of how "as an African American I was obviously starving for simple acceptance." The trip succeeded, he concluded, in "ma[king] us all aware of our sickness, which is a direct result of the U.S.A. and its way of life." Woven into Roach's text was a poem written by Lincoln, focused almost entirely on the impact of this trip on Roach's self-esteem. Lincoln's poem represented Japan as a site where manhood could be redeemed but which also provided experiences that made clear the limitations that U.S. society placed on black men.[63]

The film *Nothing But a Man* was released at the end of that year. Co-starring Ivan Dixon and Lincoln, it told the story of a young couple (Duff and Josie) trying to make it through the everyday difficulties of life in the Jim Crow South of the 1960s. Much of the film focused on Duff's struggle to gain respect while fulfilling his prescribed role as a husband and father (of a son from a prior relationship) and on how Josie supported him in his struggle and gained a measure of self-confidence in the process—that is, it depicted an African American couple's mutual investment in the redemption of black manhood. The release of the film brought renewed attention to Lincoln and provided a platform for her to voice her ideas about gender relations, human dignity, black politics, and art.

In a March 1965 conversation with Pauline Rivelli of *Jazz* magazine, Lincoln spoke at length about the position of African Americans in the United States and concluded the discussion with strong words about the U.S. government's complicity in maintaining social hierarchies. Like a growing number of African American musicians and artists, Lincoln decried the fact that black people had been distanced from African cultures and languages. She endorsed the term "African American" as a signifier of identity that promoted an ethnic bond with the African continent and challenged the Eurocentrism of American culture. And at a time when the term was increasingly falling out of favor with musicians, Lincoln expressed discomfort with the word "jazz," equating its use with the animus directed toward black people: "It's a word that passes from the Creole 'jass' which literally means sexual intercourse. A slang word, disgusting, having something to do with prostitution. When it's applied to the music it's supposed to mean something great, yet it's used daily to describe some confused condition, having nothing to do with the music, where the word 'crap' would better apply." Although such comments about jazz may not have signaled a new direction in her art, they do suggest that by 1965 the idea of jazz had lost some of its luster as a signifier for a politicized, respectable black musical art and as a means for distinguishing her work from the realm of the supper club. Still, Lincoln continued to make sense of her role as an artist much the way she had in previous years.[64]

When the discussion with Rivelli turned to *Nothing But a Man,* Lincoln linked her relationship with Max Roach to that of Josie and Duff. A woman must be patient and understanding toward her man, "who is compelled to continually prove his worth as a contributor and world builder on the outside." Thus, "her greatest task is to understand him and to take his word for what exists out there, and there's nothing simple about that."[65] Lincoln expressed similar views in an interview for Canadian television. She talked about her concern for the political situation in the United States, criticizing government inaction, expressing admiration for Martin Luther King Jr. and Malcolm X, and articulating a vision where "all the people" would be treated with respect. Much of the conversation, however, revolved around the question of the message she hoped to convey through her music. She did not see herself on the front lines of the black freedom struggle, but she did believe she and her husband could play a role. "As a performer, with the help of Max Roach, I'm Mrs. Max Roach, we try to portray in our music, something that gives our people an incentive to go on and to persevere."[66]

Lincoln believed that by expressing herself she also made "a statement on other women and on other black Americans because that's who I am." At this moment, one of the things she hoped to do was to represent black relationships in a way that was respectful to black men *and* women. Speaking of her decision to stop performing "My Man," which spoke of a "lazy," unfaithful protagonist, Lincoln repeated the story of her rejection of the song: "I couldn't love a man like that and I think about my husband, who's wonderful to look at, he's extremely bright, taught me everything I know, and he's not the least bit lazy. And I have five brothers and my father and none of these men were like that so every time I would stand on the stage and sing this song, I was making a statement, whether I knew it or not, and when I realized that was the statement I was making, I just wouldn't make it any more."[67]

Like the words of other black women activists and artists working in the early 1960s, Lincoln's comments positioned racism and economic inequality as more pressing issues than sexism and maintained an investment in black male empowerment. African American feminist politics of that day were constrained by the androcentric elements of the rhetoric of black freedom and, to some extent, by a growing popular discourse focused on the idea of a "black matriarchy," which held that black men were in danger of being emasculated not only by the broader society but by domineering black women as well. During and after 1964, when the Civil Rights Act gave a legal foundation to women's rights and male chauvinism was on the rise, many black women became less tolerant of sexism and more vocal about specific issues facing them as women. Assertions of black feminist thought and activism, however, elicited even more anxiety about a supposed "black matriarchy." Such fears were given official validation by the 1965 release of Daniel Patrick Moynihan's *The Negro Family: The Case for National Action,* issued by the U.S. Department of Labor's Office of Policy Planning and Research. The so-called Moynihan report identified a "tightening tangle of pathology" in African American families. The report explained racial, economic, and social inequalities as products of black cultural deficiencies, while accusing black women of emasculating black men by making their own gains in education and employment and by failing to live up to their prescribed gender roles as dutiful wives and mothers. The release of the Moynihan report did not create male chauvinism; but, as Paula Giddings suggests, it certainly helped to validate it.[68]

As the discourse concerning matriarchy helped to foment a backlash against black women, it also presented a challenge that black women activists and intellectuals would take up with increasing frequency in the late 1960s and 1970s.[69] But this response in fact began in the mid-1960s. While many women continued to assert that the liberation of black women and that of black men were inextricably linked, African American women activists, artists, and intellectuals expressed a growing concern with the redemption of black women. In April 1965, a month after the release of the Moynihan report, Lincoln joined poet Sarah Wright, novelist Paule Marshall, and playwright Alice Childress for a panel discussion entitled "The Negro Woman in American Literature," as part of The Negro Writer's Vision of America conference at the New School for Social Research in New York.[70] The panelists' concerns with the public image of black women and their differing perspectives on the need to affirm black manhood reflected this crucial juncture in the history of black feminism.

In her introduction to the discussion, Sarah Wright objected to the representations of women as sex objects in art and literature. She also drew attention to the current emphasis on "manhood": "I am convinced that most American men, and unhappily, far, far too many of our Afro-American men, are walking around begging for a popular recognition of what is fictitiously called 'manhood,' a begging which takes the form of attacks on women launched from many different directions." Alice Childress voiced similar fears, adding that there was a need to recognize the variety of ways black women continued to be oppressed within and outside their families. She suggested that it was incumbent upon activist writers to challenge negative representations of the black woman by publicizing "her constant, unrelenting struggle against racism and for human rights." Paule Marshall observed that black women writers had a twofold problem: being women in a society that did not take them seriously, and being black women in a society that viewed them through a web of stereotypes. She differed from Childress somewhat, stating that they also faced the "challenge" of providing the black man with "the kind of love and support he so desperately needs in a society that has conspired over the past 400 years to take from him the sense of his manhood."[71]

Unlike some of the other panelists, Lincoln was not openly critical of how the focus on black manhood and the matriarchy debate had caused a backlash against black women. Before stating her intent to explore black women's perspectives on "the African-American image in music," she expressed her belief that "masculine and feminine principles" were "interdependent."[72] Yet, even as she further articulated a concept of black womanhood rooted in heterosexual love relationships, Lincoln argued that black music offered insight into the specifics of the marginal position of African American women in society and could be a site for black women's activism.

Lincoln was sanguine about the limitations of music as a site for social struggle. She realized she was not on the front lines of the black freedom movement, but she did think her music could play an affirmative role. "We try to portray in our music, something that gives our people an incentive to go on and to persevere," she had declared in her 1965 interview with Canadian television.[73] At the New School panel, Lincoln described the role that the "black female singer-artist" might play in society and gave specific readings of songs associated with Billie Holiday, Bessie Smith, and Mahalia Jackson. In discussing these vocalists, Lincoln critiqued and affirmed her own position as a jazz interpreter of popular songs as well. She also provided a nuanced reading of the politics of black female vocal art that anticipated the work of feminist scholars such as Hazel Carby and Angela Davis, who have explored in their own work the subtle and sometimes contradictory politics of singers like Smith and Holiday.

Lincoln placed African American women vocalists at the center of "contemporary" black music, contending that they had become "symbol[s] of depth, vitality, strength, and sincerity" for a global audience. Lincoln saw blues singer Bessie Smith as a "trailblazer," whose "Gimme a Pigfoot and a Bottle of Beer" described "the fight to keep body and soul together in a white and hostile society." Smith sang about the social dislocation facing her people in "Black Mountain Blues" and criticized political corruption and the gulf between the haves and have-nots in "Poor Man Blues." Mahalia Jackson was "a monument to black feminine virtue and morality." Lincoln called attention to Jackson's rendition of Ellington's "Come Sunday," which Lincoln herself had performed on *Abbey Is Blue.* Lincoln discussed several compositions Billie Holiday had purportedly written. Calling her a poet, Lincoln described how Holiday's lyrics provided social commentary. "God Bless the Child" spoke of the "importance of economic independence," while "Strange Fruit" was an obvious critique of lynching. Holiday's music also offered insight into relationships between black men and women. "Don't Explain," which Lincoln included on *That's Him,* "told of the glorious and enduring love black women have for their men."[74]

Lincoln's treatment of Holiday's lyrics was more charitable here than some of her comments in the press had been. If Holiday and other singers presented imperfect representations of black men, Lincoln suggested, it was because the black woman vocalist was a "realist": "The man she sings of is a flesh and blood man, a man with positive and negative aspects, of a give and take relationship, of responsibilities to that relationship and of the resulting rewards. She has not demanded that he be the 'ideal man.' Recognizing her own human frailties, she candidly acknowledges his, and loves him none the less for all that." Black women vocalists were able to fulfill this role even when working within the popular song genre. Lincoln castigated the writers of two songs she recorded on *That's Him* for their racist representations of black men. Both Gershwin's "Porgy" (she noted that Porgy was a "cripple") and Harold Arlen's "Happiness Is a Thing Called Joe" (she suggested that the reference to a man as a "thing" was intentional) were products of a "hostile, racist-oriented white poet [who] could find no excellence or worth to portray in the black man." In spite of the limitations of this material, black women vocalists successfully rewrote white male-authored texts. They affirmed black heterosexual relationships through their interpretations of songs within the popular genre; and, in addition, the strength of black women's feelings about their men influenced the pop songs of a racist society. "Still there was always that certain something that had to be conceded, and that was that the 'Negro' woman loved her man . . . that he was the source of her fulfillment and happiness."[75]

Again, Lincoln's cultural politics were invested in the redemption of black men; but when she described the "functional" role that the "black female singer-artist" might play in society, she did so with an eye toward the specific ways black women were positioned in society. The vocalist is a "sophisticated woman" who "has been a secretary, a record keeper, a positive catalyst." She has come into political consciousness through the "school of hard knocks," recorded in her lyrics the exigencies of life in a racist society, and passed along this information to other women. Her songs ultimately provide "equipment for living," serving as "preparations for what to expect in the business of living in the U.S.A."[76]

The concerns Lincoln articulated in her New School presentation were consistent with those she had expressed for several years as a self-proclaimed "jazz singer." By discussing songs she herself had recorded, Lincoln made sense of her own musical past and described the role that she could play in the political moment. Her comments also provide a snapshot of the convergence of several trajectories of thought. They reflected the challenges she faced as a socially committed vocalist and resonated with other black female activists' concerns about gender relations and representations of black womanhood. Lincoln sought to present the "black female singer-artist" as someone who could call attention to inequality and racism in society, express a cultural politics based on pleasure and community building, and comment favorably on black heterosexual relationships. The critique of "Porgy" and "Happiness Is a Thing Called Joe" reaffirmed her rejection of material she had recorded in the late 1950s, even though its celebration of black heterosexual relationships clearly held some meaning for her at that time. Yet, if she was to validate a functional role for black female vocal artistry in general, she must also come to terms with the ideological contradictions in much of the lyrical material that black women vocalists chose to (or were asked to) perform. She lent more importance to lyrics written by African Americans that provided some measure of social commentary, but she left open the possibility for meaningful expression through the established repertoire of popular songs. She defined a tradition of vocal cultural politics based on explicit critique as well as innuendo. Therefore, Lincoln located an affirmation of black women's love for their men even in the songs she considered "racist," and she found something of value in the portrayals of "positive and negative aspects" of black manhood in the songs of Billie Holiday. She continued to advocate favorable representations and affirmations of black manhood, yet her participation in the discussion and her description of black women as a "symbol of depth, vitality, strength, and sincerity" also suggests her linked and growing concern that African American women be viewed positively in a negative climate.

The following year, Lincoln made a much stronger statement about the image of black women. In an essay entitled "Who Will Revere the Black Woman?" published in *Negro Digest,* Lincoln spoke to black men in uncompromising terms about negative representations of black women in a culture swept up in the debate over the supposed black matriarchy. She began by talking about the resilience of black men *and* women in a racist American society. She then expressed her dismay and anger that black men not only had "belittled" black women's appearances and pursued relationships with white women but also had cast black women as "domineering" and "evil" and blamed them for their own predicaments. Lincoln criticized both the discourse of black matriarchy and its official sanction through the Moynihan report, while expressing feelings of betrayal over black men's perceived failure to reciprocate respect. "Then, to add guilt to insult and injury, she (the Black woman) stands accused as the emasculator of the only thing she has ever cared for, her Black man. She is the scapegoat for what white America has made of the 'Negro Personality.'"[77]

If black women were "evil," Lincoln argued, then that perspective should be understood as a healthy reaction to their predicament in society and the backlash against them by black men. She wrote: "We 'black, evil, ugly' women are a perfect and accurate reflection of you 'black, evil, ugly men.'" Ultimately, her essay held out an olive branch for reconciliation. "Let it further be understood," she wrote, "that when we refer to you we mean, ultimately, us. For you are us, and vice versa." Pointing out that, matriarchy myths to the contrary, black women faced economic and sexual exploitation, Lincoln closed with a series of questions asking that someone take action:

> Who will revere the Black woman? Who will keep our neighborhoods safe for Black innocent womanhood? Black womanhood is outraged and humiliated. Black womanhood cries for dignity and restitution and salvation. Black womanhood wants and needs protection, and keeping, and holding. Who will assuage her indignation? Who will keep her precious and pure? Who will glorify and proclaim her beautiful image? To whom will she cry rape?[78]

Lincoln's charged response to the hostility being directed toward black women in the mid-1960s was an important document in a womanist trajectory of black feminist thought as outlined by Collins. Although more concerned about the specific oppression of black women than she had been in earlier comments, Lincoln was still invested in the mutual liberation of black women and black men and in the binding ties of black families.[79] We may understand this as yet another articulation of her multilayered search for dignity—one she first began to voice publicly in her transition from supper club singer and one that had been conditioned by her experience in the music industry as well as by the social and ideological context in which she had been living.

## Coda

For the next several years, Lincoln continued to perform as a singer. In 1968 she was featured in the romantic comedy film *For the Love of Ivy,* opposite Sidney Poitier. Thereafter, her life took a brief downward turn. She never received the regular work in film she hoped would material-ize, and she separated from Roach in 1969, divorcing in 1970. After the breakup, Lincoln checked herself into an upstate New York psychiatric institution for five weeks. Yet, separating from Roach also led to what Farah Jasmine Griffin describes as the third stage in Lincoln's musical journey, during which she took greater control of her career and moved away from nationalist politics and romantic concerns, increasingly defining her repertoire with songs of personal affirmation and spiritual quest.[80]

In 1972 she told *Jet* that she was now at peace with herself and that she still remained close to Roach. She also described how she had adopted a more universal political perspective and harbored less anger over inter-racial relationships. "I'm tired of cutting off parts of myself," she said. "I know I'm everybody. This humanism has been coming for a long time. At one time, I couldn't see beyond Blackness. But that was a phase I had to go through—we all have to pass through." In 1973 she recorded the album *People in Me* in Tokyo, with a group of Miles Davis's sidemen. On this album of original compositions, some of which she had written quite a bit earlier, she continued her project of performing socially rele-vant music. "Africa" invoked the continent as an Edenlike homeland, while "Naturally" urged women to ignore socially constructed standards of appearance and find beauty in their "natural" appearances. The title track expressed the humanism she described to *Jet,* as it described soli-darity across ethnic and national divides.[81]

For the rest of the 1970s, Lincoln was largely absent from the jazz world. In 1973 she moved to California to care for her ailing mother and stayed for several years, teaching drama at California State University at North-ridge and performing community work. With the support of Miriam Makeba, she went to Africa in 1975, where she was given the name "Am-inata" by Guinean president Sékou Touré and "Moseka" by the Zairean minister of information. Performing as both Abbey Lincoln and Ami-nata Moseka, she returned to the stage in 1979, which coincided with the delayed release of *People in Me.* Over the next several years, as the fortunes of the jazz industry improved, Lincoln resumed her recording career, continuing to provide social commentary in her original compositions on her 1983 release *Talking to the Sun* and resuming her engagement with the legacy of Billie Holiday with her two-volume 1987 tribute to the singer. In 1988 she signed with Verve records and during the 1990s reestablished herself as a major figure in jazz singing.[82]

Lincoln's aesthetic transformations in the late 1950s and 1960s provided important and interesting commentary on the genre of jazz singing and the challenges presented to female practitioners of this art form. In addition to her contributions to jazz history as a vocalist, Lincoln, like Mingus, remains significant for bringing broader social concerns to bear on an understanding of jazz during the era of the civil rights movement. Both alone and in cooperation with Roach and other socially oriented musicians, Lincoln called attention to African American issues within and outside the sites of jazz performance. She was instrumental in the early 1960s in fashioning the artist-activist persona that many musicians would try to build upon in later years. Her public comments about jazz singing reflect her negotiation of a constellation of politics, aesthetics, economic and social relationships, and racial and gendered ideas about artistry. This array of ideas and relationships structured the culture of the jazz community of the late 1950s and early 1960s and was also a refraction of ideas and social structures that permeated African American life and culture.

# Practicing "Creative Music"

## The Black Arts Imperative in the Jazz Community

**ON DECEMBER 29, 1965,** a group of commentators gathered at St. Paul the Apostle School in New York to debate the relationship between "jazz and revolutionary black nationalism."[1] Participating in this roundtable discussion were tenor saxophonist and playwright Archie Shepp; pianist Steve Kuhn; longtime *Down Beat* jazz critic Nat Hentoff; poet, playwright, and cultural critic Amiri Baraka (then known as LeRoi Jones); Newport Jazz Festival impresario George Wein; history graduate student and jazz columnist Frank Kofsky; Yale professor Robert Farris Thompson; and Father Norman J. O'Connor, who served as moderator.

The conversation was both humorous and combative, much of it focusing on the definition of terms and the question of the efficacy of black nationalist philosophy in creating social transformations in the United States. When the participants turned their attention to music, the discussion illustrated the extent to which new styles in jazz—commonly described as "free jazz," "the new thing," or "the avant-garde"—had been inscribed with political and racial meanings and just how contentious these associations had become. Many viewed the new music both as an expression of the increasingly militant black freedom struggle and as a reaction to the music industry's continuing mistreatment of African American artists. While some of the white participants on the panel expressed distinct displeasure that jazz had become loaded with such connotations, other white speakers embraced the "revolutionary" implications of the avant-garde and were quick to voice their own criticisms of industry practices. The gender composition of the panel demonstrated that this public aesthetic and political discourse about jazz continued to be primarily a masculine one. Most significant, however, the panel discussion offered evidence of an important dialogue within the musicians' community, and between African American musicians and other black intellectuals, over the meaning and function of jazz in the creation of a liberatory black aesthetic—evidence that can be seen most clearly in the comments of the panel's two African Americans, Shepp and Baraka.

This chapter examines how a Black Arts imperative—what Larry Neal described as a duty to "speak to the spiritual and cultural needs of black people"—developed in the jazz community during the 1960s and 1970s.[2] This discussion builds upon recent scholarship that explores the conversations, artistic collaborations, and mutual aesthetic and political concerns of musicians and members of the better-known Black Arts movements in literature and theater.[3] By no means did all musicians from this era—not even all members of the avant-garde—seek to align their music with a deeper political purpose, but different individuals and groups of musicians tried in various ways to make their music relevant. The Black Arts movement in the jazz community was not a cohesive ideological or aesthetic program; rather, it was a diverse and often contradictory complex of words, deeds, and music.

This chapter also explores how activist musicians' search for a functional aesthetic was intertwined with the challenge of making a living during a period of tremendous institutional change and ideological and aesthetic debate in the jazz community. To chart this history, it is necessary to link musicians' aesthetic philosophies, considerations of jazz history, and visions for the future to their anxieties over economic displacement, new technologies, and shifting institutional relationships. This complex of words, deeds, and music indeed must be understood in relation to the processes of deinstitutionalization and reinstitutionalization in the jazz world during the 1960s and 1970s. The years of the early and mid-1960s were a period of crisis in the jazz community, and not only because of the musical and political challenges its members faced. Music education networks disintegrated, and performance opportunities in African American communities and other urban areas became scarcer, as nascent deindustrialization, urban renewal programs, discriminatory housing loan policies, highway construction, and other factors led to the degeneration of urban infrastructures and encouraged middle-class flight to the suburbs. To make matters worse, after postwar jazz had reached an apex of popularity and profitability in the early 1960s, growing competition from other media and music ushered in a period of decline in the jazz business, as the music industry increasingly directed its resources to more "popular" forms such as rock and roll and soul.

Some musicians responded to this crisis by forming alternative institutions through which they addressed their concerns and developed ideas about black music, politics, and the responsibilities of artists to their communities. Musicians also allied themselves with other organizations. During the late 1960s and the 1970s, local, state, and federal governments, academic institutions, and corporations acknowledged black activism and political struggle and began to provide a limited amount of institutional support for African American intellectual and cultural work, including jazz. This chapter pays particular attention to jazz collectives (with a focus on the Collective Black Artists in New York) in which the Black Arts imperative was articulated in distinct ways. As musicians participated in such collective organizations and other institutions, they developed new ideas about the jazz tradition and new identities as activists, intellectuals, and artists.

## Defining Black Music, Searching for Relevance

In his comments at the 1965 roundtable, Amiri Baraka expressed a biological and ontological conception of blackness that drew upon a Négritude philosophy and the work of Martinican psychologist and revolutionary Frantz Fanon.[4] Baraka claimed the existence of a unitary people, culture, and race, whose ideas were products of their physical selves. He asserted that there was a "distinct black understanding of the world, black interpretation of the world, black definition of the world." "It goes back to the body," he argued, "your organs hanging in that black space have a life of their own, and they predict your attitudes and predict your life." Baraka envisioned cultural nationalism as an attitude and an emotional concept that would eventually determine the way the world operates. He invoked Fanon as he claimed this ideology would bring about "a new species, a new sensibility, a new attitude." And avant-garde jazz, in Baraka's mind, was an expression of this spirit and life force, which transcended the material conditions under which it was performed.[5]

Baraka would explore his cultural nationalist claims further in his 1966 essay "The Changing Same (R&B and New Black Music)," in which he again theorized the place of music in African American communities and consciousness. He described black music's central role in the formation of black identities and professed its liberatory function at the level of intellect, spirituality, and the racial body. Baraka presented the "new music" of the 1960s as an extension of African culture and spirituality and as a cultural arm of the black liberation struggle, a force that would achieve its ends through transcendence rather than polemics. Black music held the key to psychic and physical liberation by maintaining a connection to black communities and avoiding appropriation by the mainstream. Baraka juxtaposed the spirit and expression of rhythm and blues and "new black music" with mass-marketed popular music such as rock and roll, "whitened" rhythm and blues, and the commercial jazz of the 1950s. Given Baraka's masculinist focus at this time, it is not surprising that the worst offenders in his eyes were female crossover stars such as Leslie Uggams and Dionne Warwick, whose work represented black music getting "whiter," and various white "minstrels," including the Beatles, whom he described as "Myddle-class white boys who need a haircut and male hormones." Even if the work of the avant-garde did not have popular appeal, these musicians remained "authentic" black artists, whose creative output paralleled, in Baraka's words, "the emergence also of the new people, the Black people conscious of all their strength, in a unified portrait of strength, beauty and contemplation."[6]

By venerating the musical, intellectual, and spiritual visions of avant-garde players and placing them at the forefront of black consciousness-raising, Baraka's essay is emblematic of how some intellectuals from the Black Arts movement updated a New Negro conversation about the spiritual and political possibilities of black music in the political context of the 1960s. As Lorenzo Thomas argues, jazz, as "an extraordinary edifice of intellectualism balanced on the working-class eloquence of the blues," was a "perfect vehicle" for young, politicized writers to explore their "social reality." Jazz served as a means of forging black identities and programmatic visions for the arts. It was commonly figured as the source of a core, African-based—and usually masculinist—black culture and spirituality that could withstand the ravages of Western material and epistemic bondage to serve as a nurturing life spring for black liberation. In the literary imagination, musicians were often cast in the role of griots, whose duty was, in Thomas's words, the "moral regeneration of African

American people." Indeed, homages to figures such as John Coltrane and Charlie Parker abound in the prose and poetry of the Black Arts movement, as do attempts to infuse writing with syncopated rhythms, tonal coloring, and an ethos of improvisation.[7]

Baraka's ideas at this juncture differed from his earlier and later thinking about black music. They represented a significant shift from his 1963 book *Blues People,* in which he grounded his treatment of music in a class analysis and a materialist conception of history. They also differed from his writings of the 1970s and 1980s, which employed a more explicitly Marxist framework. At the time of the roundtable, Baraka had recently left the interracial arts scene in Greenwich Village to move to Harlem, where he helped found the Black Arts Repertory Theater/School in 1964. In 1966 he moved to Newark, where he founded Spirit House. By theorizing the role of music in spiritual liberation and by eschewing its role as "protest," Baraka validated a separatist cultural nationalism that rejected white society and, at least temporarily, historical materialism. But it is important to keep in mind, as Thomas also makes clear, that Baraka's militant attitudes and aesthetic ideals were formed in dialogue with musicians, in Greenwich Village and elsewhere, who were simultaneously trying to fuse art and politics. These relationships were reciprocal, as the artistic projects and theoretical visions of their contemporaries in other intellectual circles influenced musicians themselves.

During the late 1950s and early 1960s, prominent black musicians challenged aesthetic and ideological convention in the jazz world and elsewhere, while explicitly and implicitly linking new developments in the music to changes in society.[8] Abbey Lincoln, Charles Mingus, and Max Roach accelerated a long-standing critique of economic inequalities in the music industry and began to challenge the institution of jazz criticism more vociferously. These artists increasingly linked their own experiences in the industry to larger social issues and performed politically explicit material. For many musicians, activist orientations coincided with an internationalist perspective, which had been evident during the 1940s and early 1950s but became more pronounced in the late 1950s and early 1960s in the context of anticolonial struggles and the invention of the "Third World." John Coltrane, for example, made efforts to incorporate "Eastern" melodic elements in his music; Lincoln, Roach, and Randy Weston used African rhythms and explicit references to African political and cultural issues in their composition titles and song lyrics. Moreover, musicians such as Coltrane, Miles Davis, Cecil Taylor, Ornette Coleman, and Eric Dolphy built upon the earlier experiments of Mingus, Monk, and others, reorienting sound and perception by breaking down the structures of established compositional forms and questioning familiar notions of harmony, rhythm, and tonality.

The public comments of members of the so-called avant-garde suggest concerns and orientations that in some ways paralleled and may have helped to shape Baraka's ideas. In the liner notes for his 1959 album *Change of the Century,* Ornette Coleman articulated the concept of "free jazz." "Perhaps the most important new element in our music," he said, "is our conception of *free* group improvisation." Coleman recognized that group improvisation was "nothing new," but he thought his work was significant because it was free of the creative limitations imposed by the jazz idiom. Referring to the album's title track, Coleman linked his project to that of the beboppers and claimed the right "to incorporate more musical materials and theoretical ideas—from the classical world, as well as jazz and folk—into our work to create a broader base for the new music we are creating." He emphasized the emotional and intellectual inspiration behind his music as well as the collaborative spirit that fueled his group's performances.[9]

Of fundamental importance to understanding the ideological dimensions of avant-garde jazz is the spiritual purpose that some musicians ascribed to their work. When musicians such as Coltrane discussed their music, they often lent sacred and transcendental meaning to it and elevated its purpose beyond entertainment or polemics. Even before he recorded albums such as *A Love Supreme* (1964), *Ascension* (1965), and *Om* (1965), Coltrane spoke of the avant-garde musician's role in communicating knowledge, experience, and a sense of human connection. In a 1962 interview, he explained what he was trying to accomplish:

> It's more than beauty that I feel in music—that I think musicians feel in music. What we know we feel we'd like to convey to the listener. We hope that this can be shared by all. I think, basically, that's about what it is we're trying to do. . . . I think the main thing a musician would like to do is to give a picture to the listener of the many wonderful things he knows of and senses in the universe. That's what music is to me—it's just another way of saying this is a big, beautiful universe we live in, that's been given to us, and here's an example of just how

magnificent and encompassing it is. That's what I would like to do. I think that's one of the greatest things you can do in life, and we all try to do it in some way. The musician's is through his music.

Eric Dolphy voiced similar thoughts in the same interview: "Music is a reflection of everything. And it's universal. Like, you can hear somebody across the world, another country. You don't even know them, but they're in your back yard, you know?"[10]

Coltrane was usually loath to have his music characterized as a distinctly political expression, and he generally embraced a universalist rather than a black nationalist orientation.[11] Yet his personal approach to art and communication lent itself to interpretations that avant-garde music was a product of an alternative, antimaterialist black epistemology and a means of constituting black identities. Similarly, Coleman's rejection of the restrictive elements of jazz (particularly the escape from European harmonic conventions) could easily be read as a rejection of the limitations imposed on black people by white society. The universalist approach to art expressed by Coltrane and Dolphy, however, still presented a challenge to those who wished to limit the meaning and function of this music to an African American context, just as Coleman's demand that musicians have the freedom to incorporate classical and folk elements was potentially at odds with a black aesthetic.

There were other potential contradictions as well. Politically oriented musicians and commentators alike were increasingly aware that avant-garde jazz was not a music that appealed to a mass black audience. We may read Baraka's "The Changing Same" as an attempt to reconcile disparities in musical styles and audience tastes. He was invested in proving the authenticity and relevance of a jazz avant-garde that had limited popularity with black audiences. Taking a "Platonic" approach to black cultural identity, he saw different musical "projections" of core cultural "forms" (that is, the blues as a "central body of cultural experience") as historically contingent upon variances in experience and degrees of ideological and material interference from white America. Acknowledging that the "form content" of avant-garde jazz differed from "what the cat on the block digs," Baraka claimed the discrepancy was not so much a distance from blackness but a difference in "consciousness." Whereas rhythm and blues musicians were more emotionally expressive, members of the avant-garde were more self-conscious; and through self-consciousness, their spiritual inclinations allowed them to transcend pure emotionalism and move to a more "complete existence."[12]

Baraka's aesthetic taxonomy may well have reflected his own anxiety over the relevance of the Black Arts movement to the African American working class, his celebration of the "self-consciousness" of the avant-garde a validation of the role of creative intellectuals in black liberation struggles. As Phillip Brian Harper observes, one of the objectives and challenges of Black Arts nationalism was to "negotiate" social divisions in the black population. Harper claims that many of the movement's artists and intellectuals operated in fear of being perceived as alienated from the masses. Poets' antiwhite rhetoric and their use of the second person, he argues, were often a strategy to have their work "heard" by whites and "overheard" by blacks, as they tried to impress other African Americans with their own righteousness.[13] By theorizing rhythm and blues and "new music" as different reflections of a core black culture, Baraka defined heady, self-consciously avant-garde expression as a socially relevant art form that was consistent with the spiritual and communal needs, if not the tastes, of a black popular audience.

Given Thomas's observation that Baraka was influenced by his musical contemporaries, it is evident that "The Changing Same" also reflects concerns particular to the lives of professional musicians. Embedded in Baraka's comments, especially those that touch upon the authenticity of the avant-garde, were musicians' own anxieties about reaching a black audience and making sense of their role in black liberation struggles. This scenario was complicated by the need to survive in the jazz community. By the middle of the 1960s, politicized musicians were contemplating black nationalist thought at a time when the limitations of the civil rights movement in confronting institutionalized racism and economic problems were increasingly clear. They also had to contend with the growing popularity of rock and roll and soul music and the disappearance of jazz performance spaces. Not only was the avant-garde's appeal to the black community tenuous, but jazz as a whole risked losing favor with audiences of all hues. With increasing frequency in the 1960s, musicians tried to rise to the artistic challenge of the avant-garde, theorize their own duty to their communities, understand the broader creative aspects of their projects, and grapple with the reality of surviving as professional musicians.

Some musicians' responses to the moment were consistent with the separatist vision that Baraka offered. In a 1965 interview with Larry Neal, drummer Milford Graves viewed exploitative economic conditions in the jazz industry and musical conventions as part of the same dominant social structure. Graves argued that Western artistic practices were fundamentally alienating, as the artist was spiritually and emotionally distanced from his or her work. He was particularly troubled by the concept that one must have "mastery" over one's art. Graves blamed white control of the music industry for the lack of mass black interest in the new music, and he argued that the short-lived Jazz Composers Guild—an interracial free jazz organization established by Bill Dixon following the successful October Revolution in Jazz concerts—should have been an all-black organization. The Black Arts Repertory Theater/School was a better site for musicians' activism, he believed, because of the links to the community that could be forged there. "The Black musician," Graves said, "must withdraw from the Western concept and economic thing, must join together . . . and realize the truth in the music . . . must not segregate against this music the way Western society segregates against us."[14]

In a January 1967 article for *Liberator,* Graves and pianist Don Pullen linked black intellectual, cultural, and economic self-reliance, as they discussed what they termed "New Afro-American Cultural Revolutionary" (NAACR) music and art.

> The first Black men were not slaves to the thought of Europeans, but were men who possessed great wisdom and mental-physical power. They produced from their own natural mental-physical energy and power. Self-reliance—Black revolutionary thought—is a recovery, a re-emergence of this energy and power. It is a confidence in the Black mind and wisdom which does not have to meet the approval or sanction of the West. It is the rediscovery of the natural self. The New Afro-American Cultural Revolutionary music and art can not be predetermined by Western laws of thought as to what is and what shall be. The NAACR music possesses the power and energy to motivate and to stimulate Black thought to search for its own true nature, to put its mind to work. This re-awakening of Black thought is music—a music free of Western tradition, a music so powerful that only a glimpse of its potential has been realized.

Graves and Pullen called for a "self-reliance program," emphasizing that one of the major mistakes artists had made was to forsake the production end of music. Taking a cue perhaps from Charles Mingus Enterprises, they announced the recent release of a self-produced album, *Don Pullen, Milford Graves in Concert at Yale University*, which was available only by mail order. They called for abandoning "Western thought" as a means of understanding black music and advocated creating new instruments and recording techniques that would do a better job of facilitating black self-knowledge than existing technologies, which were products of white society.[15]

Even at this moment, when much of the cultural nationalist discourse collapsed the differences within African American communities and emphasized the separation between black and white society, other politically oriented musicians nevertheless attempted to balance a belief in black self-determination with an aversion to certain aspects of racial categorization and an embrace of the universal purpose with which African American musicians had long associated their music. Avant-garde pianist Cecil Taylor articulated some of these goals in a 1964 *Liberator* interview. Taylor characterized jazz as a product of African American experience that historically served an affirming role in black communities. But he too recognized that modern jazz had lost much of its African American audience. He stressed the need to bring jazz back to black communities, a project he saw as a means to personal fulfillment. "Jazz . . . has been separated from the audience it is most responsive to," he said. "I want to live and keep my work going, I can't live in an ivory tower. I want to make something beautiful." Taylor juxtaposed a black (or spiritual) approach to music with the concern for profit that characterized white society. Like Mingus and Harlem Renaissance aesthetes before him, he characterized black music as an antidote to the materialism of the West: "In my music I am searching for a new truth—a truth beyond the money principle—a truth that will make people treat each other like human beings. America needs what the Negro has for survival." According to Taylor, then, jazz was simultaneously a product of a distinct black experience and spiritual orientation while nonetheless being relevant, and even necessary, to the broader American public.[16]

Archie Shepp was another practitioner of avant-garde music, who by 1965 was one of its most ardent supporters and was also among the most

"Father of the Blues" W. C. Handy in a 1941 portrait by
Carl Van Vechten. (Courtesy of the Library of Congress,
Prints and Photographs Division, Carl Van Vechten
Collection.)

*Above:* Louis Armstrong swings with his band, circa 1937. (Courtesy of the Library of Congress, Prints and Photographs Division, New York World-Telegram and the Sun Newspaper Collection.)

*Opposite, top:* Duke Ellington and NAACP Executive Secretary Walter White pose with a poster for a benefit for the organization, circa 1938. This was one of many benefit concerts that swing-era musicians performed for civil rights and left-wing causes. (Photograph by Morgan and Marvin Smith; courtesy of Monica Smith and the Photographs and Prints Division, Schomburg Center for Research in Black Culture, The New York Public Library, Astor, Lenox, and Tilden Foundations.)

*Opposite, bottom (left to right):* Milt Orent, Mary Lou Williams, Tadd Dameron, and Dizzy Gillespie gathered at Williams's New York apartment, where bebop players often met in 1947 to discuss musical ideas. (Photograph by William P. Gottlieb; courtesy of William P. Gottlieb, Ira and Leonore S. Gershwin Fund Collection, Music Division, Library of Congress.)

Dizzy Gillespie and Charlie Parker performing at Gillespie's Carnegie Hall concert, September 29, 1947. This concert demonstrated that bebop had achieved a certain measure of artistic prestige, that its fans had a great deal of enthusiasm about the music, and that many of its practitioners maintained broad-minded artistic visions. (Photograph by William P. Gottlieb; courtesy of William P. Gottlieb, Ira and Leonore S. Gershwin Fund Collection, Music Division, Library of Congress.)

*Left:* Charles Mingus presents himself as a serious artist in a publicity shot from the 1950s. (Courtesy of the Institute of Jazz Studies, Dana Library, Rutgers University, Newark, New Jersey.)

*Below:* Charles Mingus regarding a 1963 issue of *Jazz* with suspicion. Over the course of his career, Mingus often rejected the term "jazz" as a means of describing his music. (Courtesy of the Photographs and Prints Division, Schomburg Center for Research in Black Culture, The New York Public Library, Astor, Lenox, and Tilden Foundations.)

*Right:* Abbey Lincoln in a publicity shot as she made her transition from supper club singer to jazz artist in the late 1950s. (Courtesy of the Michael Ochs Archives.)

*Below:* Abbey Lincoln singing at a 1963 Harlem Week celebration, one of many instances when she lent her name and time to social causes during the decade. (Photograph by O'Neal L. Abel; courtesy of O'Neal Abel and the Photographs and Prints Division, Schomburg Center for Research in Black Culture, The New York Public Library, Astor, Lenox, and Tilden Foundations.)

Archie Shepp in a publicity photo, circa 1965. (Courtesy of the Schomburg Center for Research in Black Culture, The New York Public Library, Astor, Lenox, and Tilden Foundations.)

Reggie Workman performing at the East Cultural Center
in Brooklyn, New York, in 1976. (Photograph by Sulaiman
Ellison; courtesy of Sulaiman Ellison and the Institute
of Jazz Studies, Rutgers University, Newark, New Jersey.)

*Left:* Yusef Lateef performing at Town Hall in 1980. (Photograph by Sulaiman Ellison; courtesy of Sulaiman Ellison and the Institute of Jazz Studies, Rutgers University, Newark, New Jersey.)

*Below:* Marion Brown in a publicity shot from the late 1960s or early 1970s. (Courtesy of the Institute of Jazz Studies, Rutgers University, Newark, New Jersey.)

Wadada Leo Smith performing with the AACM band, circa 1970.
Smith joined the AACM shortly after arriving in Chicago in 1967
and has built upon its philosophies in his written and performed work.
(Photograph by Diane Allmen; courtesy of the Prints and Photographs
Division, Schomburg Center for Research in Black Culture, The New
York Public Library, Astor, Lenox, and Tilden Foundations.)

Anthony Braxton during a performance at The Kitchen,
New York City, 1978, showcasing his proficiency on multiple
instruments. (Photograph by Sulaiman Ellison; courtesy of
Sulaiman Ellison and the Institute of Jazz Studies, Rutgers
University, Newark, New Jersey.)

Wynton Marsalis at the 1996 Sunrise Jazz Festival.
(Copyright 2001 by Lonnie Timmons III.)

vocal and outspoken critics of the discrimination and economic exploitation facing African American musicians. Shepp had originally gone to New York to work in theater, after graduating from Goddard College. Although he had some success there, he soon turned his focus to music and became a central figure in avant-garde jazz circles. He played with Cecil Taylor's quartet from 1960 to 1962, co-led a quartet with Bill Dixon in 1962 and 1963, and from 1963 to 1964 was a member of the New York Contemporary Five, along with Don Cherry and John Tchicai. During this period, Shepp remained active in Lower East Side intellectual circles, associating with the Umbra literary group and appearing at public forums with Baraka.[17]

At the December 1965 roundtable, Shepp voiced an assessment of black cultural identity and the position of black musicians in American society that differed somewhat from Baraka's view. Shepp warned against romanticized notions of blackness and continued to see the importance of dialogue between blacks and whites. He tried to find a synthesis of the belief in an ontological black cultural nationalism and the recognition that material conditions determined culture and identity. He asserted that a distinct black outlook and intuition were rooted in historical experience and necessity. Whereas Baraka was moving away from this position, Shepp believed that black nationalism represented the historical struggle of black people "to emancipate themselves economically, socially, culturally." Shepp viewed his identity as an artist and intellectual as a product of the historical relationship of African Americans to work. He even invoked W. E. B. Du Bois's *Black Reconstruction* when arguing that cultural difference had an economic basis. And he said that when he played his horn or wrote an article, "it has to do with the cotton crop economy of the South; it's got to do with the *Ballad of John Henry;* it's got to do with what Lightnin' Hopkins sings about." Even jazz as a contemporary expression was constrained by power relationships: "The reason we talk about jazz today is interesting, you know, because that was the only language you allowed us."[18]

Shepp's differences with Baraka and his attempt to reconcile a historical materialist perspective with cultural nationalism reflected a quandary many black intellectuals faced circa 1965. As Larry Neal argued: "Art exists in relation to other social, economic, and political forces, and cannot be separated from them. Here is where Marxism is a proper instrument for analyzing cultural movements. But Marxism fails, and miserably, when it confronts the internal spiritual aspects of art; especially non-Western, which is very spiritual in content and function. Our art exists above examination by Western analytical methods."[19] Yet Shepp's attention to historical materialism also symbolized a fundamental problem facing activist musicians who were trying to chart a functional black aesthetic for themselves and their community: they would have to accomplish their goals while trying to make a living during a period of tremendous flux in the jazz world.

In other conversations that year, Shepp publicly described the conflicting issues raised by avant-garde music, the responsibilities of black musicians, and the economic inequality and discrimination in the jazz community. In a 1965 *Down Beat* profile written by Baraka, Shepp articulated a revolutionary aesthetic philosophy that embraced the jazz avant-garde. Using Cecil Taylor's percussive approach to piano as a referent, Shepp described a collective movement away from the strictures of Western harmony and a reemphasis on rhythm and melody. Rather than a "projection into some weird future," he argued, the new music was a "throwback in the direction of the African influences on the music," which "reaches back to the roots of what jazz was originally. In a way, it's a rebellion against the ultra sophistication of jazz."[20]

Shepp linked this musical revival to the position of black musicians and black people in society. Later that year, in a *Down Beat* essay entitled "An Artist Speaks Bluntly," Shepp described his own experience in nightclubs, referring to them as "the crude stables (clubs) where black men are groomed and paced like thoroughbreds to run till they bleed or else are hacked up outright for Lepage's glue." While the music itself was a black creation, jazz as a construct and commodity was produced by whites. Shepp linked the marketing of music and musicians to the slave trade, oppression in South Africa, and the conditions facing black people in the "vicious, racist social system" of the United States. He articulated an affirming artistic vision grounded in an internationalist, anticolonialist, and Marxist perspective. He asked: "Don't you ever wonder just what my collective rage will—as it surely must—be like, when it is—as it inevitably will be—unleashed? Our vindication will be black as the color of suffering is black, as Fidel is black, as Ho Chi Minh is black." He concluded by stating:

I leave you with this for what it's worth. I am an antifascist artist. My music is functional. I play about the death of me by you. I exult in the life of me in spite of you. I give some of that life to you whenever you listen to me, which right now is never. My music is for the people. If you are a bourgeois, then you must listen to it on my terms. I will not let you misconstrue me. That era is over. If my music doesn't suffice, I will write you a poem, a play. I will say to you in every instance, "Strike the Ghetto. Let my people go."

As he did later at the roundtable, Shepp expressed ideas that were derived from Négritude's focus on black culture as a panacea for the ills facing humanity. He imagined America as an alienating and dehumanizing society that was in need of musicians' liberatory services: "The Negro musician is a reflection of the Negro people as a social and cultural phenomenon. His purpose ought to be to liberate America esthetically and socially from its inhumanity. . . . I think the Negro people through the force of their struggles are the only hope of saving America, the political or the cultural America."[21]

Yet Shepp admitted to Larry Neal the difficulty of reaching African American working people through avant-garde music. "I think it would be very difficult for Cecil or Ornette or myself to just go up to Harlem and expect to be accepted right away—as good as our intentions may be." Like other musicians, Shepp believed that the separation of the "Black artist" from the "Black community" stemmed from "economic reasons." He made an oblique reference to the economic restructuring that moved entertainment venues out of black communities and inspired artists to follow them. Shepp said he was willing to do what it took to reach black people through music. "Even if the artist has to forsake some of his most cherished things—then he must forsake them. If I have to get into rock and roll, somehow, I've got to slide into that, and refer to the people so that they'll know what I mean."[22]

But Shepp also said that the music itself could accomplish only so much. "There are limitations—music has its limitations, especially in *intense* political times. Some people may call them revolutionary times. At times simply to play is not enough; but that's a personal judgment. At times we must do more than play." He advocated a "rational approach" to the circumstances in which musicians found themselves. Although he welcomed celebrations of black identity and culture, he also believed cultural nationalism had confused matters. "The solution of our problems," he argued, "is one that requires and will require a practical, sound political strategy."

> I could advocate more musicians listening to rock and roll . . . I dig Dionne [Warwick] and them . . . but we have to take advantage of a certain overview which we have that others don't have. Other people may have an intuitive working class instinct, but it takes the intelligentsia to give that order and to make it meaningful. So a person like Dionne, who we can see, who we can dig, is where that's at. We can dig what that means, but that's easily misconstrued in 1965. No, we can't settle on that. For that reason, if for no other reason then, the avant-garde musician can't save his message; he must state it. Dionne, her message is groovy; but Cecil can talk, and I can talk, and Dixon can talk. And we have to have musicians who can speak. That is important because things are too easily misconstrued. Things are too easily interpreted if left to the imagination. Art must not be left to the imagination any longer.

Although Shepp was more charitable to Warwick than was Baraka, the juxtaposition of Bill Dixon's, Cecil Taylor's, and his own ability to "talk" with Warwick's "groovy" message suggests that this validation of jazz intellectualism was as masculinist as that of Mingus and others before him.[23]

Shepp's ideas in 1965 represented an important synthesis of existing discourses into a call for action at a politically charged moment. His ability to express such ideas in public, even if he alienated some of the critical establishment, revealed how some African American musicians understood themselves and were positioned by others as oppositional cultural workers in the 1960s.[24] Although Shepp was more polemical than most, he articulated commonly held ideas about the role of black music and the responsibilities of musicians. He also voiced common dilemmas about being a socially committed African American artist. Whereas Baraka easily reconciled differences in black musical styles and audience tastes through his Platonic model of black culture and identity, Shepp and other musicians would find it more of a challenge to come to terms with these discrepancies in practice.

Shepp's 1965 album *Fire Music* is a good example of how difficult it was to synthesize avant-garde aesthetic goals with what he termed a socially responsible and popular music that would be relevant to a wide range of people. In the liner notes for this album, Shepp discussed the desire to create a music that could conform to the tastes of a larger audience without being too "commercial." Interrogating the word "popular," Shepp asserted: "What it really means, after all, . . . is the people. We have to get into their lives which is one way of saying we have to get more and more into our own lives and know who we are so that we can say all that's on our minds."[25]

Shepp expressed this vision through the five tracks of *Fire Music.* The recording included versions of Duke Ellington's ballad "Prelude to a Kiss" and Antonio Carlos Jobim's "The Girl from Ipanema," a version of which—as recorded by Jobim, Stan Getz, and Astrud and João Gilberto—had been a hit single in 1964. Shepp saw "The Girl from Ipanema" as a kind of "pop art." The tune "Hambone," a Shepp original, was inspired by a character on a New York children's television show who was both a mime and a practitioner of "urban folk motifs." Shepp derived the title of "Los Olvidados" (The Forgotten Ones) from a 1950 Luis Buñuel film that was released in the United States as *The Young and the Damned.* Shepp's inspiration for the tune came from his work as a counselor and music teacher with Mobilization for Youth, a government-funded program on the Lower East Side. Finally, "Malcolm, Malcolm—Semper Malcolm" combined music and poetry as a eulogy for the recently assassinated Malcolm X. The composition emphasized Shepp's belief that the "significance of what [Malcolm] was will continue and will grow." Shepp's comments about this piece illustrate how music, politics, and the people were connected in his mind. He intended the composition to speak to the "life and spirit" of Malcolm X, which he connected to the "life and spirit" of all African Americans.[26]

Despite the populist claims that Shepp articulated in the liner notes, the fusion of avant-garde jazz with a popular appeal was difficult to pull off. He confronted the same dilemma faced by poets and playwrights in the Black Arts movement: one could put one's art out there for "the people," but they would not necessarily like it. "Hambone" is a multisectional piece of music with changing time signatures. Although the middle section of the composition is centered on a swinging ostinato bass and a repeated blues figure by the horn players, much of it is based on an urgent riff played over a compound meter (7/4 + 5/4) that disrupts any standard notion of jazz time. "Los Olvidados" shifts tempo several times, and its "harmonic" movement is rooted in distinct tones and melodic figures rather than defined chords. While "Malcolm, Malcolm— Semper Malcolm" has an identifiably political message through its spoken-word embrace of "Malcolm" and "my people," the music itself is dissonant, nonlinear, and impressionistic, with the primary movement supplied by the bass's bowed lines. The piece does not have a set tempo; the drums serve only to punctuate the notes offered by the bass and Shepp's tenor saxophone. "Prelude to a Kiss" is a relatively straightforward rendition of the standard, with Shepp employing a bowed bass and three horns to play the chords and give it lush, Ellingtonian textures. However, the band turns "The Girl from Ipanema" inside out, using changing tempos and the minor sevenths as staging grounds for modulating riffs. Shepp said the composition exemplified the sophisticated use of the minor seventh chord in Brazilian music, which gave him an interesting basis for improvisation. When Shepp does play the melody "straight" or when he improvises alone over the changes, the effect alternates between mockery and kitsch.

This is not to say that the music does not work or that a working-class audience would not understand it. Shepp's blending of diverse musical elements and the spoken word are impressive in their own right, and his arranging provides a strong foundation for his soloists. Yet, as an avant-garde expression of a popular sensibility, there is a great distance between this music, inspired by "the people," and one that would actually reach a mass audience. There was certainly no danger of Shepp's version of "The Girl from Ipanema" becoming a best-selling single. Thus, like many of the works composed by the poets and playwrights of the Black Arts movement, Shepp's version of African American expressive culture was probably "relevant" only to a small audience.

The inability to reach a mass black audience would prove frustrating. Three years later, Shepp expressed displeasure that he sold more records on college campuses than in black communities.[27] *Fire Music* nevertheless served as a blueprint of sorts for an aesthetic vision Shepp returned to on occasion during the late 1960s, one that encompassed avant-garde elements, a repertory impulse, and a populist ethos. On a series of recordings for Impulse! and other labels, he balanced avant-garde instrumentals with Ellington-composed standards and funk and blues tunes. Shepp's 1969 release *For Losers,* for example, goes a step further in reaching "the people." Although the title track is a Shepp original, featuring his modal soloing and collectively improvised passages, the album also features fairly straightforward versions of Duke Ellington's "I Got It Bad" and Cal Massey's "What Would It Be Without You." Two additional tracks, "Stick 'em Up" and "Abstract," are solidly, if mechanically, in the funk idiom. The first features Leon Thomas's kinetic vocals, while "Abstract" is an instrumental number with a steady organ and guitar groove, supporting Shepp and trumpeter Jimmy Owens's soloing above.

Albums such as this, whether recorded by Shepp or others, may well have reflected both the desires of record companies that their artists reach a wider audience through more "popular" sounds and the need of musicians to sell more records to support themselves. Yet it is also clear that, for some artists, the exploration of multiple genres was motivated by a desire to balance one's own creative aspirations, a veneration for one's musical predecessors, and the need to reach out to one's community. This vision, difficult as it was to implement effectively, can be understood as a reflection of the Black Arts movement in the jazz community, where making a living went hand in hand with making music relevant.

## Institutionalizing Aesthetic Activism

Shepp called on musicians to do more than create a socially relevant art form. He wanted them to become spokespeople and to engage in practical programs to address issues within and outside the jazz community. Shepp himself participated in the Jazz Composers Guild, although he soon left after Impulse! offered him a recording contract. His work with Mobilization for Youth and a later position with New York City's welfare department were attempts to address broader social issues. Shepp was just one of a growing number of musicians during the 1960s and 1970s who created their own institutions and participated in others, as they sought to make themselves relevant and address the conditions under which they labored.

The compulsion to bring jazz to the black community, to explore its spiritual elements, and to alleviate the economic and social hardships facing musicians was not restricted to musicians associated with the current wave of avant-garde music. Musicians across the ideological, generational, and stylistic spectrum tried in various ways to address these issues. Charles Mingus, who had a vexed relationship with free jazz, proposed the School of Arts, Music, and Gymnastics in 1963, with anticipated funding from Harlem Youth Opportunities Unlimited. Mary Lou Williams, who had challenged jazz convention with her "Zodiac Suite" in the 1940s and her lengthy sacred compositions of the 1960s and 1970s, was hardly a proponent of the "new thing." In 1964 she suggested that free jazz players were "making people sick all over town," and she later equated the avant-garde with "black magic" and "cults." After embracing Catholicism in the 1950s, she established a charitable organization, The Bel Canto Foundation, as a means of helping drug-addicted musicians. In the late 1960s, she began distributing flyers around Harlem that detailed the history of black accomplishment in jazz across stylistic lines. She called on fans to save an art form that was both "born of the suffering of the early American black people" and "the only true American art form." Jazz was also, in her view, "spiritual and healing to the soul."[28]

Musicians participated in various kinds of community-based cultural institutions both to preserve the music for the enjoyment of black people and to solve their own employment problems. Shepp, Marion Brown, and others played in avant-garde concerts put on by Baraka's Black Arts Repertory Theater/School, which gave Harlem audiences a chance to experience the new music and allowed its practitioners an opportunity to reach out to a mass audience. Calvin Strickland, who had been a trumpeter with Benny Carter, told *Liberator* in 1964: "Jazz is an embodiment of the truth, you can't be a good jazz musician unless you know the truth. . . . Older musicians have a duty to the younger ones coming up. Any youngster who is striving to become a jazz musician is my child, and it's my duty to see that he gets it right." Earlier that year, Strickland had undertaken a lecture-concert tour of black colleges and high schools in Louisiana. He also helped to establish Pomusicart, Inc., a New York organization whose primary goal was providing funding for young people to pursue poetry, music, and art. Pianist Billy Taylor helped to found the Harlem Cultural Council in 1964, in order to implement arts programs in black neighborhoods in New York. One of the council's projects was Jazzmobile, which under the direction of Taylor—and with sponsorship from Coca-Cola, Chemical Bank, and Ballantine Beer—brought musicians and a mobile stage to neighborhoods in Harlem, the Bronx, and Brooklyn, beginning in 1965.[29]

African American musicians also responded to these political, aesthetic, and economic challenges by forming several collective musicians' organizations during the 1960s. A few of these musician-run collectives were committed to a free jazz aesthetic, whereas others were founded upon more general principles of artistic expression. Most groups shared varying levels of commitment to black nationalist and utopian visions, economic self-determination and collective business practices, education programs for musicians and community members, and political activism. As Ronald Radano notes, musicians' collectives are rooted in a long history of self-help organizations in African American communities, dating back to antebellum slave culture. Antecedents in the jazz community are found in New Orleans ensembles associated with men's clubs and fraternal organizations and in various instances of collective business practices among jazz groups, including James Reese Europe's Clef Club, some of the "territory" swing bands that worked west of the Mississippi during the 1920s and 1930s, Mingus's Jazz Composers Workshop, Gigi Gryce's attempt to form a collective musicians' publishing organization in the 1950s, and Sun Ra's cultlike, Chicago-based Solar Arkestra (organized in the 1950s).[30]

One of the first collective musicians' organizations to emerge during the 1960s was Los Angeles pianist Horace Tapscott's Union of God's Musicians and Artists Ascension (UGMAA). Tapscott was a product of Los Angeles's music education circles, having studied with Sam Browne at Jefferson High School. Tapscott's first instrument was the trombone, which he played in a school band with Don Cherry and Eric Dolphy. Tapscott was a member of the U.S. Air Force from 1953 to 1957, where he learned to play piano. (Eventually this instrument would become his primary means of expression after he suffered injuries in an automobile accident.) He played trombone for a few years in Lionel Hampton's orchestra, but he was dissatisfied with life on the road. Returning to Los Angeles, he devoted himself to aesthetic activism and musical preservation. Along with trombonist Lester Robinson and pianist Linda Hill, Tapscott founded the Underground Musicians Union in 1961.

This organization, which later became the UGMAA, was organized around spiritual principles and dedicated to community education and the preservation of black music and culture. One of the group's primary goals was to channel the energies of Los Angeles youth into activities that would benefit the community, principally through playing music. The organization performed in local community venues as the Pan Afrikan People's Arkestra. They attempted to bring peace to their neighborhood during the 1965 Watts riots, performing outdoor shows on a flatbed truck. The UGMAA also responded to the lack of opportunities for both aspiring and established musicians who were trying to perform avant-garde jazz in the local club scene. Thus they linked the idea of preserving black culture to the desire to find work.[31]

Emergent collective organizations in other cities during the 1960s included the Black Artists Group in St. Louis and the Detroit Creative Musicians' Association. The best-known group was Chicago's Association for the Advancement of Creative Musicians (AACM), which was established in 1965. Early members of this organization included pianist Muhal Richard Abrams, members of the Art Ensemble of Chicago, and multi-instrumentalists Anthony Braxton and Wadada Leo Smith. The AACM developed out of the collective atmosphere of musical exploration and spiritual orientation that existed in Chicago's jazz community, the declining employment opportunities in Chicago nightclubs in the early 1960s, and the broader political climate. The early history of this organization illustrates how artistic and activist concerns were linked in the activities of a group committed to avant-garde music. Although the AACM was—and still is at the time of this writing—the most successful of the musical collectives from the 1960s, its early history also demonstrates some of the difficulties of putting the Black Arts imperative into practice.

The AACM owed its existence in part to the collaborative, experimental aesthetic orientation established in Chicago by Sun Ra and his Arkestra and also, as Robin D. G. Kelley suggests, to the "black bohemian" artistic and intellectual networks operating in Chicago during the 1950s. More specifically, the organization's roots lay in a rehearsal band established by Muhal Richard Abrams and several others in 1961. This ensemble initially concentrated on music from the hard bop idiom, but by 1963 it had taken the name Experimental Band, with Abrams as its primary visionary influence. The Experimental Band served as a vehicle for creating original music, and it responded to the shortage of opportunities in Chicago's music scene by providing a forum for musical development. The group operated with a distinct musical and philosophical agenda. John Litweiler has described the music of the Experimental Band as falling somewhere between third stream's mix of Western art music and jazz and the complex multisectional and multi-instrumental improvisation that would characterize the work of AACM members in the late 1960s. In addition to influencing the group's musical direction, Abrams, like many jazz educators, promoted a catholic appreciation and understanding of a variety of music and encouraged musicians to educate themselves, explore other art forms, and generally engage in a process of self-discovery.[32]

Abrams and other members of the Experimental Band transformed these visions into an alternative institutional structure with the formation of the AACM in 1965. The idea of a collective organization took off when Abrams met Phil Cohran, a former trumpeter for Sun Ra, in 1964. Abrams and Cohran hoped to achieve creative freedom and autonomy for black musicians through the organization. At first, the group was committed to an ideal of "original music" but was not beholden to any specific style. Groups initially associated with the AACM included Jodie Christian's hard bop quintet, Cohran's "pop-jazz" Artistic Heritage Ensemble, the more avant-garde Experimental Band, and combos led by Joseph Jarman and Roscoe Mitchell. By 1966, however, the AACM had developed a stronger identity as an organization devoted to avant-garde music. Its prominent members, at least, drew upon the theory and performance of improvised African American music as well as the work of various modern European or Euro-American theoreticians (Anton Webern, Joseph Schillinger, Paul Hindemith, and John Cage, for example) in creating collectively improvised music based on various types of melodic, rhythmic, tonal, and organizational ideas. AACM musicians were also encouraged to explore other media and to combine avenues of expression such as dance, theater, poetry, and painting with their music.[33]

The AACM's musical projects were accompanied by ideological and practical programs. The group developed its ideas in dialogue with the successes and failures of the black freedom struggle, currents of black nationalist and Afrocentric thought, and community-based self-help and arts and education programs. Its mission included a commitment to develop an "atmosphere" for communal artistic exploration; to create employment opportunities for musicians and "mutual respect" between artists and industry workers; "to uphold the traditions of elevated cultured musicians handed down from the past"; and to inspire spiritual development and self-respect among musicians. The AACM also aimed to promote the music and maintain ties with Chicago's black community by, among other endeavors, presenting community performances and providing free instruction in theory, technique, and African American music history to youngsters. Although the group would later draw upon government funding, it initially sought to accomplish these goals without such assistance, hoping instead to derive its support from its membership dues and Chicago's black community.[34]

As the Art Ensemble of Chicago's motto, "Great Black Music," suggests, the members of the AACM saw themselves as practitioners and historians, in a sense, of a grand improvisational musical tradition that stretched back to precolonial Africa.[35] Various AACM members articulated different ways one might tap into the roots of the tradition. The organization's use of "little instruments" (bells, rattles, and other types of percussion) attempted to reconnect to a glorious African past, as did the focus on spirituality advocated by some of its members. Joseph Jarman told an interviewer that incorporating dance and theater into performance was a way of reviving African artistic practices, in which musicians were also actors and dancers. Muhal Richard Abrams argued that by moving away from chord progressions, AACM members were able to return to the roots of what later became known as jazz, when artists were playing "original" music rather than interpretations of popular songs. As in earlier attempts to chart a "classical" black musical tradition, the ideal of "Great Black Music" inverted the established hierarchical relationships between racially defined traditions (that is, white or European versus black or African). In the mid- and late 1960s, this ideal was also a response to the economic marginalization of avant-garde music and an attempt to expand its reputation in black communities.[36]

At the core of the enthusiasm for "Great Black Music" was an ideal Ronald Radano terms "aesthetic spiritualism." With roots in African American spirituality, observation of African musical practices, and a "counter-cultural quest for self-expression and spiritual freedom," this doctrine linked musicians' personal development through the practice of improvised music to the political and ideological program of the AACM. Imbuing the AACM music with a transcendent purpose purportedly challenged critical misrepresentation and labeling as irrelevant. It simultaneously provided an implicit critique of the materialist concerns of white society. As a component of an alternative, black epistemology, the spiritual ideal would also enable musicians themselves to transcend a Western mindset and to realize the extent to which they had been compromised by a system of economic exploitation and racist thinking. In early interviews, Roscoe Mitchell and Muhal Richard Abrams viewed vertical harmony as an impediment to spiritual fulfillment and, as such, a manifestation of European domination.[37]

As AACM members tried to put their ideals into musical and social practice, a number of contradictions arose. Not the least of these, as Radano points out, was that the cultural nationalist rejection of Western aesthetic ideals was, in fact, based on Western notions of virtuosity and greatness, just as the group's musical innovations were beholden to European and Euro-American concert music.[38] In addition, universalist as well as nationalist ideals were influential in the group's vision, as sources of both conflict and inspiration.[39] Anthony Braxton, for example, drew from the musical catholicism of Abrams, Jarman, and others; but he found himself in conflict with other members when he insisted on emphasizing Western theory and compositional elements. He later stated that some in the AACM believed he was not sufficiently devoted to African music, suggesting the existence of not only both universalist and nationalist orientations in the minds of AACM members but also a certain arbitrariness about just what constituted "black music" among the members of an organization who self-consciously drew upon multiple musical influences. Moreover, the very notion of a spiritually oriented "Great Black Music" could, in practice, conflict with the evasion of boundaries implicit in certain spiritually based musical projects. Even as Art Ensemble members Joseph Jarman and Lester Bowie embraced the concept of "Great Black Music," they disavowed any prescriptions on music as antithetical to self-discovery.[40]

Such conflicts were played out in the everyday practices of the AACM. According to Leslie Rout Jr., who interviewed some of its members in 1967, the inclusion of one white member, Gordon Emmanuel, created a huge rift in the organization. Some cultural nationalist members, who considered the inclusion of a white member antithetical to the idea that jazz was "our thing," felt compelled to leave the group. Rout also believed that the refusal to take money from government agencies and corporations, in the name of cultural autonomy, was self-defeatist and a bit hypocritical, given that the group continued to rely on predominantly white audiences on college campuses for support. Roscoe Mitchell told Rout that the kind of audience was not important, "so long as they drop their bread." Although such a contradictory position may have been based on the belief that institutional funding sources would impose aesthetic constraints that the college audience would not, it also points to the larger issue of whether the group's avant-garde aesthetic goals were consistent with its community focus. Rout himself saw the AACM's inaccessible music and their reliance on college audiences doing very little to further their goal of imparting knowledge of their cultural heritage to black people. He concluded that, like other black nationalist organizations, the AACM was better at generating self-respect among its members than at creating substantive changes.[41]

Indeed, as Radano suggests, the career goals of some of the more prominent AACM members conflicted with the community orientation and the insistence on autonomy that made up a central part of the group's vision. Although the group maintained its commitment to bringing music to young people in schools and community centers, Chicago's black community ultimately could not adequately support the AACM financially during the late 1960s. Moreover, the community's growing impoverishment made it an increasingly dangerous place to live. Lester Bowie explained the Art Ensemble members' move to France in 1969 as a result of the difficulty they were having making a living in Chicago and the desire to spread their music to a broader and perhaps more appreciative audience. Even Abrams had to balance his AACM duties with work as a sideman in various groups performing in Chicago and on tour; by the mid-1970s, he had moved to New York. In the late 1960s, other prominent members of the group, including Wadada Leo Smith and Anthony Braxton, left Chicago for Europe or the East Coast. The AACM continues to exist today, however; and, after obtaining funds from organizations such as the National Endowment for the Arts (NEA), the group has been able to carry out its activist mission more successfully, namely through its community education program.[42]

## The Collective Black Artists

Turning to musicians' collective activity in New York allows us to see how the Black Arts imperative was put into practice with a greater focus on the employment issues faced by musicians, a less stylistically specific aesthetic vision, and a greater reliance on outside sources of funding. New York finally produced an enduring jazz collective when bassist Reggie Workman and other musicians launched the aptly named Collective Black Artists (CBA) in 1970. The CBA quickly became a focal point for the challenges Shepp and members of the UGMAA and the AACM had articulated earlier. The group operated for several years as a collectively run clearinghouse for support services for musicians, as a vehicle for artists' activism, and as a locus for the production of socially relevant music. The CBA provided transportation, rehearsal space, and booking and management services for its members. It also engaged in outreach programs for musicians and the broader African American community in New York through its newspaper, *Expansions,* as well as through a radio show and a variety of concert and education programs.

At the levels of activism, repertoire, and educational philosophy, the CBA linked the desire to liberate musicians with the desire to liberate black people. The history of the organization illustrates that activist jazz musicians faced some of the same fundamental dilemmas confronted by other black intellectuals during the period. At a time when jazz's popularity with working-class and young black audiences had long been eclipsed by commercial dance music, CBA members were trying to make themselves relevant to "the masses." Members of the group tried to seize radical intellectual identities by defining themselves as defiantly black cultural workers in a politicized era. Yet they also put forth a utopian and universalist vision, hoping that jazz was still relevant to a broader spectrum of humanity. In the end, they developed a collective aesthetic vision—expressed through words, deeds, and musical performance—that fused avant-garde experimentation with an ethos of historical preservation and a repertory exploration of the jazz tradition.

An examination of the CBA's endeavors demonstrates that this vision was bound up in the complex process by which jazz was reinstitutionalized in the late 1960s and 1970s. While musicians were looking inward for solutions to the challenges of the day, they were emboldened by the attention that other black intellectuals were paying to their music as a force in social change and were concomitantly influenced by the ideas of these intellectuals. Moreover, outside institutional support for jazz and avant-garde music gradually became more available. In addition to participating in their own organization's activities, CBA members held positions in colleges and universities and with archives, foundations, and funding agencies. As these musicians created their own institution and were incorporated into others, they were validated in new, yet incomplete, ways as thinkers and activists—and their music and politics reflected this growth.

Reggie Workman points to several factors that encouraged his own involvement with the CBA. Musicians in New York had earlier made several attempts to form alternative institutions by organizing themselves around economic and aesthetic issues. This activism reached critical mass in the mid-1960s; but Workman argues that it began much earlier, and he emphasizes the influence of Gigi Gryce's efforts to start a collectively run publishing firm in the late 1950s. As the jazz market in New York became more precarious in the mid- and late 1960s, some musicians decided to try their luck in Europe, as some of the AACM members in Chicago had done. Others, however, stayed and created organizations that dealt specifically with their concerns as musicians. Workman remembers that in addition to experiencing a "void" in their employment, musicians had difficulty with their "ability to communicate with one another and their audience and, as a matter of fact, to make an audience." Recognizing these problems, Workman and others began to form organizations to address them.[43]

Workman emphasizes the importance of other emergent institutions that encouraged networking, the development of ideas, and, occasionally, employment opportunities. He was influenced by the activities of the Jazz Composers Guild and its offshoot, The Jazz Composer's Orchestra Association, led by Carla Bley and Mike Mantler. Although the guild was short-lived, the orchestra association, whose goal was to provide its participants with "money, facilities, and encouragement," continued to operate into the 1970s, with Workman serving on its board of directors for a time.[44] Workman also remembers The East, a community-based cultural and education center in New York, as a site for musical performance and community activism. Similarly influential was Billy Taylor's work with the Harlem Cultural Council and Jazzmobile. Among

Jazzmobile's early administrators was Chris White, who was a member of the CBA and director of the Institute of Jazz Studies during the late 1960s and early 1970s. Also providing inspiration for Workman were bassist Warren Smith's Composer's Workshop Ensemble and the Jazz Musicians' Association, led by John Lewis and Ron Jefferson, an organization that served as an alternative to the American Federation of Musicians Local 802 in the late 1960s.[45]

Workman himself participated in several musician-run organizations just prior to the formation of the Collective Black Artists. In these activities, we can see more precise precedents for the CBA's activist and aesthetic agenda. Using money he earned from touring with Herbie Mann, Workman, along with his wife, Elaine Workman, and Hart LeRoi Bibbs, started a group called Art Expansions and presented Sunday afternoon "multi-media" concerts in 1967 and 1968 at Olatunji's cultural center on 125th Street in Harlem. Although they renovated the space to make it more "respectable" for a downtown audience, the Workmans and Bibb were primarily interested in reaching Harlem's community. Concerts fused music with theater, poetry, photo exhibits, and fashion shows in an effort to reach the people in the area. An Art Expansions flyer set forth the group's vision: "Our aim is to incorporate the many areas of artistic endeavor and with all people involved, build an artistic repertory which will create needed outlets and develop new incentive. [F]inally, we will place real emphasis on what we (The Black Race) have in *our own culture*." Like members of the AACM, Workman developed an artistic vision that was intended to bring music to the community while viewing other artistic media as a means of extending the project.[46]

Early members of the CBA also participated in the instrument-specific organizations that musicians established in New York during this period. Several members were associated with Bill Lee's Bass Violin Choir, an ensemble Lee founded in 1968 that consisted of a rhythm section, a vocalist, and seven basses. Workman and other bassists started an organization called Professionals Unlimited. Members of this group responded to a variety of issues as they attempted to "better professional and economic development through the collective strength of the organization." The group addressed issues specific to bassists, such as the need to find more efficient ways to transport instruments and amplifiers to and from gigs, as well as concerns relevant to other instrumentalists. The charter of Professionals Unlimited called for the acquisition of a loft space where musicians could practice, teach, and run workshops. The organization also wanted to keep track of job opportunities. Perhaps most important, members of the group hoped to create a common dialogue on subjects pertaining to their music, the expectations of bassists, and economic concerns.[47]

According to Workman, members of Professionals Unlimited and groups organized around other instruments gathered at percussionist Warren Smith's studio on Twenty-first Street and discussed the need for collective professional organizing on a larger scale. Initially, this was an interracial and international dialogue, representing musicians who performed a variety of styles. Eventually, distinct groups followed their own agendas. Some put more emphasis on the production or financial end of the music, whereas others emphasized artistic development. Many of the black artists determined that their needs differed from those of the larger group and decided to organize along racial lines. In addition to economic and logistical concerns, black artists in this circle recognized that members of their community "weren't listening to the jazz." The CBA was born out of the need to address these dilemmas. Some observers claim that the CBA was fueled by antiwhite, separatist ideals. Although the existence of the CBA may have had a divisive impact on the interracial jazz community in New York, Workman stresses that the group was forged in dialogue with white musicians, with an agreement that the members of each group would go into their "own backyard" to address the particular problems they faced.[48]

The CBA's membership consisted of individuals and groups who performed across stylistic and generic boundaries and in different artistic media. The group's decision-making process and its vision rested fundamentally with a revolving group of about ten musicians who sat as the group's executive board, with added input from the general membership. A 1971 brochure boasts of thirty-six "contemporary instrumental groups" as members, as well as additional performers involved in rhythm and blues, pop, African dance and percussion, poetry, theater, fashion, and steel drum music. In addition to bands led by the board members, "contemporary instrumental" members of the group included well-known figures such as Sam Rivers and Archie Shepp. Workman remembers that the musicians on this list were the dues-paying members of the CBA, but he adds that members had different levels of participation. Some attended regular meetings, while others were primarily interested in the CBA as a vehicle for finding work or getting a particular project off the ground. The brochure also listed a number of "supporting groups," who probably did not need the CBA's services but supported its vision on one level or another. Musicians in this category included Lee Morgan, Alice Coltrane, Freddie Hubbard, Sun Ra, and McCoy Tyner.[49]

The CBA and its executive board were staging grounds for dialogues with other organizations. The CBA hosted a conference in April 1972 at the Bedford-Stuyvesant Restoration Corporation. The meeting, which featured panels on problems facing professional musicians, African retentions in African American music, and the ethics (or lack thereof) of the mass media, ended with a call for individual musicians and other organizations to use the CBA as a clearinghouse for collective action.[50] Many of the CBA executive board members were simultaneously involved in other organizations. Bassist Chris White, director of the Institute of Jazz Studies and affiliated with Jazzmobile, also had his own organization, called Rhythm Associates, which brought instrumental instruction into schools throughout New York State. Rhythm Associates established the Muse Jazz Workshop at the Brooklyn Children's Museum under the directorship of tenor saxophonist and clarinetist Bill Barron. Pianist Stanley Cowell was one of the principal forces at Strata-East, a musician-owned independent recording company established in 1971. Trumpeter Jimmy Owens was one of the original members of the CBA and perhaps the artist who had the most impact on the organization's focus on economic development. During his involvement with the CBA, Owens was on the board of directors of George Wein's Jazz Repertory Company, the Newport Jazz Festival advisory board, the Jazz/Folk/Ethnic Music panel of the NEA, and the New York State Council for the Arts music panel. Owens also worked during this period as an artist and repertoire representative for Polydor Records.[51]

Although some women participated in the CBA as part of its general membership, no women served on the group's executive board. The exclusion of women from the board mirrored the historical marginalization of women in the jazz community and the ideas of male musicians about jazz artistry as a sphere of male activity. Moreover, when artistic identities were reconceptualized to include an activist orientation, they may have incorporated some of the masculinist focus of the civil rights and Black Power movements—not to mention the American political mainstream—that generally exalted the role of men in political struggle and imagined political activism as a means of reclaiming masculinity. As was the case in many activist groups, the wives of male members did much of the administrative work, often on a voluntary basis or for whatever low wages the organization could afford. Some women did participate in the group's organizational structure, however. Elaine Workman and other women played a large role in the publication of the CBA's newspaper and used it as an opportunity to voice their own views about community issues. The group eventually hired a Japanese American woman, Cobi Narita, as executive director, although her position appears to have been primarily geared toward fund-raising and administration rather than charting the group's artistic vision.

The CBA's "aims and goals" consisted of a ten-point program (likely inspired by the AACM's mission and perhaps by the Black Panther Party's ten-point platform of 1966) that resonated with many of the goals of other black activists but also illustrated the particular needs and desires of the musicians' community. Recognizing a history of collective organizing among musicians, the CBA claimed that previous efforts had failed because of too narrow a focus on economic issues, without a grasp of "the need to encompass an understanding of politics, community and social development." The CBA saw that its own creative and economic progress was connected to that of the larger black community and that its success also depended upon the personal growth of musicians and an analysis of the conditions they faced in society. The CBA hoped to "enhance and assist in the development of Black Creative Music and Art" and "secure [the music's] destiny" by improving "conditions and communications." This enterprise would be carried out through "publishing, production and managerial techniques," which in turn would lead to the "enhancement and cultural development of the Black community." The CBA emphasized an ethos of brotherhood, self-determination, and personal growth, linking the development of the artist to that of the people and the "well being of our Youth." The CBA would pursue these goals through a variety of musical and extramusical projects intended to benefit musicians and reach out to their community.[52]

The CBA's newspaper, *Expansions,* put forth the group's vision and publicized its activities. Edited at various times by members of the CBA's executive board, Elaine Workman, and Gladstone Yearwood (New York University student, CBA member, and future film scholar), *Expansions* began publication in December 1970 and continued with quarterly or monthly installments in 1971, 1973, and 1975. The CBA used its newspaper to educate and politicize fellow artists and as a vehicle for its members to articulate the group's visions and voice their own ideas about issues of particular concern. The newspaper carried descriptions of union activities and articles on contracts, copyright laws, and "Monies Due the Creative Musician." Early issues of the publication reported on programming decisions at local radio stations and the efforts of Rahsaan Roland Kirk, Archie Shepp, and other members of the New York–based "Jazz and the People's Movement" to protest WLIB-FM's decision to cut back on its jazz programming.[53]

*Expansions* also provided a means of networking with other activists and reaching out to the broader black community in New York through stories of mutual concern. The newspaper expressed the views of CBA members on community and political issues and served as a mouthpiece for other activists. *Expansions* featured poetry by Elaine Workman and others, reviews of books and "Blaxploitation" films, reports on Harlem and Brooklyn community affairs, and features on fashion and black-owned businesses. The newspaper validated group members as activists in their community by juxtaposing stories about the state of affairs in black neighborhoods and the conditions facing musicians. *Expansions* also shows how the CBA's commitment to community activism was linked to a "preservationist" ethos and a historical vision about the development of black music. The CBA sought to educate the readership about a tradition of what it often termed "creative black music" or "classical black music." The newspaper included a series of features on renowned artists such as Leadbelly, Paul Robeson, Bessie Smith, Billie Holiday, Louis Armstrong, and Charlie Parker. These stories venerated black artistry by describing these musicians' achievements in the context of racial and economic oppression and characterizing their work as politicized responses to their experiences.

The doctrines of education, activism, and the historical preservation of a classical yet liberating art form were also found in the CBA's radio program, "The Anthology of Black Classical Music." This half-hour show, which aired on WYNC, was hosted by Bill Barron and written by Genghis Nor. Described as the "radio voice of the CBA," the show primarily consisted of an exploration of African and African American music through interviews and recordings. The program came about after Barron wrote an article in the April 1971 issue of *Expansions* about the need to introduce black programming at WYNC, a public radio station that played mostly classical music. Barron's call to action inspired Nor, who was affiliated with an organization called Strong-Light Productions, to present Barron and the CBA with a proposal for the show. Nor conceptualized "The Anthology of Black Classical Music" as a way for black musicians to put forth their own version of the history of the music. Echoing the gendered politics that shaped many assessments of black artistry, Nor wrote, "Only men who have experienced the problem first hand as both Black men and Black musicians can put real feeling into the presentation of the series." The show, which first aired in October 1972, was designed to present a coherent history of black music that followed a "natural course" from African music through spirituals to avant-garde and "neo-African" musics. Underlying the program was an understanding that jazz was both a classical art music and a folk expression whose history ultimately reflected "the people." Seeking to reconcile both resistant and nurturing elements of the music, Nor described jazz as "bittersweet in temperament, that is, harsh in its description of the white world outside, while at the same time, soft in its visual portrayal of the people inside."[54]

*Expansions,* "The Anthology of Black Classical Music," and other CBA activities were intended to be vehicles for radical nationalist politics and community education. These activities were also designed to receive—and, to some extent, were made possible by—limited amounts of federal and state funding as well as local sources of grant money available to alternative black-run institutions. The preservationist imperative underlying these activities thus became a critical element in validating both black music as an art form worthy of support from governmental institutions and musicians' roles as cultural workers in black communities.

As George Lipsitz has shown, government policies and practices such as highway building programs and discriminatory loan processes augmented collective white privilege and furthered the degradation of urban communities after World War II. In the 1960s, the federal government established a series of urban renewal programs that were intended to revive cities; in effect, however, these programs perpetuated the marginalization of African Americans and helped to shift the U.S. urban economy away from factory production and toward an economy based on producer services. Hoping to encourage corporate investment in cities, for example, the federal government instituted programs that encouraged the construction of luxury housing and centers for the production and display of culture, including symphony halls and art museums.[55]

The process Lipsitz describes contributed to the cultural and financial marginalization of jazz and the social dislocation of many of its African American practitioners. Take the creation of the National Endowment for the Arts. Established in 1965, the NEA provided funding for a variety of arts programs but was heavily oriented toward what was considered "serious" art. It began funding jazz in 1970, but even then the resources made available did not compare to those allocated to other areas. In 1971, for example, the NEA earmarked more than $3.5 million for symphony orchestras, whereas the budget for jazz was about $50,000. Grants ranged from $1,000 to $500,000 for symphonies, whereas those for individuals or organizations in jazz topped out at $1,000. Such hierarchical practices also existed at the state and local levels of government funding and with private foundations and corporations.[56]

The changes in the urban American cultural infrastructure not only created a crisis for musicians, however; it also eventually presented them with some opportunities. Despite the relative lack of resources for jazz as compared to classical music, private and state funding for jazz grew during the 1970s, a period of overall growth for the funding of African American art and culture. The civil rights and Black Power movements had increased the visibility of and veneration for black culture, and various government agencies and corporations responded to conditions in inner cities and the demands of organizations by accommodating cultural activism through funding programs for the arts. Funding for jazz in particular also increased because of concerns, rooted in part in the proliferation of jazz styles (avant-garde, funk, jazz-rock, fusion), that a "jazz tradition" was in danger of being lost.

In addition to lobbying for changes in television and radio programming policies, for example, Jazz and the People's Movement staged a protest at the Guggenheim Foundation in March 1971 because of the foundation's paucity of funding for jazz musicians. A month later, Charles Mingus received a $15,000 fellowship. In the summer of that year, Ortiz Walton, Ishmael Reed, and Albert Dennis prepared a sixty-page report entitled "Ending the Western Established Church of Art: A Report on Cultural Racism." In his book *Music: Black, White, and Blue,* Walton suggests that after the publication of the report, the NEA decided that funding would be set aside to "concentrate on the arts of the 'ghetto.'" Although funding for jazz was minuscule compared to that available to classical musicians, activism on behalf of the jazz community appears to have paid off. The $50,000 jazz budget for 1971 was better than the $5,000 that had been allocated in 1970. By 1976 the amount of the funds available to jazz musicians had grown to more than $670,000, and by 1979 it reached $1 million.[57]

Because such government and corporate intervention stemmed, in part, from fears over urban uprisings and radical activism, it can be seen as diffusing the radical or transformative potential of activist arts groups such as the CBA. By validating black artistry and activism through the distribution of limited funds, however, the grants given by various cultural institutions provided a vehicle by which the CBA could further its aesthetic and political vision and try to survive economically, all the while balancing its own needs with those of its funding sources. Corporate and state policy, then, which contributed to the economic and institutional degradation of black communities through white entitlement programs, also provided limited amounts of economic and institutional capital that would enable musicians to further explore their intellectual and artistic projects within established and alternative institutions.

Although government and philanthropic funding never supplied an adequate means of support for the vast numbers of unemployed and underemployed musicians, it did provide tangible material assistance. By 1970, funding programs offered a limited way for activist musicians to replace the declining means of support in the music industry and black communities and to gain prestige in the process. As musicians formed their own alternative institutions, they often sought support from these programs, which in turn could influence their visions. Throughout this period, New York, as the center of the jazz community, was home to many groups who sought support from various agencies. In January 1975, an organization calling itself the Consortium of Jazz Organizations requested of New York Governor Hugh Carey that its members be included on a newly formed Task Force on the Arts. The primary moving force behind the consortium appears to have been Jazzmobile, although no fewer than twenty-five individuals and groups were listed as members of the organization. The consortium membership crossed racial lines and represented a wide array of aesthetic and ideological visions. The CBA was listed as a consortium member; and several individuals from the CBA executive board, including Jimmy Owens, Christopher White, and Stanley Cowell, represented themselves or other organizations. The consortium justified its request to participate in the task force with the claim that "jazz has contributed significantly to the quality of life for residents of New York State in serving their economic, cultural, and educational needs."[58]

An examination of the CBA's concert and education programs illustrates more precisely how economic self-determination, community outreach, and an aesthetic vision balancing preservation with experimentalism were influenced by changing institutional relationships and financial concerns. Once the CBA secured permanent office space, it offered classes and symposia through its Institute of Education. These programs served both utilitarian and ideological functions. CBA courses were primarily intended for professional musicians, but they were also geared to interested community members.[59] Much of the impetus for these classes came from a desire to provide skills for survival in the music industry, and they gave activist musicians a chance to share their knowledge with their peers. The CBA designed the curriculum to disseminate information that might not be learned in music schools, universities, or the declining informal jazz education networks. Jimmy Owens's course on "Business Aspects of the Music Industry," for example, tried to give musicians the tools to work within the legal and economic structures of the jazz world. Moreover, the existence of the educational program legitimized the group in the eyes of funding institutions. When limited grants were obtained from such organizations, teaching and concert appearances provided additional income for CBA members.

These programs also allowed members to strike a precarious balance between preserving jazz and challenging its conventions. Education programs in particular extolled the grand tradition of creative black music while giving musicians a chance to stretch the limitations of genre and expand their artistic visions. Improvisation classes taught by Stanley Cowell and Robert Williams explored a "unique set of unwritten rules to the creative process" and shared them with community members. Dr. Leonard Goines's "History of the Music Commonly Known As 'Jazz'" was "designed to bring forth to the aspiring professional musician, educator and composer a better understanding of the work and influence of those creative musicians who are living (i.e., Dizzy Gillespie, Max Roach, Thelonious Monk, etc.) as well as those musicians who are deceased (i.e., John Coltrane, Charlie Parker, Art Tatum, etc.)." As Reggie Workman said: "You can always teach a person how to play, but now is the time to educate people to what has gone on historically in an attempt to better the music tomorrow."[60]

Youseff Yancy ran the CBA Electro-Acoustic chamber group and taught a class called "Electro/Acoustical Composition and Notation." Yancy's course explored the use of electronic instruments and sound-manipulating devices such as synthesizers and tape recorders as well as modern Western classical techniques such as twelve-tone composition and serialization, with the assumption that any of these elements could be used in the composition and performance of creative black music. According to Workman, Yancy "devised a method of notation which allows a musician to write notes for Eastern, African, and electronic instruments and unusual sounds, other than traditional Western ones." The course description put a positive spin on electronic technologies that were threatening to many musicians; it argued that such devices could "expand the composer's area of communication through combining personal/visionary creativity with a unique written musical language, whereby each musician can produce a complete transcription of his new ideas."[61]

Many CBA members maintained a firm belief in the spiritual and intellectual demands of what they called "creative music." Bassist Robert Cunningham, for example, in a short essay for a 1973 collection of writings by members of Yusef Lateef's quartet, voiced his deep spiritual connection to the music. He also described the mental acuity and personal integrity that "creative music" demanded, as well as the musician's duty to convey this to his or her listener. "Today's world of music calls for a superb mental tool, a mind which is alert, able to ingest, absorb, retain, recall, synthesize, dissect, evaluate, formulate, regulate, and convey an intelligible execution to the listener. The developing musician has a great need to be thetic and aggressively progressive, doing all that is within his power to continuously improve the state of his physical, mental and spiritual health and strength."[62]

The CBA's education programs facilitated such communication with an audience, while simultaneously presenting music as a vehicle for social transformation. In doing so, the programs allowed musicians to create identities as activist cultural workers who could fulfill their responsibility as black artists while appealing to funding institutions. Jimmy Owens described government institutions as potential allies in CBA activities that involved the economic struggles of musicians. He articulated a vision for the CBA's education program that emphasized empowering musicians as cultural workers and intellectuals who could provide service to the black community as well as the broader society. In a 1974 document supporting a continuation of funding for the CBA's educational programs, Owens stated: "'Jazz' is a music that, unlike other music, contains a large degree of elements that can and do aid the development of human wholeness and self confidence." He continued: "The creative musician learns through this music 'how to think' instead of 'what to think.'" Moreover, the elements important to excellence in musical performance could also be used to help students build motor skills and create a "positive self-concept." Owens went on to suggest that by imparting these lessons into daily life, African American "jazz musicians" could join other intellectuals, educators, and psychologists in improving our "multi-cultural society."[63]

CBA members embarked on a number of different programs in an attempt to reach their community. They conducted workshops at Greenhaven State Prison in upstate New York and presented concerts in New York City jails in an attempt to reach out to incarcerated individuals and assist in their rehabilitation. They supplemented such efforts by donating copies of *Expansions* to various penal institutions in the New York area.[64] The CBA also instituted programs to reach young people. Pursuing these connections through its education program served several interlocking purposes in the CBA's vision. The CBA linked its own development to the health of its members and its community. Like figures from the Black Arts movement and the AACM, members of the CBA seized the opportunity to validate their roles as agents of black liberation by reaching out to young people who occupied a precarious position in urban centers. The focus on black youth was also a means of creating an audience and a future generation of musicians. As an alternative institution operating with outside institutional support, the CBA tried to replace the languishing informal educational networks that had enabled the jazz community to perpetuate itself by disseminating knowledge to young people. In an abridged restatement of its mission, the CBA claimed it was committed to "give particular attention to the exposure and development of our Youth, the continuum of the Creative Artists."[65]

To connect with young people, the CBA put on a series of concerts and lectures in public schools. Among these was a twenty-five-concert program for School District #4 in East Harlem. CBA members brought their own groups to schools to engage students with music and ideas that might generate interest in the idiom. As part of this program, Angeline Butler's ensemble performed a concert that included a discussion of the elements of composition and various styles and influences from Africa, South America, and India. Reggie Workman's group explored "music in the African Continuum" through illustrations of African cultural survivals in contemporary music, the ways language could be incorporated into music, and the role of African-inspired instruments in African American music. The Jimmy Owens Quartet explored emotion and its effect on everyday music, and the Paul Ortiz ensemble examined the history of rhythms and instrumentation in "contemporary Latin music."[66] This concert/lecture series also demonstrates how the CBA collectively maintained a catholic understanding of the musical and linguistic elements that made up the "continuum" of black creative music and employed this vision when they attempted to connect to and transform their community.

The CBA's pursuit of this broad-minded vision is most evident in the concert performances of the CBA Ensemble, an eighteen-piece group that was formed around the time of the organization's inception as its "main performing sector." *Down Beat* magazine described the group as a "lusty and joyous band . . . quite firmly in the Basie and Ellington traditions." However, the ensemble also performed, in the CBA's words, a "widely diversified Black Music—contemporary, traditional, R&B, Calypso, gospel and avant-garde." By forging an expansive concept of a historically imagined black classical music, the group simultaneously explored the "revolutionary" aspects of newer music and legitimized itself as a keeper of a musical tradition that expressed a collective African American social and cultural experience.[67]

The activities of the CBA Ensemble, especially its community concert program, show more precisely how economic and ideological concerns shaped the CBA's aesthetic vision. The CBA said that its ensemble was engaged in a process of "collectivizing, archiving and perpetuating the music of great black composers," an assertion reflecting its classicist and preservationist orientation. Generally, the CBA's book defined a creative music "tradition" by maintaining arrangements of compositions by a variety of artists. The CBA sought to "retain the style and feeling intended by each composer" but also used the pieces for aesthetic and utilitarian purposes by extending them from a small group context to a big band. Concerts featured compositions from the bebop idiom by artists such as Tadd Dameron and J. J. Johnson and gave "greatness" a decidedly current flavor by including the work of artists such as John Coltrane, Archie Shepp, Donald Byrd, and Lee Morgan. Members of the ensemble also wrote themselves into this tradition by featuring their own compositions.[68]

The CBA Ensemble performed tribute concerts to venerable bandleaders such as Duke Ellington and Lionel Hampton as well as to more contemporary players such as Coltrane, Shepp, and Randy Weston. Some of these tributes were undertaken to celebrate the work of artists who were deceased or otherwise in absentia, whereas other performances were collaborative affairs during which the featured artist shared the stage with the CBA. On these latter occasions, members of the CBA Ensemble often contributed their own arrangements of the guest artist's music. For example, a February 28, 1975, tribute to Ahmad Jamal featured Jamal's own quintet on some pieces, with other numbers performed by the quintet and the CBA Ensemble. CBA members Stanley Cowell, Jimmy Owens, and Roland Alexander provided arrangements for the compositions on which the ensemble performed.[69]

Defining its project in classical terms legitimized the ensemble in the eyes of funding institutions and other benefactors at a time of a growing repertory jazz movement. The CBA Ensemble was intended to be a vehicle for getting more musicians involved in the music and fostering communication among them. It was also created as a means of generating work for local musicians, some of whom were living in despair. Workman thought of the CBA Ensemble as something of a jobs program for musicians; its preservationist and classicist orientation served as a way to get limited funding from cultural organizations to pay musicians' expenses. The ensemble also functioned as a mutual aid society, performing benefits for ailing musicians and the families of recently deceased musicians. And by expanding the definition of jazz classicism to include "creative contemporary" music and its members' own compositions, the CBA sought to legitimate some of its more avant-garde proclivities and continue to take the music in new directions.[70]

The CBA's vision of a great black musical tradition and its drive to find work for its membership were also tied to its desire to cultivate an audience. The CBA Ensemble presented concerts in performance spaces whose variety illustrates a dual desire to reach audiences in black communities as well as a larger fan base. The ensemble presented concerts at well-known clubs such as the Village Vanguard and Top of the Gate, larger venues such as Town Hall, loft spaces, and more "community"-oriented spaces such as plazas, churches, and parks. The CBA Ensemble played its first public performance on April 9, 1971, at Muse in Brooklyn. When it played its second concert at New York University's Bronx campus eight days later, however, it was already clear that the concert endeavor had caused some anxieties among CBA members about their ability to reach the black community. The New York University performance was preceded by a lecture presented by Reggie Workman that was intended to facilitate communication between performers and the audience. The turnout was small, however, and, much to the CBA's dismay, "few if any" members of New York University's Black Students Union, with whom the group had been in contact before the show, were in attendance.[71]

The CBA Ensemble's size and its repertoire were also geared toward reaching a black audience whose attentions were directed elsewhere. Like many musicians in the early 1970s, some CBA members had a vexed relationship with electronic technologies (amplified instruments, synthesizers, and so on). Although jazz musicians had seen electrified musical genres as a threat to their livelihood since the rise of rhythm and blues and urban blues styles during World War II, the tremendous popularity of socially relevant soul and funk in the 1960s and early 1970s posed a particular problem for musicians who saw themselves as agents of social change. Moreover, the popular electrified jazz fusion styles, stemming in part from Miles Davis's electric turn at the end of the 1960s, which provided increased employment opportunities for some musicians, were also threatening to those whose aesthetic and ideological visions and livelihood were connected to acoustic instruments. Although CBA members saw electronics as a means of moving the jazz tradition in new directions, they also considered it a corrupting influence. They recognized that there was a gap between their activist-aesthetic project and an audience that they believed had been conditioned by electronic instrumentation.

Therefore, the CBA theorized its ensemble as a means of preserving the role and function of classical black music in the face of electronic technologies. In 1974, Workman claimed: "The idea behind a large ensemble is first of all to get more musicians involved, and in learning how to listen and hear together; and second, to help offset the artificial prana [a Yogic term for life-force] of the electronic age." Workman acknowledged that musicians created good music with amplified instruments, a perspective that his own music and the CBA's curriculum would bear out. However, electronic technologies could still have a pernicious effect on this music's profitability and liberatory potential: "When you're listening to four or five musicians playing that way," he argued, "you're really listening to Con Ed."[72]

Yet Workman hoped that the prevalence of amplified popular music might lead to the resurgence of acoustic big bands by preparing audiences for their dynamic sounds. It was hoped that by "incorporating various facets of the arts as cultural stimuli," the ensemble would "offset the limited response to small acoustical ensembles due to today's electronic age and marketing techniques and . . . draw large audiences." When CBA Ensemble concerts were intended for New York's black community, the group often merged contemporary music, multimedia presentations, and historical explorations of jazz standards and other forms in order to appeal to the audience and expose listeners to creative music in the process. For example, the CBA put on a January 26, 1975, performance entitled "'Ritual': The Evolution of Afrikan-American Music (a musical journey)," at Janes United Methodist Church in Brooklyn. The concert featured the CBA Ensemble and a number of "Ethnic Expressionists," including the church choir with additional singers, a poet, a light show, slide collages, and comments by musicologist Horace Boyer. The presentation featured a survey of spirituals and folk songs, with arrangements by CBA members and narration by Dr. Boyer; several performances of the blues; a version of Duke Ellington's "Come Sunday"; and several original compositions by CBA members.[73]

Midnight shows at the Apollo also featured diverse types of expression as a means of communicating with the younger audience who frequented the theater. These shows often showcased African themes in order to reach a young audience that was influenced by an Afrocentric popular imagination. A June 1, 1973, performance featured the CBA Ensemble, vocalists Dee Dee Bridgewater and Leon Thomas, Hubert Laws's Afro-Classic Ensemble, and a group of African dancers. An April 13, 1973, show included a sextet led by Donald Byrd, who had recently tried to reach out to young people—and made some money in the process—with his best-selling album *Black Byrd*. The inclusion of Machito's Orchestra and La Lupe on the bill with Byrd illustrate the CBA's desire to connect with a Latino audience and its recognition of Harlem as a Latino, as well as an African American, space.[74]

The juxtaposition of various styles of black music at such performances paralleled attempts to appeal to a mass audience and foster a devotion to a black musical tradition. The CBA Ensemble released a single recording on its short-lived OBE label entitled "Ali Is the Champ for Me," written and sung by Babs Gonzalez, with the backing of the ensemble. The song celebrated Muhammad Ali's return to the ring and his hero status in black communities. The flip side of the recording was the CBA Ensemble's performance of a Stanley Cowell original, "Abscretions," an instrumental number based on a pentatonic figure that the composer described as a spontaneous expression of self, meant to be a gift to "the people." A 1970 recording of Cowell's big band arrangement of "Abscretions" on *Music Inc. and Big Band,* the first release on Strata-East, has a decidedly contemporary flavor, driven by electric bass riffs, funky drumming with a heavy backbeat, and intricate yet catchy riffs by the brass and reeds.[75]

Other extant recordings by CBA members exhibit such an approach. During the 1970s, Strata-East released more than fifty albums, including a number recorded under the names of CBA members or on which members appeared as sidemen. Today the "Strata-East sound" is often defined as the blend of avant-garde leanings and jazz funk that characterized many of these releases. *Music Inc. and Big Band* also features extended free soloing by Cowell, Charles Tolliver, and others on pieces whose arrangements owe more to Ellington than to contemporary rhythm and blues or soul. And on more pop-oriented recordings, one often hears in the lyrics an emphasis on personal and spiritual development or community uplift that was crucial to the CBA's vision.

The CBA aesthetic can also be heard on recordings its members made for other labels. Jimmy Owens's 1970 Polydor album *No Escaping It!!!* is a collection of pieces performed by Owens's quartet (Owens, Kenny Barron, Chris White, and Billy Cobham), with assistance from four additional musicians, including tenor saxophonist Billy Harper. On this album, Owens and other future CBA members explore music that disrupts established genres and appears to be an attempt to reach a heterogeneous audience. "Complicity" is an up-tempo number by the quartet, clearly in the hard bop idiom, while "Milan Is Love" is a straightforward ballad by the same group of musicians. The aptly named "Lo-Slo-Bluze" is a slow-tempo, funky blues by the quartet, with Chris White's electric bass and Kenny Barron's electric piano giving it a more contemporary feeling. This exploration of contemporary popular forms is taken even further when Owens uses the full complement of musicians. "Put It All Together," "Didn't We," and "Chicago Light Green" all feature steady funk rhythms and catchy riffs by the horns. Perhaps the most interesting piece on the album is the title track, which begins as a hard bop piece with complex horn arrangements and then smoothes itself into a spare funk groove. A similar approach is found on tenor saxophonist, composer, and CBA member Frank Foster's 1974 album *The Loud Minority,* which combines free jazz, swing, electric instruments, vocals by Dee Dee Bridgewater, and spoken word.[76]

Certainly multigeneric efforts like Owens's album—as well as more straightforward attempts to create a popular sound, such as Miles Davis's *On the Corner,* Donald Byrd's *Black Byrd,* or Archie Shepp's *Attica Blues*—must be understood in the context of the commodification of the Black Power movement and the desires of record companies to reach a larger public. In the late 1960s and early 1970s, the recording industry viewed the celebration of blackness and the creation of a more populist repertoire as ways to sell more records. But the record companies' bottom line paralleled musicians' own desires to reach their community, and musicians themselves recognized this connection. In 1972 Donald Byrd said that blackness was "up for grabs and can be utilized by anyone from the entrepreneurs to the critics to the performers." For Byrd, as for members of the CBA, the critical issue was being able to play an active role in defining this commodified blackness to make it relevant for musicians and their communities.[77]

Another venue where issues about music, social relevance, and economics were explored was academia. The CBA's activities and vision, as products of and responses to changing institutional relationships, can also be examined in light of its members' roles as teachers and students in colleges and universities. The CBA's participation in academia was part of an influx of black musicians into colleges and universities in the late 1960s and 1970s with the emergence of black studies programs. To the extent that jazz had become institutionalized as a "legitimate" art in the postwar era, sporadic opportunities had arisen for musicians to pursue their artistic projects in the academy. But with the advent of black studies programs, increasing numbers of musicians—even those with radical aesthetic or political visions—had more opportunities to work in educational institutions as students or as visiting or permanent faculty members. Because of the revolutionary meanings associated with their music, jazz musicians who became teachers had an appeal across racial lines to politicized students who sought alternative intellectual training and a validation of black cultural practice. Ben Sidran notes that by 1966 the new jazz and other black musics had gained increasing popularity with white college students who wanted to identify with black liberation struggles or who linked black musical expression to their own antiestablishment orientation. Horace Tapscott's 1968 appointment to a teaching position at the University of California at Riverside came about as a result of protests by the university's Black Student Union.[78] Moreover, jazz had enough trappings as "respectable" artistic expression to appeal to more conservative university administrators who were willing to incorporate black art and culture into their curriculum.

Academic affiliation presented challenges for musicians committed to creating and preserving a liberatory art form. Teaching positions were often temporary or part-time and could be contingent upon uncertain funding sources and academic politics. Some musicians recognized that their inclusion on an academic faculty smacked of tokenism, while others found that their own notions of jazz education could not easily be transposed from informal networks to collegiate settings. Entering the academy presented even more difficulties for those committed to creating an art form relevant to black communities. Working in such institutions removed musicians both metaphorically and physically from their imagined constituencies. During the 1960s and 1970s, black musicians across generic lines struggled over how to make their academic lives relevant to the "cat on the corner." Archie Shepp, for example, joined the faculty of the black studies program at the State University of New York (SUNY) at Buffalo in 1969, moving to the University of Massachusetts in 1974. There, Shepp continued developing his ideas about the role and function of black music. But working in the academy raised a fundamental question for Shepp: how could one use the university as a space for perpetuating the development of black music if that music was dependent upon the support of African American communities for its very existence? Still, positions at colleges or universities often gave musicians institutional support for their creative projects and could provide a respite from the hardships of trying to generate an income from nightclubs and recording work. In addition, they put musicians in contact with other intellectuals, many of whom were interested in African American music. They also provided a vehicle to preserve the music through the teaching of technique, theory, and history. And once musicians were established at various schools, some were able to arrange institutional support for their fellow musicians by bringing them into higher education as teachers, fellows, or students.[79]

For CBA members, the University of Massachusetts was a primary site of academic participation. Ken McIntyre completed a doctorate in education at the university in 1971, before he and Warren Smith cofounded the Afro-American studies department at SUNY, Old Westbury. During the 1970s, CBA members participated in the black studies, education, and music programs at the University of Massachusetts. Jimmy Owens pursued a degree there, as did Bill Barron, who went on to teach at City College of New York and Wesleyan University, where he became chairman of the music department in 1984. Reggie Workman taught at the University of Massachusetts between 1971 and 1974; and other CBA members further developed their ideas about art, education, and social change at this institution. The University of Massachusetts was a particularly rich site for intellectual exchange for CBA members because of the presence of other musicians who taught or studied there. Max Roach and Archie Shepp both joined the faculty in the early 1970s; and Julian "Cannonball" Adderley, Yusef Lateef, and Billy Taylor pursued graduate degrees during this period. CBA members at the university also interacted with intellectuals whose expertise lay in other fields of study. As Workman put it: "Just having the experience of being on campus and in the company of folks like that and having the opportunity to pursue some of your ideas will influence you. And indeed it did."[80]

Workman's teaching duties included bass instruction and conducting courses that were consistent with the CBA's simultaneous embrace of preservation and experimentation. Extant course descriptions and exams also show how Workman's and the CBA's ideas were formed in dialogue with those of other musicians and intellectuals who theorized the role and function of black music and the factors that produce it. In a series of courses titled "Anthology of Black Classical Music," Workman explored the work of "black creative musicians" commonly identified as important stylists of the jazz tradition. Workman explored the work of "amalgamators"—those musicians whose skills lay in fusing existing musical sources and techniques—and "innovators," who took the music in new directions. Yet Workman also branched out to explore the poetics and politics of contemporary artists such as Marvin Gaye, Miriam Makeba, and Jimi Hendrix.[81]

Workman's classes explored different black musics as products of particular historical contexts and geographic spaces. He drew upon a number of recent texts by black authors, including Eileen Southern's *The Music of Black Americans*. Southern herself characterized this new scholarship as "help[ing] somewhat to fill the abyss" created by a shortage of "quality" work about black music from which a politically minded scholar could draw.[82] The publication of studies acceptable to politicized black educators shows the development of a critical mass of ideas that defined vernacular culture as the object of serious study and linked it to its social context. One of Workman's course descriptions stated that students would explore music in light of the "socioeconomic experience of Africans dispersed on the North and South American continents." Toward this end, Workman relied on Baraka's *Blues People* and University of Massachusetts colleague Ortiz Walton's *Music: Black, White, and Blue,* both of which connect the function of black music in vernacular culture to the effects of economics and the media upon its development. By employing this scholarship, Workman demonstrated the reciprocal dialogue between musicians and other black intellectuals. Musicians' ideas had influenced the scholarship on black music during this period. In return, the work of these commentators validated these musicians as artists and intellectuals and provided them with tools as they taught and engaged in their own studies.

Workman's analysis of the social and economic context of black music paid particular attention to issues that affected the professional musicians' community. His courses appear to have resonated with the anxieties of musician-activists who were trying to theorize music as liberatory for musicians and audiences, garner respect for it in relationship to academic and culture-producing institutions, and still make a living. Workman taught his students about the "business aspects of the music industry" and used the CBA's own literature, as well as Walton's book, to explore copyright, contracts, the vicissitudes of government funding for black arts, and the need to maintain collective organizations. He also problematized the relationship of black creative music to the academy. Drawing on written work by David Baker and a published interview with Max Roach, Workman explored how distinct aesthetic approaches for appreciating African American and European music had a palpable effect on the livelihoods of black musicians trying to find legitimacy within institutions like the universities. He self-reflexively explored the dilemma of teaching black music in a predominantly white institution, arguing that the process separated the music from its referent (that is, the black community) by incorporating it into a space where too few African Americans had access.[83]

While examining the cultural politics and conditions under which creative black music functioned, Workman's courses also addressed the spiritual elements of black music and, for that matter, all music in a way that was consistent with the rehabilitative and transformative aspects of the CBA's program. In addition to being a product of a socioeconomic context, black music was also a product of one's innermost thoughts, one's spirit, and interpersonal communication. Workman theorized this function in Afrocentric terms—arguing that black music created a distinct aesthetic system—as well as through a universal understanding of "music as a science of sound [that] will require the philosophical analysis as it relates to man and society." Drawing from Yogic philosophy and the literature of musical therapy, Workman examined the relationship of music to spiritual well-being and its regenerative purpose for black people and a larger world community. Workman and other CBA members may well have developed some of their ideas about the transformative effects of black music in dialogue with University of Massachusetts professor Roland Wiggins, who appeared at the CBA's conference in Bedford-Stuyvesant to speak about the need for a "content oriented" system of education in which music played a central role.[84]

## Coda

Despite the fervor with which members pursued their vision, the CBA began to disintegrate in the mid-1970s. Although the group continued to exist on paper beyond that date, its programs largely ceased in 1976. As in many grassroots organizations, internecine conflicts appear to have played a role in the group's demise. State and local funding opportunities also began to dry up, a situation compounded when Cobi Narita left the group to found the interracial Universal Jazz Coalition and took her grant-writing skills with her. Workman himself went on to succeed Bill Barron as the director of the Muse jazz program and since then has become director of the jazz program at the New School in New York, where at the time of this writing Jimmy Owens also teaches. Other members continued to work in community organizations and as educators.

The legacy of the CBA and other collective organizations is perhaps best measured by their less recognized accomplishments. Although CBA activities presented difficulties for the group's members, Workman says they were ultimately worthwhile:

> And of course the artistic endeavor is compromised when you get involved with all these things, because you can't practice, study, and create as much when you're divided like this. It took a lot out of my family, took a lot out of my art; but it was important, it was necessary. That's part of the thing. And you know what I think is that when you do things like that, it adds something to your being, so that when you

pick up your instrument, you have more to talk about anyway, more to say, and a stronger base to work on. So it's positive.

Despite the CBA's short history, Workman also claims that elements of the group have survived in the camaraderie among musicians who participated in its activities and in the current resurgence of jazz activism. As he puts it: "The feeling never dissolved, because all of the tentacles that were an outgrowth of that organization always point back toward the Black Artists." And every once in a while, on a staircase or in a hotel lobby, in the United States or elsewhere, Workman encounters someone who took a class offered by the CBA or at the Muse and who now greets him heartily. "And this is something that is rewarding, because you know something that you want to see has found fertile soil, which is nothing more than the fact that this person is moving around the world, standing tall, holding his own, a healthy individual, because of an experience that they had in the community. These things are important."[85]

# Writing "Creative Music"

## Theorizing the Art and Politics of Improvisation

**DURING THE 1970S AND 1980S,** a handful of prominent members of the community of creative musicians turned to the written word and moved the discussion about the social function of African American music in new directions. In a series of works published independently or by small presses, Yusef Lateef, Marion Brown, Wadada Leo Smith, and Anthony Braxton built upon their community's conversation about the spiritual, aesthetic, and political aspects of improvised music. Drawing from their experiences as professional musicians—as well as from their roles as scholars, activists, and educators within and outside universities—these multi-instrumentalists engaged in philosophical, ethnomusicological, and historical investigation of improvised music, in which they saw personal, culturally specific, and universal meanings.

These artists seldom considered themselves "jazz musicians." They generally rejected the label because of the musical, social, and philosophical constraints it imposed. Yet their ideas were rooted in a long conversation in the jazz community and, to varying extents, in their positions as workers within the jazz industry. Implicitly and explicitly, these writings operated as critical interventions in the jazz discourse; they remain a testament both to the continuing difficulties avant-garde musicians experienced while trying to make a living and to the effect of pejorative reporting from jazz critics and other commentators. Like many of their contemporaries, these musicians engaged in a quest for social relevance, spiritual purpose, and culturally specific meanings, although they rejected some of the prescriptive aspects of cultural nationalism when it seemed to present impediments to the broad-minded, functional aesthetic orientation they sought to explore.

By the time they committed their thoughts to paper, each of these musicians had long been analyzing and theorizing the art of improvisation, with an eye toward his own artistic projects. All of them were, in a sense, developing a new musical language. Yet each sought to extend this language into something larger. Lateef and Brown provided interesting commentary on the communicative aspects of improvised music, its role in musicians' personal growth and that of their audiences, and the possibility that this music might usher in social transformations. We find an even stronger political vision in the work of Smith and Braxton, as well as a simultaneous embrace and rejection of racial and geographic boundaries. Even as these two AACM members placed precise definitions on the role and function of black music, they recognized that imposing meaning on this sonic expression could have a pernicious effect on black musicians' lives. Their desire to transcend racial categories and geographic boundaries was closely linked to their desire to challenge the constraints of genre and style as well as the limitations imposed by "jazz" as an idea and a marketing category.

The works are also significant because they actively explore the intellectual aspects of creative musical expression, reflecting the way these authors assumed the role of intellectuals and sought to capitalize on the limited status they attained by doing so. In 1975 Robert Farris Thompson described Smith, Braxton, and Brown as "black musicians of the vanguard [who] are deliberately dissolving all manner of restrictions upon their creativity. Their travels are indices to the fact that back-home roots and European exposure and New York competition and academic teaching and writing, plus many other experiences, are all grist to the mills of liberation."[1] Each of these avant-garde players drew upon experiences in various geographic and institutional spaces while seeking to forge new aesthetic visions. Their writings document a self-conscious investigation into the power and function of improvisation that speaks eloquently to the precarious position of avant-garde music in American culture and the difficulty of defining just what its emancipatory function might be. Yet these musicians resolutely embraced its utopian possibilities during an era that promised cultural, spiritual, and social transformations. Their writings again updated a New Negro belief in the unique contributions of African-derived improvised music and fused it with a broad-minded, politicized sensibility derived from a rapidly changing world.

## The Therapeutic Dimensions of Improvised Music

In his 1970 instructional book *Yusef Lateef's Method on How to Improvise Soul Music,* the multi-instrumentalist briefly sets forth some of the spiritual principles that guide the "art of improvised music." Although he had studied music for more than three decades, Lateef had been inspired to produce this volume by his recent experiences as a student teacher. Born in Chattanooga, Tennessee, in 1920 and raised in Detroit, Lateef began his years of study in 1938, when he took up the tenor saxophone under the tutelage of Ted Buckner. After leaving Detroit to work with Dizzy Gillespie and other groups during the late 1940s and early 1950s, he returned to the city to study flute and composition at Wayne State University in 1955. Like a number of other musicians of his generation, Lateef adopted Islam in the late 1940s, changing his name from William Evans. Primarily known for his skills on tenor saxophone, Lateef also made a name for himself by incorporating flute, oboe, and bassoon—as well as Asian, African, and Middle Eastern instruments, rhythms, and melodies—into jazz. At the time he wrote his instructional book, he had resumed his education, earning a B.A. in 1969 and an M.A. in music education in 1970 at the Manhattan School of Music. He had recently begun student teaching, and he would go on to work for six years at Manhattan Community College while pursuing a doctorate in education at the University of Massachusetts, which he received in 1975.[2]

Lateef was among the growing number of musicians in the 1960s and 1970s who rejected the word "jazz." In a 1970 interview with Leonard Feather, he objected to the term because of its ambiguity and its association with sexual behavior. Like Mingus, he also believed that the term held the power to divide musicians and audiences, just as "mankind has said white man–black man and thereby divided mankind, instead of looking at men as being just men." Instead of "jazz," Lateef preferred the term "autophysiopsychic music," which he defined as "music that comes from the physical, mental, spiritual, and intellectual self." This take on music and racial division is evident in his instructional volume. Nowhere does he mention the word "jazz"; instead, he uses "autophysiopsychic" to refer to improvisation as a universal set of artistic principles—"a vital element in music for ages"—whose "prime form for expression" is and always will be found in the blues.[3]

Lateef begins his book with a section on "soul," a discussion that suggests an educator's engagement with the spiritual and populist underpinnings of that musical genre as well as the contemporary jazz community's desire to create a socially relevant and financially viable improvised music. One can hear a musical expression of this effort on his 1968 album *The Complete Yusef Lateef.* In addition to a striking investigation of the blues on oboe, he explores both the church-inflected "soul" music that came to prominence in the jazz community in the late 1950s and a variety of rhythmic frameworks stemming from more recent musical definitions of the term. He moves even further in this direction on his 1969 album *Yusef Lateef's Detroit,* on which he leads a big band with electric guitar, electric bass, synthesizer, and strings through a series of compositions driven by funk bass lines and catchy horn arrangements. In the 1970s, Lateef made a series of recordings featuring funk rhythms and electric instruments; and he spoke in the press about his desire to produce recordings that contained elements of improvisation but employed contemporary instrumentation and "danceable tempos" as a means of enlarging the audience for his music.[4]

Lateef's written exploration of "the soul" situates it in spiritual terms at the center of the therapeutic dimensions of music. "The soul is the genesis to human life," he asserts; and an artist "must strive to gain the highest level of consciousness and awareness by developing his mind, body and soul on an even balance. What follows is pure, individual, creative expression." Believing in the interconnectedness of all things in the universe, Lateef explains that "vibrations of the soul" provide a powerful means of communication ("like an electric current"), revealing deeper truths about human beings and their relationships with one another.[5]

According to Lateef, musicians facilitate these connections by tapping into their own thoughts and emotions and articulating them through music. Lateef emphasizes the importance of striking a balance between thought and emotion. He describes the jazz community's common expression "you have got to say something" as a directive to "incorporate a proper balance of thinking and feeling." But the ability to tap into one's emotions does not necessarily make one a skilled musician. "If the manifestation of emotion were all that was required," Lateef writes, "than [*sic*] the civil servant, the carpenter and the bus driver could compete with the mature musician." Moreover, he considers the notion that improvisation is solely a product of emotion to be a primitivist misconception. "The point is that the skilled improvisor[6] is not just a mechanical, emotional dispenser but an interpretive artist creating organically." The term "autophysiopsychic," then, not only describes the self-consciousness, emotional and spiritual depth, and physical abilities required of the successful improviser but also rejects a narrow definition of jazz as the product of emotion.[7]

In a gesture similar to the CBA's description of the therapeutic aspects of "creative music," Lateef describes the spiritual benefits that result when musicians forge a connection with their audiences. "Improvization allows the performer to deliver his message or say what he has to say musically. With his soul attuned to other souls he is capable of giving deep and far reaching experiences. If the improvizor is in harmony with himself and fellowmen, he too, will reach great spiritual heights with the tools he uses to improvize." Lateef concludes his assessment with a discussion of "emotional memory," which he describes as "a vital tool in the science of improvization." Through emotional memory, a musician attempts to access a "highly emotional experience" from his or her past and use it to produce a sonic expression of feeling in the present. Lateef describes this practice as a self-conscious enterprise involving the coordination of intellect, emotion, and physical skill. "The musician . . . is expected to skillfully filter his profoundest sensations in order to extract their properties and recompose them in performance. This is a process which compels the musician not only to recall his feelings but, to analyze and understand. If we look at the emotion-memory squarely, we see not only an improvizational tool but, a great boon for the ego, a therapeutic toy."[8]

Three years later, Lateef published a collection of writings by members of his quartet. Among his own contributions were short plays, pieces of fiction, and several meditations on aesthetics. One piece, "The Constitution of Aesthetics, the Declaration of Genius, and the Aesthetic Address," stands out as an extension of Lateef's earlier comments on the art of improvisation. This brief homage to Charlie Parker validates the African American tradition of improvised music through reference to this trilogy of documents from American nation building. By invoking the rhetoric of Jefferson, Lincoln, and the framers of the Constitution, Lateef places Parker and three decades of African American improvised music at the center of American life—a move that simultaneously rejects the historical marginalization of the music and also speaks of the possibilities occasioned by the gradual recognition of the music in universities and other cultural institutions during the 1970s.

Lateef describes Parker as a "Genius of this century," an appellation that stems both from Parker's own intellect and spiritual purpose and from the multilayered aesthetic function his music performed for listeners. Parker's music was a product of "intuition, academic and scientific comprehension," "spiritual enunciation," and "an integrated personality." He inspired artists, writers, musicians, and others "prone to cognitive thinking" as well as a broader population of "human beings upon earth [and] perhaps beyond." Parker also, Lateef argues, provided a prime example of an improvising musician's ability to work as a healer: "The noble quality of tenderness that he projected so adeptly in his autophysiopsychic rendition of the song 'Embraceable You' was and is therapeutic each time it is heard."[9]

Lateef, notably, finds no inconsistency between the functional aesthetic of improvised music and a definition of aesthetics based on the idea that success in art stems from an art object's intrinsic beauty and its ability to appeal to the "higher" reaches of the mind. Lateef writes that Parker's work had the elements "present in all great works of art": "He expresses the fathomless fascination of the soul, the instrument that lifts mind to higher regions, the gateway into the realm of imagination." In addition to simultaneously challenging and abiding by the Eurocentric aesthetic taxonomy that had marginalized improvised African American music, Lateef's validation of Parker as an improviser links a community-oriented responsibility, which permeated many musicians' intellectual projects during this period, with a duty to be true to one's own avant-garde artistic goals.[10] Ultimately, Lateef saw in Parker's music a challenge for contemporary musicians and perhaps society in general:

> WE CANNOT IGNORE THE AESTHETIC EDUCATION HE GAVE US. . . .
> IT IS FOR US TO BE DEDICATED HERE TO THE GREAT AESTHETIC
> TASK WHICH REMAINS BEFORE US—THAT FROM HIS COGENT
> MUSICAL SCIENCE, WE TAKE INCREASED DEVOTION TO THAT WHICH
> IS BEAUTIFUL AND SUBLIME WITHIN NATURE AND THE SOUL—THAT
> HE WILL NOT HAVE DIED IN VAIN—THAT THE WORLDS UNDER GOD
> SHALL HAVE A NEW BIRTH OF SOULS—AND THAT THE SOULS OF A
> PEOPLE, BY LOVE, FOR GOD, SHALL NOT ABSTAIN FROM LOVE.[11]

Lateef thus looked forward to a new day and a new people, both of which would be products of a collective spiritual awakening facilitated by the therapeutic work of improvising musicians.

## The Language of Music

Saxophonist Marion Brown was similarly interested in the therapeutic and transformative aspects of improvised music during this period. Brown's musical and written projects, however, more specifically examined the connections between music, speech, and the written word. Brown's work in this area is particularly interesting in the way it embraces music as a form of communication while nevertheless questioning its ability to convey specific meanings and challenging the ability of verbal language to represent musical experience. Brown also took Lateef's considerations of the functional qualities of music in a somewhat different direction by linking aspects of improvised music to West African practices and by considering the role of improvised music in producing African American cultural identities.

Born in Atlanta in 1935, Brown served in the U.S. Army from 1953 to 1956 before enrolling at Clark College, where he studied under multi-instrumentalist Wayman Carver. In 1960 he entered a pre-law program at Howard University, where he was a contemporary of Claude Brown and Stokely Carmichael. Brown soon decided, however, that he did not have the "emotional outlook" for a career in law or political activism and decided to put more emphasis on his music. He moved to New York in 1962 and was a prominent figure in the city's "new music" scene during the mid-1960s. Brown's artistic energies were not limited to the music world. Like Archie Shepp, he was active in black intellectual circles on the Lower East Side and was a "running buddy" of Amiri Baraka. He had a minor role in the original production of *The Dutchman* and was among the members of the jazz avant-garde who performed at the Black Arts Repertory Theater/School in Harlem. Brown also wrote a little jazz criticism and was commissioned to write an essay, "The Negro in the Fine Arts," for the *American Negro Reference Book,* published in 1965.[12]

Like many of his contemporaries, Brown addressed the lack of opportunities in avant-garde music by joining the exodus to Europe. He moved to Paris in 1967, where he recorded with European and expatriate American musicians, including AACM founding member Steve McCall and German vibraphonist Günter Hampel. Brown also obtained a position as an American Fellow in Music Composition and Performance at the Cité Internationale des Artistes in Paris, which gave him firsthand experience with the French government's relatively generous institutional support for African American improvised music. His return to the United States in 1970 took him to Atlanta, where he experienced what he described as an artistic awakening. He then moved to New Haven, where he worked briefly as a music consultant with the city's public school system. In New Haven, he performed with Wadada Leo Smith, who relocated there at Brown's suggestion. Brown took an assistant professorship at Bowdoin College from 1971 to 1974, where he completed a B.A. in music education while also teaching courses at Brandeis University and Colby College. Between 1974 and 1976, Brown undertook an M.A. in ethnomusicology at Wesleyan University, where he was once again a colleague of Smith.[13]

Institutional support in Europe and the United States gave Brown the opportunity to develop his music and ideas. In Paris he began to sketch out an aesthetic philosophy, and he started building his own percussion instruments (on the order of the AACM's "little instruments"). In a 1972 interview, Brown said his appointment at Bowdoin allowed him to pay the rent, "stretch out" and work on his music, build new instruments, and continue his investigations into the history and function of black music. His research into black aesthetics was based on ethnomusicological inquiry, oriented toward exploring music's role in psychic liberation and personal transformation, and interested in the relationship between music and written and spoken language. Describing himself as a "self-styled musicologist," Brown described his artistic project as "a personal view of my past culture . . . I'm constantly referring to my past . . . I'm like a man walking into the future backwards." This journey involved both an imagined African past and his own experiences growing up in Georgia. Acknowledging that he had no direct access to Africans' cultures, he claimed that "through listening to their music and reading, I've become a part of their environment. When I play, I'm a narrator—an essayist."[14]

Brown connected the introspective aspects of his art to a broader interpretation of the function of black expressive culture and a validation of avant-garde music. Yet he also complicated assumptions about the social relevance and communicative aspects of music. He was particularly wary of the meaning people outside the community of avant-garde musicians imposed on their music. In the 1972 interview, he rejected the idea that artists had any particular political responsibility. When asked about the role of black artists in "the revolution," Brown responded: "I don't philosophize about art at all. I don't know what the artist's job is. The only people who think they know what his job is are the people who study artists."[15] Brown clearly did "philosophize about art"; here he merely rejected the idea that black musicians had to conform to the "revolutionary" roles prescribed for them by critics and other commentators. But elsewhere, even as he infused his music with a literary sensibility and emphasized the written word as a tool in diasporan black cultural production, he pondered the limits of music as a form of communication and raised provocative questions about the ability of language to represent musical experience. These questions reflected his engagement both with scholarly discussions about music and literature and with the constraints that academic and journalistic discourse placed on musicians.

In August 1970, Brown went into the studio with Anthony Braxton, Chick Corea, Andrew Cyrille, Jeanne Lee, and a half dozen other musicians. The result was the album *Afternoon of a Georgia Faun,* which consists of two lengthy pieces of collectively improvised music: the title track and "Djinji's Corner."[16] The album generated little attention and even less praise from mainstream jazz critics. Three years later, Brown published a booklet to accompany the recording. *Afternoon of a Georgia Faun: Views and Reviews* consists of Brown's own description of the music, an interview with the artist, a poem about the music by Steven James, and six reviews of the album—including four that had appeared in foreign magazines. Through *Views and Reviews,* Brown responded to the critical vacuum by creating a dialogue about the album. In doing so, he not only set forth his avant-garde aesthetic philosophy and artistic agenda but also positioned the artist as the ultimate arbiter of the meaning of his or her music.[17]

The title track of *Afternoon of a Georgia Faun* has an ambient quality, with multiple layers of instrumentation, considerable use of silence, and minimal rhythmic propulsion. In the liner notes, Brown describes it as a "tone poem" that depicts the natural environment in Atlanta. The opening percussion suggests "wooden rain drops," "metallic" sounds represent light, and the entrance of the Zomari (a Tanzanian double reed instrument) and flutes evokes forest animals. In *Views and Reviews,* Brown provides additional ideas about the music, setting it in more specific cultural contexts. He describes the track as an extended improvisation based on two structured sections. The first symbolizes nature, with simulations of rain, wind, running water, and animal calls. Brown also describes these sounds as "feelings of loneliness in an imaginary forest of the mind," which he links to Nigerian writer Amos Tutuola's novel *My Life in the Bush of Ghosts.* Brown's reference to Tutuola bespeaks his investigations into African music and spirituality. Like Tutuola's novel, "Georgia Faun" is meant to be an introspective, "first person experience" of the world of spirits and memories, "told collectively in the musical third person."[18]

If this piece is a meditation on an African spirit world, the connection is mediated through a Georgia landscape and Brown's personal history. The music is a return home to his everyday childhood experiences in Atlanta: the smell of magnolia and honeysuckle, the songs of birds, the barks of dogs, and the sounds of the black church, whose music played a functional and spiritual role in community life. Brown contends that the musical narrative evokes these quotidian images of the South through mental and physical movement. He describes an ideal performance of "Georgia Faun" as a spectacle, involving music, song, and dance.[19]

As Lateef did in his theory of emotional memory, Brown specifically links improvisational music to personal experience and training, wherein "mind and body are unified through memory and muscle." "In memory lie the seeds of improvisation: in technique, the means by which to cultivate the memory." By connecting his physical skills as an improviser (that is, his technique) to his cultural memories and identity, he asserts that improvisation, as the height of black musical expression, connects the artist to his people. But "Georgia Faun" also reconciles these cultural memories with the conditions of modern life. The second section of this piece begins with a solo by Chick Corea, which he performs on both the keyboard and strings of the piano. According to Brown, it represents the "contemporary world of electricity and electro-magnetic energy." This movement signifies a temporal shift from a "primitive" past, in Brown's words, into an electronic future, indicating some reconciliation with the effect of electronic technologies on improvised music.[20]

Whereas "Georgia Faun" is an exploration of Brown's personal experiences and the symbolic cultural links between Atlanta and West Africa, the second piece on the album, "Djinji's Corner," is an attempt to recreate the elements of West African community-based musical performance. "Georgia Faun" is contemplative, but "Djinji's Corner" is meant to be recreational, a kind of "ring-game" that combines "music, speech, song and movement." Brown facilitates the recreational aspects of the piece through the arrangement of the recording studio. He employs "performance stations," each consisting of several instruments, including traditional band and concert instruments as well as homemade "constructions" (percussion instruments whose manufacture Brown considers an extension of improvisation). Musicians move from station to station, stopping briefly at each one to play new musical phrases or to develop those that have previously been stated. Their physical movement is intended to replicate dance, and their sharing of instruments allows them to engage in a "freer" type of collective improvisation. The musicians are supposed to have fun as well: "It is enjoyed for the sheer fun of engaging in a particular kind of exchange on which it is based."[21]

Brown augments the recreational function of the piece by using "assistants" (nonmusicians who play simple percussion parts). The idea is to reproduce traditional Ghanaian practices, in which music is performed by a nucleus of skilled musicians, with help from community members of lesser ability. As Brown describes the interaction between the two groups, he affirms the therapeutic role of participation in improvised musical performance. He tries to create a "sane sociology of contemporary music" by bringing skilled and unskilled musicians together in an appropriate setting. "This does not mean," he argues, "that every time a musician is performing, he or she may be interrupted by someone who feels like joining in." But in the right setting, these people "might be provided with musical instruments, which, when played properly, will express their emotions. In this way energy is transformed into harmless and positive activity."[22]

Brown's description of this album in *Views and Reviews* demonstrates his practical implementation of an investigation into the functional qualities of West African–derived improvised music, at both a personal and a social level, for skilled musicians and nonmusicians alike. It also illustrates his demand that this music be taken seriously. Like Lateef, Brown seeks to dismantle the hierarchical boundaries between composed and improvised music and between an aesthetic that elevates art as an object of intrinsic beauty and one that is defined by functional purpose. Brown argues not only that improvised music is as "valid" as composed music but also that, even when "arrived at through mutual cooperation at a folk level, [it] may be as successful as any other kind of music."[23]

Brown's writings are also significant for the way they interrogate the relationship between verbal or written language and musical texts. In the interview in *Views and Reviews,* Brown resists the interlocutor's repeated attempts to draw connections between "Georgia Faun," Stéphane Mallarmé's poem "Afternoon of a Faun," and Claude Debussy's musical rendition of the poetry. Although he acknowledges familiarity and some inspiration, Brown says that the narrative in the music should be understood not as an explicit plot but as a musical movement with shifting visual images. He complicates matters further by stating that meanings for performers and audience are generally different and that even he often imposes meanings on a performance after the fact. "Criticism" is by definition a product of the gulf between musicians' ideas and those of the audience. Once a listener determines that his or her interpretation does not match the performer's, Brown argues, "one becomes a critic."[24]

Brown's comments point to his simultaneous interest in and suspicion of the connections between music and language. Brown was influenced by a scholarly and creative interest in the connections between West African and African American oral and musical cultures. In "Improvisation and the Aural Tradition in Afro-American Music," a 1973 essay written for *Black World,* for example, Brown discusses the role of the spoken word in West African cultural practice and describes how this survived in the African American art of improvisation. He charts the development of an orally based African American musical tradition, from the moment when enslaved Africans began making their own instruments until it was developed to its fullest by Ornette Coleman and other free jazz players during the 1960s.[25]

Brown explores the connections between African and African American oral traditions on his 1973 recording *Geechee Recollections.* Like

"Georgia Faun," this recording evokes a southern culture and landscape, which again provide a connection to the wellspring of African culture.[26] Among the musicians joining Brown are Wadada Leo Smith, Steve Mc-Call, and Ghanaian drummer A. K. Adzenyah, a member of the ethnomusicology department at Wesleyan. Brown explores African musical orality in a four-part composition entitled "Tokalokaloka." According to the liner notes, the title comes "from the Congo" and literally means "little bits of firewood." Brown uses it as an onomatopoeic description of the "speech patterns" presented by the four percussionists on the piece and as a reference to the vocal qualities of African instrumental music. Parts One and Two of "Tokalokaloka" are largely devoid of regular meter, instead operating as a spatial exploration of the multiple textures of the musical voices (horns, rattles, gongs, chimes, autoharp, bass). Part Three marks a dramatic shift, with a steady polyrhythmic groove punctuated by Brown's saxophone and African drums. The piece is bracketed by multitrack, multi-instrumental solo performances by Brown and Smith on horns and little instruments, which offer additional examples of a self-conscious investigation of the African oral expression through the practice of improvisation.

Brown also investigates the connections between music and orality on "Karintha," a piece that combines the use of thumb piano, freely played horn lines, dissonant bowing on cello, and percussion as background and commentary for Bill Hassan's dramatic reading of a vignette from Jean Toomer's novel *Cane.* Brown had been introduced to the Harlem Renaissance writer's work by Amiri Baraka and was in the process of writing compositions based on the poetry and prose of *Cane,* with the help of NEA grants in 1972 and 1976. "Karintha," a nostalgic and lush description of a woman's physical presence and a Georgia landscape, was perhaps an ideal vehicle for evoking Brown's own memories; but it also exemplified his interest in music as a narrative form and its relationship to the written and spoken word. Brown drew upon Jean Toomer's work again on his 1975 album *Sweet Earth Flying,* and he explored music and spoken word in collaborations with poet and critic Joanne Braxton during this period as well.[27]

Yet, as Brown's comments in *Views and Reviews* indicate, he also complicated the relationship between music and the written and spoken word. He recognized the inherently limited ability of language to represent musical experience; and he used this knowledge to respond to writers who favored composed music and who held the power, by virtue of their institutional positions, to affect the lives of black avant-garde artists. In his 1972 essay "Music Is My Mistress: Form and Expression in the Music of Duke Ellington," Brown challenges the idea that improvised music is somehow less legitimate as art. Citing aestheticians and critics who demand that a legitimate piece of music display a balance of personal expression and form, Brown argues that they maintain this belief because they "cannot reconcile the fact that music does not convey propositions, as literal symbols do." If the sounds themselves contain no inherent meanings, he suggests, one is prone to judge a piece of music by its formal, or compositional, elements. Because this presents problems when analyzing fully improvised music or compositions that include improvisational elements, Brown proposes that a different set of aesthetic principles must be invoked when evaluating such music. "Balance" is achieved in improvised music not through a compositional structure but through musicians' personal expressions and the emotional bond they create with their audience.[28]

In his discussion of Ellington's work that follows, Brown says that when evaluating jazz, one must take into account spontaneity and emotion, which do not run contrary to form, as some aestheticians suggest. Ellington's music, which highlights the individual qualities of his band members' playing, does in fact maintain an "aesthetic balance" or "symmetry of form." Ellington accomplishes this precisely through his ordering of musical elements (blue notes, improvised melodies, and so on) that express, albeit only in an "abstract sense," his emotional experiences, and those of his musicians, in ways that "rhyme with emotions that are part of the everyday language of his listeners." Brown places Ellington on the same pedestal as Charles Ives, claiming that through their work, a homegrown American music "reached its highest levels of development and achievement . . . [Ellington] is to jazz, what Ives was to American folk music: a master of all its forms and idioms!"[29]

By giving Ellington's work—and, by extension, African American improvised music as a whole—status as a serious art and relevance as a functional enterprise, Brown voices an argument familiar to both musicians and critics who have tried to give the music this dual legitimacy. But even as he examines the denotative powers of improvisational music, Brown understands its limitations as an expression of specific emotions and ideas. He differs from Lateef by restricting music's ability to convey emotional meanings to the "abstract." And this basic indeterminacy in the relationship between music and "propositions" means that it is all the more important for musicians to lend meaning to their own artistic projects, especially when performers and their audiences may have such different readings. The essay concludes with a brief discussion of Ellington's autobiography, *Music Is My Mistress,* in which Brown emphasizes the importance of the artist's own interpretations of his music. Brown concludes by asking: "What makes Ellington's music so great? . . . The answer to that question lies in the realm of imagination, his imagination. To get to it, we would have to have the honor of Mr. Ellington's presence."[30]

Brown thus emphasizes the role of music in communication between performers and audiences and the importance of African and African American linguistic traditions in the aesthetics and function of black music. Yet he also explores the slipperiness of language in describing music, which itself serves as an elusive semiotics of experience, memory, and emotion. Although these might seem to be a contradictory set of suppositions, they exemplify his attempts to reconcile scholarly assessments of the relationship of music to language with an understanding of how the labeling and categorization of music is a field of power with tangible effects on members of the avant-garde and other black musicians. Brown describes music as a kind of discourse in order to validate its social and personal worth; yet he also tries to liberate it from language in order to free it from the effects of misrepresentation. But even with the latter project, he maintains a belief in the ability of musicians to create the terms by which their own music should be understood.

## A "New World Music"

AACM veteran Wadada Leo Smith addresses similar themes in his 1973 self-published aesthetic manifesto *Notes (8 Pieces) Source a New World Music: Creative Music.* Like his colleague and collaborator Marion Brown, Smith explores the relationship of improvised music to language, emphasizes the musician's role in defining the art of improvisation, and argues for its social relevance. In Smith's work, however, we find a more explicit vision of social transformation. In *Notes,* and in his essay "(Mɪ) American Music," published in the Fall 1974 issue of *The Black Perspective in Music,* Smith argues that improvised music will help to usher in a new sociopolitical order. His project is a continuation of the AACM's struggle to reconcile cultural nationalist and universalist ideas through an aesthetic philosophy that celebrates the art of improvisation. Thus "new world music: creative music," in Smith's formulation, represents both a hybrid, homegrown African American tradition of improvised music and an emergent global musical configuration that points to a utopian world community.

Born in Leland, Mississippi, in 1941, Smith moved to Chicago in 1967 after his discharge from the army. A friend put him in touch with Anthony Braxton, who introduced him to the AACM. Smith brought his own ideas about improvisation to the group, but he was also influenced by its expansive musical vision; its attention to history, philosophy, and spirituality; and its commitment to activism. Smith formed the group Creative Construction Company (CCC) with Braxton and fellow AACM member Leroy Jenkins and, with Braxton and Joseph Jarman, participated in a study group that analyzed and discussed music, philosophy, and politics. Although this was a period of artistic and intellectual growth, it was a difficult time as well. Chicago's limited jazz audience and an increasingly hostile urban environment caused many members of the black musical avant-garde to consider the city an artistic dead end. Like other AACM artists, the members of CCC looked to Europe as a source of greater economic reward and critical respect, and the group moved to Paris in 1969.

Unlike the enthusiastic response accorded the Art Ensemble of Chicago upon its arrival in Europe, the CCC's reception was tepid, in part because the group's music did not conform to French critics' and audiences' expectations of what authentic, "revolutionary" black music should sound like.[31] Smith and Braxton also had creative differences in Europe. Smith returned to the United States in 1970, settling first in New York and then in New Haven, where he formed the group New Dalta Ahkri, with pianist Anthony Davis among its members. In 1971 Smith established his own label, Kabell Records, on which he would make several recordings with this group and as a solo performer. He also achieved a certain status as a source of wisdom in artistic and intellectual circles in New Haven.[32] As he embraced this role as a teacher, Smith wrote and published *Notes* as a means of educating his audience about the transformative role of black music and remedying the errors of other commentators.

The organization and style of *Notes* reflect Smith's desire to fuse "poetic reasoning" and "Mississippi common sense" in an inquiry into the "practical" and "contemplative" aspects of improvisation. Arranged as a series of brief, thematically linked discussions about the power and parameters of improvised music, *Notes* uses storytelling and meditative reflections in an attempt to make the text "enjoyable" for the reader while remaining as "complex as possible theoretically." The general omission of capitalization in the text lends to its informality, as does the lack of footnotes. The latter device, Smith later said, also allowed him to showcase his personal investment in these issues as an African American practitioner of experimental improvised music.[33]

Smith begins his text by situating himself as heir to a tradition of "creative musicians." He dedicates his manifesto to the "great master musicians, the pioneers of creative music in america." Smith honors the memory of trumpeters Joe Smith, Fats Navarro, Booker Little, and Louis Armstrong and adds a "special dedication" to Edward Kennedy Ellington, a "sustainer of creative music" and "master musician." Smith's invocation of these musicians positions him by chosen instrument as part of a patrilineal legacy of improvising musicians, which he uses to chart the development of a creative expression of the intellect. He writes that "these unique pioneers liberated the performer to a creativity of direct deliverance of a creative thought: music."[34]

Creative music, at one level, is the art of improvising in the moment, which may or may not be based on preexisting musical structures:

> improvisation means that the music is created at the same moment it is performed, whether it is developing on a given theme or is improvisation on a given rhythm or sound (structures) or, in the purest form, when the improvisor creates without any of these conditions, but creates at that moment, through his or her wit and imagination, an arrangement of silence and sound and rhythm that has never before been heard and will never again be heard.

But creative music also signifies an analytical approach to the art of improvisation and a devotion to extending it in new directions. Smith's text is striking in the way he embraces an intellectual identity, a move that both legitimates his authorial voice in critical discussions about music and affirms his role as an agent in social transformations. The creative musician expresses thought through music but is also "dedicated to developing a heightened awareness of improvisation as an art form." In Smith's vision, this involves a critical perspective on music and its position in society.[35]

Smith situates this perspective in AACM doctrine and a broader Black Arts imperative. The epigraph of his manifesto is a quote from the introduction to Addison Gayle's *The Black Aesthetic,* in which Gayle argues that a "critical methodology has no relevance to the black community unless it aids men in becoming better than they are." Smith appears to have felt some trepidation about putting his ideas on paper, which is not surprising given the critique of avant-garde black music as overly intellectualized and irrelevant to a mass black audience. Yet his reference to Gayle's work affirms his role as thinker and agent for social change— and Smith adds that all black people need to self-consciously record their own history in order to challenge the "present social-economic-political syndrome." A few pages later, he connects Gayle's imperative to the goals and activities of the AACM, whose work, according to Smith, is exemplary of the way black musicians have made music a vehicle for social change. He emphasizes the group's desire "to integrate all the known properties of the performing arts into a total expression as indicated in the historical roots of the black man"; its cooperative commitment to community education, personal growth, and economic development; and its devotion to preserving and promoting "traditional" and "creative contemporary" black music.[36]

Like some of his AACM colleagues, Smith understands creative music as a field that owes much of its development to African Americans working inside and outside the genre known as jazz. Yet creative music is also a product of other cultures and is representative of African American musicians' refusal to have their creativity constrained by the limitations of racial identity or genre. As Smith discusses the creation of this "new world music," he tries to reconcile a veneration of African American music with a more internationalist perspective, just as he balances tenets of cultural nationalism with a universalist philosophy.

Even as he seeks to challenge the boundaries of geography and cultural categories, Smith maintains Négritude's attention to black culture—

and a black aesthetician's attention to African American culture—as an antidote to the world's ills. While questioning the idea that black music is a hermetic field, he maintains a focus on African American creativity and his own racial identity. Although his own music is informed by "the wonder and gorgeousness of nature" and "the universal principles of all when created through the cosmic powers of the all," it is still an expression of "a black man, a creative improvisor," striving to "pay homage" to black people. Smith's inspiration "unfolds from the (u.s.) north america to those ancient lands of africa and this present day modern africa—*that* is the lineage of my *music* . . . it is through this heritage that I find the most vital and creative energy for me as a person."[37]

As he charts the development of African American improvised music as a core element of the broader tradition of creative music, Smith presents a familiar view of the history of this idiom, one that moves from spirituals through the contemporary avant-garde. Like Baraka, Smith sees the blues as an originating moment of African American cultural production. Evoking Du Bois's characterization of black people in *The Souls of Black Folk,* Smith writes that the blues signals the emergence of African Americans as the "'seventh son,' the newest of earth-beings." By the beginning of the twentieth century, he argues, European instrumental and vocal music had reached the end of its development because of the limitations of the chromatic scale; however, the twentieth century also saw the arrival of a new "classic art music" (jazz) that "forecast the end of european music (composition) as the dominant form of expression." Bebop marks the close of the first stage of the development of creative music. Validating the AACM and his own musical project, Smith claims that the second period of creative music began with free jazz, which brings the improviser "back to the original intention of all great music: to create and express original ideas without being inhibited by certain prescribed forms." Although several forms of free music are determined by the character of the structures that guide the improvisation, at its highest level improvisation is unstructured, as in the "solo-form," in which musicians perform entire improvisations on single-voiced instruments or in a multi-instrumental arrangement.[38]

Despite this African American focus, Smith's vision for social transformation depends on a sense of internationalist solidarity and universalist beliefs. He looks forward to the creation of a new world music, an emergent form that is rooted in the experiences of Africans in the "new world" but that will also develop in dialogue with musical cultures from throughout the world. Ultimately, creative music provides a means for global consciousness-raising and the creation of an emancipatory future. Smith asserts that European composition reflects the political and cultural dominance of the West. Improvised creative music, in turn, holds the key to dismantling Western domination by challenging its musical conventions. Smith links creative African American musics to improvised musics from India, Bali, and the Islamic world. He predicts that together these musics "will eventually eliminate the political dominance of euro-america in this world" by creating "a balance in the arena of world music (africa, asia, europe, euro-america, afro-america)." In the end, musical transformations will lead to "meaningful political reforms in the world: culture being the way of our lives; politics, the way our lives are handled."[39]

Smith builds upon the work of theorists such as Gayle, who wove together tenets of cultural nationalism and pan-Africanism with universal principles. His work parallels that of AACM members who had rejected some of the prescriptive tenets of cultural nationalism. Smith's ideas were also a product of his experiences as a musician. North America was still Smith's primary landscape, and African American culture was his life spring of creativity, though through his travels and study he had developed affinities for other cultures. But even if black creative music were to bring about the end of Western domination and the regime of composition, these transformations would require further movement out of the economic, discursive, and aesthetic limitations imposed on the music and its practitioners in the United States. Interrogating the boundaries of national and racial identity, as well as appealing to a universal spirituality and epistemology, provided a means of negotiating these constraints.

As Smith puts forth a program for a new world music, he places much of the responsibility on musicians themselves. Drawing on the AACM's tenets of self-improvement, Smith argues that creative musicians must learn to listen and perform with all their faculties. They must become familiar with the principles governing the relationship of sound and silence and the process by which sound operates in physical spaces. Creative musicians must strive to master improvisation at its highest level—

that is, to improvise without any planning and still be able to engage in technically proficient and emotionally satisfying performance. Only then can these musicians adopt their role in producing social transformation through improvisation. The musician who creates a new world music must also be "a sensitive being who feels a higher calling and responds by seeking to enter into proper attunement with mind and body." The musician thus connects the self to a universal intelligence that "unifies the whole of creation."[40]

This transformation will not be undertaken through consciousness-raising alone. Because the music industry constrains musicians' creative output, Smith calls for sweeping changes in its institutions. The economic empowerment of musicians is a precondition of aesthetic freedom and political change. The first step involves musicians freeing their artistic selves from the "commercial business-production-journalism and the likes of the powerMAN." Smith calls for a more collective approach to copyrights and royalties: every musician who is responsible for a "substantial amount of improvising" on a record should be given credit for authorship and a share of the royalties. When some semblance of economic justice is achieved, "master improvisors," who will no longer have their creativity hampered by "man-made laws concerning creation," will be able to "bring about the needed change of consciousness in the masses and the deliverance of creative music."[41]

Like other musicians active during this period, Smith hopes that government intervention might address some of the problems facing musicians. He predicts that recent government funding for black art will lead to liberation from the "commercial business-production-journalism." No doubt buoyed by the limited, but growing, levels of financial and institutional support provided to a select number of black improvising musicians by governmental and private funding sources in Europe and the United States, Smith advocates a "conscientious cultural program," financed through taxes, that "would enable all segments of these united states to become fully aware of and experience this great classical art music of afro-america" and challenge the idea that "our" classical music is rooted in Europe.[42]

Laws and emergent technologies might also play an emancipatory role. Smith refers to an October 1971 Congressional act that, beginning in February 1972, established copyright through sound recordings and provided civil and criminal protection against record piracy; and he sees this as a means for improvisers to empower themselves by registering and retaining rights of authorship over their creations. Smith also rethinks, on some level, the idea of improvisation as a product of an oral tradition. He claims that an "oral-electronic tradition" is currently being born, one that can be transmitted through the media and "satellite techniques" anywhere in the world, communicating its liberating effect more quickly to a larger audience. Smith argues that we must set up cultural ties and "seek out other cultures that have improvisation as their classical art music (india, pan-islam, the orient, bali, and africa) and make lasting cultural commitments to them." For the world can survive only if "we, as humans, become earth-beings committed in our cultural and political aspects to a pan-world future."[43]

Smith's simultaneous veneration of a black musical vision and embrace of universal principles also reflect his negotiation of the discourse surrounding jazz and classical music. *Notes* is in some ways a direct response to jazz criticism as well as a program for social transformation. Smith responds to the double bind in which music criticism had placed black avant-garde musicians: their art was derided by some for being too derivative of European concert music, whereas others thought it could never approach the artistic legitimacy of classical music. In a 1975 interview, Smith reacted testily when asked to comment on the comparison between his music and contemporary classical music. Although he acknowledged mutual influence and agreed that "the fundamental laws of each music are the same," he maintained a belief in distinct traditions and insisted that his roots lay in what is commonly defined as the jazz tradition. By giving greater attention to the artistry of African Americans, Smith rejected his supposed connections to European concert music and placed himself within a jazz tradition that has been a site of black accomplishment and a source of artistic validation. And when Smith argued that improvised music maintains the spirit of the drum—even if the drum itself is not present—he refuted the charge that his lack of "swing" distanced him from this tradition.[44] But Smith also recognized that, regardless of its form, improvised music performed by black musicians would never be more than "jazz" in the eyes of certain critics and music scholars. Theorizing black music's role in the formation of a new world musical tradition, which is itself a corrective to European cultural and political hegemony, is also a means of dismantling the aesthetic barrier between classical and black improvised music.

Smith also asks in *Notes* whether creative music can even be criticized. Evoking Brown's *Afternoon of a Georgia Faun* as an example of a recording that critics were unable to fit into prescribed categories, he demands that creative music be taken on its own terms. Smith echoes a long-standing frustration of jazz musicians who suffered the "real and drastic effect-influence of false interpretation (words) on music," and he uses the written word as a means of challenging the derisive effect of jazz criticism. Like other black aestheticians, Smith calls for establishing new critical criteria that are based upon the function of black music instead of its adherence to prescribed forms. Although some musicologists and critics have recognized the importance of improvisation in the development of "art-music," using critical tools from the world of composition is fruitless. Ultimately, Smith agrees with Marion Brown that creative music facilitates the communication of meanings that are determined by the improviser, the listener, and the performance environment at the moment of its production. Language cannot adequately capture this experience and communicate it to a nonparticipant. "So the answer is *no*," he concludes, "creative music cannot be criticized."[45] Although arguing that creative music is beyond criticism and then offering a written interpretation of the music are somewhat contradictory, Smith's antinomic position, like Brown's, recognizes that the written word has the power both to constrain avant-garde musical projects and to give them broader purpose.

Smith moves his discussion of improvised music in a somewhat different direction in his essay "(M1) American Music." Here he envisions a lineage of North American classical music composers, whose work was often marginalized in musicological circles, as potential allies in his critique of Eurocentrism. Like Brown, Smith was drawn to the music and written work of Charles Ives. He saw in Ives's incorporation of thematic material from blues and ragtime a validation of creative music as well as a model for an expansive aesthetic vision. Smith was also influenced by Ives's *Essays Before a Sonata*, first published in 1920, in which the composer ascribed meaning to his own music.[46]

In "(M1) American Music," Smith gives more attention than he did in *Notes* to the contributions of "classical" composers in the development of a new world music. He argues that "the late nineteenth century marks the beginning of the history of America's serious art music." He identifies two traditions, creative music and classical music, both of which incorporate African *and* European elements. Smith locates the origins of this "art music" in Scott Joplin's compositions for piano and Ives's American-centered classical music. Responding to Eurocentric music scholarship, Smith argues that both artists successfully challenged the notion that European music is the national music of the United States, a supposition that was "politically and racially motivated." Also important are Duke Ellington's innovations in voicings for orchestral forms and the tonal and timbral contributions of his soloists. On the classical side, Smith creates a genealogy, beginning with Ives's "Unanswered Question" and highlighting African American contributions to classical music. He mentions the work of Henry Cowell, William Grant Still, Harry Partch, Thomas J. Anderson, Henry Brant, John Cage, Milton Babbitt, Edgard Varése, and Ollie Wilson. The inclusion of Mexican composer Carlos Chavez extends the tradition of American music beyond the southern border of the United States.[47]

Smith nevertheless views creative music as playing the central role in creating a new world music, for it is improvised music that best fulfills Ives's ideal that it "absorb from its environment" while maintaining its identity. Moreover, it is the practitioners of improvised music who have best incorporated multiple elements into their work. Smith explains that the "average" creative musician is versed in the "fundamental laws" of "at least one Asian music, in the classical music of Europe and Euro-America, and in African music." Yet Smith also asserts that a progressive, liberating aesthetic can be forged from an amalgamation of the two distinct American traditions. After outlining the way these genres developed on American soil, Smith calls for a "wider American music" in which the "laws and aesthetic principles underlying creative music" would be merged "with the most positive discoveries" of classical music. The result would be an emergent art form and a new type of artist. Smith argues that the new music must be different from the third stream, which he considers merely an attempt to combine existing forms by musicians grounded in distinct traditions. Rather, the new musicians would have equal understanding of both musical trajectories.[48]

The success of this hybrid American music for the "advancement of humanity in America," however, depends on interactions with people in other countries. The new American music must ultimately become a world music: "a different and wholly new music derived from the musics of the many different peoples of earth (earth-beings)." Smith, who began studying ethnomusicology at Wesleyan University in 1974, maintains an ethnographer's belief that one must be immersed in a culture's practices as a precondition of understanding its music. The creation of a new world music cannot be achieved through the random sampling of musics from different cultures, he cautions:

> What is happening now in music represents a crossing and exchange of influences in a kind of mingling of extractings from other musics' cultural-environments and lumping of them together. Those who perform this music seem to be ill-informed as to the true nature of the different musics being used. At present the elements of these musics are handled out of context and the results clearly show that music is not the "universal language."

One must approach the music of other cultures by first gaining an understanding of the philosophy, religion, and social interactions of the people who produce it. Then one can analyze the "mechanics" of the music. At that point, a new music can develop that transcends improvisation and composition and the commonly recognized roles of musicians and ensembles. This music will be created by a group of knowledgeable and educated creators who will "be able to give form to it through consciousness manifested in intellect, emotion, and intuition." Smith concludes that "we are indeed in a position to form a world community, and it is from this community that the new music will arise. All peoples of earth (earth-beings) and their respective cultures and arts will be equally represented."[49]

Smith's interest in fusing the creative musical ideal with "the most positive discoveries" from classical music, as well as his interest in cross-cultural musical exchanges, resonates in his parallel project of creating a symbolic language to organize and analyze improvisation. In 1970 Smith began working with two musical systems: the "rhythm-unit concept" and "Ahkreanvention." The rhythm-unit concept holds that any single sound, rhythm, or combination of sounds and rhythms may be understood as a complete "piece." Smith envisioned Ahkreanvention as an alternative notation system for scoring sound, rhythm, silence, and improvisation. It is a somewhat open-ended symbolic framework, designed so that musicians can analyze in the moment of creating their own improvisations. Its purpose, Smith said in 1978, was "to create and invent musical ideas simultaneously utilizing the fundamental laws of improvisation and composition." Ahkreanvention includes symbols designating duration, improvisation, and "moving sounds of different velocities." These symbols are arranged on "two types of staffs: sound staffs divided into low, medium and high; and sound staffs of adjustable sound partials."[50]

In *Notes,* Smith articulates the basis of his rhythm-unit concept. He states that each "single rhythm-sound" or series of "sound-rhythm[s]" is a "complete improvisation" unto itself. "Each element is autonomous in its relationship in the improvisation," he writes, "therefore, there is no intent towards time as a period of development." Without expectations of rhythmic continuity, resolution, or closure, musicians are free to explore a more spatially centered way of performing music as a product of the instant. In performances involving more than one musician, such as those by his group New Dalta Ahkri, each performer is a "complete unity," operating independently yet creating together. Ideally, each creator responds only to his or her own playing, even though the creation occurs within a group. "This attitude frees the sound-rhythm elements in an improvisation from being realized through dependent re-action." Although Smith does not mention Ahkreanvention in *Notes* or give any details of how the music might be scored, he offers two "forms" that suggest a way of structuring musical performances that both preserves the improviser's autonomy and demands a degree of interpretation of musical ideas put forth by the "composer." "EeLO'jsZ" refers to a way of organizing musicians into groups so that the autonomy of each improviser is maintained. "aFmie" is an "art-dance-music form," in which a dancer and a musician respond to the same set of symbols but are given the freedom to interpret them as they see fit.[51]

Smith goes on to describe the use of these concepts on his first Kabell Records release *Creative Music-1,* a collection of six solo improvisations, five of which are multi-instrumental pieces. Each piece is based upon a different musical principle. "Nine Stones on a Mountain" is an exploration (or "image-vision," in Smith's words) of how "sound-thought permeates our mind." The musical statements on this piece are connected by this common theme; but in accordance with Smith's theory, each "sound rhythm" is a distinct musical thought and therefore unencumbered by a need for structural unity. "aFmie, poem, solo-dance #3" is written for musician and dancer. Following the dictates of Smith's improvisational form, both dancer and musician are supposed to operate as "total entities in themselves" and not rely on each other for inspiration. As a soloist, Smith contributes the dancer's part by moving his body (for example, the manipulation of embouchure, the way he strikes a gong) while playing the piece. "Egotommeli" is dedicated to the Dogon sage of the same name. This multiple percussion piece features Smith's use of the steel-o-phone, a homemade instrument consisting of chimes and a "keyboard" made of fifteen bars of different types of metal (aluminum, cast iron, copper). The improvisational character of the piece is enhanced by the mechanics of the steel-o-phone. The player has the freedom to rearrange the keys of the instrument so that it produces different tones when struck in the same way on successive performances. On this piece, Smith bases his improvisations on a "score" of basic musical structures; but, as he notes, the beginning and the end of the piece, which are based on the same symbols, sound "very different on both ends because of the scoring of sound which allows for improvisation."[52]

Smith's second Kabell release is *Reflectativity*, a live recording of a 1974 New Dalta Ahkri performance in New Haven. Smith plays trumpet, flügelhorn, piccolo trumpet, Indian and bamboo flutes, and percussion, a complement of instruments that illustrates his desire to create a new world music by incorporating musical elements from throughout the globe. Joining him are Anthony Davis on piano and Wes Brown on bass and Ghanaian flute. *Reflectativity* consists of two pieces of music: the title track, performed in memory of the recently deceased Duke Ellington; and "t wmukl-D," dedicated to "the fishermen of the world." In the liner notes, Smith again describes an approach to "scoring" improvisation that encourages and demands a creative engagement (on the part of musicians and audiences alike) with the formal qualities of his music: "I am deeply thankful to Anthony Davis and Wes Brown for giving their breath in order that the music could live, for the burden of music-making is not the sole responsibility of a one mind, but the collective mind of participants and non-participants, even though the initial creative energy for scoring an improvisation can be the work-task of one person."[53]

One can hear Brown's and Davis's engagement with Smith's score when listening to both pieces on this record. There appears to be little in the way of "dependent re-action" among the musicians, but this music clearly does not involve musicians playing unstructured improvisations without regard to form. Although the piece lacks regular meter and time-keeping instruments, the use of silence, punctuating clusters of sound by the ensemble, and Smith's brief passages on percussion suggest temporal movement, though not movement that depends upon cyclical repetitions or regular rhythmic activity. This movement through time, as well as the harmonic and melodic elements of the piece, suggests that Smith's scores provide a basic soundscape of mood and transition, while leaving the performers free to explore their own ideas independently within this framework. Each of the three musicians takes center stage at different moments, with the others adding supporting musical fills. At clearly orchestrated transitions, often marked by Smith switching instruments, the musicians begin exploring new themes in unison.

Smith was finally able to record a fully developed Ahkreanvention composition for ensemble on his 1978 ECM release *Divine Love*. "Tastalun" is music for three muted trumpets. Joining Smith on the recording are Kenny Wheeler and AACM colleague Lester Bowie. The basic framework of "Tastalun" creates an environment where the instruments support one another while engaging in independent improvisation. The counterpoint is not based upon harmonic resolution or the dictates of call and response; instead, the lines move independently, coming together at intermittent points. These convergences show how Smith controls tonal effects and temporal movement with his musical directions. The following year, Smith released his aptly titled solo album *Ahkreanvention,* on which he performed a series of Ahkreanvention works. Two compositions for Ghanaian flute, "Sarhanna" and "Kashala," showcase his drive to immerse himself in the music of other cultures. On "Life Sequence I," Smith moves between steel-o-phone, percussion, flügelhorn, and several types of trumpets—an example of his practice of creating structures for solo improvisations to be performed by individual musicians on multiple instruments.[54]

Eventually Smith supplanted the Ahkreanvention system with one he termed "Ankhrasmation," the development of which paralleled his embrace of Rastafarianism (and the name Wadada) in the 1980s. Whereas

Ahkreanvention provided a means of analyzing and scoring the "art object" itself, Ankhrasmation added still other philosophical and cultural dimensions to the project. "Ankh" referred to a "vital life force" as symbolized by the Egyptian ankh cross. "Ras" was the Ethiopian male honorific, embraced by the Rastafarian religion as a sign of respect; it was also a reference to the Egyptian sun god Ra. "Ma" simply referred to "mother." According to Smith, the component elements of Ankhrasmation reached back to Egyptian cultural and philosophical traditions, while its embrace of male and female elements of the family signified "a connection with all things the human makes." This musical language thus connected the art of improvisation to the Afrocentric and universal utopian vision Smith expressed in *Notes*. As he said in 1998, this system "conjure[s] up these kinds of utopias, like the ones that Martin Luther King built, which was about human rights, or the one Gandhi built, which was about human rights. It's a manipulation of feeling and ideas that you want to be able to connect to something of value when you live in a hostile environment."[55]

## The "Crisis" of the Black Creative Intellectual

In a contribution to Graham Lock's 1995 festschrift for multi-instrumentalist and composer Anthony Braxton, on the occasion of Braxton's fiftieth birthday, Smith describes some of the major elements of both the score and the recording of Braxton's "Composition 113." His brief essay illustrates how the Ankhrasmation system lent itself to analyzing improvisations scored by other musicians. Like Ahkreanvention, the later system organizes music on two types of staffs. The first staff depicts the "fundamental structure" of a composition, which comprises the basic harmonic and rhythmic movement and the general contours of the melodic line; while the second staff indicates the "structure activity," which involves particular melodic figures, tonal effects, and other elements the improviser is to explore. Ankhrasmation thus provides not only two sets of information for an improviser to interpret but also a means of analyzing a recorded piece of music in terms of its basic "organic" musical ideas as well as its elaboration.[56]

Braxton's work was perfect for Ankhrasmation analysis. He had developed his own original system for scoring improvisation, which also allowed and demanded interpretation from musicians. Moreover, he and Smith had been intellectual allies and musical collaborators since their days with the AACM. Both had written about their music and in doing so fused Afrocentric principles with a liberating, universalist vision. Smith's analysis of "Composition 113" (a composition for soloist, large photograph, and prepared stage) drew from Braxton's score and narrative description of the piece. In a performance of this composition, the improvising musician is instructed to participate in "mythological" fantasy by taking on the roles and musically expressing the attitudes of six shadowy characters who embody six human characteristics (humor, acceptance, strength, dependability, courage, and belief). The composition is part of a series of "ritual and ceremonial musics and stories" Braxton began to develop in the 1980s, which he viewed as "an individual effort to establish motives for world change."[57]

The remainder of this chapter focuses on Braxton's writings about creative music. The sheer volume of Braxton's written work makes it tremendously difficult to come to terms with the scope of his ideas. An entire book does not provide adequate space, let alone a chapter section. In 1985 Braxton independently published the *Tri-axium Writings,* a three-volume, 1,700-page project that set forth his aesthetic philosophy and an account of the history of music on earth. Three years later, he released *Composition Notes,* a five-volume, 2,400-page collection of commentary about his own music. In addition, Braxton has made numerous statements about music and its position in society in liner notes, interviews, and other venues; and the growing body of scholarship on Braxton has made the discursive field around his music even larger.[58] Nevertheless, the following pages attempt to describe the general contours of Braxton's vision for creative music, emphasizing how his aesthetic and philosophical systems position this music as a mode of African American intellectualism in the face of narrow definitions of black creativity.

A native of Chicago, Braxton joined the AACM upon returning to the city in the fall of 1966 after a stint in the military, which included service in the Eighth Army Band in Korea. Braxton had previously encountered AACM members Henry Threadgill, Joseph Jarman, and Malachi Favors in 1963 at Wilson Junior College in Chicago. That same year, Braxton met Roscoe Mitchell, who introduced him to free jazz and early bebop recordings. By the time Braxton joined the AACM, he had become something of an activist—he worked for a short while with the

Congress of Racial Equality (CORE)—and had taken classes and educated himself in European philosophy and African American letters. Braxton had also developed an aesthetic vision that blurred the distinctions between jazz and concert music. Braxton continued these projects as a member of the AACM, as he joined its members in their investigations of avant-garde jazz, modern concert music, mysticism, and a commitment to social transformation.[59]

Like Smith, Braxton extended the AACM's aesthetic, spiritual, and social vision into alternative social and musical expressions. In the preface to the first volume of *Composition Notes,* Braxton describes his "life's work objectives": "(1) to establish a music and music system for *extended* functionalism; (2) to establish a philosophical basis that respects and clarifies a world view perspective; and (3) to erect a mythological and *[fantasy]* context to portray this information."[60] "Extended functionalism," to simplify and paraphrase the definition Braxton offers in the *Tri-axium Writings,* refers to a "discipline" that gives insight into the spiritual or metaphysical dimensions of social experience and extends these insights into personal transformation and social change.[61]

The first part of Braxton's "life's work objectives," then, involved the creation of an alternative, socially transformative musical system. Like some of his AACM colleagues, he drew upon aspects of avant-garde jazz and modern concert music; but as Ronald Radano argues, Braxton was the AACM member who "most radically challenged the constraints distinguishing concert music from jazz."[62] He rejected the limitations of both, dismantling the wall between them as well as that between composed and improvised music. As saxophonist Evan Parker put it:

> It's clear that, unlike me, AB never made the category error of dialectically opposing composition and improvisation as though they were mutually exclusive. He has always seen and presented his music as composition in which the notational and improvisational methods may be used in combination to arrive at a particular result. Given his universalist appetites, it is natural that he should have worked across the spectrum from completely notated to completely improvised compositions with all the hybrid possibilities in between.[63]

In the late 1960s, Braxton began to devise a "language music system" as a means of integrating what he termed the "extended improvisations" of

Coltrane and Cecil Taylor and the "structural dynamics" of Webernian serialism. Braxton developed a series of "language types" (for example, long sounds and trills) and "sound classifications" (such as "gurgle sounds"). When woven together through a process of "conceptual grafting," these language types provided "an elastic approach to composition for solo improvisation." Braxton also developed a system of geometric shapes and mathematical diagrams for describing these language types.[64]

Throughout the late 1960s and 1970s, Braxton developed this "language" in solo contexts and in ensembles ranging in size from duos to large orchestras. He worked with a variety of forms and compositional principles that simultaneously spoke of an engagement with modern concert music and avant-garde jazz and a rejection of the boundary between them. In his series of Kelvin compositions, he used complicated rhythmic patterns instead of chord changes as the building blocks for his compositions. On other pieces, he employed the concept of a "gravallic base," a cyclical pattern of rhythms, as a way of outlining the structure of his compositions. Some pieces combined sections of standard notation with passages employing shapes and diagrams that provided flexible guidelines for improvisation. In his compositions for "creative orchestra," for example, Braxton combined notated parts with diagrams that defined textures but gave musicians some choice in tempo, pitch, tone color, phrasing, and timbre in ensemble sections. A striking example of this approach can be heard on the recording *Creative Orchestra Music 1976,* where Braxton leads an orchestra featuring well-known jazz avant-garde players (Muhal Richard Abrams, Dave Holland, Roscoe Mitchell, Wadada Leo Smith) and several musicians from experimental concert music (Frederic Rzewski, Richard Teitelbaum). The musicians work with notated material and structured group improvisation on six compositions that Braxton linked to the big band tradition of the "Ellington's-Hendersons-Mingus's-Colemans—etc."[65]

Like Smith, Braxton saw his music, and that of his AACM colleagues and other genre-challenging musicians, as a tool for global social transformation. For three decades, he has expressed the belief that the logic of his hybrid music points in the direction of erasing the boundaries and labels that are symbolic of racism, sexism, and European and American political domination of people of color throughout the globe. By the 1980s, Braxton moved further in this direction through the creation of ritual and ceremonial musics. His desire to "erect a mythological and *[fantasy]* context to portray this information" is perhaps most evident in his self-referential *Trillium* operas, in which various characters discuss Braxton's beliefs, comment on his music, and enact his vision of social change. The librettos, as Graham Lock notes, "each address a specific concept taken from the *Tri-axium Writings*" and describe coming ethical conflicts pitting the forces of individualism and materialism against spiritual, universalist beliefs.[66]

Braxton discusses the philosophical and social implications of his musical vision in the most detail in the *Tri-axium Writings*. Here we can see Braxton's complex extension of the AACM's "aesthetic spiritualism" in his own articulation of a world system of creativity, as well as the intellectual influence of writers ranging from Afrocentric scholar Yosef ben-Jochannan to Wadada Leo Smith to composer Karlheinz Stockhausen.[67] In the context of Braxton's career and various comments he has made over the years, the *Tri-axium Writings* can also be viewed as an attempt to carve out a creative space for his hybrid music. In fact, Braxton has seen "world change," or at least some kind of global consciousness-raising, as a necessary step for his hybrid musical vision to be accepted. Braxton tries to establish what he terms a "perception context that respects and allows for both the disciplines (improvisational/fluid musics and notated/stable musics) to exist and evolve—as unified and independent realities (with its own secrets and particulars)."[68] But it is his destruction of the boundary between improvised and composed music and his simultaneous reification of these categories as manifestations of distinct, culturally specific philosophical systems that most directly challenge some of the racialized assumptions of music criticism—for Braxton has been deeply concerned with the reputation of African American avant-garde artists and the inability of African American and nonblack observers to come to terms with his particular brand of black intellectualism.

Although Braxton's intellect, eccentric personality, and iconoclastic mixture of avant-garde jazz and concert music practices won him many admirers over the years, he has remained a controversial figure since the early days of his career. The cultivated intellectual approach through which he developed his hybrid musical vision made him all the more appealing and controversial as his career progressed. Reflecting upon the Creative Construction Company's lukewarm reception in Europe after their arrival in 1969, Braxton said: "There was a great debate in Paris that lasted maybe six months, and the verdict was that our music didn't swing, while the Art Ensemble represented the real gains of the AACM—in fact, the two became virtually synonymous. . . . Our music was viewed as cold, intellectual, borrowing from Europe or something. We were not acceptable African-Americans."[69]

Such a reaction should not have been surprising, given the often-primitivistic expectations of European audiences, but it was a source of great disappointment nonetheless. Upon his return to the United States in 1970, Braxton settled in New York, where he stayed for a brief period with Ornette Coleman. In New York, Braxton played with a variety of performers, including Frederic Rzewski's Musica Elettronica Viva. In 1971 he joined Chick Corea's group, Circle (with Jack DeJohnette and Dave Holland), and toured with them in Europe, gaining greater notoriety. He moved back to Paris, where he performed with a variety of musicians (modern concert and jazz) and eventually obtained a residency at the American Center.[70]

Braxton's hybrid vision brought him increasing attention from French and American jazz critics, which eventually enabled him to secure a contract with Arista Records when he returned to the United States in 1974. Despite his critical renaissance during the 1970s, however, his work simply did not appeal to many listeners. Speaking of one of Braxton's longer compositions for a large ensemble, Peter Niklas Wilson argues:

> The traditionally oriented jazz listener is obliged to do without the security of the time-worn formal and harmonic frameworks. . . . The more adventurous jazz fan will miss the visceral excitement of extended virtuoso solos or displays of collective "energy" and be repelled by the relative restraint of the music. . . . The New Music Expert is . . . bound to criticize the absence of a large-scale formal concept and Braxton's failure to be "innovative"—innovation being measured by criteria like complexity, advanced systems of pitch or rhythmic organization, sophistication of formal design, newness or difficulty of instrumental techniques or timbres employed.

Of course, as Wilson additionally notes, racism was a major factor in determining concert music devotees' interpretation of Braxton, just as it is also clear that certain conceptions of race—more specifically, expectations about a certain kind of blackness—influenced how he was perceived in the jazz world.[71]

As Radano shows, Braxton was celebrated during the mid-1970s by jazz writers who wanted to reinvent a jazz tradition and revive the flagging jazz industry. Braxton seemed to be an ideal artist to champion because he was experimental and eccentric but still seemed to adhere to the jazz tradition. Yet Braxton's critical favor was contingent on his continuing ability to be seen as a jazz artist. Although his eccentricities and intellectual proclivities fit the primitive/intellectual homology that had long pervaded the jazz mythology around black musicians, jazz critics seldom took his ideas (as opposed to his image as an intellectual) or his affinity for concert music seriously. And even when they did, they rarely had a sufficiently sophisticated knowledge of contemporary concert music to understand his range of referents. Once Braxton shifted his jazz recordings to European labels, while keeping his "serious" concert music on Arista, he ceased to fit into prescribed categories, and his popularity declined.[72]

Braxton believed he was misrepresented by the critical fervor surrounding him, and he recognized the impact that journalism and commodification had on the lives of artists. In a 1979 interview, Braxton articulated a familiar challenge to the "one dimensional" journalism of white critics. Although he carefully avoided saying that white critics should not write about black music (a position that he would consider racist), he advanced a culturalist argument, noting that problems arose when the vast majority of people documenting the music, no matter how well intentioned, were white people whose viewpoints might be culturally biased. In Braxton's view, it was a major problem that African Americans, women, and people in other countries were given little opportunity to define their art and intellects. Echoing Ellington, Mingus, and others before him, he argued that the word "jazz" obscured an understanding of the complexity of black lives: "I don't know what they mean by 'jazz' with the exception of saying 'nigger.'" He also connected the idea of jazz to a discourse of primitivism that explained black accomplishment as the result of "natural ability."[73]

White jazz writers were not the only ones with whom he took issue in this interview. Some black critics thought Braxton's hybrid music and intellectualism distanced him from black culture. In reference to recent criticism he had received from Stanley Crouch and Ted Joans, Braxton claimed black writers could be just as misdirected as whites. Thus, part of the impetus for creating the *Tri-axium Writings* had been to correct the errors of black commentators: "That's why I've gone on to write these three books, because nobody else would do it. I'm tired of waiting for the black literary community to take a position that I can understand." When asked why he sought to develop a black aesthetic when he was derided by African American writers for not being black enough, Braxton replied that there was nothing wrong with trying to create such an ideal; the problems occurred when black identity and culture were defined in narrow terms. As a means of expanding the definitions of blackness, he rejected a biological definition of race, preferring to understand it in spiritual and intellectual terms. He described blackness as a "spirit factor" that emerged from a particular place (Africa) and was reinvented "as it travel[ed] through a particular physical and vibrational route." Black aesthetics were to be understood in terms of "information and how it's colored methodology."[74]

In the introduction to the *Tri-axium Writings,* Braxton describes the three volumes as a "snapshot of what I have been thinking and feeling from a period of September 1973 to March 1980." These dates begin with the tail end of his expatriate days in Paris and continue through a period of artistic exploration on both the European and American continents at the margins of both the jazz and concert music worlds.[75] Speaking of the text in 1989, Braxton said:

> My philosophical and world view perspective is documented and demonstrated in the *Tri-axium Writings.* I felt by 1968 that the only way to continue my work was to clarify and give a perspective that I could use to evolve and learn in, based on what I was experiencing in my life. Or, at least, I sought to erect a platform that would make sense, an evolutionary platform that I could use to continue with my work, in learning how to live, learning what attraction means to me, and learning what role creative music would have in my life. So, the *Tri-axium Writings* is a foundation of the philosophical system, which demonstrates individual-to-group logics. I'm interested in the dynamic implications of what's happening in this time period, with extended technology, extended architecture, possibilities for extended communication and correspondence, and to learn from those fundamentals that

unite us as a species on this planet, to better understand value systems and the role of beauty and wonder in the discipline we call music.[76]

In other words, Braxton tries to devise an aesthetic philosophy that recasts his identity as an intellectual; redefines the role of black intellectualism in the face of critical misrepresentations of "black creativity" and "creativity in general"; and theorizes the interaction of spiritual, historical, and geographic forces on intellect and art. All of this serves as a means of crafting a space for his own musical project. Although space does not permit a summary of the intricacies of Braxton's complex, often abstruse, and exhaustingly repetitive arguments—which are not made any clearer by the wide array of neologisms he employs to make his points—we can make sense of their broader scope in the context of Braxton's career during the 1970s.

The first volume of the *Tri-axium Writings* shows how Braxton's ideas about music, culture, race, economics, and geography reflect his complex position as an African American musician and intellectual situated in the margins of genre, place, discourses, and economics. The term "tri-axium" refers to a tripartite method of describing and making sense of the world. Braxton describes the historical development of three broadly defined musical traditions (world music, Western art music, trans-African music) that have developed in a reciprocal cause-and-effect relationship with human societies. He begins by setting forth the "underlying philosophical bases" for these distinct musical traditions and then explains how they are converging to facilitate the emergence of a transformative global music.

World music is the sonic equivalent of a core "world creativity," a kind of metaphysical and spiritual component of human existence that helps to guide one's thoughts and to determine how life is experienced. World music in practice serves a ritualistic function and holds the key to global transformation. Braxton roots this world creativity in dynastic Egypt. He figures precontact Africa as an idealized and undifferentiated place and time, where music was deeply woven into the cultural fabric. Our distance from African music, which at this point in the text is a metonym for world music, is a result of its disruption by the cultural and philosophical systems of the West and their underlying economic systems of slavery, colonialism, and neocolonialism. Yet despite its obfuscation, world creativity still exists at an often-unrealized level as part of a collective consciousness of the world community. Like Wadada Leo Smith, Braxton argues for focusing on improvisation as an expression of world creativity and a vehicle in bringing about social transformation. In Braxton's words, "this then is the actual 'isness' of improvisation as conceived and offered to us from the progressional continuance of world culture— as opposed to present day concepts which view this subject as an end in itself. . . . It is important that this factor is understood if we are to view the realness of world creativity as a potential transformational tool."[77] Improvisation is thus a philosophical enterprise and a central ritualistic and aesthetic element of a global musical culture that has been marginalized by the West.

Part of Braxton's quest in this text is to document and validate the existence of world music in order to challenge the errors of critics, historians, and others who have been unable to grasp the spiritual and aesthetic aspects of non-Western music and have therefore diminished its importance. Racism and primitivism create this "misdocumentation," but the problem is ultimately one of epistemology: "The western affinity to what it would call 'logical' can become a straitjacket for comprehending world creativity (or culture). Thus, it comes as no surprise that many western historians have little or no respect for many areas of world creativity." In response, Braxton calls for an alternative approach that is rooted in the "meta-realness of world creativity." In other words, Braxton seeks to redefine the study of music by basing its investigation in its functional and aesthetic aspects and empowering the practitioners of world music to define their own terms.[78]

Braxton presents a history of music that culminates with world music reemerging as a progressive force and musicians like himself occupying center stage as practitioners and commentators. Like other black aestheticians, he describes an alternative epistemological orientation that is both pan-African and universalist. However, in order to define and validate his role as a stylistic synthesizer (a "restructuralist," in his words), he must come to terms with other musical traditions and systems of thought in which he is immersed. The history of Western art music, at one level, is an indicator of the Western "attitude," which Braxton describes as a hierarchical worldview dependent upon the separation of ideas from spirituality and upon a reliance on "empiricism to validate ideas."

As reflected in music, the Western ideal has been characterized by a dependence on uniform tonal scales, indicating a shift away from an integrative spirituality; a hierarchy of specialization, wherein composers and performers play distinct roles; a lack of improvisation; and an emphasis on "investigation" as a means of musical erudition. Braxton defines this Western art music tradition in reductionist terms as a single musical and intellectual tradition running from Bach to Schoenberg. Although this description is somewhat at odds with his universalist aspirations and commitment to dismantling musical categories, Braxton describes Western music as an aberration of the world system in order to theorize both a long history of cultural domination and the critical misrepresentation, prejudice against, and economic exploitation of African American musics.[79]

But Western art music is in a state of flux, Braxton believes. Although he maintains a critique of the Western "attitude" and the classical music tradition, he asserts that modern concert music composers have challenged the parameters of the genre. Braxton believes Schoenberg's serialism marked the end of the "solid period" of Western art music, just as existentialist philosophy challenged Enlightenment assumptions about order and objectivity in the world. Although Western art music is still a separate tradition, Anton Webern and John Cage ushered it into a period of transition. The musical "continuums" established by these composers signaled a "return to basic essences—or to the world group," as composers from European and American classical music began to employ improvisation in their work. The shift from "empiricism" connected these artists to the world system of creativity, thereby challenging the idea of Europe as the sole site of legitimate creativity: "The solidification of serialism in Webern's understanding would reveal a renewed awareness of universal consciousness, and while this awareness would not necessarily be seen in his perception of its functional science, it would permeate the nature and spirit of its later exploration tendencies." Thus, it is left to Braxton and other "restructuralists" to take these explorations a step further.[80]

The changes in Western art music are, on some level, a product of its composers' interaction with the music of black artists and, more specifically, with practitioners of "trans-African music." Braxton defines "creative black music" from the trans-African tradition as music that transcends generic or marketing categories such as jazz, rhythm and blues, soul, and avant-garde. Nevertheless, it is also clear that African American "jazz" is at the center of this musical practice. Braxton tries to balance an understanding of creative black music as an oppositional extension of a universalist world cultural system with a viewpoint that African American music specifically responds to a history of Western domination. On the one hand, Braxton says that trans-African music actively attempts to reformulate a unified African cultural and "vibrational" tradition: "the story of creative black music [in the twentieth century] would be the evolution of process as a means to cast off every remnant of the white aesthetic and reinsert its own definitions." On the other hand, Braxton casts trans-African music as a projection of a world creativity that holds the promise for future transformations. Although black musicians rejected a "white aesthetic," they have drawn upon Western culture and ideas, especially when they are European or North American subjects themselves. Even as he criticizes the way methodological inquiry into creative black music misrepresents it—he cites both "general insensitivity" and "deliberate intent"—he believes that "western methodological tools" may be used to restore its place in the world.[81]

Braxton theorizes the hybridity of black music and culture in the West, while maintaining a belief in an African aesthetic as an idealized locus of power and identity. Western art and philosophy may be suffocating forces, but they also provide the tools for forging a liberating aesthetic. Here we begin to see more clearly the connections between his aesthetic philosophy and his own life and music. Braxton's analysis demonstrates how he negotiated the realities of race, power, and his particular experiences as an African American intellectual and musician. He had been trained in African American and European musical practices; had experienced discrimination, critical denigration, and economic exploitation on two continents; had been criticized for not being authentically black; and had maintained some tenets of a black cultural nationalist ideology. His model of musical systems expresses a belief in the universality of creativity and musical expression while recognizing that discursive and material boundaries do indeed dictate experience.

Some commentators argue that Braxton's hybrid musical vision and aesthetic philosophy and his aversion to static social identities make him a consummate postmodernist.[82] Yet his critique of the oppression of black people, other minorities, and women is still dependent on historically stable notions of identity. He understands how power comes into play when boundaries are tested and the expression of people on the margins is commodified and textualized. Although he has sought to disrupt formal categories of art and challenged assumptions about ethnic and racial identity, he also understands that the ephemerality and plasticity of definitional categories in the late twentieth century still reflect hierarchical power relationships. We might therefore consider Braxton a critic *of* postmodernity as well as a postmodern critic. In 1979 Braxton claimed that one of the problems of the past fifteen years—roughly the period of his public musical career— has been an "acceleration surrounding the definitions," with artists unable to create meanings on their own terms. When queried, Braxton agreed that this acceleration may be a result of recent developments in technology and capitalism, but he also situates these "many various levels of *spectacle*" in what he has termed "the grand trade off," the long-standing belief in the superiority of Western culture and the denigration of the cultural and intellectual traditions of others. Ultimately, this proliferation of discourses and labels is still a product of a "misbalance of forces that we're dealing with, the position of white people and the suppression of black people and Indian peoples. . . . we deal with words and concepts but we don't seem to be able to find essences any more."[83]

In the *Tri-axium Writings,* then, Braxton presents an analysis that defies musical categories while reifying the "essences" of others. By doing so, he challenges ideas about culture and identity even as he depends upon rather monolithic ideas of the same. Underlying historical events, cultural interactions, and the spectacle of journalism are philosophical and spiritual essences that provide modes of understanding and acting in the world. Braxton forges an aesthetic philosophy and a "transformational" journalism that validate his role as an intellectual and artist during what he sees as a time of momentous change. This project provides a means for him to oppose what he sees as the limitations placed on African American musicians and allows him to validate his own desire to seek out others in the world community of musicians.

The material and cultural domination of the West, Braxton argues, is in jeopardy. As he said in the 1979 interview: "the collective forces of world culture will move to make a situation where change will be inevitable on many different levels." This transformation began to take shape in the

1940s. Developments in serialism and in what he terms "neoclassicism" began the transformation in Western art music. In trans-African music, Charlie Parker and other bebop performers marked a critical juncture with their music, as they expressed the rising militancy of black Americans during World War II and a self-conscious artistic turn among black artists. This musical expression also had an impact on white artists and audiences. In Braxton's words:

> Parker's activity also represented the juncture where white people found the necessary conceptual factors to employ source-shift as a means to have creative music from the black aesthetic correspond to the dictates of what is commonly referred to as "art music" . . . bebop had to do with understanding the realness of black people's actual position in America and understanding the seriousness of what was being raised in creative music as a separate entity in itself.

Although the cultural interaction of this "source-shift transfer" was exploitative for black musicians, bebop accelerated the process by which black jazz musicians could reshape a Western culture in dire need of such transformation. The implication is that, in the utopian future, boundaries that were constructed around cultural groups and musical styles will be eliminated in favor of a world community and its attendant creative expressions. Thus, black creativity is both empowering for African American subjects and a panacea for a degenerating West.[84]

Braxton discusses creative black musicians whom he considers important and transitional: Thelonious Monk, Charles Mingus, John Coltrane, Cecil Taylor, Miles Davis, Art Tatum, George Russell, and Sun Ra. These figures are important for their self-consciously produced musical innovations. By creating a "separate information reality of black methodology," their work also challenges the Western idea that African American creativity is not valid. Braxton also describes the significance of Ravi Shankar and Indian musicians in shaping the spiritual and musical visions of African American and American musical practice and the impact of various "popular" forms on creative music. While mentioning the privilege that many white musicians have enjoyed in the jazz community, Braxton also recognizes the contributions of white improvisers—he often mentioned the influence of Paul Desmond on his own development—to the creation of a global creative music.[85]

Braxton identifies the musical movements coming out of New York and Chicago and other cities in the 1960s as providing the next step toward world creativity. Avant-garde musicians offer the clearest expression of the aesthetic and political position of black music, as well as a coherent shift toward the reestablishment of world community. The New York school, which consists of figures such as Marion Brown, Archie Shepp, and Albert Ayler (Braxton alternatively refers to it as the "post-Ayler continuum"), engaged the musical challenges of bebop and the early free jazz players while inscribing their own work with spiritual and political meaning. The AACM, in contrast, "could be understood as the movement which scientifically met the dynamics that this transformation implied." "Science" in this sense, refers to research, as evidenced by Roscoe Mitchell's and Lester Bowie's study of minstrelsy; Muhal Richard Abrams's research into the spiritual elements of black aesthetics; Joseph Jarman's and Malachi Favors's historical investigations of African American music; and Wadada Leo Smith's and Braxton's focus on an "alternative scientific functionalism for structure (composition)."[86]

When these musicians and others interacted with or influenced classical performers such as Stockhausen and Cage, they created a powerful shift toward a "solidification" of a world creative community. Braxton argues that the most "incredible" period of this interaction occurred in Paris between 1968 and 1973, which was, not surprisingly, the period when Braxton spent most of his time abroad. In a 1977 interview, Braxton saw his own experience in Europe as a chance to dismantle boundaries through musical interaction: "That's why I've been running around the planet, going out of my way to meet European musicians, to learn their music, to play with them. Because it's time to knock down these barriers and come together to play music. It's past time actually but we may as well start now." At the end of the first volume of the *Tri-axium Writings,* Braxton notes the influence of Ornette Coleman, Cecil Taylor, Mingus, Wadada Leo Smith, Stockhausen, Cage, and Xenakis on one another and on other musicians living in or passing through Paris during this period. When expatriate and traveling American musicians returned to the United States in the mid- and late 1970s, it also had a profound impact on the direction of the music. In Braxton's mind, the multiracial group of musicians who shaped the development of world music during this period were Steve Lacy, Andrew White, Dave Holland, Anthony Davis, Günter Hampel, Jeanne Lee, Warne Marsh, Keith Jarrett, and James

Newton. Braxton's tone in this section is celebratory as he writes of his experiences in Europe and the directions his own career and creative output have taken.[87]

In the second volume of the *Tri-axium Writings,* Braxton examines in greater detail the development of creative music in Europe and Japan and the experiences of African American musicians overseas. He more systematically explores the relationship of music and social transformations in ways that resonate with the discussions ongoing in his musical community for much of the 1960s and 1970s. He examines the economic problems facing musicians and questions why "extended black creativity" is so removed from African American communities. In an attempt to come to terms with a paradox that many politically committed, black avant-garde artists had addressed before him, he casts blame on a general lack of recognition of artistic creativity as well as on market forces that promote popular music to black audiences. Braxton champions the role of groups like the AACM in educating black people (and other communities) and in spreading knowledge about creative music. He also directly addresses another question that had accompanied the production of black music during this period: is music an explicit form of politics? He is particularly concerned with the supposed politics of the avant-garde. To state that the music of the 1960s represents a major shift in political purpose, he argues, overemphasizes the intent of many musicians. Moreover, such a position does not adequately address the political acumen of previous generations of musicians. Nor does it come to terms with the subtler role of black creativity over "the last two hundred years—and I would even guess, the last two thousand years" in perpetuating a world system of creativity and spirituality. What is important about the 1960s, however, is that a large number of musicians recognized "that a new order was needed to restore positive functionalism" in the music.[88]

Braxton's commentary on the avant-garde also addresses the gender politics of the jazz world. Whereas many members of his generation recognized the need to establish a new racial order, Braxton is one of the few male musicians who publicly recognized the oppression of women in artists' communities and the larger society. In fact, his discussion of women in the third volume of the *Tri-axium Writings* self-consciously offers a corrective to the shortsightedness of his colleagues' visions. Braxton theorizes the liberation of women as a precondition for the social changes to which he looks forward. He recognizes that male members of musicians' communities have defined creativity as a male sphere of activity. Although he links the oppression of women to general patterns in Western culture, he acknowledges the specific ways that women have been marginalized in the jazz community. As a general rule, he argues, the subordinate role of women in jazz circles is a result of patriarchy in the black community, the physical hardships of life on the road, and other factors. In practice, the lack of respect for female creativity has meant that women are discriminated against in hiring decisions and usually do not receive the word-of-mouth recognition that translates into good nightclub gigs and recording dates. Braxton also finds it ironic that politicized and "super-mystical" musicians of the 1960s could also "function as chauvinist and oppressor."[89]

Braxton asserts that black women have helped to build the legacy of creative music. Women not only have made important contributions to jazz tradition but also have been integral to the perpetuation of creativity and spirituality in black communities. Braxton sees the marginalization of African American women in contemporary jazz as part and parcel of the "source-shift transfer" of bebop, which helped to reassert the primacy of a world system of creativity. Before bebop, Braxton argues, the church was the primary site of the production of African American creative music. The church was also a site where women had some measure of equality as artists. Bebop, as music and as an expression of a philosophical position, disrupted the primacy of the church in the perpetuation of creative music. As this process unfolded, women were often (though not always) excluded from production of creative music. Moreover, bebop was a form that was both understood and expressed in sexist terms, which had profound implications for years to come: "The realness that the social reality surrounding bebop was also sexist would be an important consideration affecting the potential of creative music in the fifties and sixties time cycle." Braxton emphasizes that sexism has always been rampant across the globe, but he stresses the sexist elements of bebop because of its impact on the jazz community, which in turn must play a crucial role in global change. Therefore, Braxton's utopian vision is dependent upon equality for women in the music world and, by extension, a feminization of the world community.[90]

## Coda

Recently, Braxton's vision has been validated by the numerous books published in the 1990s that focus on his life and work and, perhaps more important, by his receipt of a MacArthur Foundation fellowship in 1994. Yet through it all, Braxton has remained controversial and has made it a point to speak out about the way creative music has been categorized. In 1994 Braxton referred to the multiplicity of influences—African, European, Asian, Hispanic—on his music and held out hope that the "dynamic implications of my processes can be reviewed with respect to its positive, universal implications . . . as it will relate to new attempts for a multiple philosophical-spiritual context." Calling on white people, black people, and others to begin to cooperate with one another, he looked forward to a period of transformation in the "post-Reagan era."[91]

Braxton was still critical of the jazz discourse, however, as well as critical of the narrow definitions that have been placed on black creativity. Recognizing that the debates about the jazz canon—which he termed "spectacle diversions"—were products of the marketplace, Braxton lamented the commercially viable orthodoxy of trumpeter Wynton Marsalis and drummer-turned-critic Stanley Crouch, Marsalis's vocal supporter. Braxton believed that jazz "neoclassicism" had a negative impact on musicians who have pursued experimental paths. Equating the veneration of a jazz tradition with a limited and very marketable kind of blackness, Braxton complained: "I'm seeing New Orleans used in this time period to crush the composite aspirations of the music. How unfortunate! That component of the alignment of the jazz musicians to the marketplace, letting the marketplace set an agenda for the music, more and more we'll be able to look at that." Moreover, Braxton saw in the critical work of Crouch the validation of a "new minstrel era," in which ideas about black identity and culture suggest a "narrowing of possibilities, not an expansion of possibilities" in art and society. The present, Braxton said, was a good time to have a comedy show on television. Speaking about music, he said:

> By chopping off the restructuralist implications of the music, by chopping off the innovation of the music, you have chopped off anything to grow from. If bebop and Dixieland is it, that's great, but that's a Eurocentric idea, anyway. . . . You can put this in your article, if you

want to get me shot, but what the heck: The African American intel-
lectual community from the 60s/70s time cycle has now embraced
Eurocentricity on a level that boggles the mind. . . . Remember now,
I'm called the "white Negro." Nobody wants to use those terms, but
I'm supposed to be the embodiment of that which has not been black,
when in fact I never gave one inch of my beliefs or experiences.[92]

In Braxton's mind, the neoclassical project, just like the idea of jazz itself, erased black difference and the complexity of black lives—a somewhat ironic assertion, considering that the neoclassical project (at least
Marsalis's and Crouch's vision of it) has been based on Albert Murray's
cultural criticism, which, like Braxton's, is invested in making sense of
aesthetic and ritualistic functions of black music and rejecting the limitations of Eurocentric and black nationalist discourse about African
American music. It is to this neoclassical project and the debates about
it that the following chapter turns.

# "The Majesty of the Blues"

Wynton Marsalis's Jazz Canon

**IN A 1999 CENTENNIAL TRIBUTE** to Duke Ellington, trumpeter, composer, and jazz spokesperson Wynton Marsalis described Ellington's music as simultaneously concerned with "the uplift of the human spirit" and emblematic of American life in the twentieth century. Ellington's music was a "synthesis," Marsalis argued, of a wide range of musical styles and cultural influences. Although the blues represented the most important color on Ellington's musical palette, indicating a firm grounding in the African American vernacular, his music, like William Shakespeare's plays, "appealed to all people." Beyond its form, Ellington's music embodied the struggles of a country trying to come to terms with its multiracial legacy. "Duke's artistic mantra," Marsalis wrote, "was integrate, integrate, integrate. He blended diverse cultural and musical ideas because he understood not only what the country was, but also what it could become." Whereas other musicians "escaped into the art world of the 'serious composer,'" "retreated to the university to rail bitterly against the establishment," or became "tired imitator[s] of pop trends," Ellington remained committed to his aesthetic project and, by association, a democratic vision of American society.[1]

No musician has been more central to the jazz renaissance in America that began during the 1980s than Wynton Marsalis. Through his work as a musician, interviewee, writer, host of programs broadcast on the Public Broadcasting System and National Public Radio, educator, and artistic director of the Jazz at Lincoln Center program, Marsalis has played a pivotal role in spreading jazz to a wider listening audience and generating an unprecedented level of respect for the music. Drawing on his authenticity as a jazz musician from New Orleans and the cultural capital of an artist skilled in both jazz and classical musical performance, Marsalis has usurped some of the authority held by jazz writers and has validated musicians' own ability to lend meaning to their artistic projects in ways previous generations of musicians could only dream about. In April 1997, Marsalis became the first jazz musician to receive a Pulitzer Prize, for his oratorio *Blood on the Fields,* which tells the story of two African slaves, Jesse and Leona, through their capture, the terrors of the Middle Passage, their sale in New Orleans, and the rigors of plantation life. The award marked a significant moment, both in Marsalis's own career and in the institutionalization of jazz in American arts and letters. In 1965 a Pulitzer Prize board had rejected the recommendation of the organization's music jury that Ellington, who had written several lengthy compositions himself, be given a special award for "the vitality and originality of his total productivity" over the course of his career. That Marsalis was given the award in 1997, combined with the Pulitzer board's decision to change the language of their requirements so that jazz could be considered for the prize, illustrates the change in the status of the idiom.

Marsalis's celebration of Ellington provides a glimpse into the aesthetic and cultural vision that has attracted so much attention. Drawing heavily on the ideas of Albert Murray and Stanley Crouch, Marsalis has portrayed Ellington as well as Louis Armstrong and other central players in jazz history as heroic figures, whose music was strongly rooted in black vernacular practice yet assembled from multiple influences and relevant to diverse audiences. Marsalis's description of Ellington's desire to "integrate" is emblematic of his embrace of Murray's "omni-American" perspective on African American life and culture: a vision that affirms the humanity of black people, places them at the center of American experience, and rejects aspects of both Eurocentrism and black cultural nationalism.

Marsalis, like generations of musicians before him, has plotted jazz along the axes of African American cultural achievement, American exceptionalism, and universal expression. By venerating the music and identifying its function in rituals of affirmation, he too has sought to improve the position of jazz in American society and make its dissemination a vehicle for social change. Yet, unlike some of the other musicians in this study, Marsalis has charted a very specific vision of what constitutes the jazz tradition. As a means of bettering music and society, he has worked to establish a canon of legitimate jazz expression and a variety of educational programs geared toward preserving it. In doing so, Marsalis has helped to win newfound prestige for jazz as an art form, but he has also found himself at the center of controversy. The litmus test for jazz artistry, in his vision, is the extent to which it conforms to certain values inscribed in musical standards as well as its ability to perform an effective ritual-istic function. For close to twenty years, Marsalis has argued that an ero-sion of cultural values has debased American society and marginalized jazz in the process. He has been particularly critical of youth culture, com-mentators who have sought to locate black experience on the margins of American life, and musicians who have strayed from jazz orthodoxy. Within this formulation, the projects of avant-garde and fusion players, hip-hop musicians, and pop stars are all judged inferior—a distinction that, many musicians and critics argue, has excluded avant-garde ex-pression and various hybrid styles from contemporary celebrations of jazz. Although Marsalis's comments about Ellington's diverse musical influ-ences and broad-minded vision indicate that in more recent years his canon has been less exclusive, his cultural gatekeeping continues to make him a controversial figure.

This final chapter discusses how Marsalis's effort to define a jazz tra-dition is another in a series of responses to the historical development of jazz, the discourses surrounding it, and its position vis-à-vis cultural institutions and the culture industry. As it has done when examining the projects of other musicians, this analysis situates Marsalis's canon-building project in its historical context, for his thoughts about race and culture, the jazz tradition, the intellectual aspects of improvisation, and male wisdom and creativity should be viewed as a strategic response to economic and social transformations in the 1980s and 1990s and the at-tendant conversations about African American culture and society.

## Marsalis's Apprenticeship

Marsalis was born in 1961 and raised in New Orleans. The son of pro-fessional jazz pianist Ellis Marsalis, he gained further jazz experience from playing in the Fairview Baptist Church band, under the direction of ban-joist and guitarist Danny Barker. As a young musician, he was initially drawn to the sounds of groups like Earth, Wind and Fire and performed in local soul and funk bands. In high school, however, Marsalis became what he terms "serious" about music through a more rigorous study of European classical music and jazz. By the time he finished high school, Marsalis had received a good deal of acclaim. At the age of fifteen, in 1977, he won the Outstanding Musician Award at the Eastern Music Festival in North Carolina; at sixteen, he performed Bach's Brandenburg Concerto no. 2 with the New Orleans Philharmonic Symphony. After Marsalis completed high school in 1979, he moved to New York, where he auditioned for the Juilliard School and was awarded a four-year scholarship. That same year, Berkshire Music Center musical director Gunther Schuller admitted Marsalis to the center's prestigious summer program at Tanglewood, where he won an award as outstanding brass student. At Juilliard, Marsalis developed his skills in both the jazz and classical idioms. He performed with local orchestras and sat in with a variety of jazz groups, including Art Blakey's Jazz Messengers. Marsalis became a regular member of the Messengers in the summer of 1980 and took time off from Juilliard in the spring of 1981 to tour with the group. That summer he traveled the United States, Japan, and Europe with Herbie Hancock's V.S.O.P quartet, with whom he recorded an album that was released in January 1982. In August 1981, he recorded his eponymous first jazz album with Columbia, also released in January 1982. That spring, Marsalis left the Jazz Messengers to work with his own quintet, which included his brother Branford on saxophone, pianist Kenny Kirkland, drummer Jeff "Tain" Watts, and bassist Charles Fambrough.[2]

The release of Marsalis's straight-ahead, bebop-inflected album and a heavy marketing campaign by Columbia immediately drew the attention of critics and fans alike. After a decade of searching for someone who might draw upon the pastiche of sounds from the avant-garde, fusion, rhythm and blues, "world," and classical music and somehow distill them into a style that was also part of the jazz tradition, critics found a traditionalist alternative in this well-tailored, articulate young man with New Orleans authenticity, a jazz family pedigree, a veneration for music history, the cultural capital of a classical musician, and the promise of developing into a virtuoso. Reflecting on the trumpeter's early popularity, jazz critic Gary Giddins claimed that Marsalis's eloquence, ability to play jazz and classical, and knack for selling records without appearing to "sell out" made him the musician of critics' dreams. On a similar note, John Szwed remarked that Marsalis carried the burden Clifford Brown had shouldered in the early 1950s. Just as Brown was a "defender of the traditional principles of swing, emotion, and heat against the cold formalism of West Coast [read, white] musicians, so Marsalis is seen as defending these principles against the excesses of the '60s and '70s."[3]

And defend these principles he did. In comments in a January 1982 *Down Beat* article that coincided with the release of his first album, Marsalis set forth ideas he would continue to develop through the 1980s and 1990s. When asked where he fit in musically, given that he also was about to release a classical album, he drew upon his family history to place himself firmly in the jazz continuum. He also distinguished his version of jazz, which resisted the music industry's commercialism, from fusion, which he considered a form of popular music that was erroneously marketed as jazz:

> I do not entertain and I will not entertain. I'm a musician. I studied the music and my music should be presented that way. I'm serious about what I'm doing. I will not play funk. I like funk, but I am not a funk musician. Funk musicians don't pay the kind of dues that jazz musicians pay to the music. . . . If Herbie [Hancock] wants to play funk, if Miles [Davis] wants to play funk, if Freddie [Hubbard] wants to play funk, or whoever is playing funk—I think it's beautiful. But the worst thing is when the record company takes a funk album, puts it out and calls it a jazz album.[4]

Marsalis's rejection of the entertainer's role was not without irony, for he was fast becoming one of the most promoted jazz artists in the history of the idiom. Nonetheless, by defining his project as a serious artistic enterprise that ran contrary to the profit-driven aesthetic of commercially successful artists, Marsalis established one of his selling points as well as an important component of his aesthetic and social vision.

Marsalis's doctrine of seriousness was also intended to counter stereotypes of black inferiority and validate a legacy of African American cultural achievement. He said his decision to return to Juilliard after securing his Columbia contract stemmed from a desire to challenge the myth that jazz musicians could not play seriously and "to get the degree for all the cats who don't think brothers can do it." When asked about race as a determinant of jazz excellence, Marsalis refuted the assumption that musical excellence was biologically based but also claimed that prescribed modes of artistic behavior pertained to cultural, if not racial, identity. Therefore, he argued, many white jazz musicians have been limited by a desire to act black, just as black musicians in the classical world have been hampered by a desire to act white. Although Marsalis would later ascribe such hard-and-fast prescriptions to youthful naiveté, a "1970s" understanding of race and culture, and misunderstandings on the part of his interlocutors, these comments also demonstrate the beginnings of his struggle to link the artistry of jazz to African American exceptionalism while simultaneously rejecting the racially deterministic belief that black accomplishment in jazz was innate.[5]

By the end of 1982, Marsalis's career as a jazz player had taken off. He won awards for both Jazz Artist of the Year and Album of the Year in the *Down Beat* poll and was nominated for a Grammy for his first jazz album. In a *Down Beat* interview that December, Marsalis drew upon his rising status as a musician and public figure as he set forth a plan for reviving jazz from the moribund state into which he believed it had fallen in the 1970s. Here he expressed the belief that the avant-garde also bore responsibility for the current position of jazz: "The problem with some of the stuff that all the critics think is innovative is that it sounds like European music—European, avant garde, classical 20th century static rhythm music with blues licks in it. And all these cats can say for themselves is 'we don't sound like anybody else.' That doesn't mean shit." As a solution, Marsalis advocated the development of jazz standards. The popular standards of the past had provided a good basis for jazz musicians' improvisations, but they had been played out. Many contemporary tunes, he said, were "sad pieces of one-chord shit." To alleviate the shortage of harmonically sophisticated popular songs, he advocated an exploration of the overlooked compositions of artists such as Ornette Coleman, Miles Davis, John Coltrane, Booker Little, and Charlie Rouse to create a new set of standards upon which contemporary artists could build. Rather than moving into the ether of abstraction, "the key is to sound like somebody else, to take what is already there and sound like an extension of that. It's not to not sound like that. Music has a tradition that you have to understand before you can move to the next step."[6]

Such comments can be understood as a product of his immersion in the community of jazz musicians and its long-standing appeal to the idea of tradition when responding to critical misrepresentation and the forging of a social vision. Like musicians before him, Marsalis validated the idea of a jazz continuum as a means of addressing the economics of the industry. With a market in which fusion players were reaping most of the limited resources, Marsalis's comments may be seen as an attempt to validate the music of those who strove to play more solidly in the straight-ahead, post-bebop style. By distancing the avant-garde from the jazz idiom and linking it to critical tastes, Marsalis not only chastised musicians who had strayed from the jazz tradition but also challenged jazz critics' role as the custodians of this tradition and bestowed that duty on musicians instead.

But Marsalis did not limit his opinions to issues solely related to the performance and institutionalization of jazz. He soon began to link his veneration of the jazz tradition and disdain for popular culture and avant-garde experimentation to broader social and cultural issues. Marsalis's intellectual project can thus be understood both as a response to the marginalization of jazz in American life and as a strategic reaction to and product of the structural dislocations, discursive formations, and media representations that have affected African American communities over the past twenty-five years. In order to understand fully the development of Marsalis's ideas, however, they must also be discussed in relation to his intellectual apprenticeship with Stanley Crouch and Albert Murray. As in Murray's and Crouch's writing, music has been for Marsalis both a metaphor for and a means of intervening in broader social issues.

Soon after Marsalis arrived in New York, Crouch took on the role of his intellectual mentor, began championing him as a symbol of jazz excellence, and introduced him to Albert Murray.[7] Although they may have been rooted in his own experiences and position as a jazz musician, Marsalis's ideas about jazz history, aesthetics, and ritual, as well as his desire to place jazz at the center of American culture, were also influenced by the claim of an African American birthright and the vernacular exceptionalism articulated most clearly in the post–World War II era by Ralph Ellison and later by Murray and Crouch.[8] Marsalis would draw upon their ideas as he attempted—through music, commentary, and his position at Lincoln Center—to lend artistic legitimacy to African American vernacular expression. In doing so, he reinterpreted the long-standing challenge of making sense of jazz in relation to high, folk, and commodified popular cultures as well as in relation to African American, American, and universal experiences.

In his 1970 collection of essays, *The Omni-Americans,* Albert Murray explores the relationship of black experience and American culture and in so doing challenges the "folklore of white supremacy" and the "fakelore of black pathology" that he believes permeate social-scientific discourse. Murray's primary quarrel is with social scientists and policy makers who have reduced African Americans to social victims. By dwelling on African American pathologies, he argues, social scientists and the welfare state have discursively and programmatically marginalized and dehumanized black people. In particular, the Moynihan report (discussed in chapter 4) "is a notorious example of the use of social science survey as a propaganda vehicle to promote a negative image of Negro life in the United States." Rejecting social science, then, Murray posits a humanist understanding of black life and offers "an affirmative rebuttal to negative allegations" rather than an appeal to liberal guilt. Building upon the pragmatist literary criticism of Kenneth Burke, the aesthetic theory of André Malraux, and Ellison's expansive treatment of African American experience in *Invisible Man* and other writings, Murray emphasizes the heroic aspects of black life and the human affirmation that informs black cultural production.[9]

But Murray is not merely concerned with the misconceptions of academics and policy makers. He takes on "race-oriented propagandists, whether black or white," who, regardless of method or ideology, exaggerate ethnic differences and distance black people from the American mainstream. Like his contemporary Harold Cruse, Murray criticizes African Americans' engagement with Marxist thought. The sea change in black self-consciousness during the 1940s—when the cultural emphasis of the New Negro movement slowly gave way to the "concern with abstract economic theory and a general politicalization of all issues"—led both Richard Wright and James Baldwin into the trap of using literature as a vehicle of social analysis. The devaluation of the black middle class by young radicals, a position Murray roots in the misconceptions of "white ghettologists," has obscured "the fact that it is the so-called middle class Negro (or Negro with so-called middle class aspirations) who represents the most fearsome revolutionary threat to the white status quo." Yet, unlike Cruse, Murray puts little faith in black nationalism. Although he supports some of its culturally affirming aspects, he rejects its adherence to a segregationist logic and the extent to which it denies the full humanity of black people. The Black Arts movement, he argues, is politically naive, playing to the stereotypes of contemporary white American audiences, just as participants in the Harlem Renaissance catered to the primitivist fantasies of theirs. Moreover, black separatists, in Murray's estimation, have given up a valuable American birthright. African American culture, identity, and experience, he asserts, are thoroughly enmeshed in the broader North American experience, and it is only through this realization that observers can "do justice to the enduring humanity of U.S. Negroes."[10]

Notwithstanding the history of economic, political, and judicial oppression in the United States, Murray believes that continued focus on the marginalization of African Americans leads to greater discrimination. Thus, any program for social change must emphasize the contributions of African Americans to a U.S. culture and society that is "incontestably mulatto." Although slavery excluded black people from citizenship, enslaved Africans were in the "presence of more human freedom and individual opportunity than they or anybody else had ever seen before." Ultimately, African Americans' quest for freedom has been decidedly American. In the lives of Harriet Tubman and Frederick Douglass, for example, one finds heroic examples of the "pioneer spirit of American womanhood" and the "American as self-made man."[11]

For thirty years, Murray has attempted to craft such a vision through his fiction and nonfiction. But our concern here is music and, more important, the way Murray, like Ellison before him, has invoked the blues (a tradition that includes jazz) as a metaphor for the heroism of African American people, as a means of affirming the "incontestably mulatto" aspects of American culture, and even as a model for social activism. Moreover, according to Murray, observers' inability to understand the meaning and function of the blues is but more proof of their misreading of the humanity of African Americans and their relationship to the broader U.S. culture.

Drawing upon Kenneth Burke's equation of stylization with strategies for living, Murray argues that survival is more than just the quest for food, clothing, or shelter. Art provides a necessary function in human life; "it is a way of sizing up the world, and so, ultimately, and beyond all else, a mode and medium of survival." As an aestheticized response to living, blues music performs a vernacular, ritualistic function; expresses a national experience; and retains a universal purpose. Whereas many see the blues as an "expression of frustration and despair," this "major American innovation of universal significance and potential" represents the most "profound assimilation" into modern American life while simultaneously "mak[ing] Negroes acknowledge the essentially tenuous nature of all human experience." Linking the form of the blues to its philosophical meanings, Murray writes that Duke Ellington's "It Don't Mean a Thing (If It Ain't Got That Swing)" is "the definitive statement of the epistemological assumptions that underlie the blues idiom." When a black musician or dancer "swings the blues," she or he provides a "heroic" and "affirmative" response to what Malraux called *la condition humaine.*

> Extemporizing in response to the exigencies of the situation in which he finds himself, he is confronting, acknowledging, and contending with the infernal absurdities and ever-impending frustrations inherent in the nature of all existence *by playing with the possibilities that are also there.* Thus does man the player become man the stylizer and by the same token the humanizer of chaos; and thus does play become ritual, ceremony, and art; and thus also does the dance-beat improvisation of experience in the blues idiom become survival technique, esthetic equipment for living, and a central element in the dynamics of U.S. Negro life style.[12]

Murray's invocation of heroism, his attention to aesthetics and ritual, his insistence that blues music represents an "assimilation" into modern American life, and his continual emphasis that this music is the product of hard work and not instinct, all challenge Eurocentric aesthetic hierarchies and a separatist mentality.

Murray moves beyond metaphor and into a more detailed exploration of the idiom in his 1976 book *Stomping the Blues.* Here he emphasizes the communal aspects and ritualistic function of the blues while challenging primitivist assessments of the music. Murray patently rejects writing about blues and jazz that reduces the music to an unconscious reflection of its social context or does not take its artistry seriously. He links the preoccupation with the music's anticommercial folk status and the belief that it is a "natural" expression to "political theories about noble savages." Musical skills represent "not natural impulse but the refinement of habit, custom, and tradition become second nature." Spontaneous expression is thus a "conditioned reflex" that is the "end product of discipline, or in a word, training." When speaking of the possibility of oppositional meanings in the blues, Murray rejects the idea that the blues or jazz directly reflects its sociopolitical context. He asserts that social historians put too much emphasis on literal meanings of lyrics that evoke suffering or social critique. Rather, the pathos of the blues is more existential or metaphysical than political. The importance of the blues is not in social commentary but in "the attitude toward experience . . . the disposition to persevere . . . that blues music at its best not only embodies, but stylizes, extends, elaborates, and refines into art." It is a historically transcendent, ritualistic stylization of experience that addresses the material conditions of life without speaking directly of them. The "primary emphasis is placed upon aesthetics not ethics. What is good in such circumstances is the beautiful, without which there can be no good time."[13]

Some of this analysis is directed toward a younger generation of intellectuals. In *The Omni-Americans,* Murray issues a challenge for young radicals to stop following the programs of "white social technicians" and instead begin playing their own "improvisations" on Marx, Mao, Guevara, and Fanon.[14] And although Murray does not address Amiri Baraka's work directly, critiques of Baraka's materialist analysis in *Blues People* and the spiritual and ontological focus of his "The Changing Same" are implicit in both *The Omni-Americans* and *Stomping the Blues.* In a review of *Blues People,* Ralph Ellison took issue both with Baraka's lack of attention to the aesthetic and ritual elements of the blues and with his suggestion that the legitimacy of black music depends on the distance of performers and audiences from middle-class mores. His discomfort with Baraka's class analysis led Ellison to conclude: "The tremendous burden of sociology which Jones would place upon this body of music is enough to give even the blues the blues."[15] Murray too rejects Baraka's class analysis as well as his characterization of the music as a form of protest. Although Murray's work from this period shares some similarities with Baraka's later formulation of black music in "The Changing Same," it differs in some important ways. Baraka pays attention to ritualistic function and aesthetics in this essay but ultimately argues that blues music bespeaks both a racialized black body and a distinct black ontology rooted in an African past. Both rhythm and blues and the jazz avant-garde are manifestations of this essential black cultural force. Such "projections" of this core expression can thus be vehicles for liberatory identities that distance black people from the American mainstream. Murray, in contrast, argues that the germination of the blues is based on culture, not race, and specifically reflects values created by African Americans as they have worked for full citizenship in the United States.

Even as Murray frees jazz and blues from Eurocentric and nationalist prescriptions, however, his aesthetic formulation imposes its own boundaries. The heroism of the blues, its artistry, and its social function are rooted in particular musical qualities and in a ritualistic role that only some musicians are capable of fulfilling. Conspicuous in their inability to express the heroic function of the blues are soul musicians and rock and rollers, who draw from the blues idiom but express "sentimentality" rather than "earthiness." Although the photographs in *Stomping the Blues* chart the idiom from Buddy Bolden through John Coltrane and Ornette Coleman, Murray rejects certain directions that the jazz avant-garde took during the 1960s and 1970s. Artifice is necessary to the blues, but too much preoccupation with "elaboration, extension, and refinement does indeed get out of control and degenerate into pretentious display and a mindless pursuit of novelty for its own sake—or in the name of some sophomoric conception of progress." Also unable to fulfill the heroic function of this music are those musicians who have sought to lend political meaning to their art or who have complained too loudly about their economic status.[16]

Success in the idiom, Murray asserts, does not come from revolution or innovation but from musicians' skill at inheriting their "roles in the traditional ritual of blues confrontation and purgation, and of life affirmation and continuity through improvisation." Musicians express this functional artistry most eloquently not in free improvisation, atonality, or funk rhythms, but simply in "swing," which Murray refers to as the "Armstrong/Ellington Principle." Indeed it is Ellington who best exemplifies the values of the blues idiom: "The preeminent embodiment of the blues musician as artist was Duke Ellington, who, in the course of fulfilling the role of entertainer, not only came to address himself to the basic imperatives of music as a fine art but also achieved the most comprehensive synthesis, extension, and refinement to date of all the elements of blues musicianship." Comparing Ellington's compositions to canonical American literature, Murray argues that his work has "converted more of the actual texture and vitality of American life into first-rate universally appealing music than anybody else," including composers such as John Cage, Aaron Copland, and Charles Ives.[17]

Murray's vision resonated deeply with cultural critic Stanley Crouch, who came to prominence as an intellectual in the 1980s after rejecting black nationalism and the work of Baraka in particular. Born in 1945 and raised in Los Angeles, Crouch entered adulthood at the height of the black freedom struggle. He cites the Watts rebellion as the moment when he moved from a philosophical and active involvement in the civil rights movement into what he terms "ethnic nationalism." Thereafter, he became deeply immersed in the work of Frantz Fanon, Négritude thinkers, African novelists and playwrights, and Amiri Baraka. Crouch joined Studio Watts, a local repertory theater group run by Jayne Cortez, and, like Baraka, wrote poetry that often featured themes of jazz and black nationalism. His work appeared in the *Journal of Black Poetry, Liberator,* and *Black World.* In 1968 he became a poet in residence at Pitzer College and was soon hired as the first full-time faculty member at Claremont College's Black Studies Center. Crouch was also, at least briefly, a member of the jazz avant-garde. A self-taught drummer, he started a group called Black Music Infinity with Pan-African People's Arkestra members David Murray, Arthur Blythe, and other musicians in Los Angeles. He later shared a loft with David Murray in New York, where they presented musical performances and poetry readings.[18]

Despite these credentials, Crouch became disenchanted with black nationalism and its manifestations in literature and art during the 1970s. He believed white paternalism encouraged "third rate" work, and his discomfort with a lack of aesthetic criteria in Black Arts movement writing was most likely augmented by the criticism he began to receive for being unduly influenced by "Western standards." But Crouch's own critique went much deeper than aesthetics. Black nationalism eventually came to represent to him a profound moral and intellectual failure on the part of African American intellectuals and activists and also of American society as a whole. Writing in 1990, Crouch describes his early embrace of this ideology in terms that speak to his rejection of it:

> Having been born in 1945, I consider myself part of an undeclared lost generation that ran into the xenophobic darkness, retreating from the complex vision of universal humanism that underlay the Civil Rights Movement. It was surely a flight that called for embracing black power, black nationalism, black studies, the racist rants that were known

as "revolutionary black art," and a comical but tragic version of leadership . . . its ideas . . . helped send not only black America but this nation itself into an intellectual tailspin on the subjects of race, of culture, of heritage.

Crouch's rejection of black nationalism was facilitated by the "work and friendship" of Albert Murray and the influence of the writings of Ralph Ellison, who, in Crouch's words, "liberated me from the influence of LeRoi Jones, whose work I once copied as assiduously as Sonny Stitt did Charlie Parker's."[19]

Since the 1980s, Crouch has drawn upon the work of Murray and Ellison as he has reformulated his own ideas about African American intellectual life, art, and politics. He places black people at the center of American morality, history, and geography; emphasizes the hybridity of African American and American art, culture, and intellectual life; criticizes black literature that is either dependent on a politics of moral outcry or that too narrowly portrays African American experience; and challenges the idea that middle-class status somehow makes African Americans less authentically black. All the while, he has reserved harsh criticism for any aesthetic, intellectual, or political projects that remain wedded to a separatist vision. African Americans are not the only ones who bear responsibility for the failures of contemporary society, according to Crouch; the women's movement and the gay liberation movement have also been shackled by the "self-righteous" and "separatist talk" that derailed black liberation movements.[20]

Crouch's cultural politics are perhaps most eloquently and forcefully expressed in his commentary on music. Building on Ellison's and Murray's "heroic" understanding of the blues, he casts the music world as a site of a profound struggle where, as Robert Boynton describes it, "the forces of barbarism and the forces of civilization compete in a battle that is at once aesthetic and ethical." In this arena, jazz holds a "transformative power" in its own right and provides a metaphor of "flexible profundity" for Crouch to engage in cultural critique. In fact, Crouch's own intellectual transformations are evident in his commentary about this music.[21]

In a 1979 *Village Voice* piece entitled "Bringing Atlantis Up to the Top," for example, Crouch criticizes the jazz avant-garde and links its perceived shortcomings to the failings of black nationalism. Yet he still ponders what might be salvaged from a Black Arts vision. He chastises avant-garde musicians for forsaking dance rhythms, for employing a limited tonal vocabulary, for playing music that "sounded very European despite the proclamations about its blackness," and simply for playing poorly. Such flaws, he argues, are rooted in the misdirected ideas about black identity promulgated by the Black Arts movement: "It infested art as well as politics and resulted in a great deal of rather simplistic and ludicrous ancestor worship, intellectual irresponsibility, primitive mask-wearing, and counterfeit militancy that frequently had more to do with renegade dilettante romance than more fascinating combinations of notes, sounds, colors, and rhythms." Yet Crouch is still beholden to Baraka's call for "unity music" and hopeful that experimental jazz musicians can provide a vibrant cultural force in black communities. He predicts a new synthesis between jazz and rhythm and blues, with an emphasis on rhythmic elements, which would infuse new life into both idioms.[22]

Although Crouch is no fan of Miles Davis's electric music and perceives a lack of seriousness among many fusion players, he remains interested in the "jazz-funk language" Davis created for electric instruments. He identifies in the work of Davis's contemporaries an ongoing "search for a combination of the sophistication of jazz and the fluidity of the polyrhythms that had developed within the black dance world over the last 15 years, or at least since James Brown's 'Cold Sweat.'" Crouch is buoyed by the members of the jazz avant-garde who have rejected some of their "pretentiously intellectual" musical visions as they try to bridge the gap with the black community. Younger jazz players were listening to George Clinton and Marvin Gaye, and "it seems as though the comprehensiveness one hears in the music of Duke Ellington, Sun Ra, Charles Mingus, the AACM, and Arthur Blythe is now coming into r&b." Crouch looks forward to the development of a "unity music" that was emerging in the work of Jerome Cooper, James "Blood" Ulmer, Ornette Coleman, David Murray, Wayne Shorter, and Olu Dara: "I am confident we are on the verge of hearing some exceptional music, music that will cut across more lines than ever, and will be much richer than the mechanical getdown music and would-be dancing of motor-booty affairs. . . . In musical terms we are moving toward what literary scholar Werner Sollors has called 'populist modernism.' I think so anyway."[23]

Yet Crouch eventually rejected the search for a "populist modernism" that linked experimental jazz and contemporary black popular culture. Instead, he began to extol the virtues of tradition and, in particular, the accomplishments of Wynton Marsalis. Writing in 1990 about Miles Davis's attempt to reach out to a popular audience, Crouch links Davis's electric turn to the failures of black nationalism and the dissolution of middle-class values:

> His pernicious effect on the music scene since he went rapaciously commercial reveals a great deal about the perdurability of Zip Coon and Jasper Jack in the worlds of jazz and rock, in the worlds of jazz and rock criticism, in Afro-American culture itself. The cult of ethnic authenticity often mistakes the lowest common denominator for an ideal. It begets a self-image that has succumbed to a nostalgia for the mud. What we get is the bugaboo blues of the noble savage, the surly and dangerous Negro who will have nothing to do with bourgeois conventions. . . . Davis's corruption occurred at about the time that the "Oreo" innuendo became an instrument with which formerly rejected street Negroes and thugs began to intimidate, and often manipulate, middle-class Afro-Americans in search of their roots, and of a "real" black culture. In this climate, obnoxious, vulgar, and antisocial behavior has been confused with black authenticity. This has led to blaxploitation in politics, in higher education, and in art. . . . The fall of Davis reflects perhaps the essential failure of contemporary Negro culture: its mock-democratic idea that the elite, too, should like it down in the gutter.

Such ideological and aesthetic transgressions, Crouch wrote elsewhere, are countered by a young generation of straight-ahead jazz players who "symbolize the resurgence of the democratic art of jazz and predict the increasing freedom from decadence we will see in American youth over the next few decades."[24]

## The Importance of Standards

With the encouragement and support of Crouch and Murray, Marsalis put their visions into practice as a spokesman for and a performer of jazz. In the 1980s, he developed a musical style incorporating elements from major figures in the jazz tradition and sought to pass along knowledge to other musicians. All the while, he tried to transcend narrow media representations of himself. In doing so, he hoped to gain a reputation as an important musician in his own right and position himself as a keeper of a jazz canon. Marsalis drew upon Crouch's and Murray's ideas as he voiced comments about the role of this music in society and its implications for black people in late-twentieth-century America.

In the liner notes to Marsalis's 1985 release *Black Codes from the Underground,* Crouch points out that the term "black codes" refers to the system of laws that regulated African slaves' lives and institutionalized their status as chattel. The term is also a symbol for the way such laws have evolved into limitations on black art in the form of commercialism and stereotypes. In his own comments in these liner notes, Marsalis, in Murray-like fashion, connects creative limitations to social restrictions, whether they are imposed by others or self-imposed:

> Black codes mean a lot of things. Anything that reduces potential, that pushes your taste down to an obvious, animal level. Anything that makes you think less significance is *more* enjoyable. Anything that keeps you on the surface. The way they depict women in rock videos—black codes. People gobbling up junk food when they can afford something better—black codes. The argument that illiteracy is valid in a technological world—black codes. People who equate ignorance with soulfulness—definitely black codes. The overall quality of every true artist's work is a rebellion against black codes. That's the line I want to be in—and I definitely have plenty of examples.

Crouch points to the music on the album as precisely this rebellion against black codes. Marsalis was, in Crouch's words, "expanding the expression of human intricacy" and "mak[ing] music in keeping with the world-spirited joy and seriousness of Armstrong, Ellington, Parker, Monk, Coltrane, and the best of Davis, Coleman, Shorter, and Hancock." Whether the music on this album meets these claims is a matter best left to the listener, but Marsalis's writing and arranging clearly reflect a self-conscious attempt to engage the jazz tradition as he and Crouch have theorized it. Marsalis employs complex chord changes, modal passages, and intricate rhythms on up-tempo songs that retain a hard-driving swing feeling. His ballads maintain a strong lyricism, even when complicated by the offbeat punctuation of the rhythm section. As Crouch points out, each composition stands on its own as a constantly evolving unit, in which subsequent sections build upon the ideas of previous ones. These are not numbers consisting of simple themes developed through a succession of solos; rather, they are a calculated attempt to create an intelligent and dynamic expression that counters the logic of the "black codes."[25]

On his 1987 release *Standard Time, Volume 1,* the first of several volumes in this series, Marsalis approaches jazz history from a somewhat different angle and puts into practice the desire to enforce certain cultural standards. Marsalis and his quartet celebrate the "jazz standard" in their performances of eleven pieces. Nine are standards by composers from both the jazz idiom (for example, Ellington's "Caravan") and the interwar popular song idiom (such as Kern and Hammerstein's "The Song Is You"). All are compositions that have produced "classic" jazz performances on record. As Crouch writes in the liner notes: "By taking on selections from the standard repertoire that have inspired a good number of classic jazz performances, Marsalis and his men are placing themselves in a situation where their work has to be judged against the best of the entire tradition." Their challenge, he continues, "is to learn how to redefine the fundamentals while maintaining the essences that give the art its scope and its grandeur."[26] Marsalis embarks on this challenge by providing fresh arrangements of familiar numbers. This album is perhaps most impressive as a reflection upon and extension of the jazz tradition in its exploration of the "essence" of swing rhythm. For example, the band plays a version of "April in Paris" that changes tempo and rhythmic feel frequently, while their arrangement of "Autumn Leaves"— written by drummer Jeff Watts—changes meter every bar over the first sixteen bars of several choruses. Marsalis also validates himself as the upholder of jazz standards by including two songs of his own: a blues, "Soon All Will Know," and a ballad, "In the Afterglow."

Marsalis also addressed the question of standards, as well as musicians' duty to uphold them, in interviews and opinion pieces. In a 1984 article entitled "In Defense of Standards," Marsalis adheres to Murray's omni-American and heroic perspectives on art and culture and mirrors Crouch's pessimistic assessments of the state of American cultural values.[27] Rejecting certain assumptions of black nationalism, Marsalis espouses a broader American cultural nationalism: "The ultimate achievement of a society is the establishment of an art form that is indigenous to that society. . . . Cultural awareness is what gives people a sense of self-pride as a group, and what defines the national character." He laments Americans' tendency to look to Europeans for "some sense of cultural worth" and champions jazz as a national artistic treasure.[28] Like Anthony Braxton, Marsalis argues that the 1940s were a critical moment for the insertion of black aesthetics into American music. This was the moment when Armstrong, Parker, Ellington, and Monk "introduced an entire range of mood and emotion into the vocabulary of Western music, an entirely new way of phrasing, an entirely new way of thinking in the language of music." Unlike Braxton's formulation in the *Tri-axium Writings,* however, Marsalis's view sees this aesthetic intervention as a product of African Americans' conformity to a broadly defined national American culture. It is not the product of an African past; nor does it signal the eventual development of an expansive, global musical culture. Thus Monk's music in particular "perfectly captures the spirit and tone of America." His use of a "short form, short phrases," and a "short thematic development" are typically American; they reflect Manhattan as a small space and the temperament of an American people who are "bombarded with millions of pieces of information every day."[29]

Jazz has seldom received adequate respect as an American art form, and Marsalis laments that its marginalization has diminished its artistic worth and obscured its function. As a result of racism in North American cultural institutions and the economic exigencies of the profession, musicians have been forced to perform in unsavory locations and have incurred the condemnation of churchgoing people. Jazz's prestige also suffers from the fallacy that it is a product of emotion and not intellect. As a response to such misunderstandings, Marsalis invokes the intellectualism of jazz practice as a means of proving its status as art. The lack of a full array of written scores does not signify a shortcoming: "What is so amazing is that they came up with as intellectual a system as was eventually developed, without the emphasis being on written music." Louis Armstrong, for example, was not the "intuitive genius" many have claimed him to be. Armstrong could not have achieved his level of consistency without self-awareness, for he always performed "with the same logic, the same impeccable taste, always structured a certain way and very well thought out. And that is what any great artist does with his material."[30]

Americans have also lost sight of the importance of jazz because of the dissolution of cultural standards. Employing an eighteenth- and nineteenth-century definition of culture as a means of uplift, Marsalis argues that most Americans "know nothing about the great improvisational artists, the records," or jazz's core values of "elevation and improvement." The primary culprits in this crisis of values are the media, which have created a popular culture "with everything reduced to the lowest common denominator." Marsalis is especially concerned with sex in music videos, the banality of rap music, and the fixation on youth culture in general:

> Rap records have no message: What you have are essentially some rhymes in iambic pentameter that express points of view that have been expressed since the 1850's. So there's rhythm—I'll give them credit for that. But as a contribution to the history of Western music? To hold up the lyrics for comparison with everything else that has been written about man, about the conditions of life in this country? After all the great polemics and poems and pieces of music that have been written? Are we really going to stoop to that level now?

Also troubling to Marsalis are older jazz musicians who have forsaken their roles as artists and sought to emulate popular performers. Although there is nothing intrinsically wrong with being versed in a multiplicity of musical expressions, "we musicians should never forget that it is our job to educate people, to stand up for excellence and quality" in the face of tastes imposed on the public by the profit-driven media. Marsalis believes musicians should draw upon vernacular practice, make art out of it, and appeal to and educate a broad audience. "To me, the test of true greatness in an artist is the ability to write or perform music that is on the very highest level but can also appeal to common people. That's the problem Beethoven, Stravinsky, Charlie Parker, and Louis Armstrong all faced."[31]

The duty of the jazz musician, and particularly the African American jazz musician, then, is to reintroduce cultural standards into American culture to counteract the relativizing effects of the mass media. Citing the paradox of democratic opinion, Marsalis suggests that cultural tastes may need to be imposed:

> Standards have become a very unpopular thing to defend in this country. Cultural education is suspect, and brings accusations of

elitism. . . . Now, democracy is a wonderful form of government—and I will say right away that I would rather live in this country than anywhere else—but it isn't terribly encouraging for cultural standards. The biggest problem with democracy, and with our education, is that every opinion becomes law and fact, just because it exists. . . . Yet we mustn't forget that beneath all those opinions there is an underlying truth and reality.

In the end, encouraging cultural standards provides a means of "educating our youth correctly" and avoiding a scenario in which "culture" is replaced by "decadence."[32]

Marsalis makes similar comments about the importance of intellectualism to jazz performance in a 1984 tribute to Louis Armstrong, entitled "Intimidation and Inspiration." And here too, like Crouch and Murray, he is particularly critical of those "pretentious" musicians (that is, the avant-garde) who mistake jazz for some kind of simple folk art and self-consciously try to elevate it above its roots. This celebration of Armstrong also makes clear the patrilineal parameters of his jazz canon. Armstrong is both a metonym for a grand artistic tradition and its patriarch:

> He was also known as Pops, because he was the father of us all. The progenitor. The spark plug . . . He showed how serious and modern the business of playing the trumpet could be. Pops. Louis Armstrong. An extremely great musician. Pops. The father. Delivered us from the Tower of Babel. Armstrong. Dropped a bomb that created instead of destroyed. The king. Armstrong. A perfectly named individual. Not to be taken lightly. I salute in my mind every time I hear his sound. Louis Armstrong. Jazz.

And by writing himself into this lineage, Marsalis taps into and perpetuates the idea of a masculinist jazz tradition.[33]

Marsalis gives further insight into the social implications of his aesthetic project in a 1986 *Ebony* article entitled "Why We Must Preserve Our Jazz Heritage." Here he puts more emphasis on the importance of jazz in an African American context than he had done in previous writings, as he encourages a black middle-class audience to pay more attention to the form:

> Jazz is an art form and it expresses a Negroid point of view about life
> in the 20th century. It is the most modern and profound expression of
> the way Black people look at the world. . . . Jazz is something Negroes
> *invented* and it said the most profound things not only about us and
> the way we look at things, but about what modern democratic life is
> really about. It is the nobility of the race put into sound; it is the sensu-
> ousness of romance in our dialect; it is the picture of the people in all
> their glory, which is what swinging is. . . . it is the highest rendition
> of individual emotion in the history of Western music.

Marsalis locates the origins of this "point of view" in Louis Armstrong's
playing in the 1920s, which not coincidentally marks the consolidation
of large black urban communities in the wake of the Great Migration.
Comparing jazz with the popular songs upon which it was often based,
Marsalis claims that it was the "weight of centuries" of African American
experience that made jazz more American than other music and allowed
black musicians of the 1920s, 1930s, and 1940s to "improve" compositions written by immigrant songwriters through a "Negro methodology
of swing."[34]

Jazz might be a product of a black engagement with modern life, but
it also expresses American exceptionalism. Like his mentors, Marsalis
locates this black point of view at the core of American values. He rejects the logic of separatism that operates in black cultural nationalism
and white supremacist racist segregation. Intolerable, too, are both the
"sociological cliches" that define the music as unreflective responses to
oppression and the mass media that are guilty of misrepresenting black
culture. Marsalis argues that "Negro" expression in the mass media (that
is, the representation of jazz) used to be an "antidote" to stereotypes,
whereas now people have been pushed back into minstrelsy. In this state
of confusion, "you have Black people who seem as though they believe
the Norman Lear version of Negroes is more valid than Duke Ellington's
version."[35]

The solution to this crisis, then, is an emphasis on standards that reflect
the grandeur of an African American cultural tradition that lies at the
center of American life and thought. Marsalis, like Crouch, reworks Murray's definition of art so that the emphasis on aesthetics providing a "style
for living" becomes one of setting an aesthetic "standard for perfor-

mance" and "standards for living." And the wellspring of these standards is jazz, which counteracts the narrow definitions that are placed on black artistry and black people, for this music rejects the devaluation of black life by speaking of excellence, responsibility, honor, and a continual striving for freedom from "limitations wrongly imposed":

> What Murray makes clear is that there was a body of ideas about human life that Black Americans brought into functional human expression with such vitality that *their* version changed the society and the image of that society in the rest of the world. That's the center of the issue: Negroes didn't accept what was handed down to them, they put those things together in the symbolic form of art and proved that you could use those same principles of respect for the individual and collective expression in artistic *performance.* That was a major event in the history of the world and in the history of art.[36]

Marsalis presents a pantheon of jazz artists, ranging from Jelly Roll Morton to Ornette Coleman—Billie Holiday is the only woman in the group—who have maintained "a commitment to the highest form of Negroid expression." He emphasizes, in particular, the roles of Duke Ellington, who, better than anyone, expressed the complexity of African American culture, and Charlie Parker, who "took Negroid improvisation to the highest level it has achieved." While Parker's music contained elements that could be traced to European and African styles, it could never be reduced to those roots; it existed only as an outgrowth of a synthetic African American expression.[37] By finding distinct roles for these central figures in modern jazz, Marsalis updates a discourse wherein musicians defined jazz and their place within it by making sense of the legacies of Parker and Ellington. As in Mingus's view, Ellington symbolizes an expansive sense of artistry—although for Marsalis he does not represent the fusion of classical *and* jazz elements that he did for Mingus—while Parker is emblematic of black genius.

Yet there is still work to be done, Marsalis claims, for "we now live in an age of aesthetic skullduggery." Cynical musicians are more concerned with profits than art, while those who maintain their integrity are dismissed as "purist," "academic," "trying to be white," or simply "old-fashioned." Such pursuits are products of a larger problem: namely, that "people stopped believing that there were any real values to be upheld that were

Negroid." Part of the responsibility for this turn of events lies with the black middle class's simultaneous quest for racial authenticity and its fixation on the cultural products deemed popular by the marketplace. Black professionals, he writes, "are so gullible and worried about being accused of not identifying with the man in the street that they refuse to discern with the interest in quality that makes for a true elite. . . . What they usually like is what's selling, and they often evaluate its significance in monetary terms." Moreover, Marsalis argues, few African Americans, regardless of class, have an intellectual orientation strong enough to get them to read critical work. He urges members of the black middle class to read Murray and Ellison and to learn about, support, and recover the "higher standards" of "Negroid style" in general.[38]

Marsalis expresses a similar vision in his commentary in the 1990s. In his 1994 book *Sweet Swing Blues on the Road,* he employs a voice that fuses the familiarity of vernacular expression with references to classical mythology and European music history, as he champions the affirmative qualities of blues (and jazz). As elsewhere, he emphasizes the role of African American artistic greatness—as a cultural practice, not a racial characteristic—in the creation and perpetuation of jazz, all the while emphasizing the music's universal purpose. A central theme in the book is the contrast between the integrity of jazz traditionalists and the banality of popular tastes imposed on people by a corporate elite and the misdirected energies of other musicians. "Enemy was the blues laid low in public by grown-ups engaged in (mere) child's play," he writes. "We are jazzmen. Playing the blues still, the jazz blues. Eight o'clock P.M. All over the world. Forever." He also uses the comments of artists such as Anthony Braxton, Cecil Taylor, and Steve Coleman, all of whom have claimed that their music moves beyond the limitations imposed by the term "jazz," as a means of casting the avant-garde outside the tradition he is trying to uphold. These musicians, he argues, know they are not jazz musicians: "it's the critics who insist that their music is jazz."[39]

In another passage, he tells the story of an older woman who encounters her grandchildren as she returns home from one of Marsalis's shows. The young people are not interested in hearing about the performance and return their attention to the television screen, where "women in drawers assume semipornographic poses while men with hands on genitalia chant rhymed doggerel to an incessant beat." Later, Marsalis describes how the media have taken advantage of teenage sexuality and used it to misinform young people:

> No mothers are they who wax fat by mining the rich fields of adolescent passion. Masquerading as "artist," using the most sophisticated tools of communication known to man, they will dick and pussy you to death. Lead you, in your vulnerable and unsophisticated state, down the road of romantic indigestion. Give you in too-large doses what you have already.
>
> This is no vaccination, it is an infection. Imposed on the young by their elders for profit at the expense of music, film, dance, and literature. And you love it. Like the many Africans given umbrellas, beads, and mirrors in exchange for humans. The joyful trading of something priceless for trinkets.[40]

In keeping with his earlier comments about Armstrong, Marsalis describes a patriarchal continuum of jazz artistry and wisdom. Although he expresses a deep respect for women as individuals and performers, he emphasizes the role of men as the carriers of the jazz tradition. In a chapter dedicated to Crouch, he speaks of "old oak tree of men" who are repositories of knowledge and dignity. This tradition of great musicians (and, we can assume, Crouch and Murray) provide a panacea to the social ills of our day: "They are what was. But they still are, like warriors forced to fight past their prime (because of weakness in the youth), who become one with their cause, proclaiming the majesty of the blues, the jazz blues. Not by playing or telling but by being big ol' oak tree of men." These men are "true hipsters"; they can see through the obfuscating forces of advertising and popular tastes and the illusions of race. They understand that America has a "mulatto culture" and that jazz is a thoroughly American response to the obstructions that black people have had to overcome.[41]

Marsalis has put this vision into practice through his role in the Jazz at Lincoln Center program. Although this chapter does not attempt to present a detailed discussion of the institutional history of this jazz program, nor of the rancorous offstage debates that have accompanied it, a brief review gives insight into the ways Marsalis's vision has provided a basis for an unprecedented level of institutional support for this music.[42] Jazz at Lincoln Center grew out of the center's yearly Classical Jazz series. Lincoln Center employee (and eventual producer of Classical Jazz)

Alina Bloomgarden began promoting the idea for the series in 1983, inspired by pianist Barry Harris's Jazz Cultural Theater, which presented jazz workshops and performances. After several years of lobbying, the series began in 1987 with three performances: a "Ladies First" concert featuring Betty Carter and Carrie Smith, and tributes to Thelonious Monk and Charlie Parker.[43]

That same year, Bloomgarden brought in Marsalis as an artistic advisor, and he in turn solicited the assistance of Stanley Crouch. Over the course of the next few summers, Marsalis helped put on a week of musical performances in line with the vision mapped out by Murray, Crouch, and himself. In "What Jazz Is—and Isn't," a 1988 editorial in the *New York Times,* Marsalis expressed the goals of a program intended to improve the position and quality of jazz as he defined it. Musicians, he argued, were continually encouraged by the market to come up with something "new" and profitable, which gave them little incentive to explore the tradition that he and his mentors held in such high esteem. There was little support for this music in the educational system, either. Marsalis also laid part of the blame for the marginalization of the music on jazz writers. On the one hand, their primitivist assumptions about musicians, their own "rebellion" against middle-class mores, and their lack of musical knowledge led them to devalue the music as a product of instinct and not intellect. On the other hand, cultural and moral relativism created a kind of myopia, where critics could not distinguish between jazz and less important forms of popular music. The solution, Marsalis argued, was to create institutional support for the jazz tradition. Musicians and fans would learn about the great artists of the past and would also gain a sense of the self-consciousness and hard work that has gone into the creation of jazz. In presentations of the work of Duke Ellington, Tadd Dameron, and Max Roach that year, Marsalis hoped, the audience at Lincoln Center would gain a sense of "two things as 'classical in jazz': the compositions of major writers and the quality of improvisation." Program notes by Stanley Crouch would explore both the "*intent* of the musicians as well as the *meaning* of the art." Ultimately, Classical Jazz was "intent on helping give to jazz, its artists and its products their deserved place in American culture."[44]

In January 1991, Lincoln Center announced the establishment of a permanent jazz department, known as Jazz at Lincoln Center, with Marsalis as artistic director and Rob Gibson as executive producer and director of programming. The center foresaw Jazz at Lincoln Center becoming an independent constituent organization on a par with the Metropolitan Opera, the Juilliard School, the New York City Ballet, and the New York Philharmonic. The creation of the program coincided with a $3.4 million grant from the Lila Wallace–Reader's Digest Fund to support a "national performing network for jazz," making 1991 a momentous year in the effort to have jazz accepted in the institutions that produced high culture. Five years later, Jazz at Lincoln Center officially became "the first new constituent created by Lincoln Center since 1969, with a mission of jazz performance, education, and dissemination."[45]

With Marsalis as artistic director and Murray and Crouch as artistic consultants, Jazz at Lincoln Center became a powerful vehicle for the linked projects of preserving jazz and disseminating jazz education. Over the past several years, this program has been carried out through concerts by the Lincoln Center Jazz Orchestra and other groups, lectures, radio and television broadcasts, a film series, a library of jazz scores, workshops, and a variety of educational programs. Early in his tenure as director, Marsalis noted that a basic function of Lincoln Center jazz was to "establish a base to get pertinent information about the music out to a wider range of people." He also made it clear that his vision for preserving jazz is linked to its development through education. Young people, he argued,

> are hungry to learn, but we need curriculum, we need a canon, we need to find ways to get the school boards interested in seeing that American culture is taught. . . . And swinging is a matter of coordination, and the coordination means that you are willing to communicate with other people. That's how swinging is—you get three or four people together, and the only way they can swing is if they work together. And that's what democracy is—freedom of expression that elevates everybody.
>
> Everybody wants it, they're ready for a change, and they're ready for positive change, and they're ready to start trying to get together. They're tired of fighting each other, they're tired of being white and black.
>
> People are ready to be Americans, and that's why it's time for jazz.

Early on, Marsalis put his ideas into practice with the Jazz for Young People series of lectures and performances, "designed to teach children and families the fundamentals of America's great indigenous art form—jazz." More recently, this program has been augmented by educational programs conducted by the Lincoln Center Jazz Orchestra while on tour and by the "Essentially Ellington" program, a competition and festival for high school jazz bands from the United States and Canada.[46]

The success of the Jazz at Lincoln Center program is emblematic of the crucial role Marsalis and his colleagues have played in asserting musicians' authority in the process of defining jazz. Yet it is important to note that the organization soon became a lightning rod for conflict, stemming from the attempt to craft a jazz canon, from personnel decisions made regarding the Lincoln Center Jazz Orchestra, and from personality conflicts between major players at Lincoln Center and the jazz press. As Richard Woodward notes, much of the struggle was simply the result of the growing prestige accorded jazz during the 1980s and 1990s, which meant that more power and money were at stake. Although Marsalis had long weathered criticism from jazz writers and musicians who found his vision exclusionary, he received more disapproval with the formation of Jazz at Lincoln Center. Now disagreements over the definitions of the jazz tradition translated into decisions about which performers were hired for the center's orchestra and whose music was featured on its programs. In a review of the 1991 Classical Jazz program, critic Whitney Balliett accused Marsalis of "reverse racism" because only six of fifty-four musicians on the program were white. Other critics raised this issue as well. An ill-conceived letter from Rob Gibson to members of the Lincoln Center Jazz Orchestra, announcing plans to replace older members with musicians under the age of thirty almost provoked a lawsuit and led to charges of racism and more charges of reverse racism. Some have also taken issue with the dearth of women instrumentalists and composers on center programs.[47]

Still others believe that Jazz at Lincoln Center's aesthetic vision has been too narrow. Some of the hostility has come from critics who support the avant-garde, but Marsalis has also received a healthy dose of criticism from musicians who saw his shepherding of the program as a direct threat to their livelihoods. Ironically, Jazz at Lincoln Center, which generally has left members of the avant-garde out of the funding and employment loop, has used as a means of exclusion the historically minded project of venerating a tradition—a project that organizations such as the AACM and the CBA used as a basis for their activism in the 1960s and 1970s. Clarinetist Don Byron has criticized Jazz at Lincoln Center and the narrowness of its vision. Speaking about Marsalis and Crouch in 1994, Byron said: "Me and most of the cats I hang around with, we're too left-wing to be around Lincoln Center. . . . They should be representing the freshest, baddest stuff. I don't even exist in jazz as these people perceive it to be."[48]

AACM trumpeter Lester Bowie also articulated a good deal of resentment toward Marsalis and criticized the practices of Lincoln Center. Bowie chastised Marsalis for disparaging popular music and the varied sources from which innovative musicians had always drawn. Although he believed the program at Lincoln Center was a good idea in theory, Bowie warned that the institutionalization of the music might stifle its creative force:

> Every city should have a jazz orchestra with a budget equal to the philharmonic. But don't negate the other things that are happening, don't stunt the growth of the music. We're not gonna sacrifice the music to get into the concert hall. . . . It's not simple music anymore. So it does belong in the concert hall. But it also belongs in the street, on the farm, it needs equal access everywhere, the same as country western, rap, anything. Because jazz is all of these. . . . C'mon, baby! Influence me! . . . Americans often look for the easy way out, and they get misinformation. . . . It's not just learning some songs; we have to learn how to live and exchange information as people.[49]

Bowie thus articulated a repertory orientation rooted more firmly in the aesthetic and social visions of the collective organizations of the 1960s and 1970s.

Yet Bowie's comments also illustrate that the doctrine of Jazz at Lincoln Center has consolidated the resolve of more experimental musicians to remain true to their own projects. And the increased funding for jazz in the 1990s, which Lincoln Center has both benefited from and helped to create, appears in the end to have helped to promulgate an ever-diverse array of jazz styles. Gene Santoro optimistically noted in 1996 that although some musicians worried that funding and institutional support would constrain the music, most were confident that this increased attention would encourage jazz's "innate, long-documented developmen-

tal urges and continuing aesthetic expansion." There have also been in-
dications that the reaction to the Lincoln Center program has resulted
in a gradual loosening of its canonical strictures. Marsalis and Crouch
have remained resolute in their ideas about the role and function of a
jazz tradition, but, as Santoro observed in 1996, Jazz at Lincoln Center
has "modified its originally narrowcast programming formulas . . . [to]
become another potentially interesting participant in jazz's fascinating
and complex internal evolutionary dynamics." Indeed, Jazz at Lincoln
Center has devoted an increasing amount of attention to Latin jazz over
the past several years and has sponsored performances by Paul Bley, Charlie Haden, Andrew Hill, Steve Lacy, Sam Rivers, and other musicians
with strong avant-garde backgrounds. Still, at the time of this writing,
the debate over Lincoln Center continues. One recent article suggests
that many musicians outside the mainstream of jazz have cooled their
critiques of the program because of the institution's resistance to change
and have directed their search for sponsorship elsewhere.[50]

## Marsalis in His Times

So what does one make of such comments and conflicts? I believe it is
important to consider Marsalis's vision, as well as those of his mentors,
as a strategic response—both to the state of jazz and to the state of African
American society. Through his celebration of the jazz tradition and his
focus on jazz education as a means of social uplift, Marsalis, along with
Crouch and Murray, has, with a good deal of success, helped to raise the
status of jazz in American culture. This project also, often in contradictory ways, addresses the economic violence being directed toward black
communities and the concomitant exclusion of their members from the
broader fabric of American society. A brief sketch of some of the economic and ideological changes occurring in the United States and their
impact on African American society can help to clarify the implications
of this vision.

As the U.S. economy continued its process of deindustrialization during the 1970s, 1980s, and 1990s, the impact on African American neighborhoods, and on urban working-class and poor people in general, was
devastating. As urban jobs geared toward manufacturing and the transportation of goods disappeared from cities, they were replaced by low-

wage employment in the service sector, if at all. As joblessness and underemployment grew, so did the crime rate. The resulting fear of criminal behavior has engendered the rapid growth of the penal system, punitive policing in communities of color, and an increase in the representation of black criminality in the media, which in turn led to an even greater increase in punishment. Such processes were institutionalized during the 1970s and then expanded in the 1980s, as the social and economic policies of Ronald Reagan and George Bush expanded poverty by crippling social welfare policies and diverting resources away from urban infrastructures.[51]

As if the direct material effects were not enough, these economic trends facilitated a conservative, racist, and antifeminist backlash against the social transformations that had been wrought during the 1960s and 1970s. The Reagan political agenda must also be understood as both a product and a skillful manipulation of the white male backlash that emerged in response to the new economic regime and the gains made by African Americans during the civil rights era. Reaganism and the mainstream media skillfully celebrated the virtues of entrepreneurial capitalism while recasting the political struggles of minorities and women as reverse discrimination. Such narratives played well both to a corporate elite and to white male workers who saw their fortunes fall in this economy. This understanding of the world was also instrumental in the creation of emergent racial ideologies. As Manning Marable argues: "Jim Crow no longer existed, but in its place stood a far more formidable system of racial domination, rooted within the political economy and employing a language of fairness and equality while simultaneously eroding the gains achieved by blacks during the second reconstruction."[52] Even in the 1990s, the "neoliberal" ideologies of the Clinton administration and various academics and policy makers, while rejecting the race-baiting demagoguery of some conservatives, still shied away from addressing racially based inequalities head on and championed what was often a naive universalism—while economic globalization and the booming high-tech and financial sectors continued to bolster an economy that disproportionately benefited elite members of American society and increasingly marginalized people of color and others at lower income levels.[53]

A central tenet of this system of domination has been what Jimmie Reeves and Richard Campbell term "cultural Moynihanism." Reeves and Campbell suggest that the Moynihan report provided a blueprint for conservative social policies in the 1980s and 1990s. Employing the assumptions of the Moynihan report, contemporary analysts and policy makers in these years blamed social inequalities on black pathologies, rather than on economic trends or institutional racism. These ideas have justified the dismantling or paring down of social welfare and affirmative action programs and the growing rate of incarceration for African Americans.[54] Even as the U.S. economy expanded rapidly in the mid- and late 1990s and the crime rate decreased, many African Americans were unable to benefit from the current job market, saw the social safety net disintegrate, or sat languishing in the ever-growing penal system.

Despite these setbacks for poor and working-class people, the 1970s, 1980s, and 1990s were periods of significant gains for the black middle class in education, electoral politics, and business. Throughout this period, American society as a whole became more integrated, even as many urban communities remained racially divided and more segregated in terms of class. The "most striking change" in terms of integration occurred, as Marable argues, in the greater visibility of African Americans in popular culture, social institutions, and the media. But in the end, the greater visibility of black people in the media proved to be a contradictory barometer of social justice. Although African Americans made significant gains that are reflected in media representations, black visibility also developed because these images help to fuel a booming culture industry that caters to black working-class and middle-class consumers and a broader American populace fascinated by blackness. Yet the growth of the entertainment sector is a function of the very economic changes that increasingly marginalized members of the black working class. Moreover, images of well-adjusted and successful African Americans, existing alongside unfavorable images of black pathology and criminality, help to justify pernicious social policies and neoracist ideologies by explaining both black failures and successes as the result of individual merit rather than as outgrowths of social policies, social movements, and economic forces. Just because racism has been tempered at face value does not mean it is not entrenched in deeper economic policies and business practices. As Marable writes, despite the "optimistic projections" of the entry of African Americans into the middle class, the "racial division of labor" remains "a primary factor in the modern capitalist economy."[55]

America in the 1980s and 1990s thus witnessed the development of a postindustrial economy and society; continued class, racial, and gender conflicts that stem from economic changes; and a concomitant growth of neoracist, antifeminist, antigay, and xenophobic ideologies and political movements. The social manifestations of structural changes have been explained away and justified by reasserting conservative or neoliberal ideologies which hold that institutional discrimination and inequality are justifiable outgrowths of fair competition in the marketplace, the unfortunate outcomes of the pathologies of those on the margins, or simply intractable problems that cannot be resolved without sabotaging the economy or injuring more "worthy" members of society. And all these trends have been represented by a proliferation of mediated images that simultaneously emphasize black participation in American society and construct urban African Americans as a threat to its fabric.

Marsalis's aesthetic vision, his popularity, and the success of his shepherding of the Lincoln Center jazz program may all be understood in relation to these social and cultural transformations. His artistic and ideological project has a particular resonance in these times. Marsalis's veneration of a heroic jazz tradition and his celebration of America's "mulatto culture" not only have increased the prestige of jazz in American cultural institutions but also have legitimated the voices of black critics and musicians. He has additionally provided a powerful defense against charges that Lincoln Center discriminates against white musicians. Beyond the jazz world, Marsalis's critique of American society and culture provides an effective rejoinder to the exclusion of African Americans from American society, although it also remains consistent with some of the discourses that have excluded them.

The economic shifts of this era have helped to promote Marsalis's popularity as a jazz musician and a spokesman. Although the jazz audience remains relatively small, it did grow over the course of the 1980s and 1990s. The jazz record business has picked up, as the entertainment sector of the economy expanded and concomitant technological advances facilitated the production, dissemination, and marketing of the music. The rise of the service-sector economy has created a growing market for jazz among its beneficiaries: namely, an ethnically diverse, well-educated, and affluent group of consumers, who patronize jazz clubs in revitalized, or gentrified, downtown areas or "public sites" such as concert halls and college auditoriums and who use their disposable income to expand their CD collections.[56]

Marsalis's contradictory project of aesthetic leveling and his implementation of Crouch's and Murray's post–black nationalist American exceptionalism also seem to have helped win new respect for jazz with the African American audience he addressed in the *Ebony* piece as well as with a broader American public. By simultaneously challenging the hierarchical distinction between classical music and jazz and then validating jazz by elevating it above popular musical forms, Marsalis provided a recipe for middle-class audiences seeking the cultural capital to validate their economic status. During a period when conservative intellectuals decried the breakdown of America's value system and the fragmentation of its social fabric in the wake of the social movements of the 1960s and 1970s, Marsalis's embrace of jazz as an African American art form that expresses national and universal values both reflected and questioned such viewpoints. Even as he challenged the Eurocentric and often racist aspects of the collective hand-wringing over the dissolution of American society, Marsalis may have, as Burton Peretti suggests, appealed to an American public that had to some extent rejected many of the cultural and social experiments of the 1960s and 1970s.[57]

Moreover, Marsalis's heroic version of jazz history and his embrace of cultural standards also addressed media representations of black social and cultural "pathologies" in urban areas, which have been part and parcel of a new chapter in the long story of America's simultaneous fear and fascination with its black presence. In the context of the hostile racial politics and anxieties about the urban underclass during the 1980s and 1990s, popular music (namely, rap) has come to represent a lack of values among the black poor and working class both in mainstream media coverage and, to some degree, in black communities. Marsalis's jazz project provided a "respectable" alternative to the youthful rebellion of rap while still catering to a broad demand for urban African American musical expression. It is difficult to gauge whether any significant number of middle-class African Americans became jazz fans because Marsalis scolded them for their inattention to the genre. Yet his heroic vision of jazz provided a class-specific means of calling attention to black contributions to society during a period that gave so much attention to black "threats" to society.

Marsalis's vision has also been instrumental in securing increased corporate and government support for the jazz idiom and has facilitated its growing presence on college campuses, even at a time when funding for the arts has been jeopardized by conservative outrage over subsidies for art considered subversive or obscene. By cultivating the role of an intellectual, demanding that jazz be understood as an intellectual practice, and rejecting the aesthetic boundary between jazz and classical music, Marsalis has helped to win prestige for the music. Marsalis's involvement with Jazz at Lincoln Center demonstrates that his particular post-nationalist, universalist, and American-exceptionalist project was a perfect fit for the stewardship of a program whose existence benefited from the kind of legitimacy he has brought to jazz. And the program promises to grow in the future. In May 2000, Jazz at Lincoln Center unveiled the design for a new home. This $103 million, 100,000-square-foot facility, scheduled to open in 2003, "will be," according to the organization, "the world's first performing arts center designed specifically for jazz."[58]

Marsalis's implementation of Crouch's and Murray's ideas has also provided a ready-made response to some of the most vocal critics of Jazz at Lincoln Center. The center, for example, was the site of a heated debate between Marsalis and jazz writer James Lincoln Collier. Marsalis fired the first salvo in the exchange by writing a scathing letter to the *New York Times,* criticizing the paper for publishing a favorable review of Collier's book *Jazz: The American Theme Song.* Marsalis claimed that Collier's biographies of Armstrong and Ellington were filled with factual errors. He also objected to Collier's lack of attention to how individual musicians drew from one another and his inability to understand the "intentional" elements of jazz creativity. Echoing Murray's critique of jazz writing in *Stomping the Blues,* Marsalis wrote: "Mr. Collier is nothing more than a pompous social scientist who for too long has passed as a serious scholar of jazz music. That is why it is unfortunate that he was reviewed by a man apparently unaware of the contempt all who are seriously engaged in jazz feel for this viper in the bosom of blues and swing." Marsalis saw Collier's work as representative of the "impoverished state" of jazz criticism. If critics were unable to police their own ranks, then musicians must take charge. So Marsalis challenged Collier to defend his ideas in public, and the two men squared off for a debate on August 7, 1994.[59]

Commenting on the exchange, Andre Craddock-Willis argues that race, power, and generation "confounded" the debate, which did little to bridge the gulf between musicians and critics.[60] True, but the debate did illustrate, on one level, how issues of critical authority were brought into question when three black men (Marsalis, Murray, and Crouch) took over the direction of Jazz at Lincoln Center and began to chart publicly the direction of jazz in the public imagination. Additionally, it showed just how well their vision served to legitimate the aesthetic projects and perspectives of African American musicians.

Marsalis devoted much of his time during the debate to the technical errors he found in Collier's books about Armstrong and Ellington. Marsalis also took issue with what he saw as Collier's blindness to the heroism of jazz creativity. Whereas Collier had written that the problems Armstrong had with his embouchure late in his life were a result of full lips and poor technique, Marsalis argued that they were the result of the trumpeter's commitment to the art form: "The real reason for his problems with his embouchure is that he was like a boxer, who would endure incredible amounts of pain. Where a normal man would stop— especially when improvising, because you have the choice to play what you want—Mr. Armstrong would just keep playing."[61]

Marsalis also emphasized the importance of recognizing the intellectualism of jazz practice. Collier opened by suggesting that Crouch had written the letter to the *Times*. Although Marsalis's vituperative attack in the letter was reminiscent of one element of Crouch's prose, this assertion played perfectly into Marsalis's hand. He had with him a draft of a manuscript he had written—almost certainly *Sweet Swing Blues on the Road*—and presented it, stating: "For those who doubt that I'm capable of writing in the English language, this is it."[62] In addition to challenging the accusation that he was a mouthpiece for Crouch, Marsalis defined himself as a capable thinker about jazz and asserted that Collier's critical vision was marred by an inability to recognize the intellectual power of jazz musicians.

Collier made the salient point that in Marsalis's vision of jazz history, certain figures, like Ellington, could do no wrong: "The problem that we have in jazz today . . . ," he argued, "is that you're not allowed to say anything about a jazz musician except what's very nice." Yet Collier's rationale for some of his comments about Ellington was questionable—

for example, his claim that the bandleader's lack of formal training led to "random" harmonic structures in his compositions. Moreover, if one writes a musical biography and grounds it in assumptions about its subject's lack of "intellectual sophistication," as Collier did with Ellington, there certainly is a danger of reducing the music to a mechanical reflection of sociological forces. Marsalis challenged such assumptions by asserting the musician's ability to set the record straight on his own terms:

> The reason I am here is because as a musician, we're constantly attacked by men who don't study our music. They don't take our music seriously enough to know it. They don't come to us and ask us about it. And then they want to know why we're mad. I've done more interviews than any musician alive and—in only two interviews in fifteen years have I ever been asked about my method as a musician.[63]

Marsalis made this assertion persuasively, drawing upon his own knowledge of jazz history and the power and prestige with which he is vested as artistic director of Lincoln Center's jazz program.

Finally, when it came to the racial politics of Jazz at Lincoln Center, Marsalis showed that Murray's paradigm of African American exceptionalism provided an effective means for validating black institutional authority at the center and for refuting charges of reverse racism that were leveled at the program by some jazz critics. Toward the end of the debate, Collier managed to turn the discussion to three major criticisms of the Lincoln Center program commonly voiced in the jazz press: first, that Marsalis primarily used black players and had never celebrated a white musician on a Lincoln Center program; second, that he had given an inordinate number of commissions to himself and his present or former associates; and third, that he had omitted members of the avant-garde from Lincoln Center events. Marsalis adamantly refuted the charge that he was enriching himself with commissions, but he made no apologies for freezing out the avant-garde. As far as he was concerned, it was his prerogative to craft a program consistent with his own taste and vision. He even suggested that his refusal to put on programs of black avant-garde music was evidence that his selections were color-blind.[64]

Marsalis responded more specifically to charges of reverse racism by producing statistics showing that 50 percent of the lectures at Lincoln

Center had been conducted by white scholars. Of the performers who had appeared on stage at Jazz at Lincoln Center, 56 percent were black, 31 percent were white, and 13 percent were Hispanic. Although Collier conceded the point, he noted that the majority of the players were black and that Lincoln Center had, at that point (although this has since changed), never put on a program highlighting the work of a white artist. Marsalis's response to this was to reverse the accusation and charge Collier with being preoccupied with race and class, a flaw he also claimed marred Collier's scholarship. Marsalis criticized Collier's use of the term "black music" and his desire to "separate things" by focusing on race and class distinctions and refusing to see the ways that Americans' lives are interconnected. If there had been a majority of black players, it was because "the basis of jazz music is in the American Negro culture. Not in race . . . Race is physiology. This is a matter of culture." By defining jazz as a cultural (that is, ethnic) and not a racial inheritance, Marsalis naturalized the centrality of African Americans to its production and justified his stewardship (and that of Crouch and Murray) of the Lincoln Center program. If jazz was both ethnically black and American, it was thus simultaneously an African American birthright and outside the economy of racism and racial separatism.[65]

The relevance of this vision of jazz heroism and denial of racial thinking went beyond the jazz world; Marsalis, Murray, and Crouch have all seen the validation of the jazz tradition as a means of responding to the economic, racial, and cultural legacy of the Reagan-Bush years. As Murray himself recently said: "America's only possible hope is that the Negroes might save us, which is what we're all trying to do. We've got Louis, Duke, Count, and Ralph, and now we're trying to do it with Wynton and Stanley. That's all we are—just a bunch of Negroes *trying* to save America."[66] Writing about hip-hop culture, Tricia Rose situates its emergence in postindustrial urban America: "It is the tension between the cultural fractures produced by postindustrial oppression and the binding ties of black cultural expressivity that sets the critical frame for the development of hip hop."[67] Although Marsalis has defined his musical project as diametrically opposed to that of hip-hop, we can understand it as a response to the same historical currents, for he has attempted to mend the "cultural fractures" produced by postindustrial oppression and the proliferation of unfavorable media images by establishing new "binding ties" through a grand African American musical tradition that replicates the often-unrealized ideals of American society.

Since the 1960s, some commentators have labeled the Ellisonian demand for African American inclusion a reactionary position. But one can argue that there is also something potentially subversive in seizing an African American birthright. Speaking of Murray's early work, Henry Louis Gates Jr. remarks:

> In Murray's hands, integration wasn't an act of accommodation but an act of introjection. . . . So, even as the clenched fist crowd was scrambling for cultural crumbs, Murray was declaring the entire harvest board of American civilization to be his birthright. In a sense, Murray was the ultimate black nationalist. And the fact that people so easily mistook his vision for its opposite proved how radical it was.[68]

Murray's embrace of the blues as a metaphor for African American heroism, which he used in the 1970s as a means of rejecting social-scientific and black separatist assessments of African American life, today presents a challenge to "cultural Moynihanism." In his 1996 collection of essays, *The Blue Devils of Nada,* Murray builds upon many of the themes he addressed in earlier writings, while refusing to accept the exclusion of black people from American life. After speaking about Duke Ellington's childhood in a Washington, D.C., occupied by the racist administration of Woodrow Wilson, Murray emphasizes that Ellington "did not grow up thinking of himself as downtrodden." This, among other stories, offers to African Americans in today's America—a racial context much different from that of the 1910s, but one still structured by the "folklore of white supremacy" and the "fakelore of black pathology"—an aesthetic for living in which individual accomplishment and a demand for inclusion go hand in hand.[69]

Although Crouch's intellectual capital has increased since he incorporated neoconservative elements into his social vision, he cannot be dismissed as merely an apologist for white supremacy, as some of his critics have suggested. He condemned the draconian social policies of the Reagan era, and his cultural criticism has ultimately sought to improve black communities and America as a whole during a period of backlash against the gains of the civil rights movement. As he came to prominence as a public intellectual, Crouch recognized the white backlash that was brewing in the United States and set forth a cultural critique that, at least in part, was meant to counter it. In a 1979 review of a Nina Simone concert, during which the singer criticized the nightclub management from the stage for failing to pay her on time, Crouch criticized her actions. "I suspect that shows of this sort feed the terrible backlash against black people that is again starting to form in this country," he wrote. "Simone played into the hands of those who would, again, disenfranchise us, using incompetence, irresponsibility, and inordinate arrogance as excuses."[70] Even some commentators on the left have identified a liberatory potential in Crouch's work.[71]

And Marsalis, too, has carefully tailored a celebration of both African American and American cultural exceptionalism which refuses the brand of racism that justifies itself by emphasizing pathological behavior and the distance of African American culture from the American mainstream. Moreover, by championing the intellectual aspects of jazz practice, he refutes racist ideas of black mental inferiority and those discourses that categorize blackness by locating pathologies on the racial body. By transforming black nationalism into a kind of American exceptionalism with a Negro core, then, Marsalis, Crouch, and Murray all have helped produce a vision that radically challenges the marginalization of black people from American experience.

Still, this vision remains consistent, in some ways, with the ideological projects it seeks to refute. During the 1980s, for example, the rhetoric of black inclusion became a tool for the right. Although Murray effectively used the image of Harriet Tubman as an American heroine to decry the exclusion of African Americans in 1970, Manning Marable describes how, at a 1981 address to the NAACP national convention, Ronald Reagan described Harriet Tubman as embodying the "glory of the American experience" in a speech that sought to justify the dismantling of government programs that addressed black needs.[72] Marsalis's project also remains consistent with the practice of accepting African Americans into U.S. society as ethnic but not racial bodies. Although American audiences have a long history of consuming black cultural forms, desegregation brought a growing absorption of elements of black culture into the mainstream. As Marable argues, however, nonblacks' "affinity and tolerance for blackness were almost always cultural and ethnic, rather than racial."[73] In other words, although many consumers have been willing to incorporate black music, language, and literature into their everyday lives, they have often not understood (or have refused to see) race as an artificial construction imposed upon people of African descent in order to facilitate and justify economic exploitation. A heroic blues affirmation of American and African American values does not necessarily challenge this.

By linking his own musical project with African American exceptionalism, and conflating and dismissing the jazz avant-garde and black nationalism, Marsalis also participates in demonizing the 1960s—an important tenet of late-twentieth-century neoconservatism and neoracism. The contradictions of this vision mirror those of his mentors. Crouch's insightful observations about the narrowness of cultural nationalist representations of black experience and his willingness to criticize the anti-white rhetoric that often replaced meaningful dialogue in effect place on the black freedom movement a heavy burden of blame for the problems of American society. By fusing their claims of an African American birthright with a blanket condemnation of black nationalism, Marsalis and company reject both its narrow-minded and bigoted aspects *and* those elements that might make sense of the way blackness as a racial identity was formed in a context of power.

Marsalis's project also remains consistent with the ideologies of social and cultural conservatism and neoliberalism when he venerates jazz by distancing it from popular culture and reduces social relations to questions of values. Marsalis's condemnation of the moral shortcomings of hip-hop is instructive. As Rose points out, the attack on black youth, which is at the heart of many critiques of rap music, stems from a "long-standing, sociologically based discourse that considers black influences a cultural threat to American society."[74] Although Marsalis's veneration of black culture attempts to subvert this discourse, it nevertheless conforms to certain elements of it. While there is a great deal to criticize in the misogyny, glorification of violence, homophobia, anti-Semitism, and just plain banality of some rap music, dismissing the entire genre on the grounds of cultural standards and morality is ultimately consistent with a discourse that condemns black youth in general.[75]

As this book has tried to make clear, musicians have long defined jazz as an intellectual practice to challenge stereotypes about black inferiority. As effective as Marsalis's definition of jazz intellect has been in winning newfound prestige for the art form, by distancing it from other forms of black popular culture and market-driven tastes, he simultaneously affirms an elitist disdain for certain black tastes and cultural affiliations. Marsalis's aesthetic vision and his program of jazz activism are rooted in a narrower vision of the jazz tradition than the ones held by members of the CBA and the AACM in the 1970s. Whereas the CBA's educational programs were rooted in a radicalized Black Arts imperative and a validation of youth culture, Marsalis's is grounded in a rejection of cultural nationalism and young people's engagement with popular culture. Some of this can be traced back to Murray's formulation in *Stomping the Blues.* By ascribing a kind of high-art capital and artistic intent to the communal function of the blues, Murray provides a successful means of dismantling the hierarchical relationship between concert music and black vernacular music. Yet to the extent that his assessment relies on formalistic and ritualistic definitions of the beautiful as a source of legitimacy, it retains the capacity to create its own aesthetic taxonomy based on specific musical elements. And by venerating Ellington's music through comparisons to Euro-American literary works with supposed universal significance, Murray's project of opposing white supremacy nevertheless invokes aesthetic standards that have been used to marginalize and trivialize African American culture. Moreover, a recognition of the problems of racial identification, representation, and social policy that arise when the lives of the black poor come to represent the sum total of black experience loses its force when Marsalis and Crouch write in condescending tones about the cultural forms and behaviors they believe have overshadowed superior bourgeois tastes and values.

Marsalis's vision also reproduces the gendered construction of the jazz tradition as male and conforms to the ideology of the contemporary antifeminist backlash. Although Marsalis criticizes the sexist representations of women in rap music, his idea of a patriarchal lineage of jazz history conforms to the history of jazz writing and the veneration of male artistic genius within the jazz community. For some observers, Marsalis has come to symbolize a healthy black masculinity. Writing about him in the *Village Voice,* Playthell Benjamin describes Marsalis as a "living refutation of all the negative stereotypes and banal clichés that have become conventional wisdom about black males, especially young black males."

Instead, the trumpeter "ennobles Afro-American manhood" and is "heir to a black male cultural heritage" that includes figures ranging from W. E. B. Du Bois to Colin Powell.[76] But by arguing that the "great men" of jazz provide the means of uplifting the black community and "saving America," Marsalis's vision is also consistent with a discourse that locates deviant aspects of African American culture in the female body and the belief—expressed by conservatives, populist religious fundamentalists, and black nationalists alike—that the problems of American society are to be solved by the reassertion of patriarchy.

## Coda: Ellington Redux

One of the striking elements of Marsalis's development as a musician and as a critic, particularly in the 1990s, has been his growing affinity for the music and vision of Duke Ellington, an affinity shared and cultivated by Crouch and Murray. Beginning with his 1989 album *The Majesty of the Blues,* Marsalis released a series of thematic albums that featured the blues, drew upon a historical knowledge of the jazz tradition, and invoked Ellington as a practitioner of both blues music and a blues ethos. Speaking in 1989, Marsalis said: "If you're not playing blues, it's not jazz. And it must also reflect or show a knowledge of history of the music in the progression of each instrument."[77]

*The Majesty of the Blues* self-consciously explores the history of jazz. The first two compositions bring the roots of jazz in New Orleans into the present by combining basic forms with more recent inventions. The title track, subtitled "The Puheeman Strut," fuses the blues tonality and polyphony of early-twentieth-century New Orleans music with modal movement through a succession of keys. The introduction features Coltrane-like playing by tenor player Todd Williams, which he reproduces in his solos. With Williams riffing underneath, Marsalis plays the head using a plunger mute, invoking the "dirty" style of Storyville trumpeting. On his own solos, Marsalis explores a range of tone colors as he growls, moans, and bends notes with the mute. This song is bottom-heavy, with a sense of rhythmic urgency that bassist Reginald Veal creates by playing a bass figure with a long bent pitch that disrupts the basic pulse. Marsalis describes the second piece, "Hickory Dickory Dock," as a children's tune that combines a march beat and a gospel shuffle. The church influence is expressed by pianist Marcus Roberts's dense chords and the call and response between the members of the band. The march passages are syncopated in a way that evokes ragtime composers' appropriations of band music in the creation of jazz.[78]

The remainder of the album is taken up by a three-part piece entitled "The New Orleans Function." The arrangement of this triptych is that of a New Orleans funeral march. The musical evocation of the idea of a jazz tradition through this most "ancient" of jazz rituals is obvious.[79] The piece begins with "The Death of Jazz," a dirgelike section that evokes the music heard by mourners on their way to the cemetery. The following segment, "Premature Autopsies (Sermon)," revolves around a sixteen-minute "sermon" written by Stanley Crouch and read by Reverend Jeremiah Wright Jr. Marsalis backs this spoken-word piece with a gospel-laden blues, with horns providing the affirming voices of the congregation. The sermon begins with an interrogation of the idea that jazz is dead. Because "we are told to mourn it," Crouch eulogizes the "noble sound," calling it a "great art" that symbolizes African American triumph over adversity and "the democratic imperatives of our birthright." Invoking Murray's metaphors, Crouch describes the music as a "knight wrapped up in the glistening armor of invention," who has successfully fought off the "despair pronounced by dragons." Unfortunately, this great art has been pronounced dead by the "money lenders of the marketplace" for not conforming to their desire to make it into a commodity. But despite such proclamations, the human spirit in the music has overcome the threats to its existence, just as the human spirit of African Americans has transcended the ignominy of slavery and taught Americans the "true meaning of democracy."[80]

The sermon locates this spirit most deeply in Duke Ellington and his successors "who will not leave the field once it becomes obvious that the sound of a cymbal swinging in celebration is more beautiful than the ringing of a cash register." With the band returning to the funeral march, Ellington's life and the perseverance of jazz are celebrated: "You had better not pay much attention to those premature autopsies. This noble sound, this thing of majesty, this art, so battered but so ready for battle, it just might lift you high enough in the understanding of human life to let you know in no uncertain terms why that marvelous Washingtonian,

Edward Kennedy Ellington, NEVER came off the road."[81] With this statement, the band launches into "Oh, But on the Third Day," which concludes the piece with an up-tempo affirmation such as a New Orleans jazz band would perform on the way home from the cemetery. In such rituals, the music serves as an affirmation of life for those remaining among the living. In this case, it serves to validate Marsalis's and Crouch's roles as champions of the "noble sound" and the Ellingtonian tradition.

In May 1992, Marsalis premiered his extended composition *In This House, On This Morning* at Lincoln Center and took his septet into the studio the next day to record the piece. The recorded version takes another step back into the history of black music, emphasizing the harmonies, rhythms, and tonalities of the church, while still speaking of the blues. As Crouch writes in the liner notes, this recording "brings the broad spiritual perspective at the root of jazz together with the intellectual achievements that have taken place in an art built upon the melody, the harmony, and the rhythms of the blues." Just as Murray wrote of the blues serving a similarly affirming function as a church service (albeit in a secular context), Crouch notes similar roles: "The blues is the sound of spiritual investigation in a secular frame, and through its very lyricism, the blues achieves its spiritual penetration."[82] The composition itself is shaped as a church service, with individual movements taking the listener from the informal prayer before the service to the "Pot Blessed Dinner," for which churchgoers gather after the worship is over. Over the course of the performance, Marsalis explores a variety of sacred musical themes. At times the band swings like a revival meeting, whereas at other moments it methodically and systematically examines the possibilities of instrumental voicings. A major emphasis is the exploration of the vocal aspects of African American religious music, both through the range of tones that Marsalis and his saxophonists explore on their instruments and with the help of guest vocalist Marion Williams.

As a look back into history, the album engages thematic works such as John Coltrane's *A Love Supreme* and Duke Ellington's suites and sacred concerts. Indeed, the extended coda of "Recessional," with Todd Williams playing a soaring tenor solo over an ostinato figure and the chanting of the other band members, seems particularly indebted to Coltrane's album. Crouch compares the music on *In This House* to the breadth of

*Black, Brown and Beige.* He also notes Marsalis's acknowledgment that the movement "Representative Offerings" is influenced by Ellington's *Afro-Bossa* and *The New Orleans Suite.* As Marsalis delves further into Ellington's legacy, however, he also must come to terms with the broader palette with which the composer explored the jazz idiom. With *In This House,* Marsalis seeks to reconcile Ellington's extended compositional forms and use of diverse musical idioms with his own ongoing project of maintaining the homegrown authenticity of the blues:

> Even though the form is definitely American, I wanted to open the interpretation up to all kinds of musical approaches. That's why the piece has the emotion of traveling and visiting many different kinds of churches and many different kinds of services, from the highly refined all the way to the backwoods, way down in the country. *In This House* moves from the feeling of the black American church to the study of Bach chorales, even the feeling of ritual in ancient religious forms [a variation of a Gregorian chant on "The Lord's Prayer"] and the sounds one hears when in Middle Eastern countries [the tonalities of "Call to Prayer"]. By using the blues as a fundamental element, I was also able to ground the music in our culture while stretching it onto an international plane.[83]

By moving further into jazz history and bringing it forward through the legacy of Ellington, Marsalis takes the vernacular into an international context but is careful to bring it back home again.

Marsalis's grandest evocation of Ellington is his oratorio *Blood on the Fields.* Here Marsalis not only creates an extended composition for a large jazz band but also, as Ellington did in *Black, Brown and Beige,* seeks to tell an epic story of African American experience. Premiered at Alice Tully Hall at Lincoln Center on April 1, 1994, *Blood on the Fields* was recorded in 1995 and finally released in 1997. The oratorio tells the story of two Africans, Jesse, an African prince, and Leona, a "commoner," who are captured, endure the Middle Passage and slavery, and finally achieve freedom, not by escape but by embracing an American identity and birthright. Musically, Marsalis draws from influences ranging from Ellington to Mingus to Stravinsky to Bernstein, as he weaves together a pastiche of jazz history through Latin and funk rhythms, march passages, bebop harmonies and melodic lines, spirituals, and New Orleans swing. Supporting everything is a heavy dose of blues forms and melodies, which Marsalis arranges in lush, Ellingtonian orchestrations that showcase the talents of individual soloists.[84]

If *Blood on the Fields* represents a self-conscious attempt by Marsalis to position himself as a modern-day Ellington, one of the striking things about this portrayal is the way that he as well as Crouch have emphasized the universal aspects of Ellington's legacy.[85] It is an evocation of Ellington that corresponds to the centennial tribute discussed at the beginning of this chapter. In a 1992 interview with Robert O'Meally, Marsalis notes Ellington's grounding in black vernacular expression and his early efforts of creating a racial expression, but he emphasizes that the composer later rejected racial prescriptions and sought to create a broader human expression.[86] Such a perspective is similarly evident in Marsalis's and Crouch's attempt to cast *Blood on the Fields,* a story of the slavery of African peoples, as a fundamentally human tragedy with implications for all of America. Marsalis told *Down Beat* that slavery was the "defining issue in our national identity. It still is a major deterrent and stumbling block on our way to really enjoying democracy, enjoying the life of our country and of us enjoying each other." Speaking to the *New York Times,* he said that even in the portrayal of slavery he was trying to portray the human spirit in tragic circumstances. "I'm not projecting anything social onto that. I'm speaking purely as a man."[87]

Chapter 1 of this book opened with a quotation from an essay Ellington wrote in 1939. In that piece, Ellington tried to create a socially relevant black aesthetic under conditions that limited black creativity. He challenged the narrow perspectives of jazz critics, as he tried to make sense of an art form that was clearly an African American and an American achievement. As he stated his intent to create "an authentic Negro music" that was a "genuine contribution from our race," Ellington's New Negro vision also held that the production and reception of black music would have an effect on the social standing of African Americans.

Like Ellington in the 1930s, Marsalis has tried to make sense of African American art in a society structured by race; like all the musicians in this study, he has made sense of the validation and restrictions involved when understanding jazz as an African American art form. And he too has tried to use jazz as a tool for promoting social change and exploring human potential. By invoking the universalist aspects of Ellington's vision and expressing them in a color-blind portrayal of slavery, Marsalis and Crouch, as Ellington did earlier, provide a commentary on the state of jazz and the state of African American society. Slavery, they argue, has profound implications for American society. As Crouch states in the liner notes for *Blood on the Fields:* "American issues of labor, of gender, of the exploitation of children, and, finally, of human rights within this society are traceable back to that phenomenon, for it defined every inadequacy that was allowed to exist within the United States." But it is in the opposition to slavery that he finds "a deeper understanding of the meaning of democracy and inspired actions that helped define the ethical grandeur of courage within our culture." "*Blood on the Fields,*" Marsalis asserts, "details in music what I feel it takes to achieve soul: the willingness to address adversity with elegance."[88]

Updating Ellington's New Negro demand for inclusion, and speaking as a purveyor of an art form that now has significantly greater respect as an African American accomplishment, Marsalis offers an argument that focuses less on assimilation via a cultural dowry than on the need to recognize that America's moral center and salvation lie in the experiences of African Americans and their allies. It is a triumphant and optimistic vision that should be understood as somewhat contradictory in the social, cultural, and ideological contexts sketched out here as well as in relation to the growing prestige of jazz as an art form. Ultimately, in his view, it is through shared human values, symbolized by a heroic jazz tradition, that mutual liberation of black people and others will occur. Marsalis is indeed linked—notwithstanding strong ideological and aesthetic differences, distinct historical circumstances, and varying levels of investment in the idea of jazz—to Ellington and the other musicians discussed in this book.

# Epilogue

**SEVENTY-FIVE YEARS LATER,** jazz is still a paradox in the terms J. A. Rogers set out in 1925. It is a music rooted in American and, more specifically, African American experience; yet it is indeed too "fundamentally human" to be racial and too international to be understood solely as a product of the United States. The racial and geographical places of jazz have been made more complex by the proliferation of musical styles that are identified as jazz, the complicated ways in which the music is marketed and distributed, and a variety of transformations in American culture and society.

Scholars, critics, artists, and fans have for close to a century tried to understand the paradoxical place of jazz in American life. But they are not the only ones. Musicians, too, have addressed the idea of jazz while negotiating their place in society as practitioners of this art form. This book has shown that when we synthesize an understanding of social, cultural, and intellectual transformations, with an attention to musicians' ideas, we see that these artists have self-consciously engaged the complicated identities, demographic shifts, material conditions, and other social forces for which their music has been seen as emblematic. In other words, musicians have not only created an expression that may be understood as a product of an African American, American, or global culture; they have tried to locate it within or across a variety of cultural boundaries. They have not merely produced music that speaks of the forces of capitalist production; they have articulated what it means to contend with these forces while trying to create an artistic expression. They have not only performed music that reflects the hybridity of black culture; they have been conscious that they have done so and have actively and publicly struggled with questions of authenticity. They have not merely served as agents of community formation or articulated emergent identities through their music; they have seized these roles, tried to make sense of how their music might perform these functions, and pondered their responsibilities to their communities.

W. C. Handy, Louis Armstrong, Duke Ellington, Herbie Nichols, Charlie Parker, Mary Lou Williams, Billy Taylor, Charles Mingus, Abbey Lincoln, Archie Shepp, Reggie Workman, Marion Brown, Yusef Lateef, Anthony Braxton, Wadada Leo Smith, and Wynton Marsalis make up a short list of the musicians who have tried to make sense of the paradoxical position of jazz and their own artistic projects. At the time of this writing, Workman, Braxton, Taylor, Smith, Lincoln, Shepp, and, of course, Marsalis actively continue this conversation through their written work, participation in educational enterprises, and public commentary about this music. As they take this conversation in new directions in the twenty-first century, they are joined by others who will, I hope, be the subjects of further investigations into the intellectual history of jazz.

Musicians have certainly made their best-known and most influential statements through sonic expressions rather than through debate or the written word. Most of the intellectual energies of the jazz community have, after all, been devoted to learning, practicing, writing, arranging, and performing music. Yet musicians have embraced the identities of intellectuals and articulated important ideas about their music and other subjects. And if we give these ideas the respect and attention they deserve, they provide a means for rethinking jazz history. Not only can we understand the intellectual history of jazz as embodying more than the ideas of critics and traditional intellectuals; in addition, musicians' ideas can add another chapter to the story of African American intellectual life.

# Notes

## Introduction

1. This broad definition of intellectual activity is critical to Gramsci's vanguardist concept of "organic intellectuals," who are created by a social group and give it "homogeneity and an awareness of its own function not only in the economic but also in the social and political fields." Gramsci contrasts these organic intellectuals with "traditional intellectuals," who occupy positions or institutions more commonly identified with intellectual life. See Antonio Gramsci, *Selections from the Prison Notebooks* (New York: International Publishers, 1971), 5–9.

Scholars have often characterized African American musicians as "organic intellectuals" as a means of describing their social role in creating group identities and resistant cultural practices. Although many of the musicians discussed here may be described as organic intellectuals (and some might also be described as traditional intellectuals), I do not employ the Gramscian categories systematically in this study, simply because my focus is not on theorizing the role of this music in social transformations. I am more interested in how musicians have perceived and theorized the political potential of their music.

2. Thomas Carmichael, "*Beneath the Underdog:* Charles Mingus, Representation, and Jazz Autobiography," *Canadian Review of American Studies* 25, no. 3 (Fall 1995): 32–34.

3. Paul Berliner, *Thinking in Jazz: The Infinite Art of Improvisation* (Chicago: University of Chicago Press, 1994); Ingrid Monson, *Saying Something: Jazz Improvisation and Interaction* (Chicago: University of Chicago Press, 1996); Ronald Radano, *New Musical Figurations: Anthony Braxton's Cultural Critique* (Chicago: University of Chicago Press, 1996); Scott DeVeaux, *The Birth of Bebop: A Social and Musical History* (Berkeley: University of California Press, 1997); Sherrie Tucker, *Swing Shift: "All-Girl" Bands of the 1940s* (Durham: Duke University Press, 2000); Graham Lock, *Blutopia: Visions of the Future and Revisions of the Past in the Work of Sun Ra, Duke Ellington, and Anthony Braxton* (Durham: Duke University Press, 2000).

## Chapter 1. "A Marvel of Paradox"

1. Duke Ellington, "Duke Says Swing Is Stagnant," in *The Duke Ellington Reader*, ed. Mark Tucker (New York: Oxford University Press, 1993), 135 (originally published in *Down Beat*, February 1939, 2, 16–17); John Hammond, "The Tragedy of Duke Ellington, the 'Black Prince of Jazz,'" in Tucker, *The Duke Ellington Reader*, 118–120 (originally published in the *Brooklyn Eagle*, November 11, 1935; and in *Down Beat*, November 1935, 1, 6).

2. J. A. Rogers, "Jazz at Home," in *The New Negro*, ed. Alain Locke (New York: Atheneum, 1977), 216.

3. Guthrie P. Ramsey Jr., "Cosmopolitan or Provincial? Ideology in Early Black Music Historiography, 1867–1940," *Black Music Research Journal* 16, no. 1 (Spring 1996): 15–21; Jon Michael Spencer, *The New Negroes and Their Music: The Success of the Harlem Renaissance* (Knoxville: University of Tennessee Press, 1997), 3, 22–26.

4. W. E. B. Du Bois, *The Souls of Black Folk*, in *Three Negro Classics* (New York: Avon Books, 1965), 378; William Banks, *Black Intellectuals: Race and Responsibility in American Life* (New York: W. W. Norton, 1996), 65–66; Hazel V. Carby, *Race Men* (Cambridge: Harvard University Press, 1998), 9–41, 91.

5. Du Bois, *The Souls of Black Folk*, 382.

6. Alain Locke, "The New Negro," in *The New Negro*, 3.

7. Ted Gioia, *The History of Jazz* (New York: Oxford University Press, 1997), 27.

8. See Amiri Baraka [LeRoi Jones], *Blues People: Negro Music in White America* (New York: Morrow, 1963; reprint, New York: Quill Paperbacks, 1983); Burton Peretti, *The Creation of Jazz: Music, Race, and Culture in Urban America* (Urbana: University of Illinois Press, 1992); Burton Peretti, *Jazz in American Culture* (Chicago: Ivan R. Dee, 1997); Kathy Ogren, *The Jazz Revolution: Twenties America and the Meaning of Jazz* (New York: Oxford University Press, 1989); Albert Murray, *Stomping the Blues* (New York: McGraw-Hill, 1976; reprint, New York: Da Capo, 1989); William Howland Kenney, *Chicago Jazz: A Cultural History, 1904–30* (New York: Oxford University Press, 1993); Ann Douglas, *Terrible Honesty: Mongrel Manhattan in the 1920s* (New York: Noonday Press, 1995).

9. Contrary to myth, most early professional jazz players received some measure of formal training—from school, church, parents, orphanages, fraternal organizations, or other musicians—that included instruction in harmony, sight reading, and composition. Most also had some familiarity with classical and religious music and with various elements of popular music. See Ogren, *The Jazz Revolution*, 29–30; Peretti, *The Creation of Jazz*, 100–106; Scott DeVeaux, *The Birth of Bebop: A Social and Musical History* (Berkeley: University of California Press, 1997), 39–45, 49–69. For an excellent, though less historically specific, discussion of the role of educational networks in the development of jazz, see Paul Berliner, *Thinking in Jazz: The Infinite Art of Improvisation* (Chicago: University of Chicago Press, 1994), especially pt. 1.

10. Ogren, *The Jazz Revolution*, 14–18, 35, 43; Baraka [Jones], *Blues People*, 51–70.

11. Sociologist C. Wright Mills defined a cultural apparatus as "all the organizations and *milieux* in which artistic, intellectual and scientific work goes on, and of the means by which such work is made available to circles, publics, and the masses" ("The Cultural Apparatus," in *Power, Politics, and People: The Collected Essays of C. Wright Mills*, ed. Irving Louis Horowitz [New York: Ballantine, 1963], 406). During the first half of the twentieth century, as Michael Denning explains, this cultural apparatus incorporated the arts in two primary areas: "a culture industry of leisure and entertainment built on new technologies of motion pictures, recorded sound, and broadcasting; and a state cultural bureaucracy collecting, subsidizing, and distributing arts, information, and education through a variety of schools and agencies" (*The Cultural Front: The Laboring of American Culture in the Twentieth Century* [London: Verso, 1996], 38–39).

12. Peretti, *The Creation of Jazz,* 50–58; James Weldon Johnson, *Black Manhattan* (New York: Knopf, 1930; reprint, New York: Da Capo, 1991), 162–180; Ogren, *The Jazz Revolution,* 56–86; Robin D. G. Kelley, *Race Rebels: Culture, Politics, and the Black Working Class* (New York: Free Press, 1995), 45; Earl Lewis, *In Their Own Interests: Race, Class, and Power in Twentieth-Century Norfolk, Virginia* (Berkeley: University of California Press, 1991), 91–92.

13. Douglas, *Terrible Honesty,* 364–368, 419–425; Ogren, *The Jazz Revolution,* 5, 35–38, 91, 100. As Douglas perceptively notes, recordings and radio broadcasts were perfect vehicles for disseminating African American music, as they conveyed distinct tonalities, rhythms, and emotional depth, which could not be done with any accuracy through sheet music or written instruction.

14. Ted Vincent, *Keep Cool: The Black Activists Who Built the Jazz Age* (London: Pluto Press, 1995), 106–160; Ogren, *The Jazz Revolution,* 113–114; Peretti, *The Creation of Jazz,* 22–32, 60–64.

15. Kenney, *Chicago Jazz,* 121–123. See also various advertisements in *The Crusader,* March, April, May, and September 1920; February, April, May, and July 1921.

16. Kenney, *Chicago Jazz,* 127.

17. Lawrence Levine, "Jazz in American Culture," in *The Jazz Cadence of American Culture,* ed. Robert G. O'Meally (New York: Columbia University Press, 1998), 431–447.

18. Ogren, *The Jazz Revolution,* 139–161. For a good sample of the responses to jazz during the 1910s and 1920s, see *Keeping Time: Readings in Jazz History,* ed. Robert Walser (New York: Oxford University Press, 1999), 3–69.

19. Douglas, *Terrible Honesty,* 5, 49–52, 217–299, 349–399; Ogren, *The Jazz Revolution,* 7, 100, 139–161; Peretti, *Jazz in American Culture,* 17, 31–43; Peretti, *The Creation of Jazz,* 76–99, 189; David Levering Lewis, *When Harlem Was in Vogue* (New York: Oxford University Press, 1981), 99.

20. Peretti, *The Creation of Jazz,* 76–82; Peretti, *Jazz in American Culture,* 32–43.

21. Paul Whiteman, press release for 1924 concert, in Henry O. Osgood, *So This Is Jazz* (1926; New York: Da Capo, 1978), 144–145; Whiteman's statement is

also reprinted in *Reading Jazz,* ed. David Meltzer (San Francisco: Mercury House, 1993), 116–117. Two years later, Whiteman published his autobiography, which did not mention African American contributions to the idiom; see Paul Whiteman, with Mary Margaret McBride, *Jazz* (New York: J. H. Sears, 1926).

22. Studies emphasizing the elitism of these intellectuals include Nathan Huggins, *Harlem Renaissance* (New York: Oxford University Press, 1971); and Lewis, *When Harlem Was in Vogue.* For studies that address the complexities of Harlem intellectuals' assessments of jazz, see Ogren, *The Jazz Revolution,* 111–138; and Spencer, *The New Negroes and Their Music.*

23. James Clifford, *The Predicament of Culture: Twentieth-Century Ethnography, Literature, and Art* (Cambridge: Harvard University Press, 1988), 215–251.

24. James Weldon Johnson, "Preface" to *The Book of Negro American Poetry,* in *Voices from the Harlem Renaissance,* ed. Nathan Huggins (New York: Oxford University Press, 1976), 281–283.

25. Ibid., 281–288. See Ramsey, "Cosmopolitan or Provincial?" 22–25, for a discussion of Johnson's cultural politics.

26. Johnson, "Preface," 283–300.

27. For interesting comments on the conundrum facing black intellectuals, see Gerald Early, "Pulp and Circumstance: The Story of Jazz in High Places," in O'Meally, *The Jazz Cadence of American Culture,* 393–430. For a discussion of New Negro intellectuals' aversion to the constraints of racial categories, see Lewis, *When Harlem Was in Vogue,* 176–178; and Ross Posnock, *Color and Culture: Black Writers and the Making of the Modern Intellectual* (Cambridge: Harvard University Press, 1998).

28. James Weldon Johnson, ed., *The Book of American Negro Spirituals* (New York: Viking, 1925), 28–32; Brent Edwards, "The Seemingly Eclipsed Window of Form: James Weldon Johnson's Prefaces," in O'Meally, *The Jazz Cadence of American Culture,* 590.

29. Langston Hughes, "The Negro Artist and the Racial Mountain," in Huggins, *Voices from the Harlem Renaissance,* 308.

30. Ibid., 305–309.

31. Zora Neale Hurston, "How It Feels to Be Colored Me," in *Folklore, Memoirs, and Other Writings* (New York: Library of America, 1995), 828–829.

32. Ogren suggests that there may have been a certain amount of irony in Hurston's description; see *The Jazz Revolution,* 136.

33. Hughes, "The Negro Artist," 307–309.

34. Hurston, "How It Feels to Be Colored Me," 829; Zora Neale Hurston, "Characteristics of Negro Expression," in O'Meally, *The Jazz Cadence of American Culture,* 304.

35. Rogers, "Jazz at Home," 217–220.

36. Ibid., 218–221.

37. Ibid., 216–217, 223–224.

38. Samuel Floyd Jr., *The Power of Black Music: Interpreting Its History from Africa to the United States* (New York: Oxford University Press, 1995), 100–107.

39. Vincent, *Keep Cool,* 62–65; Eileen Southern, *The Music of Black Americans,* 2d ed. (New York: W. W. Norton, 1983), 343–345.

40. Ogren suggests that this description may have been based on the experiences of Tom Brown's Dixieland Jass Band; see *The Jazz Revolution,* 142.

41. "A Negro Explains Jazz," in *Readings in Black Music,* ed. Eileen Southern, 2d ed. (New York: W W. Norton, 1983), 239 (originally published in *Literary Digest,* April 26, 1919, 28–29); Early, "Pulp and Circumstance," 416–420.

42. Europe is quoted in Southern, *The Music of Black Americans,* 288.

43. "A Negro Explains Jazz," 240–241.

44. See W. C. Handy, *Father of the Blues,* ed. Arna Bontemps (New York: Macmillan, 1941), 33. For additional comments on the restrictions faced by black musicians during the late nineteenth and early twentieth centuries, see Southern, *The Music of Black Americans,* 242–245, 296, 424.

45. Handy, *Father of the Blues,* 75–77.

46. Ibid., 78–79, 97–100, 119–121.

47. "Men of Our Times," *Crusader,* January 1919, 11; advertisements for the Pace and Handy Music Company in *Crusader,* January 1919 (back cover) and September 1920 (33); advertisements for the Handy Brothers Music Company, Inc., in *Crusader,* June 1921 (inside front cover) and October 1921 (inside front cover).

48. Handy, *Father of the Blues,* 210, 230; Abbe Niles, "Introduction" to *Blues: An Anthology,* by W. C. Handy (New York: Albert and Charles Boni, 1926), 1, 14.

49. Niles, "Introduction," 1–6, 10–13.

50. Ironically, Handy would later celebrate the role that white Harlem Renaissance patron Carl Van Vechten, who has frequently been criticized for his primitivistic outlook, played in promoting the blues. In his autobiography, Handy mentions the essays about music by Alain Locke and J. A. Rogers in *The New Negro* and the references to the blues in the poetry of Langston Hughes and Sterling Brown. Handy thought, however, that Van Vechten had done more to draw attention to the idiom; see *Father of the Blues,* 229–230.

51. Niles, "Introduction," 1, 14–16; Handy, *Father of the Blues,* 119–121.

52. Niles, "Introduction," 8, 17–18.

53. Peretti, *The Creation of Jazz,* 22–75, 100–119.

54. Niles, "Introduction," 17–22, 31–32, 39. Niles and Handy also saw validation in Harry Yerkes' 1925 performance of "Jazz America," a four-movement symphony written by Albert Chiaffarelli and based in large part on a Handy blues composition.

55. Angela Davis, *Blues Legacies and Black Feminism: Gertrude "Ma" Rainey, Bessie Smith, and Billie Holiday* (New York: Pantheon, 1998), xvii, 3–41; Hazel Carby, " 'It Just Be's Dat Way Sometime': The Sexual Politics of Women's Blues," in *Unequal Sisters: A Multi-Cultural Reader in U.S. Women's History,* ed. Ellen Carol DuBois and Vicki L. Ruiz (New York: Routledge, 1990), 238–249.

56. Niles, "Introduction," 22–23; Handy, *Father of the Blues,* 209. Women with credits in Handy's *Blues: An Anthology* include Handy's daughter Lucille, who penned the music to "Deep River Blues"; Mercedes Gilbert, who wrote the lyrics to "Friendless Blues"; and Ethel Neal, who cowrote "The Blues I've Got."

57. Carby, *Race Men;* Kevin Gaines, *Uplifting the Race: Black Leadership, Politics, and Culture in the Twentieth Century* (Chapel Hill: University of North Carolina Press, 1996).

58. Sherry Ortner, "Is Female to Male as Nature Is to Culture?" in *Women, Culture, and Society,* ed. Michelle Zimbalist Rosaldo and Louise Lamphere (Stanford: Stanford University Press, 1974), 67–87.

59. Sally Placksin, *Jazzwomen, 1900 to the Present: Their Words, Lives, and Music* (London: Wideview, 1982; Pluto Press, 1987), 41; Linda Dahl, *Stormy Weather: The Music and Lives of a Century of Jazzwomen* (London: Quartet Books, 1984), ix–x; Peretti, *The Creation of Jazz,* 35–36, 123–124, 160.

60. Peretti, *The Creation of Jazz,* 35–36, 123–125.

61. Patrick Hill, "Furious Style: Jazz, Sporting Life, and the Forging of a Masculinist Cultural Politics in Black Chicago, 1912–1923," working paper, University of Michigan, 1998.

62. Edward Kennedy Ellington, *Music Is My Mistress* (New York: Doubleday, 1973; reprint, New York: Da Capo, 1976), 21–22.

63. For a description of clubwomen's aversion to jazz and other popular entertainments, see Evelyn Brooks Higginbotham, *Righteous Discontent: The Women's Movement in the Black Baptist Church, 1880–1920* (Cambridge: Harvard University Press, 1993), 200.

64. Susan McClary, *Feminine Endings: Music, Gender, and Sexuality* (Minneapolis: University of Minnesota Press, 1991), 7–8, 17, 57.

65. Ibid., 81–82, 101–103.

66. Ibid., 25.

67. Marlon B. Ross, "Romantic Quest and Conquest: Troping Masculine Power in the Crisis of Poetic Identity," in *Romanticism and Feminism,* ed. Ann K. Mellor (Bloomington: Indiana University Press, 1988), 26–51.

68. Douglas, *Terrible Honesty,* 409.

69. Ogren, *The Jazz Revolution,* 98.

70. Peretti, *Jazz in American Culture,* 47–51; Gioia, *The History of Jazz,* 49–66, 106–122.

71. Ogren, *The Jazz Revolution,* 87; Peretti, *The Creation of Jazz,* 71, 115–116, 151–155.

72. Ogren, *The Jazz Revolution,* 50–51, 105, 115; Kenney, *Chicago Jazz,* 56–57.

73. Dave Peyton, "The Musical Bunch," *Chicago Defender* (national edition), January 23, 1926, 6; March 19, 1927, 6; April 16, 1927, 6. Peyton was not without his criticisms of Armstrong, however; in his March 19, 1927, column, Peyton praised Armstrong's musicianship but said the trumpeter did not have the discipline or organizational skills to be a leader.

74. Peyton, "The Musical Bunch," *Chicago Defender* (national edition), March 10, 1928, 6.

75. Peyton, "The Musical Bunch," *Chicago Defender* (national edition), May 21, 1927, 6; April 14, 1928, 6; March 9, 1929, 6; March 23, 1929, 6. The March 9 column is quoted in Kenney, *Chicago Jazz,* 127.

76. Peyton, "The Musical Bunch," *Chicago Defender* (national edition), August 17, 1926, 6; May 12, 1928, 6; March 10, 1928, 6; June 30, 1928, 6.

77. Tucker, *The Duke Ellington Reader,* 3–22.

78. Ibid., 31–40; Graham Lock, *Blutopia: Visions of the Future and Revisions of the Past in the Work of Sun Ra, Duke Ellington, and Anthony Braxton* (Durham: Duke University Press, 2000), 77–88. For a lengthier treatment of Ellington's ideas during the 1930s and 1940s, see Lock's two chapters on Ellington in *Blutopia.*

79. Mark Tucker, "The Renaissance Education of Duke Ellington," in *Black Music in the Harlem Renaissance,* ed. Samuel Floyd Jr. (New York: Greenwood Press, 1990), 111–117, 121–122. Tucker mentions that Henry Lee Grant expressed such views about popular music in the journal *Negro Musician,* which he edited in 1921. For a similar take, see Albert Murray, *The Blue Devils of Nada: A Contemporary American Approach to Aesthetic Statement* (New York: Random House, 1996), 83–96.

80. Janet Mabie, "Ellington's 'Mood in Indigo': Harlem's 'Duke' Seeks to Express His Race," in Tucker, *The Duke Ellington Reader,* 41–43 (originally published in *Christian Science Monitor,* December 13, 1930); Lock, *Blutopia,* 77–88.

81. Florence Zunser, "'Opera Must Die,' Says Galli-Curci! Long Live the Blues!" in Tucker, *The Duke Ellington Reader,* 44–45 (originally published in *New York Evening Graphic Magazine,* 27 December 1930).

82. Duke Ellington, "The Duke Steps Out," in Tucker, *The Duke Ellington Reader,* 46–50 (originally published in *Rhythm,* March 1931, 20–22). Tucker suggests that the editors may have changed Ellington's prose for this essay, but, as he also notes, the ideas seem consistent with Ellington's project.

83. Ibid., 48–49.

84. Ibid., 49.

85. Ibid., 50; Gioia, *The History of Jazz,* 131; Lock, *Blutopia,* 104–109.

86. David Stowe, *Swing Changes: Big Band Jazz in New Deal America* (Cambridge: Harvard University Press, 1994), 1–38; Lewis Erenberg, *Swinging That Dream* (Chicago: University of Chicago Press, 1998), 120–149; Denning, *The Cultural Front,* xiv–xviii, 4–9, 324–337.

87. Denning, *The Cultural Front,* 42–48, 337–338.

88. Stowe, *Swing Changes,* 21–24; *Down Beat,* June 1937, 1, 3; Samuel B. Charters and Leonard B. Kunstadt, *Jazz: A History of the New York Scene* (Garden City: Doubleday, 1962; reprint, New York: Da Capo, 1981), 259.

89. Scott DeVeaux, "The Emergence of the Jazz Concert, 1935–1945," *American Music* 7 (Spring 1989): 7–12, 24–25.

90. Mark Naison, *Communists in Harlem During the Depression* (Urbana: University of Illinois Press, 1983; reprint, New York: Grove Press, 1985), 193–212, 298–301; Denning, *The Cultural Front,* 333–334; "Harlem After Dark," *Amsterdam News,* February 11, 1939, 20.

91. "Thousands Jam Great Hall at City College for Musical Fete," *Amsterdam News,* January 7, 1939, 12; "Harlem After Dark," *Amsterdam News,* February 4,

1939, 16; "Artists Set for Concert," *Amsterdam News,* February 11, 1939, 20. Determining the extent to which participation in a benefit reflected a musician's politics is difficult. Some musicians indeed were active in unions or more radical Popular Front organizations during the 1930s. Pianist Teddy Wilson, for example, taught at the left-wing Metropolitan Music School in New York. Other musicians' connections to the left were more tenuous, but, as Denning suggests, artists who participated in these benefits "recognized the social crises of the depression and fascism, and were attracted to the hopes and energies of the Popular Front social movement" (*The Cultural Front,* 333). As Handy himself put it in a 1938 letter that discussed a birthday party given for him by a "Spanish Democracy organization": "I am no communist but I have taken part in their programs for the Scottsboro Boys and felt very good in doing so. I have taken part in benefits for the flood sufferers, Jews, Catholics, Negroes, whites and everybody else and at the time I was sympathetic with the Loyalists of Spain" (W. C. Handy, letter of November 4, 1938, reprinted in *Father of the Blues,* ix).

92. Stowe, *Swing Changes,* 102–109, 122–123.

93. Scholars generally point to Horace Gerlach, an arranger who worked with Armstrong and contributed an analysis of Armstrong's music at the end of the text, as the ghostwriter. Dan Morgenstern suggests that Armstrong wrote or dictated some of the earlier passages, with later parts adapted from interview notes. Similarly, Thomas Brothers says: "I find it likely that the relationship between the published text and Armstrong's original text was somewhat close, that Armstrong was edited and embellished and altered, but that we can read a great deal of him in this book." William Kenney believes the ghostwriter had a larger role. See Dan Morgenstern, "Foreword" to *Swing That Music,* by Louis Armstrong (London, New York: Longman's, Green, 1936; reprint, New York: Da Capo, 1993), vii, x–xi; Thomas Brothers, *Louis Armstrong in His Own Words: Selected Writings by Louis Armstrong* (New York: Oxford University Press, 1999), 203; William H. Kenney, "Negotiating the Color Line: Louis Armstrong's Autobiographies," in *Jazz in Mind: Essays on the History and Meanings of Jazz,* ed. Reginald T. Buckner and Steven Weiland (Detroit: Wayne State University Press, 1991), 38–59.

94. Armstrong, *Swing That Music,* 9, 12, 29–30, 74, 105, 122.

95. Ibid., 32, 72–75, 104–105, 121–122.

96. Alain Locke, *The Negro and His Music* (Washington, D.C.: Associates in Negro Folk Education, 1936; reprint, New York: Kennikat Press, 1968), 78–79, 93–94, 98–99.

97. Ibid., 96, 130.

98. See, for example, Paul Burgett, "Vindication as a Thematic Principle in the Writings of Alain Locke on the Music of Black Americans," in Floyd, *Black Music in the Harlem Renaissance,* 29–39; Lorenzo Thomas, "The Bop Aesthetic and Black Intellectual Tradition," *Library Journal of the University of Texas* 24, nos. 1 and 2 (1994): 105–117.

99. Locke, *The Negro and His Music,* 4, 86, 100–103, 129.

100. Ibid., 130–137.

101. See Bernard Gendron, "'Moldy Figs' and Modernists: Jazz at War

(1942–1946)," in *Jazz Among the Discourses,* ed. Krin Gabbard (Durham: Duke University Press, 1995), 31–56.

102. For extended discussion of the complicated issues involved with jazz criticism in the 1930s, see Stowe, *Swing Changes,* 50–93; John Gennari, "The Politics of Culture and Identity in American Jazz Criticism" (Ph.D. diss., University of Pennsylvania, 1993), chaps. 2 and 3.

103. "White Man's Music Started Jazz—Says Nick," *Down Beat,* March 1937, 1–2; Paul Eduard Miller, "Roots of Hot White Jazz Are Negroid," *Down Beat,* April 1937, 5; Paul Eduard Miller, "Critic Deplores Recording of the 'Jazzed-Up' Classics: Real Swing Is Ellington's Jungle Jazz—Not Semi-Classical Music," *Down Beat,* June 1937, 14; Gennari, "The Politics of Culture and Identity in American Jazz Criticism," 78–87, 102–103, 123; Stowe, *Swing Changes,* 54, 62–80, 89–93.

104. Stowe, *Swing Changes,* 86–92.

105. Ibid., 87–88; Benny Carter, "Do Critics Really Know What It's All About?" *Metronome,* May 1937, 17.

106. Like James Weldon Johnson's reference in his discussion of spirituals, Ellington's comments here anticipate Baraka's later critique of swing; see the chapter titled "Swing—From Verb to Noun," in Baraka [Jones], *Blues People.*

107. Ellington, "Duke Says Swing Is Stagnant," 132–135.

108. Ibid., 134; Duke Ellington, "Duke Becomes a Critic," in Tucker, *The Duke Ellington Reader,* 138–140 (originally published in *Down Beat,* July 1939, 8, 35).

109. Duke Ellington, "'Situation Between the Critics and Musicians Is Laughable'—Ellington," in Tucker, *The Duke Ellington Reader,* 136–137 (originally published in *Down Beat,* April 1939, 4, 9); Duke Ellington, "Duke Concludes Criticism of the Critics," in Tucker, *The Duke Ellington Reader,* 137–138 (originally published in *Down Beat,* May 1939, 14); Hammond, "The Tragedy of Duke Ellington," 120. For a discussion of the feud between Ellington and Hammond, see Stowe, *Swing Changes,* 50–54; and Lock, *Blutopia,* 119–125.

110. Stowe, *Swing Changes,* 52, 61.

111. Ellington, "Duke Says Swing Is Stagnant," 135.

## Chapter 2. "Dizzy Atmosphere"

1. For a concise discussion of bebop's musical elements and their antecedents in the work of an earlier generation of players, see Thomas Owens, *Bebop: The Music and Its Players* (New York: Oxford University Press, 1995), 3–10.

2. Scott DeVeaux, "Constructing the Jazz Tradition," *Black American Literature Forum* 25, no. 3 (Fall 1991): 525–560; Scott DeVeaux, *The Birth of Bebop: A Social and Musical History* (Berkeley: University of California Press, 1997), 1–31; Amiri Baraka [LeRoi Jones], *Blues People: Negro Music in White America* (New York: Morrow, 1963; reprint, New York: Quill Paperbacks, 1983), 175–236; Eric Lott, "Double V, Double-Time," *Callaloo* 11, no. 3 (1988): 597–605. Similar accounts of the politics of bebop are found in Ben Sidran, *Black Talk* (New York: Holt, Rinehart and Winston, 1971; reprint, New York: Da Capo, 1981), 78–115;

and Acklyn Lynch, *Nightmare Overhanging Darkly: Essays on Black Culture and Resistance* (Chicago: Third World Press, 1993).

3. Bernard Gendron, "'Moldy Figs' and Modernists: Jazz at War (1942–1946)," in *Jazz Among the Discourses,* ed. Krin Gabbard (Durham: Duke University Press, 1995), 31–56; Bernard Gendron, "A Short Stay in the Sun: The Reception of Bebop (1944–1950)," *Library Chronicle of the University of Texas* 24, no. 1/2 (1994): 137–160; David Stowe, *Swing Changes: Big Band Jazz in New Deal America* (Cambridge: Harvard University Press, 1994), 230–233, 239, 243–244.

4. DeVeaux, *The Birth of Bebop,* 20–31, 39–69. DeVeaux emphasizes an ethos of "progress" in the jazz community as a major motivation for the beboppers. Rooted in the early jazz community and developed during the swing era, progress linked musical experimentation, respectability, and racial uplift strategies.

5. Ibid., 219; Ralph Ellison, "The Golden Age, Time Past," in *Shadow and Act* (New York: Signet Books, 1966), 198–210.

6. Ellison, "The Golden Age, Time Past," 199–200.

7. Kenneth Clarke, quoted in Dizzy Gillespie, with Al Fraser, *To Be or Not to Bop* (New York: Da Capo, 1979), 142.

8. Gillespie and Fraser, *To Be or Not to Bop,* 287–291.

9. Manning Marable, *Race, Reform, and Rebellion: The Second Reconstruction in Black America, 1945–1990,* rev. 2d ed. (Jackson: University of Mississippi Press, 1991), 13–27; Robin D. G. Kelley, *Race Rebels: Culture, Politics, and the Black Working Class* (New York: Free Press, 1995), 55–75; George Lipsitz, *The Possessive Investment in Whiteness: How White People Profit from Identity Politics* (Philadelphia: Temple University Press, 1998), 188, 195.

10. Roi Ottley, *"New World a Coming": Inside Black America* (Boston: Houghton Mifflin, 1943), 101–112; Penny Von Eschen, *Race Against Empire: Black Americans and Anticolonialism, 1937–1957* (Ithaca: Cornell University Press, 1997), 19–21; Kelley, *Race Rebels,* 128–133; Lipsitz, *The Possessive Investment in Whiteness,* 195–210.

11. Von Eschen, *Race Against Empire,* 5, 41; W. E. B. Du Bois, *Dusk of Dawn: An Essay Toward an Autobiography of a Race Concept* (New York: Harcourt, Brace, 1940); Zora Neale Hurston, *Dust Tracks on a Road,* in *Folklore, Memoirs, and Other Writings* (New York: Library of America, 1995); Alain Locke, "Who and What Is 'Negro'?" *Opportunity* 20 (1942): 36–41, 83–87. For a discussion of texts that challenged assumptions about race in the 1940s, see Ross Posnock, *Color and Culture: Black Writers and the Making of the Modern Intellectual* (Cambridge: Harvard University Press, 1998), 130–134, 208–215.

12. Ottley, *"New World a Coming,"* 167–185.

13. This perspective should not be confused with the sometimes naive and often oppressive color-blindness of Cold War liberalism, in which government officials and intellectuals assumed that racism was a product of psychology rather than social structure and consisted of individual acts that were aberrations in a fundamentally fair and just society. The adoption of the latter marked a retreat from a critical engagement with a historical legacy of racism and changed the di-

rection of African American intellectual life and popular culture in the late 1940s and 1950s. For a discussion of this turn, see Von Eschen, *Race Against Empire,* 145–166.

14. Stowe, *Swing Changes,* 28–29; Ted Vincent, *Keep Cool: The Black Activists Who Built the Jazz Age* (London: Pluto Press, 1995), 199; DeVeaux, *The Birth of Bebop,* 39–45, 49–69.

15. Browne's prominent students in the late 1930s and the 1940s included Chico Hamilton, Horace Tapscott, Jackie Kelso, Frank Morgan, Cecil McNeely, Dexter Gordon, and Sonny Criss. Hightower also taught Cecil McNeely and Melba Liston. See Clora Bryant et al., eds., *Central Avenue Sounds: Jazz in Los Angeles* (Berkeley: University of California Press, 1998); Robert Gordon, *Jazz West Coast: The Los Angeles Scene of the 1950s* (London: Quartet Books, 1986), 28; Ted Gioia, *West Coast Jazz: Modern Jazz in California, 1945–1960* (New York: Oxford University Press, 1992), 40–41, 124; Linda Dahl, *Stormy Weather: The Music and Lives of a Century of Jazzwomen* (London: Quartet Books, 1984), 253–254.

16. Among Reese's prominent students were Charles Mingus, Dexter Gordon, Buddy Collette, Eric Dolphy, and Hampton Hawes. Even Ben Webster came around for instruction on occasion. Dexter Gordon is quoted in Gordon, *Jazz West Coast,* 28. See also Charles Mingus, *Beneath the Underdog: His World as Composed by Mingus* (New York: Knopf, 1971; reprint, New York: Vintage Books, 1991), 76–77; Bryant et al., *Central Avenue Sounds;* Brian Priestley, *Mingus: A Critical Biography* (London: Quartet Books, 1982; reprint, New York: Da Capo, 1983), 11–16; Gioia, *West Coast Jazz,* 41–43; Gene Santoro, *Myself When I Am Real: The Life and Music of Charles Mingus* (New York: Oxford University Press, 2000), 36–37.

17. DeVeaux, *The Birth of Bebop,* 143–164.

18. Ibid., 236–253; Stowe, *Swing Changes,* 114–117, 145, 157–162; Sherrie Tucker, *Swing Shift: "All-Girl" Bands of the 1940s* (Durham: Duke University Press, 2000), 348. For a fictionalized account of Lester Young's experience in the army, see Geoff Dyer, *But Beautiful: A Book About Jazz* (New York: North Point Press, 1996), 7–28.

19. DeVeaux, *The Birth of Bebop,* 169, 284–294, 302–306.

20. Herbert Nichols, "The Jazz Life," *New York Age,* June 28, 1941, 10; August 2, 1941, 10; August 16, 1941, 10; August 23, 1941, 10.

21. Nichols, "The Jazz Life," August 2, 1941, 10; August 23, 1941, 10.

22. "Editorial," *The Music Dial,* June 1943, 3; "Editorial," *The Music Dial,* July 1943, 3–4; Wington Thompson, "Post War Planning," *The Music Dial,* September 1943, 3; Ray Parker, "Opinion," *The Music Dial,* October 1943, 3, 5.

23. Herbie Nichols, "A Case for the Jazz Purist," *The Music Dial,* April 1944, 19; Herbie Nichols, "The Jazz Purist," *The Music Dial,* November 1944, 21; Herbie Nichols, "Jazz Purism," *The Music Dial,* July 1944, 7.

24. See A. B. Spellman, *Four Lives in the Bebop Business* (New York: Pantheon, 1966; reprint, New York: Limelight Editions, 1994), 158–164. A. B. Spellman notes that Nichols also wrote a lot of poetry before going into the service and that he

believed enough in the "war on two fronts" to have written patriotic songs during the war.

25. DeVeaux, *The Birth of Bebop*, 291–294; Gillespie and Fraser, *To Be or Not to Bop*, 203; Stanley Crouch, "Max Roach: Drums Unlimited," *Village Voice*, December 17, 1979, 106–107; Owens, *Bebop*, 10; Leonard Feather, *Inside Jazz* (New York: J. J. Robbins, 1949), 28; Billy Taylor, *Jazz Piano: A History* (Dubuque: William C. Brown, 1982), 127.

26. Taylor, *Jazz Piano*, 116, 130, 133; Miles Davis, with Quincy Troupe, *Miles: The Autobiography* (New York: Touchstone, 1989), 49; Bryant et al., *Central Avenue Sounds*, 221.

27. DeVeaux, *The Birth of Bebop*, 273–274, 281, 428.

28. Ibid., 320, 334–348, 371–381.

29. Gillespie and Fraser, *To Be or Not to Bop*, 371; Richard O. Boyer, "Profiles: Bop," *New Yorker*, July 3, 1948, 31.

30. Lott, "Double V, Double-Time," 598–601; Steve Chibnall, "Whistle and Zoot: The Changing Meaning of a Suit of Clothes," *History Workshop* 20 (Autumn 1985): 62.

31. Boyer, "Profiles: Bop," 28, 30.

32. "Bebop Called Music in Tune with the Times," *Baltimore Afro-American*, July 3, 1948, 6.

33. Boyer, "Profiles: Bop," 30; Dave Hepburn and Nard Griffin, "Bebop: Music or Madness," *Our World*, January 1949, 34; Ralph Ellison, "On Bird, Bird-Watching, and Jazz," in *Shadow and Act*, 221.

34. My analysis of "Koko" is based, in part, on Barry Kernfeld, *What to Listen to in Jazz* (New Haven: Yale University Press, 1995), 53–61; and Owens, *Bebop*, 18–19, 39–40.

35. Bryant et al., *Central Avenue Sounds*, 145–150, 184–185, 268–271.

36. Charlie Parker and Dizzy Gillespie, *Diz 'n Bird at Carnegie Hall*, Roost CDP 7243 8 57061 2 7.

37. Ira Gitler, liner notes for Parker and Gillespie, *Diz 'n Bird at Carnegie Hall*; Russell is quoted in Gillespie and Fraser, *To Be or Not to Bop*, 324. George Russell, *The Lydian Chromatic Concept of Tonal Organization for Improvisation* (New York: Concept Publishing, 1959).

38. Leonard Feather, "A Bird's-Ear View of Music," *Metronome*, August 1948, 14, 21–22.

39. Michael Levin and John S. Wilson, "No Bop Roots in Jazz: Parker," *Down Beat*, February 1994, 24–26 (originally published in *Down Beat*, September 9, 1949).

40. Ted Gioia, *The History of Jazz* (New York: Oxford University Press, 1997), 205, 230–231.

41. Dan Morgenstern, liner notes for Mary Lou Williams Trio, *Zodiac Suite*, Folkways FTS 32844; Linda Dahl, *Morning Glory: A Biography of Mary Lou Williams* (New York: Pantheon, 1999), 159–176.

42. Although James Hall suspects that this article may have been ghostwrit-

ten by a critic or musician friend (possibly Milt Orent or Marshall Stearns), he suggests that the ideas were those of Williams (James Hall, personal correspondence with the author, March 5, 2001).

43. Mary Lou Williams, "Music and Progress," *Jazz Record,* November 1947, 23–24. Williams made similar comments about the need for continual experimentation in music in a 1949 interview in *Metronome.* Speaking about the development of her own approach, she said: "I pushed, I broadened, I moved, I experimented. That's what I've always taught the kids who come to me. You've got to keep going. There's only one reason, really, to stop. That's to take account, to get new sounds, to get the sounds you're not hearing" (Barry Ulanov, "Mary Lou Williams," *Metronome,* July 1949, 24). Williams made similar comments about young people in "Music Can Help Youth, Says Mary Lou Williams," *People's Voice,* June 1, 1946, 39.

44. Williams, "Music and Progress," 23–24; "Passion for a Piano," *Negro Digest,* March 1945, 29 (reprinted from *New York Post,* December 11, 1944). According to her biographer, Williams never worked out a deal with Syracuse University, although she did perform sections of the suite with a trio as a benefit for the NAACP at the school (Dahl, *Morning Glory,* 175).

45. Announcement, *New York Age,* March 2, 1945, 10; Gillespie and Fraser, *To Be or Not to Bop,* 290–291, 311; Gioia, *The History of Jazz,* 222–224.

46. Norman Weinstein, *A Night in Tunisia: Imaginings of Africa in Jazz* (New York: Limelight Editions, 1993), 51–54. Blakey's albums with African themes include *Drum Suite* and *The African Beat.* Blakey said his reason for going to Africa also stemmed from the fact that he "couldn't get any gigs," which points out the ongoing financial difficulties many innovative musicians experienced.

47. Boyer, "Profiles: Bop," 31; "Moslem Musicians," *Ebony,* April 1953, 104–111; Gillespie and Fraser, *To Be or Not to Bop,* 293, 343. Gillespie was talked into posing as a Muslim for a 1948 *Life* photo spread that cast bebop in a disparaging light.

48. Gillespie and Fraser, *To Be or Not to Bop,* 291–293; "Moslem Musicians" (*Ebony*).

49. For discussions of masculinist representations of African American modern jazz musicians, see David Ake, "Re-Masculating Jazz: Ornette Coleman, 'Lonely Woman,' and the New York Jazz Scene in the Late 1950s," *American Music* 16, no. 1 (Spring 1998): 25–44; Herman Gray, "Black Masculinity and Visual Culture," *Callaloo* 18, no. 2 (1995): 401–405; Ingrid Monson, "The Problem with White Hipness: Race, Gender, and Cultural Conceptions in Jazz Historical Discourse," *Journal of the American Musicological Society* 48 (Fall 1995): 397–422.

50. Tucker, *Swing Shift,* 19, 119–120. A sampling of the numerous discussions of the limited gains African American women made during World War II includes the following: Karen Tucker Anderson, "Last Hired, First Fired: Black Women Workers During World War II," *Journal of American History* 69, no. 1 (June 1982): 82–97; Paula Giddings, *When and Where I Enter: The Impact of Black Women on Race and Sex in America* (New York: Morrow, 1984; reprint, New York: Bantam Books, 1985), 231–258; Maureen Honey, ed., *Bitter Fruit: African American Women*

*in World War Two* (Columbia: University of Missouri Press, 1999), 1–33; Jacqueline Jones, *Labor of Love, Labor of Sorrow: Black Women, Work, and the Family from Slavery to the Present* (New York: Basic Books, 1985; reprint, New York: Vintage Books, 1986), 232–260.

51. Tucker, *Swing Shift,* 97–224.

52. Ibid., 141–142, 174, 182–187.

53. Gillespie and Fraser, *To Be or Not to Bop,* 282.

54. Hazel V. Carby, *Race Men* (Cambridge: Harvard University Press, 1998), 135–165; Kelley, *Race Rebels,* 175–176.

55. Valerie Wilmer, *As Serious as Your Life: The Story of the New Jazz* (London: Allison and Busby, 1977; reprint, London: Pluto Press, 1987), 205.

56. Liston is quoted in Dahl, *Stormy Weather,* 256.

57. Gendron, "A Short Stay in the Sun," 154–156.

58. Ibid., 138–139; Feather, *Inside Jazz,* 34; announcement, *New York Age,* April 21, 1945, 10.

59. Gendron, "A Short Stay in the Sun," 139–141; Feather, *Inside Jazz,* 36; Stowe, *Swing Changes,* 207–209; Catherine Ramírez, "The Pachuca in Chicana/o Art, Literature and History: Reexamining Nation, Cultural Nationalism and Resistance" (Ph.D. diss., University of California, Berkeley, 2000).

60. John L. Dower, *War Without Mercy: Race and Power in the Pacific War* (New York: Pantheon, 1986), 173.

61. Stowe, *Swing Changes,* 141–160, 166–167; Bruce M. Tyler, *From Harlem to Hollywood: The Struggle for Racial and Cultural Democracy* (New York: Garland, 1992), 124, 137.

62. "Jazz Symposium," *Esquire,* September 1944, 93; Paul Edward Miller, *Esquire's 1945 Jazz Book* (New York: A. S. Barnes, 1945), 115; Paul Edward Miller, *Esquire's 1946 Jazz Book* (New York: A. S. Barnes, 1946; reprint, New York: Da Capo, 1979), 186–187; Stowe, *Swing Changes,* 157.

63. Duke Ellington, "We, Too, Sing America," in *The Duke Ellington Reader,* ed. Mark Tucker (New York: Oxford University Press, 1993), 146–148 (originally published as "Speech of the Week," *California Eagle,* February 13, 1941); John Pittman, "The Duke Will Stay on Top!" in Tucker, *The Duke Ellington Reader,* 148–151.

64. Scott DeVeaux, "The Emergence of the Jazz Concert, 1935–1945," *American Music* 7 (Spring 1989): 15–22; DeVeaux, *The Birth of Bebop,* 202–205; "Jazz Concerts: Ex-Speakeasy Music Wins Firm Beachhead in Symphony Halls," *Ebony,* September 1946, 29–34. See also *New York Age,* May 24, 1941, 10; March 7, 1942, 10; April 10, 1943, 10.

65. DeVeaux, "The Emergence of the Jazz Concert," 7–12, 24–25.

66. Gendron, " 'Moldy Figs' and Modernists," 32–34, 49.

67. "Jazz Concerts" (*Ebony*), 29–34.

68. Lipsitz, *The Possessive Investment of Whiteness,* 206, 208; Elaine Tyler May, *Homeward Bound: American Families in the Cold War Era* (New York: Basic Books, 1988), 58–91; Anderson, "Last Hired, First Fired," 82–97; Dominic J.

Capeci, *The Harlem Riots of 1943* (Philadelphia: Temple University Press, 1977), 9, 134–145.

69. Tyler, *From Harlem to Hollywood,* 214–220; Stowe, *Swing Changes,* 146–147, 228–229.

70. Gillespie and Fraser, *To Be or Not to Bop,* 210–211, 282; Gordon, *Jazz West Coast,* 16.

71. Gendron, "A Short Stay in the Sun," 142–153; Stowe, *Swing Changes,* 189–199, 214–219; "Bebop Fashions," *Ebony,* November 1948, 31. For a good discussion of how demographic shifts and labor flows engendered new forms of music during and after World War II, see George Lipsitz, *Class and Culture in Cold War America: "A Rainbow at Midnight"* (New York: Praeger Scientific, 1981), 195–225.

72. Ross Russell, "Bebop Instrumentation," *Record Changer,* November 1948, 13, 22.

73. Gilbert McKean, "The Jazz Beat: Memo on Bebop," *Saturday Review,* August 30, 1947, 18–19.

74. Dave Banks, "Be-Bop Called Merely the Beginning of a New Creative Music Form," *Down Beat,* February 11, 1948, 16; Marshall Stearns, "Rebop, Bebop, and Bop," *Harper's,* April 1950, 92.

75. L. D. Reddick, "Dizzy Gillespie in Atlanta," *Phylon* 10, no. 1 (First Quarter 1949): 45–48.

76. Langston Hughes, "Bop," in *The Best of Simple* (New York: Hill and Wang, 1961), 117–119; Nicholas Evans, "Langston Hughes as Bop Ethnographer in 'Trumpet Player: Fifty-second Street,'" *Library Chronicle of the University of Texas* 24, no. 1/2 (1994): 130.

77. Amy Lee, "Figs Might Do Well to Take a Hint from Bop—Make New Dixie Sounds," *Down Beat,* May 6, 1949, 2; Stearns, "Rebop, Bebop, and Bop," 96.

78. Sidney Finkelstein, *Jazz: A People's Music* (New York: Citadel Press, 1948), 191–238.

79. Ted Gioia, *The Imperfect Art: Reflections on Jazz and Modern Culture* (New York: Oxford University Press, 1988), 113. For a less than serious consideration of bebop as intellectual practice, see Ted Hallock, "Bop Jargon Indicative of Intellectual Thought," *Down Beat,* July 28, 1948, 4. For more serious interpretations, see "Professor Explains Bop," *Down Beat,* February 25, 1949, 3; McKean, "The Jazz Beat"; and Boyer, "Profiles: Bop."

80. Orrin Keepnews, "Thelonious Monk's Music May Be First Sign of Be-Bop's Legitimacy," *Record Changer,* April 1948, 5, 20; Bill Gottlieb, "Thelonious Monk—Genius of Bop," *Down Beat,* September 24, 1947, 2; George Hoeffer, "Pianist Monk Getting Long Awaited Break," *Down Beat,* February 11, 1948, 11; Boyer, "Profiles: Bop," 30–31.

81. Monson, "The Problem with White Hipness," 412; Ronald Radano, *New Musical Figurations: Anthony Braxton's Cultural Critique* (Chicago: University of Chicago Press, 1996), 261–263; Andrew Ross, *No Respect: Intellectuals and Popular Culture* (New York: Routledge, 1989), 78–85. Radano builds on the work of

Mariana Torgovnick, who argues that the idea of the primitive developed in Western culture during the twentieth century as a composite of the modern and the Other. Radano's discussion pertains most specifically to the 1950s and 1960s, but his analysis is relevant to the 1940s as well.

82. Robin D. G. Kelley, conversation with the author, April 1997.

83. Steven Elworth, "Jazz in Crisis," in Gabbard, *Jazz Among the Discourses,* 58.

84. My assessment of the black press was derived by surveying articles in *Ebony,* the *Amsterdam News,* the *New York Age,* and *Negro Digest.* See also Stowe, *Swing Changes,* 223–224; Gendron, "A Short Stay in the Sun," 145–147.

85. Billy Taylor is quoted in Sharon A. Pease, "Taylor One of Creators Among Progressives," *Down Beat,* August 11, 1950, 12.

86. Billy Taylor, *Basic Be-Bop Instruction for Piano* (New York: Charles H. Hansen Music, 1949), 2.

87. Ibid.

88. Ellison, "The Golden Age, Time Past," 202; Irving Louis Horowitz, "Authenticity and Originality in Jazz: Toward a Paradigm in the Sociology of Music," *Journal of Jazz Studies* 1, no. 1 (October 1973): 60; Leonard Feather, "Yardbird Flies Home," *Metronome,* August 1947, 44; Levin and Wilson, "No Bop Roots in Jazz," 24–26.

89. Tadd Dameron, "The Case for Modern Music," *Record Changer,* February 1948, 5, 16; Barry Ulanov, "Fats Navarro," *Metronome,* November 1947, 19, 38.

90. DeVeaux, *The Birth of Bebop,* 22–24; Ross, *No Respect,* 69–70.

91. Dameron, "The Case for Modern Music"; Levin and Wilson, "No Bop Roots in Jazz," 24, 26.

92. Gendron, "A Short Stay in the Sun," 154–156; Stowe, *Swing Changes,* 218–220; DeVeaux, *The Birth of Bebop,* 440–441; "Oldest Negro Night Club," *Ebony,* October 1949, 44–45; "Louis Jordan," *Ebony,* January 1949, 39–41; "Blues Singers," *Ebony,* August 1950, 35–39.

93. Babs Gonzales, "What's What with Bop," *New York Age,* December 24, 1949, 41.

94. DeVeaux, *The Birth of Bebop,* 438–440.

95. John S. Wilson, "Bird Wrong; Bop Must Get a Beat: Diz," *Down Beat,* February 1994, 26–27 (originally published in *Down Beat,* October 7, 1949).

96. "Bop at End of Road, Says Dizzy," *Down Beat,* September 8, 1950, 1.

97. Ralph Gleason, "Dizzy Getting a Bad Deal from Music Biz: Gleason," *Down Beat,* November 17, 1950, 14; "Folks Find a New Word to Mangle," *Down Beat,* December 15, 1950, 10.

98. Gillespie interview in Art Taylor, *Notes and Tones: Musician-to-Musician Interviews* (1982; New York: Da Capo, 1993), 126.

## Chapter 3. "Passions of a Man"

1. Ralph J. Gleason, "Charlie Mingus: A Thinking Musician," *Down Beat,* June 1, 1951, 7. Another version of this letter, with the heading "Noted For Ralph,"

can be found in box 45, folder 3, Charles Mingus Collection, Library of Congress Music Division (hereafter cited as CMC).

2. Gene Santoro, *Myself When I Am Real: The Life and Music of Charles Mingus* (New York: Oxford University Press, 2000), 56. Mingus was referred to the Hollywood job by Lloyd Reese.

3. Mingus later claimed he was most productive as a composer during the early 1940s: "That was when I was energetic and wrote all the time. Music was my life" (Charles Mingus, liner notes for *Let My Children Hear Music,* Columbia 31039; quoted in Brian Priestley, *Mingus: A Critical Biography* [London: Quartet Books, 1982; reprint, New York: Da Capo, 1983], 12).

4. Ted Gioia writes that Mingus's music in the mid- and late 1940s "reflected an unusual mixture of 'avant-garde' and 'derriere-garde'" (*West Coast Jazz: Modern Jazz in California, 1945–1960* [New York: Oxford University Press, 1992], 336–337). For other descriptions of Mingus's music during this period, see Priestley, *Mingus: A Critical Biography,* 29–39; Ralph Gleason, "Swinging the Golden Gate," *Down Beat,* March 25, 1949; and Santoro, *Myself When I Am Real,* 65–86.

5. Nat Hentoff, *The Jazz Life* (1961; New York: Da Capo, 1975), 167; Priestley, *Mingus: A Critical Biography,* 14, 32; Charles Mingus, *Beneath the Underdog: His World as Composed by Mingus* (New York: Knopf, 1971; reprint, New York: Vintage Books, 1991), 67; Santoro, *Myself When I Am Real,* 40–45.

6. Priestley, *Mingus: A Critical Biography,* 40–42.

7. Priestley points out that this comment is a reference to Hampton (ibid., 37).

8. Clora Bryant et al., eds., *Central Avenue Sounds: Jazz in Los Angeles* (Berkeley: University of California Press, 1998), 131–132, 154–158, 247–249, 403; Santoro, *Myself When I Am Real,* 89.

9. Ronald Radano, *New Musical Figurations: Anthony Braxton's Cultural Critique* (Chicago: University of Chicago Press, 1996), 12–16. Radano says this "classifying" discourse reached its highest expression in State Department–sponsored tours of American musicians overseas, which reinforced the Cold War idea that the United States was a raceless, classless society.

10. John Gennari, "The Politics of Culture and Identity in American Jazz Criticism" (Ph.D. diss., University of Pennsylvania, 1993), 177–206.

11. See John Panish, *The Color of Jazz: Race and Representation in Postwar American Culture* (Jackson: University Press of Mississippi, 1997). Panish talks at length about how color-blind ideologies in the jazz discourse marginalized black musicians' contributions to jazz and depoliticized their work.

12. Gleason's strategy was consistent with the practices of other jazz writers who saw the incorporation of musicians' voices into the critical dialogue as a means of legitimizing jazz. See, for example, Leonard Feather, "Jazz Achieves Social Prestige," *Down Beat,* September 21, 1955, 11; Nat Hentoff, "Voices of Silence," *Down Beat,* September 21, 1955, 12; Billy Taylor, "Billy Taylor Replies to Art Tatum Critic," *Down Beat,* September 21, 1955, 17.

13. Priestley, *Mingus: A Critical Biography,* 44–49; Gioia, *West Coast Jazz,* 338–339; Santoro, *Myself When I Am Real,* 94.

14. Priestley, *Mingus: A Critical Biography,* 46–47. Other musician-run labels from the period included those started by Dave Brubeck, Dizzy Gillespie, Duke Ellington, Woody Herman, and Lennie Tristano.

15. Hal Zogg, KUTA, Salt Lake City, to Charles Mingus, September 1, 1952, box 57, folder 7, CMC.

16. Celia Mingus to Dorothy Sachs, *Mademoiselle* magazine, June 2, 1956, box 57, folder 18, CMC. For a more in-depth discussion of Debut Records and, in particular, Celia Mingus's role in the company, see Nichole T. Rustin, "Mingus Fingers: Charles Mingus, Black Masculinity, and Postwar Jazz Culture" (Ph.D. diss., New York University, 1999), 183–243.

17. Charles Mingus, *Debut Rarities, Volume 4,* Debut 1829–2.

18. Poet and novelist Al Young first heard these sides as a teenager in Detroit in 1954. He recalls that Mingus's music "was ready-made for someone like myself—a late-blooming teenager, who read and read and probably thought too much" (Janet Coleman and Al Young, *Mingus/Mingus: Two Memoirs* [Berkeley: Creative Arts, 1989; reprint, New York: Limelight Editions, 1991], 116–118).

19. Priestley, *Mingus: A Critical Biography,* 39.

20. Ibid., 49; J. Bradford Robinson, "Lennie Tristano," in *The New Grove Dictionary of Jazz,* ed. Barry Kernfeld (New York: St. Martin's, 1994), 1218–1219; Ira Gitler, liner notes for *Debut Rarities, Volume 4.*

21. Charles Mingus to Mr. Kahn, Jazz Disques, Paris, France, undated, box 57, folder 17, CMC. Nichole Rustin suggests that Celia Mingus may have written many of the letters sent out under Charles Mingus's name. Whatever the case, the ideas expressed in these letters appear to be those of Charles Mingus and are consistent with the aesthetic vision he put forth in his music, other writings, and commentary. See Rustin, "Mingus Fingers," 207.

22. Charles Mingus to Barry Ulanov, May 9, 1952, box 57, folder 20, CMC.

23. Charles Mingus to Charles Delauney, *Jazz Hot,* June 2, 1952, box 57, folder 17, CMC. Mingus made similar comments to a representative of a French distributor, whom he approached about handling distribution of Debut records (Mingus to Kahn, undated, CMC).

24. Charles Mingus to Howard Garland, KFMB, San Diego, undated, box 57, folder 17, CMC. Mingus saw Garland's letter in the May 7, 1952, issue of *Down Beat.* Mingus expressed similar sentiments to other disc jockeys, some of whom he learned about through their letters to *Down Beat;* see Mingus's letters to Hal Zogg, October 2, 1952, box 57, folder 7, CMC; to "Phil" of WERE, Cleveland, Ohio, February 6, 1953, box 57, folder 18, CMC; to Don Williams, WFAH, Alliance, Ohio, undated, box 57, folder 18, CMC; and to Jack Grant, WJQS, Jackson, Mississippi, box 57, folder 18, CMC.

25. In the words of Celia Mingus, Debut was trying to encourage interest in jazz as an "American art" with a "higher level" of audience as opposed to "wild-eyed, screaming, frantic bobby-soxers" (Celia Mingus to "Flo," undated, box 57, folder 17, CMC).

26. The engagement with Ellington lasted only a few weeks at the beginning of 1953 and was marred by Mingus's physical confrontations with at least two band members. The incident that terminated his employment was a fight with trombonist Juan Tizol, which culminated with Tizol and Mingus chasing each other around the stage with weapons in hand (a machete and a fire axe); see Priestley, *Mingus: A Critical Biography,* 50–51.

27. Ibid., 54–57; Charles Mingus, liner notes for *Pithecanthropus Erectus,* Atlantic 1237.

28. Priestley, *Mingus: A Critical Biography,* 58–60; Charles Mingus, liner notes for *Jazz Composers Workshop,* Savoy MG-12059. Mingus explored similar material in a session conducted a month later for Period; see/hear Charles Mingus, *Intrusions,* Drive 41023.

29. Mingus, liner notes for *Jazz Composers Workshop.*

30. Coleman and Young, *Mingus/Mingus,* 130. Young was referring specifically to Mingus's reception in the late 1940s, but the reference applies to the early 1950s as well. Young borrows this reference from Amiri Baraka's *The System of Dante's Hell* (New York: Grove Press, 1965).

31. Priestley, *Mingus: A Critical Biography,* 50–51.

32. Nat Hentoff, "Mingus in Job Dilemma Vows, 'No Compromise,'" *Down Beat,* May 6, 1953, 21; Priestley, *Mingus: A Critical Biography,* 46. Mingus had met Hentoff while performing in Boston in late 1951.

33. Leonard Feather, "50 Stars for Bird! Mingus Exclaims," *Down Beat,* June 15, 1955, 25, 33.

34. Gennari, "The Politics of Culture and Identity in American Jazz Criticism," 190–191.

35. Mingus took another swipe at Brubeck during the "Blindfold Test" when commenting on a song called "Margo" by Teddy Charles. Mingus gave this record "45 stars," juxtaposing it with Brubeck's music: "The composition is the kind of thing people should be listening to. . . . Dave Brubeck can never do that, man. He could play the notes—but it wouldn't sound like that. But he wouldn't want to play like that anyway."

36. "The Man on Cloud No. 7," *Time,* November 8, 1954, 67–76. The article does describe Brubeck as having engaged in a "philosophical inquiry" into the value of mescaline (which he eventually rejected). But even this foray into drug use is legitimized by defining it as an academic pursuit and comparing it to the psychedelic experimentations of literary figure Aldous Huxley, as documented in *The Doors of Perception.*

37. Ibid., 67, 70.

38. Mingus appears to have been aware of the article at the time of its publication. He discussed it in his "Open Letter to Miles Davis," published later in 1955 (discussed later in this chapter) and almost certainly was familiar with it at the time of the "Blindfold Test."

39. W. T. Lhamon, *Deliberate Speed: The Origins of a Cultural Style in the American 1950s* (Washington, D.C.: Smithsonian Institution Press, 1990), 12, 39–40,

44; David Rosenthal, *Hard Bop: Jazz and Black Music, 1955–65* (New York: Oxford University Press, 1992), 22–23, 28–29, 39–43.

40. Priestley, *Mingus: A Critical Biography,* 64–65.

41. Nat Hentoff, "Miles," *Down Beat,* November 2, 1955, 13.

42. Charles Mingus, "An Open Letter to Miles Davis," *Down Beat,* November 2, 1955, 12–13.

43. Mingus, liner notes for *Pithecanthropus Erectus.*

44. Mal Waldron, liner notes for *Mingus at the Bohemia,* Debut 123; Priestley, *Mingus: A Critical Biography,* 66–68.

45. Waldron, liner notes for *Mingus at the Bohemia.*

46. Mingus, liner notes for *Pithecanthropus Erectus;* Priestley, *Mingus: A Critical Biography,* 68–70. Priestley calls this composition, with sections of "indefinite length," "the first fully integrated example on record of Mingus's 'extended form.'"

47. Mal Waldron claims that "Work Song" was Mingus's first attempt to ascribe specific political meanings to a composition: "In particular, I think Mingus thought of the men who worked out their bondage by driving stakes or laying railroad ties. In a broader sense, he thought of the whole Negro race with its oppressions and problems" (liner notes for *Mingus at the Bohemia*).

Mingus recorded "Haitian Fight Song" again in 1957 for the album *The Clown.* In the liner notes, he said the song could just as easily have been called "Afro-American Fight Song." "My solo in it is a deeply concentrated one. I can't play it right unless I'm thinking about prejudice and hate and persecution, and how unfair it is. There's a sadness and cries in it, but also determination" (quoted in Nat Hentoff, liner notes for *The Clown,* Atlantic 90142–2).

48. The fact that there are five choruses on the 1956 recorded version complicates this a bit. Some commentators claim that each section of the A/B/A/C chorus represents a movement. See Priestley, *Mingus: A Critical Biography,* 69; and Andrew Homzy, "Charles Mingus: The Atlantic Years," liner notes for *Passions of a Man,* Rhino R2–72871, 26–27.

49. In March 1958, Mingus's group backed Langston Hughes's poetry recitations at a series of Sunday afternoon concerts at the Village Vanguard. That same month, Mingus and his band provided the accompaniment for one side of *Weary Blues* (Verve 841 660–2), a Hughes recording of poetry. The title track to the 1957 recording *The Clown* included an improvised narration by radio personality Jean Shepherd, based on a semi-autobiographical narrative created by Mingus. *A Modern Jazz Symposium of Music and Poetry with Charlie Mingus* (Bethlehem 20–40092) had one spoken-word piece, "Scenes of the City," which featured a poem written by actor Lonnie Elders, with the assistance of Langston Hughes, and read by actor Melvin Stewart. See Priestley, *Mingus: A Critical Biography,* 78–79, 89–90.

50. Andrew Homzy, *More Than a Fake Book: Fifty-Five of Mingus' Compositions with Musical Analyses by Andrew Homzy* (New York: Jazz Workshop, 1991); quoted in Homzy, "Charles Mingus: The Atlantic Years," 34. See also Hentoff, liner notes for *The Clown;* and Priestley, *Mingus: A Critical Biography,* 78–79.

51. See, for example, Max Roach's *We Insist! The Freedom Now Suite* (1960, Candid 9002) and *Percussion Bittersweet* (1961, Impulse! 8); Abbey Lincoln's *Straight Ahead* (1961, Candid 9015); Randy Weston's *Uhuru Africa* (1960, Roulette 65001); and Sonny Rollins's *The Freedom Suite* (1958, Riverside 258).

52. Although the song was originally untitled, it received its name during a 1957 performance when drummer Dannie Richmond spontaneously responded, "Governor Faubus!" to Mingus's query: "Tell me someone who's ridiculous" (Priestley, *Mingus: A Critical Biography,* 86–87, 102–104; Rosenthal, *Hard Bop,* 139–141).

53. Santoro, *Myself When I Am Real,* 179–182.

54. Ralph Gleason, "Your Chance to Watch a Virtuoso Play Bass," *San Francisco Chronicle,* December 18, 1956, 21.

55. C. H. Garrigues, "Discognizant: The Bold Experiment," *San Francisco Examiner,* December 30, 1956.

56. Barry Ulanov, "Barry Ulanov," *Down Beat,* October 3, 1956, 16.

57. See, for example, "M + M at Monterey," *Newsweek,* October 5, 1964, 120–121; Nat Hentoff, "A Volcano Named Mingus," *HiFi/Stereo Review,* December 1964, 52–55.

58. Priestley, *Mingus: A Critical Biography,* 82; Charles Mingus, liner notes for *Pre-Bird,* Mercury SR 60627.

59. Charles Mingus (as told to Diane Dorr-Dorynek), liner notes for *Blues and Roots,* Atlantic 50232; Priestley, *Mingus: A Critical Biography,* 100–101.

60. Various drafts, liner notes for *Blues and Roots,* box 46, folder 6, CMC.

61. Ibid.

62. For a discussion of how Mingus's business dealings put him uncomfortably close to underworld figures, see Santoro, *Myself When I Am Real,* 192–193.

63. John Corbett, *Extended Play: Sounding Off from John Cage to Dr. Funkenstein* (Durham: Duke University Press, 1994), 13–18. Corbett builds on bell hooks's concept of "radical creative space"; see bell hooks, *Yearning: Race, Gender, and Cultural Politics* (Boston: South End Press, 1990), 153. During the period in question, Bob Reisner described Mingus as "a controversial storm center for his outspoken views" ("Jazz," *Village Voice,* November 6, 1957, 12).

64. Diane Dorr-Dorynek recorded one of Mingus's tirades during a 1959 performance at the Five Spot; see Diane Dorr-Dorynek, "Mingus . . . ," in *The Jazz Word,* ed. Dom Cerulli, Burt Korall, and Mort L. Nasitir (New York: Ballantine, 1960; reprint, New York: Da Capo, 1987), 14–18.

65. Priestley, *Mingus: A Critical Biography,* 81; Charles Mingus to George Varriale, Unemployment Insurance Accounts Bureau, October 10, 1958, box 60, folder 4, CMC.

66. Charles Mingus to President Dwight Eisenhower, March 25, 1959, box 45, folder 5, CMC. That Mingus actually sent this letter is confirmed from an April 22, 1959, response he received from the U.S. Treasury (box 60, folder 4, CMC).

67. Charles Mingus, "What I Feel About Jazz," *Jazz News,* July 26, 1961, 10; Robert Shelton, "Jazz Man Is Changing His Beat," *New York Times,* August 27,

1962, 19; Stanley Dance, "Mingus Speaks," *Jazz,* November/December 1963, 12–13.

68. Ira Gitler, "Mingus Speaks—and Bluntly," *Down Beat,* July 21, 1960, 68.

69. Priestley, *Mingus: A Critical Biography,* 149.

70. Santoro, *Myself When I Am Real,* 206; Charles Mingus to William Chance, October 7, 1963, box 63, folder 3, CMC. In another letter, Mingus expressed his frustration over the union's failure to support him in his claim against Shaw Artists Company. He appropriated Patrick Henry's slogan "give me liberty or give me death," employed militant racial rhetoric, and suggested that atomic weapons might solve all of society's problems (Charles Mingus to Max Aron, Local 802, AFM, February 11, 1962, box 48, folder 1, CMC).

71. Charles Mingus to Goddard Lieherson, President, Columbia Records, November 6, 1964; Charles Mingus to Legal Department, United Artists, November 10, 1964; both in box 54, folder 14, CMC. Mingus informed these companies that he was willing to give them a special deal on the recordings.

72. Flyer, Charles Mingus Record Club, box 55, folder 16, CMC.

73. Shelton, "Jazz Man Is Changing His Beat."

74. A recording of this interview may be heard as a "bonus track" on the CD version of *Oh Yeah* (Atlantic 90667–2).

75. Dan Morgenstern, "Rotating with Satchmo and Miles," *Metronome,* June 1961, 20.

76. Mingus was so affected by the fervor Coleman generated after his arrival in New York at the end of 1959 that he volunteered unsolicited comments about Coleman at the end of a 1960 *Down Beat* "Blindfold Test"; see "Another View of Coleman," *Down Beat,* May 26, 1961, 21.

77. Mingus, "What I Feel About Jazz," 10. For a discussion of Mingus's "love-hate affair" with Coleman's music, see John Litweiler, *Ornette Coleman: A Harmolodic Life* (New York: Morrow, 1992), 83.

78. Dave Solomon, *Playboy,* to Charles Mingus, January 13, 1965, with attached *Playboy* interoffice memorandum, Solomon to Spectorsky, Kessie, and Budrys, November 11, 1964, box 54, folder 7, CMC; "Mingus Changes Mind—Will Stay Here," *Down Beat,* October 15, 1962, 15; "Charlie Mingus Tells Why He's Quitting the Scene," *New York Post,* August 28, 1962; Shelton, "Jazz Man Is Changing His Beat"; Coleman and Young, *Mingus/Mingus,* 3–4, 86–88; Priestley, *Mingus: A Critical Biography,* 135–136; Thomas Carmichael, "*Beneath the Underdog:* Charles Mingus, Representation, and Jazz Autobiography," *Canadian Review of American Studies* 25, no. 3 (Fall 1995): 34; Santoro, *Myself When I Am Real,* 178, 194, 219, 284

79. Santoro, *Myself When I Am Real,* 131; Robin D. G. Kelley, *Race Rebels: Culture, Politics, and the Black Working Class* (New York: Free Press, 1995), 215–216. Kelley links the celebration of the pimp in black popular culture during the Black Power era to the Moynihan report (discussed in chapters 4 and 7), suggesting that young black men valorized the pimp because he was the ultimate refutation of the matriarchy thesis.

80. The *Playboy* memorandum suggests that the 875-page manuscript in existence in 1964 was the version that Lomax worked on for McGraw-Hill. This indicates that the 875-page "original" in the Charles Mingus Collection (box 45, folders 2–10) at the Library of Congress is the same version (hereafter cited as Mingus, "Beneath the Underdog" manuscript [1964]). The archived copy of the 875-page version is missing pages 89 to 180. Included with the manuscript are an additional thirty-one pages of introductory material, which do not appear to be part of either the 875-page original or the published version. It is unclear whether these were written earlier or later than the original.

I should also note that many of the characters in the autobiography have different names in the two versions. The apocryphal story is that the names of some characters were changed to prevent embarrassment or potential libel suits. Out of respect for Mingus, his family, and the individuals described in the autobiography, I refer to all characters by the names used in the published version.

81. Scholars writing about this text differ as to how closely Mingus's interrogation of his own identity should be connected to his music. Christopher Harlos, for example, argues that "overshadowing the initial search for the musical self is the search for the racial/ethnic self" ("Jazz Autobiography: Theory, Practice, Politics," in *Representing Jazz*, ed. Krin Gabbard [Durham: Duke University Press, 1995], 131–161). I am more in agreement with Thomas Carmichael, who also situates the text in the late 1950s and early 1960s and who argues that it negotiates relations of dominance and resistance through "a series of affiliations and disavowals that connect the trials of the subject in the text with the cultural practices of jazz itself" ("*Beneath the Underdog*," 30–32).

82. For a more in-depth reading of the racial and gender politics of *Beneath the Underdog*, see Rustin, "Mingus Fingers," 13–115. Rustin's discussion is particularly important for theorizing the connections among race, gender, economics, and madness in the book.

83. See Panish, *The Color of Jazz*, 42–78, for a good discussion of representations of Charlie Parker in postwar jazz criticism and literature.

84. Mingus, *Beneath the Underdog*, 188–189.

85. Mingus, "Beneath the Underdog" manuscript (1964), 199.

86. Ibid., 390–401.

87. Rustin, "Mingus Fingers," 13–70.

88. Hazel V. Carby makes a similar observation about Miles Davis's autobiography. She explores how Davis "seeks freedom *from* a confinement associated with women, and freedom *to* a world defined by the creativity of men." Women are also figured as sources of contamination with the potential to disrupt male creativity. See Carby, *Race Men* (Cambridge: Harvard University Press, 1998), 138–141.

89. Mingus, *Beneath the Underdog*, 316.

90. Coleman and Young, *Mingus/Mingus*, 29–30, 154; Santoro, *Myself When I Am Real*, 50.

91. Michael M. J. Fisher, "Ethnicity and the Post-Modern Arts of Memory,"

in *Writing Culture: The Poetics and Politics of Ethnography*, ed. James Clifford and George Marcus (Berkeley: University of California Press, 1986), 214; Mingus, *Beneath the Underdog*, 267.

92. David Ake, "Re-Masculating Jazz: Ornette Coleman, 'Lonely Woman,' and the New York Jazz Scene in the Late 1950s," *American Music* 16, no. 1 (Spring 1998): 25–44; Ingrid Monson, "The Problem with White Hipness: Race, Gender, and Cultural Conceptions in Jazz Historical Discourse," *Journal of the American Musicological Society* 48 (Fall 1995): 412–415; Norman Mailer, "The White Negro: Superficial Reflections on the Hipster," *Dissent* 4, no. 3 (Summer 1957): 276–293.

93. Carby, *Race Men*, 143–146.

94. Ibid., 156.

95. Mingus imagines a "seeming new being, this self made being from the creative mind of two people feeling, loving, knowing the same exact goodness of life, expressing their joy in having conscious desire at being able to touch and feel the same together within, know[ing] they have communed out the sacred threshold of life" ("Beneath the Underdog" manuscript [1964], 681).

96. Mingus, *Beneath the Underdog*, 343.

97. Ibid., 298, 312.

98. Ibid., 353.

99. Ibid., 131.

100. Mingus, "Beneath the Underdog" manuscript (1964), 606–609.

101. Ibid., 664–665.

102. Mingus, *Beneath the Underdog*, 85, 360–362. In the unpublished manuscript, Mingus makes the connection between Monk, Parker, and Jesus in more explicit terms. These men are "dying for what they believe the same as Christ while they fish and play with their nets and sets" (861–862).

103. Mingus, "Beneath the Underdog" manuscript (1964), 710.

104. Ibid., 768.

105. Charles Mingus, liner notes for *The Black Saint and the Sinner Lady*, Impulse! 174; Santoro, *Myself When I Am Real*, 210.

106. Mingus, *Beneath the Underdog*, 339–340.

## Chapter 4. "Straight Ahead"

1. Abbey Lincoln has stressed to me that she was never a "political" person but rather a "social" one (Abbey Lincoln, telephone interview by the author, tape recording, September 13, 2000). However, her definition of "political" is fairly narrow and assumes participation in electoral politics. And the activities in which Lincoln was involved during the late 1950s and early 1960s clearly fit within the domain of the political, in both a cultural and a social sense, as I have defined it in this book. Out of deference to Ms. Lincoln's assessment of her past, I use the term "social" whenever possible to describe her activities and orientation, but in some instances I use "political" or "politics" when it seems necessary.

2. Michael Bourne, "For the Love of Abbey," *Down Beat,* February 1992, 20–21; John S. Wilson, "Miss Lincoln Sizes Up Women's Place in Jazz," *New York Times,* June 17, 1983, C20; *Jet,* November 11, 1954, 34–35; *Affair: A Story of a Girl in Love,* Liberty 3025.

3. Francis Davis, "Leading Lady," *High Fidelity,* May 1986, 66; Chester Higgins Sr., "Abbey Lincoln Talks of Breakup with Max Roach," *Jet,* May 25, 1972, 16–17; Lincoln interview, September 13, 2000.

4. Bourne, "For the Love of Abbey," 20–21; Davis, "Leading Lady," 66; Dom Cerulli, "Caught in the Act," *Down Beat,* February 20, 1957, 12; Dom Cerulli, "The Arrival of Abbey," *Down Beat,* June 12, 1958, 19; "The Girl in the Marilyn Monroe Dress," *Ebony,* June 1957, 27–31; "New Acts: Abbey Lincoln," *Variety,* July 4, 1956, 55; "Nightclub Reviews: Black Orchid, Chi," *Variety,* August 21, 1957, 55; "Music," *Time,* July 14, 1956, 45.

5. Davis, "Leading Lady," 66.

6. Cerulli, "The Arrival of Abbey," 19.

7. Evelyn Brooks Higginbotham, *Righteous Discontent: The Women's Movement in the Black Baptist Church, 1880–1920* (Cambridge: Harvard University Press, 1993), 185–229; Darlene Clark Hine, "Rape and the Inner Lives of Black Women in the Middle West: Preliminary Thoughts on the Culture of Dissemblance," *Signs* 14 (Summer 1989): 912–920.

8. Lincoln interview, September 13, 2000; Cerulli, "The Arrival of Abbey," 19; "Abbey Lincoln Found Happiness in Jazz," *Jet,* May 28, 1959, 58; Nat Hentoff, liner notes for *Straight Ahead,* Candid 9015. In 1958 Lincoln told Dom Cerulli of her recurring desire to become "a dignified colored woman on-stage. I wanted to be earthy and basic but with dignity." The following year Lincoln told *Jet* that she left the supper club lifestyle because she "demanded [to] be respected as a dignified Negro woman." *Jet's* correspondent added: "Abbey's views are so strong on race issues until sometimes she enters engagements with her hair in its natural state—insisting that white standards of beauty are only one of many."

9. Cerulli, "The Arrival of Abbey," 19; "Abbey Lincoln Found Happiness in Jazz," 58; Lincoln interview, September 13, 2000.

10. "Abbey Lincoln Found Happiness in Jazz," 58; Lincoln interview, September 13, 2000; Wilson, "Miss Lincoln Sizes Up Women's Place in Jazz"; G. Vercelli, "Profile: Aminata Moseka/Abbey Lincoln," *Down Beat,* September 1, 1979, 42; Hentoff, liner notes for *Straight Ahead;* Cerulli, "The Arrival of Abbey," 19. Helen Hayes King, associate editor of *Jet,* recalled that Lincoln said during this period that her decision to go "natural" came in part as a result of her husband's advice; cited in Robin D. G. Kelley, *Yo' Mama's Disfunktional!: Fighting the Culture Wars in Urban America* (Boston: Beacon Press, 1997), 27–28.

11. Will Friedwald, *Jazz Singing: America's Great Voices from Bessie Smith to Bebop and Beyond* (New York: Collier Books, 1992), xi–xiv; Robert G. O'Meally, liner notes for *The Jazz Singers: A Smithsonian Collection of Jazz Vocals from 1919 to 1994,* Smithsonian Institution RD 113, AS–28978, 11–19.

12. Friedwald, *Jazz Singing,* 143–144, 146; Nat Hentoff, "Ella Fitzgerald: The

Criterion of Innocence for Popular Singers," in *The Ella Fitzgerald Companion: Seven Decades of Commentary,* ed. Leslie Gourse (New York: Schirmer Books, 1998), 38–41 (originally published as liner notes for *The Best of Ella . . .* , Decca MCA2–4047).

13. Robert O'Meally, *Lady Day: The Many Faces of Billie Holiday* (New York: Arcade, 1991), 9, 27–31, 37–53, 159–161; Friedwald, *Jazz Singing,* 135–138; Angela Davis, *Blues Legacies and Black Feminism: Gertrude "Ma" Rainey, Bessie Smith, and Billie Holiday* (New York: Pantheon, 1998), 161–180; John S. Wilson, "Billie Holiday—Jazz Singer, Pure and Simple," *New York Times,* July 6, 1958, 13; "The Paradox of Billie Holiday," *Variety,* July 22, 1959, 39; Richard Gehman, "Lady (for a) Day," *Saturday Review,* August 29, 1959, 39.

14. Davis, *Blues Legacies and Black Feminism,* 181–197; Michael Denning, *The Cultural Front: The Laboring of American Culture in the Twentieth Century* (London: Verso, 1996), 346–348; Friedwald, *Jazz Singing,* 137; O'Meally, *Lady Day,* 21, 67, 95; Whitney Balliett, "Billie, Big Bill, and Jelly Roll," *Saturday Review,* July 14, 1956, 32–33; Nat [Hentoff], " 'Lady Sings the Blues' Is Tough, Revealing Story," *Down Beat,* August 8, 1956, 9; Billie Holiday with William Dufty, *Lady Sings the Blues* (New York: Doubleday, 1956).

15. Gerald Early, "Pulp and Circumstance: The Story of Jazz in High Places," in *The Jazz Cadence of American Culture,* ed. Robert G. O'Meally (New York: Columbia University Press, 1998), 427–428. For a contemporary review of these concerts, see Nat Hentoff, "Caught in the Act," *Down Beat,* December 12, 1956, 10.

16. Gehman, "Lady (for a) Day," 39.

17. See Leslie C. Dunn and Nancy A. Jones, *Embodied Voices: Representing Female Vocality in Western Culture* (New York: Cambridge University Press, 1994), 1–3, for a discussion of the limitations of female voice in systems of artistic representation in Western culture.

18. Bourne, "For the Love of Abbey," 20–21; Lincoln interview, September 13, 2000.

19. In a discussion of the thwarted possibility of starring in a film version of Billie Holiday's *Lady Sings the Blues,* Lincoln spoke of knowing firsthand about Holiday's mistreatment by men: "Billie came into Birdland one night to see Dizzy Gillespie play . . . Max and I were there, too. 'I'm so lonely,' she told me. 'Louis [McKay, her husband] is in California on business, and I'm sitting at home polishing my nails and going crazy.' And everybody knew that Louis was living it up a few blocks away with a woman who called herself Broadway Betty" (Davis, "Leading Lady," 66).

20. Wilson, "Miss Lincoln Sizes Up Women's Place in Jazz."

21. Patricia Hill Collins, *Black Feminist Thought: Knowledge, Consciousness, and the Politics of Empowerment* (New York: Routledge, 1991), especially 3–40; Patricia Hill Collins, *Fighting Words: Black Women and the Search for Justice* (Minneapolis: University of Minnesota Press, 1998), 22–28, 61–66. Collins is more explicit about problematizing a single black feminist voice in the second work, *Fighting Words.*

22. Farah Jasmine Griffin, "A Morning Song: Abbey Lincoln—Diva of the

Dawn," unpublished chapter manuscript, 7–8. The author wishes to thank Dr. Griffin for her generosity in sharing this piece.

23. Collins, *Black Feminist Thought,* 37–38, 183–185.

24. Davis, *Blues Legacies and Black Feminism,* xvii.

25. For a discussion of the debates over damage imagery in social science discourse, see Daryl Scott, *Contempt and Pity: Social Policy and the Image of the Damaged Black Psyche, 1880–1996* (Chapel Hill: University of North Carolina Press, 1997). Although he does not discuss Frazier's *The Negro in the United States,* Scott points out how Frazier began to adopt a more pessimistic account of the black family in the 1950s.

26. *That's Him,* Riverside 251; *It's Magic,* Riverside 277; *Abbey Is Blue,* Riverside 1153.

27. Lincoln asserts that she had "complete control" of the material on the Riverside albums (Lincoln interview, September 13, 2000).

28. Ibid.; Ron Dyke, "Abbey Sings About Men and Love," *Metronome,* July 1958, 14.

29. For a discussion of the history of these songs and Holiday's recordings of them, see Donald Clarke, *Wishing on the Moon: The Life and Times of Billie Holiday* (New York: Viking Penguin, 1994), 108, 117, 153–154, 196, 242, 287.

30. Dyke, "Abbey Sings About Men and Love," 14.

31. Davis, *Blues Legacies and Black Feminism,* 161–180.

32. Lincoln interview, September 13, 2000; Davis, "Leading Lady," 66.

33. Speaking a decade later, vocalist Betty Carter argued that the move away from standards into avant-garde expression had alienated a large part of jazz's female audience (Betty Carter, interviewed in Art Taylor, *Notes and Tones: Musician-to-Musician Interviews* [New York: Da Capo, 1993], 279).

34. Lincoln interview, September 13, 2000.

35. Friedwald, *Jazz Singing,* 389; Orrin Keepnews, liner notes for *Abbey Is Blue.*

36. Nat Hentoff, liner notes for *We Insist! The Freedom Now Suite,* Candid 9002; Jack Cooke, "We Insist! The Max Roach Group Today and The Freedom Now Suite," *Jazz Monthly,* July 1962, 7; Congress of Racial Equality press release, clipping file "Max Roach, 1960–69," Institute of Jazz Studies, Rutgers University, Newark, New Jersey.

37. Hentoff, liner notes for *We Insist!*

38. Cooke, "We Insist!" 4–8. Cooke states that the "texture" of Lincoln's voice had "thickened and become richer. . . . Her obvious identification with the material provided for her by Brown and Roach has led her to an altogether higher standard of interpretation than she could ever bring to the average show tune or pop song, and has given her voice a range of inflection and tone with ranges from a pure lyricism to a deep, edgy snarl."

39. Hentoff, liner notes for *We Insist!*

40. Ibid.; Cooke, "We Insist!" 7–8.

41. Max Roach is quoted in Margo Guryan, liner notes for *Percussion Bittersweet* (Impulse! 8), 5.

42. Ibid., 5, 9; Cooke, "We Insist!" 8.

43. The musicians include Lincoln, Roach, Walter Benton (tenor saxophone), Coleman Hawkins (tenor saxophone), Eric Dolphy ("reeds"), Booker Little (trumpet), Julian Priester (trombone), Mal Waldron (piano), Art Davis (bass) Robert Whitley (congas), and Roger Sanders (congas).

44. See O'Meally, liner notes for *The Jazz Singers,* 92–93, for a description of this performance.

45. Lincoln interview, September 13, 2000.

46. In the album's liner notes, Nat Hentoff suggests that this song expresses "a sardonic view of the ambivalences of romantic attachments." Yet Lincoln confirms that the lyrics address broader social issues (Lincoln interview, September 13, 2000).

47. Wilson, "Miss Lincoln Sizes Up Women's Place in Jazz"; Vercelli, "Profile," 43; June L'Rhue, "The New Abbey Lincoln: A Voice of Protest," *Pittsburgh Courier,* May 27, 1961, 20; Barbara Gardner, "Metamorphosis," *Down Beat,* September 14, 1961, 18–20.

48. Gardner, "Metamorphosis," 20.

49. Lincoln interview, September 13, 2000; Bourne, "For the Love of Abbey," 20; Wilson, "Miss Lincoln Sizes Up Women's Place in Jazz"; Davis, "Leading Lady," 66; Frank Kofsky, "Abbey Lincoln," *Radio Free Jazz,* February 1977, 11. Davis suggests that Lincoln's cool treatment had more to do with record companies' "antipathy" to jazz than with an aversion to her politics. Kofsky, however, says Lincoln was ostracized by critics and recording companies because of the political nature of her work. Lincoln agrees with Kofsky's assessment.

50. John S. Wilson, "Singer in Focus: Abbey Lincoln Grows as Jazz Musician," *New York Times,* October 29, 1961, sec. 2, 23.

51. Ira Gitler, "Gitler's Review," reprinted in *Down Beat,* March 15, 1962, 21.

52. Ibid.

53. "Racial Prejudice in Jazz, Part I," *Down Beat,* March 15, 1962, 20–26; "Racial Prejudice in Jazz, Part II," *Down Beat,* March 22, 1962, 22–25; Lincoln interview, September 13, 2000.

54. "Crow Jim," *Time,* October 19, 1962, 58–60.

55. "Racial Prejudice in Jazz, Part I," 21–22.

56. Ibid. Lincoln concurred with Hentoff. She argued: "All art must be propaganda; all art must have an attitude; and all art must reflect the times you live in."

57. See Amiri Baraka [LeRoi Jones], "Jazz and the White Critic," in *Black Music* (New York: Morrow, 1967), 11–20. For the most obvious example of the move to establish a "black aesthetic," see Addison Gayle Jr., ed., *The Black Aesthetic* (New York: Doubleday, 1971).

58. "Racial Prejudice in Jazz, Part I," 24.

59. Ibid.

60. "Racial Prejudice in Jazz, Part II," 22–23. Like other musicians discussed in this book, Lincoln asserted that art could be racially specific while remaining invested in a humanist vision. "Why is it that because I love my people and I

want human dignity, must I be a racist?" Lincoln asked. "Because I say my people are worthwhile and should be free, does this mean I hate the white man?" (23).

61. Dave Hepburn, "No Nationalist, Says Abbey, She Just Wants Dignity . . . ," *New York Amsterdam News,* June 30, 1962, 18; George T. Simon, "Singer Proud to Be Different," *Herald Tribune* (New York), July 8, 1962.

62. Hepburn, "No Nationalist, Says Abbey."

63. Max Roach and Abbey Lincoln, "Black Man in Japan," *Liberator,* January 1964, 12–13, 19.

64. Pauline Rivelli, "Abbey Lincoln: Proud and Confident," *Jazz* 4, no. 7, July 1965, 10.

65. Ibid., 12.

66. "Abbey Lincoln, Mississippi John Hurt," *Coda,* April/May 1965, 6–8. This interview was conducted by Patrick Watson and was broadcast on the CBC network on March 7, 1965.

67. Ibid., 8.

68. Daniel Patrick Moynihan, *The Negro Family: The Case for National Action* (Washington, D.C.: U.S. Government Printing Office, 1965); Collins, *Black Feminist Thought,* 73–74; Jacqueline Jones, *Labor of Love, Labor of Sorrow: Black Women, Work, and the Family from Slavery to the Present* (New York: Basic Books, 1985; reprint, New York: Vintage Books, 1986), 311–312; Paula Giddings, *When and Where I Enter: The Impact of Black Women on Race and Sex in America* (New York: Morrow, 1984; reprint, New York: Bantam Books, 1985), 299, 309–311, 325–335. Collins suggests that the Moynihan thesis was developed in part to thwart white women's feminist activism.

69. A number of essays published a few years later that distilled these issues can be found in *Words of Fire: An Anthology of African-American Feminist Thought,* ed. Beverly Guy-Sheftall (New York: New Press, 1995), 145–176, 185–197.

70. The conference was cosponsored by the New School and the Harlem Writers Guild. This particular panel was dedicated to Lorraine Hansberry (who had recently died). Lincoln recalls having previously been in dialogue with the other panelists (Lincoln interview, September 13, 2000).

71. "The Negro Woman in American Literature," *Freedomways,* First Quarter 1966, 8–10, 14–25.

72. Ibid., 11.

73. "Abbey Lincoln, Mississippi John Hurt," 7.

74. Lincoln did not claim that the song "Strange Fruit" had been written by Holiday, but she did say that Holiday "helped create" it. Lincoln also discussed "Billie's Blues" as a tune that "revealed [Holiday's] retiring disposition and impish modesty." See "The Negro Woman in American Literature," 11–12.

75. Ibid., 12–13.

76. Ibid., 13.

77. Abbey Lincoln, "Who Will Revere the Black Woman?" in *The Black Woman: An Anthology,* ed. Toni Cade (New York: New American Library, 1970), 80–82 (originally published in *Negro Digest,* September 1966).

78. Ibid., 83–84.

79. I draw here from Farah Jasmine Griffin's more detailed reading of this essay in "A Morning Song," 4–9.

80. Ibid., 32–38.

81. Higgins, "Abbey Lincoln Talks of Breakup With Max Roach," 17; Wilson, "Miss Lincoln Sizes Up Women's Place in Jazz." *People in Me* (Inner City 6040) was not released by Inner City Records until 1978.

82. Liner notes for *People in Me;* Jack E. White, "Lincoln's Emancipation," *Time,* May 17, 1993, 59; Davis, "Leading Lady," 79; *Talking to the Sun,* Enja 4060; *A Tribute to Billie Holiday,* Enja 6012; *Abbey Sings Billie: Volume 2,* Enja 7037. For a more detailed description of Lincoln's engagement with Billie Holiday's legacy in the 1980s and 1990s, see Griffin, "A Morning Song," 38–45.

# Chapter 5. Practicing "Creative Music"

1. These comments were serialized in *Jazz* magazine under the title "Jazz and Revolutionary Black Nationalism" over the course of fourteen issues between April 1966 and July 1967.

2. Larry Neal, "The Black Arts Movement," in *The Black Aesthetic,* ed. Addison Gayle Jr. (New York: Doubleday, 1971), 257.

3. For examples of scholarship that explores the connections between Black Arts movements in music and other fields, see Robin D. G. Kelley, "Dig They Freedom: Meditations on History and the Black Avant-Garde," *Lenox Avenue* 3 (1997): 13–27; Lorenzo Thomas, "Ascension: Music and the Black Arts Movement," in *Jazz Among the Discourses,* ed. Krin Gabbard (Durham: Duke University Press, 1995), 256–274; Aldon Lynn Nielsen, *Black Chant: Languages of African-American Postmodernism* (Cambridge: Cambridge University Press, 1997); Samuel Floyd, *The Power of Black Music: Interpreting Its History from Africa to the United States* (New York: Oxford University Press, 1995); and Ronald Radano, *New Musical Figurations: Anthony Braxton's Cultural Critique* (Chicago: University of Chicago Press, 1996).

4. Négritude, as articulated by Aimé Césaire, Léopold Senghor, and others, was a mid-twentieth-century attempt to define a distinct, diasporic black identity in cultural, philosophical, and sometimes biological terms. Although Fanon was a student of Césaire, he largely rejected the essentialist aspects of Négritude. Still, as Baraka's comments suggest, Fanon's work was often invoked by cultural nationalists seeking to describe a distinct black sensibility.

5. "Jazz and Revolutionary Black Nationalism," *Jazz,* June 1966, 28–29; April 1966, 30.

6. Amiri Baraka [LeRoi Jones], "The Changing Same (R&B and New Black Music)," in *Black Music* (New York: Morrow, 1967), 192, 205.

7. Thomas, "Ascension," 257–259, 270.

8. For another account of some of the major issues being articulated during this time, see Radano, *New Musical Figurations,* 63–73.

9. Ornette Coleman, liner notes for *Change of the Century,* Atlantic 1327.

10. Don DeMichael, "John Coltrane and Eric Dolphy Answer the Critics," *Down Beat,* April 12, 1962, 22.

11. See, for example, the interview with Coltrane in Frank Kofsky's *Black Nationalism and the Revolution in Music* (New York: Pathfinder Press, 1970) in which the saxophonist resists Kofsky's attempts to characterize his music as a militant expression (221–243). For a discussion of how Coltrane's ideas were appropriated and made to serve divergent ideological interests, see Gerald Early, "Ode to John Coltrane: A Jazz Musician's Influence on African-American Culture," *Antioch Review* 57, no. 3 (Summer 1999): 371–385.

12. Baraka [Jones], "The Changing Same," 187–189.

13. Phillip Brian Harper, "Nationalism and Social Division in Black Arts Poetry of the 1960s," *Critical Inquiry* 19 (Winter 1993): 234–253.

14. L. P. Neal, "Black Revolution in Music: A Talk with Drummer Milford Graves," *Liberator,* September 1965, 14–15. In his comments, Neal linked Graves's ideas to Neal's own vision for the Black Arts movement, "which is focusing its attention on evolving a true art that meets the spiritual and social needs of black people."

15. Milford Graves and Don Pullen, "Black Music," *Liberator,* January 1967, 20. There was, of course, a certain irony that a musical project defined in juxtaposition to "Western thought" would be recorded at Yale University.

16. Charlie Russell, "Has Jazz Lost Its Roots?" *Liberator,* August 1964, 4–7.

17. Amiri Baraka [LeRoi Jones], "Voice from the Avant-Garde: Archie Shepp," *Down Beat,* January 14, 1965, 18–19; Barry Kernfeld, "Archie Shepp," in *The New Grove Dictionary of Jazz,* ed. Barry Kernfeld (New York: St. Martin's, 1994), 1111–1112; Nielsen, *Black Chant,* 180–181; Harold Cruse, *The Crisis of the Negro Intellectual: A Historical Analysis of the Failure of Black Leadership* (1967; reprint, New York: Quill, 1984), 484.

18. "Jazz and Revolutionary Black Nationalism," *Jazz,* April 1966, 30; May 1966, 29; August 1966, 29; November 1966, 38; December 1966, 44.

19. Neal, "Black Revolution in Music," 14.

20. Baraka [Jones], "Voice from the Avant-Garde," 18–20, 36.

21. Archie Shepp, "An Artist Speaks Bluntly," *Down Beat,* December 16, 1965, 11, 42.

22. Lawrence P. Neal, "A Conversation with Archie Shepp," *Liberator,* November 1965, 24–25.

23. Ibid.

24. Radano argues that the polemical styles of Shepp and others and their oversimplification of "the ideological dimensions of the music" made it easy for conservative critics to dismiss their music and social critiques (*New Musical Figurations,* 69).

25. Shepp is quoted by Nat Hentoff in the liner notes for *Fire Music* (Impulse! 86). See also Nielsen, *Black Chant,* 201–204, for a discussion of *Fire Music.*

26. Hentoff, liner notes for *Fire Music.* "Malcolm, Malcolm—Semper Mal-

colm" was originally a section of a longer piece of music called "The Funeral," which Shepp had dedicated to Medgar Evers. After Malcolm's assassination, Shepp rewrote the section. Malcolm X was killed on February 21, 1965; Shepp and his group recorded this piece of music on March 9. The other tracks were recorded on February 16.

27. Ben Sidran, *Black Talk* (New York: Holt, Rinehart and Winston, 1971; reprint, New York: Da Capo, 1981), 145.

28. "Jazz: The Prayerful One," *Time,* February 21, 1964, 58–59. Several of the flyers Williams distributed can be found in the clipping file "Mary Lou Williams" at the Institute of Jazz Studies (Rutgers University, Newark, New Jersey); see "History of Jazz" and "Jazz Is Your Heritage." For further information about how musicians across the stylistic spectrum responded to this political moment, see Art Taylor's *Notes and Tones: Musician-to-Musician Interviews* (New York: Da Capo, 1993).

29. Charlie L. Russell, "Minding the Cultural Shop," *Liberator,* December 1964, 12–13; Valerie Wilmer, *As Serious as Your Life: The Story of the New Jazz* (London: Allison and Busby, 1977; reprint, London: Pluto Press, 1987), 218; "Jazzmobile," in *The New Grove Dictionary of Jazz,* 608.

30. Radano, *New Musical Figurations,* 84–85; Bob Rusch, "Reggie Workman Interview," *Cadence,* July 1995, 7.

31. Rico Mitchell, "Horace Tapscott," *Down Beat,* January 1988, 13; Mike Davis, *City of Quartz: Excavating the Future in Los Angeles* (London: Verso, 1990), 64.

32. Kelley, "Dig They Freedom," 17–25; Radano, *New Musical Figurations,* 77–81; Wilmer, *As Serious as Your Life,* 116–118; Graham Lock, *Forces in Motion: Anthony Braxton and the Meta-Reality of Creative Music* (London: Quartet Books, 1988), 33–35; John Litweiler, "A Man with an Idea," *Down Beat,* October 5, 1967, 23, 26, 41.

33. Radano, *New Musical Figurations,* 77–87; Terry Martin, "The Chicago Avant-Garde," *Jazz Monthly,* March 1968, 12–18.

34. Radano, *New Musical Figurations,* 83, 86–98; Lock, *Forces in Motion,* 33–35; John Litweiler, *The Freedom Principle: Jazz After 1958* (New York: Da Capo, 1984), 173–174; Wilmer, *As Serious as Your Life,* 116–118; Leslie B. Rout Jr., "AACM: New Music (!) New Ideas (?)," *Journal of Popular Culture* 1, no. 2 (1967): 130.

35. For a provocative discussion of the significance of the African orientation in the Art Ensemble of Chicago's music, see *Lenox Avenue* 3 (1997), which devotes the entire issue to the group.

36. Radano, *New Musical Figurations,* 99–100; J. B. Figi, "Art Ensemble of Chicago," *Chicago Sundance,* November/December 1972, 44; Gary Giddins, "Muhal Richard Abrams and the AACM," *Radio Free Jazz,* June 1978, 7.

37. Radano, *New Musical Figurations,* 101–105.

38. Ibid., 108–112.

39. Radano acknowledges the AACM's universalism at various points in his study, especially in his comments about Anthony Braxton, but he focuses on the

nationalist elements of the group's philosophy. At times, his discussion of cultural nationalism as the "official position" of other members of the AACM seems geared toward constructing them as a foil for what he views as a more hybrid, eclectic, postmodernist, and ultimately "egalitarian" vision that Braxton pursued as a soloist during the 1970s and 1980s. Although, as Braxton and others have pointed out, some members of the group were no doubt guilty of a pernicious brand of "blacker than thou" militancy and antagonistic separatism, Braxton was not the only AACM member to explore utopian and catholic approaches to art and culture. Interviews with Abrams and other members of the AACM, as well as the writings of Wadada Leo Smith, Joseph Jarman, and George Lewis, illustrate this point. Lewis emphasized the centrality of the conflict between universalism and nationalism in the life of the AACM in a personal communication with the author (March 17, 1999).

40. Lock, *Forces in Motion,* 47–48; Figi, "Art Ensemble of Chicago," 48.

41. Rout, "AACM," 131, 135–137.

42. Radano, *New Musical Figurations,* 112; Figi, "Art Ensemble of Chicago," 47; Martin, "The Chicago Avant-Garde," 17; Litweiler, "Man with an Idea," 41.

43. Reggie Workman, interview by the author, tape recording, Oakland, California, August 18, 1995; Rusch, "Reggie Workman Interview," 7.

44. Workman interview, August 18, 1995; Ed Hazell, "Jazz Composers Guild," in *The New Grove Dictionary of Jazz,* 607; Wilmer, *As Serious as Your Life,* 213–214; flyer from Jazz Composer's Orchestra Association, Inc., box 2, "Future Publications" folder, Reggie Workman/Collective Black Artists Papers, Institute of Jazz Studies, Rutgers University, Newark, New Jersey (hereafter cited as CBA Papers).

45. Wilmer, *As Serious as Your Life,* 218; Workman interview, August 18, 1995; "Jazzmobile," in *The New Grove Dictionary of Jazz.*

46. Workman interview, August 18, 1995; Rusch, "Reggie Workman Interview," 13; Roy Bikhs, "Letter to Harlem," May 15, 1968, box 2, "Future Publications" folder, CBA Papers; Reggie Workman, Art Expansions fund-raising letter, September 30, 1968, box 2, "Future Publications" folder, CBA Papers.

47. Miscellaneous flyers and notes pertaining to Professionals Unlimited, box 2, "Future Publications" folder, CBA Papers; Workman interview, August 18, 1995.

48. Workman interview, August 18, 1995; Rusch, "Reggie Workman Interview," 13. Radano says that the CBA "asserted an exclusionist ideology that, however justified, exacerbated racial tensions in the jazz community" (*New Musical Figurations,* 156).

49. Workman interview, August 18, 1995. A list of the membership is found in *Expansions* 1, no. 3 (May 1971): 19.

50. Robert Rusch, "CBA Conference Seeks Unity of Black Artists," *Down Beat,* July 20, 1972, 10–11.

51. Workman interview, August 18, 1995. See also the following entries in *The New Grove Dictionary of Jazz:* Paul Rinzler, "Bill Barron," 76; Frederick A. Beck, "Jimmy Owens," 947; and "Christopher White," 1283. See also Christopher White,

"Check Yourself," an essay from an unknown source (1972), 197–198, box 2, "BA Blanket Proposals" folder, CBA Papers. According to *Expansions,* members of the CBA Executive board in 1971 were Stanley Cowell, Bob Cunningham, Billy Harper, Jimmy Heath, Don Moore, Jimmy Owens, Tyrone Washington, Reggie Workman, and Kiane Zawadi. Board members in 1973 were Cunningham, Owens, Workman, Bill Barron, Frank Foster, Jimmy Rogers, and Robert Williams. In 1975, the members were Owens, Rogers, Workman, Hamiet Bluiett, John Carter, Leonard Goines, and Ed Williams.

52. "Aims and Goals," *Expansions* 1, no. 1 (December 1970): 8.

53. Jazz and the People's Movement began in 1970 with a series of disruptions of network television shows to protest the dearth of black jazz musicians on television. After disrupting the Merv Griffin, Dick Cavett, and Johnny Carson shows, the group was given a half-hour of air time on Cavett's show to discuss their grievances and subsequently secured a few televised network performances. They also turned their attention to radio programming in the New York area. See Wilmer, *As Serious as Your Life,* 215–218.

54. Grant proposals for 1973–1974, 1974–1975, Collective Black Artists to New York State Council on the Arts [NYSCA], box 1, "NYSCA" folder, CBA Papers; Bill Barron, "We Are Not All Mozart Lovers," *Expansions* 1, no. 2 (April 1971): 2; Genghis Nor, Strong-Light Productions, proposal to Collective Black Artists for "The Anthology of Black Classical Music," June 9, 1971, box 4, "Brooklyn - All Education" folder, CBA Papers.

55. George Lipsitz, "The Possessive Investment in Whiteness: Racialized Social Democracy and the 'White' Problem in American Studies," *American Quarterly* 47, no. 3 (September 1995): 372–377.

56. Ortiz Walton, *Music: Black, White, and Blue* (New York: Morrow, 1972), 144–146.

57. Ibid., 150; Wilmer, *As Serious as Your Life,* 247; Lee Underwood, "Jimmy Owens: Creating the Business Legacy," *Down Beat,* October 19, 1978, 15–16, 46, 48; NEA Annual Reports (Washington, D.C.: U.S. Government Printing Office, 1971–1980). Owens, who was a member of the NEA panel on jazz and ethnic music, suggested that he too played a role in this increase in funding.

58. Consortium of Jazz Organizations to Governor Hugh Carey, January 2, 1975, box 2, "BA Blanket Proposals" folder, CBA Papers.

59. Workman interview, August 18, 1995.

60. 1974–1975 CBA Institute of Education registration form and course description, box 1, "NYSCA" folder, CBA Papers; Diane Weathers, "The CBA: A Grass Roots Movement," *Black Creation* 5, no. 1 (Fall 1973): 34.

61. 1974–1975 CBA Institute of Education registration form and course description, box 1, "NYSCA" folder, CBA Papers; Diane Weathers, "The Collective Black Artists," *Black World* 23, no. 1 (November 1973): 74–76.

62. Robert Cunningham, "Why a Life of Music?" in Yusef Lateef, Kenneth Barron, Albert Heath, and Robert Cunningham, *Something Else: Writings of the Yusef Lateef Quartet* (New York: Autophysiopsychic Partnership, 1973), 92.

63. Jimmy Owens, untitled document supporting 1974–1975 NYSCA grant proposal, October 16, 1974, box 1, "NYSCA" folder, CBA Papers.

64. 1974–1975 NYSCA grant proposal, box 1, "NYSCA" folder, CBA Papers; Reggie Workman to Denise Spalding, November 30, 1972, box 4, "Brooklyn - All Education" folder, CBA Papers. Workman's letter indicates that the CBA was to perform two concerts a day between December 20 and 22 at the Brooklyn House of Detention and between December 26 and 28 at the Manhattan House of Detention. See also *Expansions* 3, no. 3 (September 1973): 2, in which a letter to the editor from Herman Green, Program Dept., Manhattan House of Detention for Men, thanks the CBA for donations of *Expansions*. Mario Escalero, a self-taught saxophonist and flautist incarcerated at Wallkill, New York, also wrote in, asserting that the CBA's mission had inspired him to pursue a career in music when he was released.

65. "Aims and Goals," *Expansions* 1, no. 1 (December 1970): 8; "Collective Black Artists, Aims and Goals," *Expansions* 3, no. 2 (June 1973): 7.

66. Jimmy Owens to Ms. Camille Taylor, April 6, 1973, box 4, "Brooklyn - All Education" folder, CBA Papers.

67. Peter Keepnews, "What Is the CBA?" *Down Beat*, February 28, 1974, 10; supporting documentation for 1974–1975 NYSCA grant proposal, box 1, "NYSCA" folder, CBA Papers.

68. Supporting documentation for 1974–1975 NYSCA grant proposal, box 1, "NYSCA" folder, CBA Papers. CBA members whose compositions were in the book included Frank Foster, Jimmy Heath, Stanley Cowell, Roland Alexander, and Jimmy Owens.

69. Concert flyers, box 1, CBA Papers.

70. Keepnews, "What Is the CBA?" 10; supporting documentation for 1974–1975 NYSCA grant proposal, box 1, "NYSCA" folder, CBA Papers.

71. "Letter to Katara Uptown," *Expansions* 1, no. 3 (May 1971): 2; "Here and There," *Expansions* 1, no. 3 (May 1971): 8.

72. Keepnews, "What Is the CBA?" 10.

73. 1974–1975 NYSCA grant proposal, box 1, "NYSCA" folder, CBA Papers; "Ritual" concert flyer, box 1, CBA Papers.

74. Concert flyers, box 1, CBA Papers; supporting documentation for 1974–1975 NYSCA grant proposal, box 1, "NYSCA" folder, CBA Papers.

75. "Feature Interview: Stanley Cowell," *Expansions* 1, no. 3 (May 1971): 4, 16; *Music Inc. and Big Band,* Strata-East 660–51–009.

76. *No Escaping It!!!,* Polydor 2425031; *The Loud Minority,* Mainstream 349.

77. Donald Byrd, "The Meaning of Black Music," *Black Scholar* 3, no. 10 (Summer 1972): 31.

78. Sidran, *Black Talk,* 144; Mitchell, "Horace Tapscott," 13.

79. "Archie Shepp," in *The Black Composer Speaks,* ed. David N. Baker, Lida M. Belt, and Herman C. Hudson (Metuchen, N.J: Scarecrow Press, 1978), 292, 296–297; Wilmer, *As Serious as Your Life,* 241–244.

80. Workman interview, August 18, 1995.

81. This information is contained in various course descriptions and syllabi for courses Workman taught at the University of Massachusetts, found in boxes 2 and 4, various folders, CBA Papers.

82. Eileen Southern, *The Music of Black Americans,* 2d ed. (New York: W. W. Norton, 1983); Eileen Southern, "Music Research and the Black Aesthetic," *Black World* 23, no. 1 (November 1973): 4–13.

83. Final exam, "Anthology of African-American Music," box 2, "Outlines on Records" folder, CBA Papers.

84. Among the titles Workman used for this area of inquiry were "The Musical Scale and the Scheme of Evolution," "Fourteen Lessons in Yogi Philosophy," "Healing and Regeneration Through Music," and "Healing and Regeneration Through Color." Workman mentioned his respect for Wiggins in my interview with him (August 18, 1995). For a discussion of Wiggins's ideas, see Robert Rusch, "CBA Conference Seeks Unity of Black Artists," *Down Beat,* July 20, 1972, 11.

85. Workman interview, August 18, 1995.

## Chapter 6. Writing "Creative Music"

1. Robert Farris Thompson, "Mambo Minkisis: The Mind and Music of Leo Smith," *Coda,* November 1975, 10–11.

2. Yusef Lateef, *Yusef Lateef's Method on How to Improvise Soul Music* (Teaneck, N.J.: Alnur Music, 1970); Lee Jeske, "Yusef Lateef," in *The New Grove Dictionary of Jazz,* ed. Barry Kernfeld (New York: St. Martin's, 1994), 680–681.

3. Leonard Feather, "Jazz Is a Four-Letter Word," *Melody Maker,* September 5, 1970, 14; Lateef, *Yusef Lateef's Method,* 4.

4. *The Complete Yusef Lateef,* Atlantic 1499; *Yusef Lateef's Detroit,* Atlantic 1525; Len Lyons, "Yusef Lateef: Life Begins at 60!" *Down Beat,* March 23, 1978, 17, 39–40; "Yusef Lateef Develops 'New Sound,'"*Billboard,* April 8, 1978, 56.

5. Lateef, *Yusef Lateef's Method,* 3.

6. Throughout the text of his book, Lateef generally employs alternative spellings of the word "improviser," which he spells "improvisor" or "improvizor." He uses a "z" in the spelling of the words "improvize," "improvization," and "improvizational."

7. Lateef, *Yusef Lateef's Method,* 5–6.

8. Ibid., 3, 6.

9. Lateef, "The Constitution of Aesthetics, the Declaration of Genius, and the Aesthetic Address," in Yusef Lateef, Kenneth Barron, Albert Heath, and Robert Cunningham, *Something Else: Writings of the Yusef Lateef Quartet* (New York: Autophysiopsychic Partnership, 1973), 21–23.

10. Ibid., 22.

11. Ibid., 23–24.

12. Linda Tucci, "The Artist in Maine," *The Black Perspective in Music* 1, no. 1 (Spring 1973): 61–62; David Such, "Marion Brown," in *The New Grove Dictionary of Jazz,* 158; Maceo Crenshaw Dailey Jr., "Introduction" to *Recollections: Es-*

*says, Drawings, Miscellanea,* by Marion Brown (Frankfurt: Juergen A. Schmitt, 1984), 17–18; Marion Brown, liner notes for *Afternoon of a Georgia Faun,* ECM 1004; liner notes for *Geechee Recollections,* Impulse! 9252; Lorenzo Thomas, "Ascension: Music and the Black Arts Movement," in *Jazz Among the Discourses,* ed. Krin Gabbard (Durham: Duke University Press, 1995), 262. Thomas suggests that expertise about African retentions in African American music influenced Baraka's *Blues People.* Thomas remembers discussing these issues with Brown himself.

13. Brown, *Recollections,* 19–20, 247.

14. Tucci, "The Artist in Maine," 60–62.

15. Ibid., 61.

16. Brown, liner notes for *Afternoon of a Georgia Faun.*

17. Marion Brown, *Afternoon of a Georgia Faun: Views and Reviews* (Nia Music, 1973).

18. Brown, liner notes for *Afternoon of a Georgia Faun;* Brown, *Views and Reviews,* 1; Amos Tutuola, *My Life in the Bush of Ghosts* (New York: Grove Press, 1954).

19. Brown, *Views and Reviews,* 16–19.

20. Ibid., 1, 5–6.

21. Ibid., 1–7.

22. Ibid., 6–7. Brown cites J. H. Nketia's *African Music in Ghana* (Evanston: Northwestern University Press, 1963) when discussing Ghanaian music.

23. Brown, *Views and Reviews,* 7.

24. Ibid., 19–22.

25. Marion Brown, "Improvisation and the Aural Tradition in Afro-American Music," *Black World* 23, no. 1 (November 1973): 14–19. Brown puts forth similar ideas in an undated essay in *Recollections,* his 1984 collection of essays, drawings, compositions, and interviews. In a piece titled "The Relationship Between Language and Texts and Language and Music in Afro-American Songs," Brown discusses the poetic aspects of African American vocal musics and validates his own use of spoken word in his musical projects (*Recollections,* 153–166).

26. In the liner notes for Brown's *Geechee Recollections,* critic J. B. Figi writes: "Just as many *down home* ways originated *back home,* Georgia is Marion's corridor to Africa."

27. Figi, liner notes for *Geechee Recollections;* Dailey, "Introduction," 21; *Sweet Earth Flying,* Impulse! 9275. Aldon Lynn Nielsen argues that Brown's fusion of poetry and music illustrates that "for black artists it is a thin line between song and speech indeed, and it is a highly permeable line" (*Black Chant: Languages of African-American Postmodernism* [Cambridge: Cambridge University Press, 1997], 218).

28. Marion Brown, "Music Is My Mistress: Form and Expression in the Music of Duke Ellington," in Brown, *Recollections,* 107–110.

29. Ibid., 109–115. Brown draws part of his analysis from Martin Williams's *The Jazz Tradition* (New York: Oxford University Press, 1970).

30. Brown, *Recollections,* 110, 124–125. Brown makes similar comments in his

1973 essay "The Spiritual Awakening of John Coltrane," in which he explores the saxophonist's spiritual transformation in relationship to different theological models of mystical experience. Comparing Coltrane's composition "A Love Supreme" with the poetic representation of the theme on the inside cover of this album, Brown suggests that Coltrane's poem gives a more refined account of emotional (and spiritual) experience than the music (*Recollections,* 127–151).

31. See Valerie Wilmer, *As Serious as Your Life: The Story of the New Jazz* (London: Allison and Busby, 1977; reprint, London: Pluto Press, 1987), 251–254, for a discussion of French critical demands of avant-garde musicians.

32. In 1975 Yale professor Robert Farris Thompson described how musicians, artists, and fans came to Smith to "seek his counsel" (Thompson, "Mambo Minkisis," 10–11).

33. Ismael Wadada Leo Smith, interview by the author, tape recording, September 12, 1998, Oakland, California.

34. Leo Smith, *Notes (8 Pieces) Source a New World Music: Creative Music* (self-published, 1973), i. Smith's text is not paginated. As a means of providing adequate reference to the reader, I have designated the dedication page as i and the following page, which consists of a quotation from *The Black Aesthetic,* as ii. I switch to Arabic pagination for the page that begins with the line "as an afterthought i realize . . ."

35. Ibid., 4.

36. Ibid., ii, 1–3; Addison Gayle Jr., ed., *The Black Aesthetic* (New York: Doubleday, 1971); Smith interview, September 12, 1998. In addition to being symbolic of the intellectual links between musicians and contemporary thinkers, *The Black Aesthetic* also put Smith in dialogue with an earlier generation of African American intellectuals. Smith remembers the specific influence of Langston Hughes's "The Negro Artist and the Racial Mountain" and W. E. B. Du Bois's "Of the Sorrow Songs," a chapter from *The Souls of Black Folk.* Both are reproduced in *The Black Aesthetic.*

37. Smith, *Notes,* 25–26.

38. Ibid., 13–19.

39. Ibid., 4–5.

40. Ibid., 5–7.

41. Ibid., 7–8.

42. Ibid., 20–21.

43. Ibid., 20–21, 36–37. For a discussion of the Congressional act (Public Law 92–140), see Russell Sanjek and David Sanjek, *American Popular Music in the Twentieth Century* (New York: Oxford University Press, 1991), 221; and United States Statute at Large, 1971 (Washington, D.C.: U.S. Government Printing Office, 1972), 85: 391–392. Smith's prophecies about instantaneous global musical exchange, of course, have to some degree come true with the growing popularity of the Internet.

44. Bill Smith, "Leo Smith Interview," *Coda,* November 1975, 5.

45. Smith, *Notes,* 11–12.

46. See Charles Ives, *Essays Before a Sonata, The Majority, and Other Writings,* ed. Howard Boatwright, rev. ed. (New York: W. W. Norton, 1989), 78–79, 92–93. Ives wanted to show the influence of transcendental philosophy on his second pianoforte sonata, "Concord, Mass., 1845"; and he championed a national music, rooted in homegrown experience yet cosmopolitan in scope. Ives also said, "A day in a 'Kansas wheat field' will do more for [an American composer] than three years in Rome." Smith told me that he was inspired by this collection and made specific reference to the "wheat field" analogy (Smith interview, September 12, 1998).

47. Leo Smith, "(M1) American Music," *The Black Perspective in Music* 2, no. 2 (Fall 1974): 111–116. Smith suggested the importance of Chavez in our interview (Smith interview, September 12, 1998).

48. Smith, "(M1) American Music," 114.

49. Ibid., 116.

50. Leo Smith, liner notes for *Divine Love,* ECM 1143; Smith interview, September 12, 1998; George Lewis, personal correspondence with the author, March 17, 1999.

51. Smith, *Notes,* 22–23.

52. Ibid., 31–36; *Creative Music-1,* Kabell-1.

53. *Reflectativity,* Kabell-2.

54. *Ahkreanvention,* Kabell-4; *Divine Love,* ECM 1143.

55. Smith interview, September 12, 1998.

56. Wadada Leo Smith, "An Ankhrasmation Analysis: Anthony Braxton's 'Composition 113' (1983)," in *Mixtery: A Festschrift for Anthony Braxton,* ed. Graham Lock (Devon, England: A Stride Conversation Piece, 1995), 93–102.

57. See Anthony Braxton, *Composition Notes, Book E* (Synthesis Music, 1988), 385–398.

58. See, for example, Ronald Radano, *New Musical Figurations: Anthony Braxton's Cultural Critique* (Chicago: University of Chicago Press, 1996); Lock, *Mixtery;* Graham Lock, *Forces in Motion: Anthony Braxton and the Meta-Reality of Creative Music* (London: Quartet Books, 1988); Graham Lock, *Blutopia: Visions of the Future and Revisions of the Past in the Work of Sun Ra, Duke Ellington, and Anthony Braxton* (Durham: Duke University Press, 2000), which devotes a third of its pages to Braxton; Mike Heffley, *The Music of Anthony Braxton* (Westport, Conn.: Greenwood, 1996); and Alun Ford, *Anthony Braxton: Creative Music Continuums* (Devon, England: Stride Research Documents, 1997).

59. Radano, *New Musical Figurations,* 47–75, 112–120.

60. Braxton, *Composition Notes, Book A,* i.

61. For full definitions of Braxton neologisms, see entries in his glossary of terms at the end of each volume of the *Tri-axium Writings.* The definition of extended functionalism is found in Anthony Braxton, *Tri-axium Writings* (Synthesis Music, 1985), 1:509.

62. Radano, *New Musical Figurations,* 128.

63. Evan Parker, untitled article in Lock, *Mixtery,* 183.

64. Graham Lock, "A Vision of Forward Motion: Notes on the Evolution of

Anthony Braxton's Solo Music," in Lock, *Mixtery,* 48–49 (quotations are from Braxton, cited by Lock); Radano, *New Musical Figurations,* 122, 134–136. Radano suggests that Braxton's alternative notation system may have been influenced by modernist concert composers John Cage, Earle Brown, and Morton Feldman.

65.  Radano, *New Musical Figurations,* 189–237; Art Lange, "Implications of a Creative Orchestra," in Lock, *Mixtery,* 125; Anthony Braxton, liner notes for *Creative Orchestra Music 1976,* Arista 4080. Lange and Radano link Braxton's combination of notated score, verbal instructions, and diagrams to the compositions of Cage, Stockhausen, and other concert music composers that allow for interpretation (though not spontaneous improvisation) by players, as well as to the fusion of oral and written instruction in "jazz."

66.  Lange, "Implications of a Creative Orchestra," 130; Bill Shoemaker, "A Wake-Up Call," in Lock, *Mixtery,* 130; Hugo de Craen, "Braxton and Kandinsky: Symbolists of the Spiritual," in Lock, *Mixtery,* 214; Lock, *Blutopia,* 185–209.

67.  Radano, *New Musical Figurations,* 229–231; Lewis, personal correspondence with the author, March 17, 1999. Radano notes that the *Tri-axium Writings* reflect ben-Jochannan's Afrocentric thought; the "mystical beliefs" of Schoenberg, Webern, Varése, and Cage; the romanticism of Stockhausen; and the "mystical writings" of Corinne Heline, Lawrence Blair, and Alice Bailey. George Lewis recalls that Braxton was influenced by the writings of ben-Jochannan, Stockhausen's *Texte I and II,* and the books of Smith, Brown, and Lateef.

68.  This quotation from Braxton's "Catalogue of Works" is cited in Francesco Martinelli, "Toward the Synthesis—Music and Philosophy in Anthony Braxton's Work," in Lock, *Mixtery,* 151.

69.  Braxton quoted in Lock, *Forces in Motion,* 82.

70.  Radano, *New Musical Figurations,* 142, 157–170, 180–183.

71.  Ibid., 186; Peter Niklas Wilson, "Firmly Planted in Mid-Air: Notes on the Syntax and Aesthetics of Anthony Braxton's 'Composition 151,'" in Lock, *Mixtery,* 143–144.

72.  Radano, *New Musical Figurations,* 238–267; Lock, *Forces in Motion,* 82–83; Lock, *Blutopia,* 149–155, 162–163; Lewis, personal correspondence with the author, March 17, 1999.

73.  Nathaniel Mackey and Herman Gray, "Spotlight Yellow: Interview 1979," in Lock, *Mixtery,* 56–69. This interview was conducted in Santa Cruz, California, on October 15, 1979.

74.  Ibid., 57–62. Ted Joans had referred to Braxton as an "Oreo" in a 1975 *Coda* article; see Ted Joans, review of Le Festival Mondial, *Coda,* October 1975, 37. For a discussion of the criticisms of Braxton raised by Joans, Crouch, and Baraka, see Lock, *Blutopia,* 159–162.

75.  Braxton, *Tri-axium Writings,* 1:iv–v.

76.  Braxton's comments from a 1989 *Down Beat* interview are quoted in Martinelli, "Toward the Synthesis," 148–149.

77.  Braxton, *Tri-axium Writings,* 1:36.

78.  Ibid., 1:29.

79. Ibid., 1:44–48, 64–69. Recognizing the potential contradictions in this view, he explains that he is forced to make this distinction so that he can establish a basis by which to examine world creativity.

80. Ibid., 1:70–75, 305–306.

81. Ibid., 1:79, 92–94.

82. This is a central component of Radano's thesis in *New Musical Figurations.*

83. Mackey and Gray, "Spotlight Yellow: Interview 1979," 58. Braxton defines "the grand trade off" in his *Tri-axium Writings:* "Slowly but surely the collected forces of western culture have moved to solidify a view point concerning humanity that has nothing to do with anything but maintaining the present social and political 'state of things.' In this concept, black people are vibrationally viewed as being great tap dancers—natural improvisers, great rhythm, etc., etc., etc.,—but not great thinkers, or not capable of contributing to the dynamic wellspring of world information. White people under this viewpoint have come to be viewed as great thinkers, responsible for all of the profound philosophical and technological achievements that humanity has benefited from—but somehow not as 'natural' as those naturally talented black folks" (1:305).

84. Mackey and Gray, "Spotlight Yellow: Interview 1979," 56; Braxton, *Tri-axium Writings,* 1:124.

85. Braxton, *Tri-axium Writings,* 1:239–282.

86. Ibid., 1:426–427.

87. Steve Lake, "Improvisations (Europe)," in Lock, *Mixtery,* 83; Braxton, *Tri-axium Writings,* 1:455–456.

88. Braxton, *Tri-axium Writings,* 2:181–197, 540–541.

89. Ibid., 3:429–441.

90. Ibid., 3:448–457, 460–468; Heffley, *The Music of Anthony Braxton,* 200–204.

91. John Corbett, "Ism vs. Is," in Lock, *Mixtery,* 198–204.

92. Ibid., 199–202.

## Chapter 7. "The Majesty of the Blues"

1. Wynton Marsalis, "Ellington at 100: Reveling in Life's Majesty," *New York Times,* January 17, 1999, sec. C, 1, 31.

2. Mitchell Seidel, "Wynton Marsalis," *Down Beat,* January 1982, 52–53; Columbia Records press release A, clipping file "Wynton Marsalis," Institute of Jazz Studies, Rutgers University, Newark, New Jersey, 1–2; Leslie Gourse, *Wynton Marsalis: Skain's Domain: A Biography* (New York: Schirmer Books, 1999), 32–60.

3. Ronald Radano, *New Musical Figurations: Anthony Braxton's Cultural Critique* (Chicago: University of Chicago Press, 1996), 238–267; Gary Giddins, "The Young Jazzman of Our Dreams," *Village Voice,* October 16, 1984, 95; John Szwed, "Wynton Marsalis's Burden," *Village Voice,* September 9, 1983, 61.

4. Seidel, "Wynton Marsalis," 53.

5. Ibid., 52–53.

6. James A. Liska, "Common Understanding," *Down Beat,* December 1982, 14–16, 64. This article is an interview with Wynton and Branford Marsalis.

7. Robert S. Boynton, "The Professor of Connection," *New Yorker,* November 6, 1995, 113–116.

8. For a discussion of the friendship and intellectual relationship between Murray and Ellison, see Henry Louis Gates Jr., *Thirteen Ways of Looking at a Black Man* (New York: Random House, 1997), 31–33. See also Jerry Gafio Watts, *Heroism and the Black Intellectual: Ralph Ellison, Politics, and Afro-American Intellectual Life* (Chapel Hill: University of North Carolina Press, 1994). Marsalis himself has often spoken of his intellectual debt to Murray and Crouch. See, for example, Wynton Marsalis and Frank Stewart, *Sweet Swing Blues on the Road* (New York: W. W. Norton, 1994), 116; Gourse, *Wynton Marsalis,* 103–113.

9. Albert Murray, *The Omni-Americans: Some Alternatives to the Folklore of White Supremacy* (New York: Outerbridge and Dienstfrey, 1970; reprint, New York: Da Capo, 1990), 1–7, 22–39; Albert Murray, "The Function of the Heroic Image," in *The Jazz Cadence of American Culture,* ed. Robert G. O'Meally (New York: Columbia University Press, 1998), 569–579. Jerry Watts describes how Murray's response to the construct of "victim status" is to validate the "heroic individualism" of African American culture and intellectual life and place them firmly at the center of American experience (*Heroism and the Black Intellectual,* 16–23).

10. Murray, *The Omni-Americans,* 3, 21, 36–54, 86–96, 142–168, 172–177.

11. Ibid., 18–22, 36–37.

12. Ibid., 55–60.

13. Murray, *Stomping the Blues* (New York: McGraw-Hill, 1976; reprint, New York: Da Capo, 1989), 42, 65–76, 98, 212. See Murray, "The Function of the Heroic Image," 577, for a description of how *Stomping the Blues* represented an attempt to explore the specific details of his metaphor.

14. Murray, *The Omni-Americans,* 53–61.

15. Ralph Ellison, "Blues People," in *Shadow and Act* (New York: Signet Books, 1966), 241–250.

16. Murray, *Stomping the Blues,* 212, 227, 245.

17. Ibid., 214, 224.

18. Stanley Crouch, *Notes of a Hanging Judge* (New York: Oxford University Press, 1990), x–xi; Boynton, "The Professor of Connection," 102–106.

19. Crouch, *Notes of a Hanging Judge,* x–xi; Stanley Crouch, *The All-American Skin Game, or The Decoy of Race* (New York: Pantheon, 1994), x; Boynton, "The Professor of Connection," 110. Boynton points out that Crouch's break from his past was made "complete" in a 1979 *Village Voice* exchange with Baraka, whom he accused of "Dick and Jane black nationalism"; see Stanley Crouch, "King of Constant Repudiation," *Village Voice,* September 3, 1979, 20–21, 33; Amiri Baraka, "What Kind of Crouch Is That?" *Village Voice,* September 3, 1979, 19, 33.

20. Crouch, *Notes of a Hanging Judge,* x–xiii.

21. Boynton, "The Professor of Connection," 116.

22. Stanley Crouch, "Bringing Atlantis Up to the Top," *Village Voice,* April 16, 1979, 65, 67.

23. Ibid., 66–67.

24. Crouch, *The All-American Skin Game,* 180, 185, 191.

25. Stanley Crouch, liner notes for *Black Codes from the Underground,* Columbia 40009.

26. Stanley Crouch, liner notes for *Standard Time, Volume 1,* Columbia 40461, 4.

27. Jane Rubinsky, "Wynton Marsalis: In Defense of Standards," *Keynote: A Magazine for the Musical Arts,* December 1984, 8–12. Although presented as an uninterrupted statement by Marsalis, this piece is an edited transcript from an interview the author conducted with him. An abridged version appeared in *Newsday* (December 30, 1984) under Marsalis's name.

28. Ibid., 9.

29. Ibid., 10.

30. Ibid.

31. Ibid., 10–12.

32. Ibid., 11–12.

33. Wynton Marsalis, "Intimidation and Inspiration," *ASCAP in Action* (Fall 1984): 22–23.

34. Wynton Marsalis, "Why We Must Preserve Our Jazz Heritage," *Ebony,* February 1986, 131. Marsalis cites *The Omni-Americans* and *Stomping the Blues* in his discussion. His intermittent use of the term "Negro" is a rhetorical device that appears to have been adopted from Crouch's use of the term as a rejection of black cultural nationalism and black power politics. Marsalis cites Max Roach as the source for the phrase "Negro methodology of swing."

35. Ibid., 132, 134.

36. Ibid., 131, 132.

37. Ibid., 132, 134.

38. Ibid., 134, 136.

39. Marsalis and Stewart, *Sweet Swing Blues On the Road,* 57, 141–145.

40. Ibid., 58, 90, 95.

41. Ibid., 150–165.

42. For an excellent and more detailed analysis of the politics of Jazz at Lincoln Center, see Herman Gray, "Jazz Tradition, Institutional Formation, and Cultural Practice: The Canon and the Street as Frameworks for Oppositional Black Cultural Politics," in *From Sociology to Cultural Studies: New Perspectives,* ed. Elizabeth Long (New York: Blackwell, 1997), 351–373.

43. Richard B. Woodward, "The Jazz: A Tale of Age, Rage, and Hash Brownies," *Village Voice,* August 9, 1994, 27–34; Susanna L. Miller, "Jazz Swings Uptown," *Down Beat,* April 1991, 12; Gourse, *Wynton Marsalis,* 189–192.

44. Wynton Marsalis, "What Jazz Is—and Isn't," in *Keeping Time: Readings in Jazz History,* ed. Robert Walser (New York: Oxford University Press, 1999), 334–339 (originally published in *New York Times,* July 31, 1988, 21, 24).

45. Miller, "Jazz Swings Uptown"; Frank Alkyer, "Jazz Begins to Get Its Due," *Down Beat,* April 1991, 12; *The New Center of the Jazz Universe,* Jazz at Lincoln Center promotional brochure.

46. Jazz at Lincoln Center press release, undated, clipping file "Wynton Marsalis," Institute of Jazz Studies, Rutgers University, Newark, New Jersey. Marsalis is quoted in Howard Reich, "Wynton's Decade," *Down Beat,* December 1992, 18–20. High school bands apply to the program by submitting taped performances of Ellington compositions arranged by Jazz at Lincoln Center.

47. Woodward, "The Jazz," 27–34; Gourse, *Wynton Marsalis,* 224, 234–235.

48. Stephen Sherrill, "Don Byron," *New York Times Magazine,* January 16, 1994, 21.

49. Kevin Whitehead, "Jazz Rebels," *Down Beat,* August 1993, 17–20. In this interview with Lester Bowie and Greg Osby, Osby basically agrees with Bowie's assessment of Jazz at Lincoln Center.

50. Gene Santoro, "All That Jazz," *The Nation,* January 8 and 15, 1996, 34–36; Peter Watrous, "A Jazz Success Story with a Tinge of the Blues," *New York Times,* September 22, 1998, sec. D, 1, 6; Gourse, *Wynton Marsalis,* ix–xiv. For a list of Jazz at Lincoln Center events during the 1997 to 2000 seasons, see the organization's Web site at *www.jazzatlincolncenter.org.*

51. This economic transition is theorized in David Harvey, *The Condition of Postmodernity: An Enquiry into the Origins of Cultural Change* (Cambridge, Mass.: Blackwell, 1989), 119–197. For a good summary of Harvey's argument, see Jimmie Reeves and Richard Campbell, *Cracked Coverage: Television News, The Anti-Cocaine Crusade, and the Reagan Legacy* (Durham: Duke University Press, 1984), 86–88. For a discussion of how deindustrialization framed African American cultural production in the 1970s, 1980s, and 1990s, see Tricia Rose, *Black Noise: Rap Music and Black Culture in Contemporary America* (Hanover: Wesleyan University Press, 1994), 27–29; Manning Marable, *Race, Reform, and Rebellion: The Second Reconstruction in Black America, 1945–1990,* rev. 2d ed. (Jackson: University Press of Mississippi, 1991), 155–156; and Robin D. G. Kelley, *Race Rebels: Culture, Politics, and the Black Working Class* (New York: Free Press, 1995), 185.

52. Michael Omi and Howard Winant, *Racial Formation in the United States: From the 1960s to the 1990s,* 2d ed. (New York: Routledge, 1994), 113–136; Reeves and Campbell, *Cracked Coverage,* 89–91; Marable, *Race, Reform, and Rebellion,* 190–191.

53. For a discussion of neoliberalism, see Omi and Winant, *Racial Formation,* 145–159.

54. Reeves and Campbell, *Cracked Coverage,* 92–100.

55. Marable, *Race, Reform, and Rebellion,* 159, 185–186; Reeves and Campbell, *Cracked Coverage,* 100–101. Reeves and Campbell base their analysis on Herman Gray, "Television, Black Americans, and the American Dream," *Critical Studies in Mass Communication* 6, no. 4 (December 1989): 376–386.

56. For a demographic portrayal of the jazz audience, see Scott DeVeaux, "Jazz

in America: Who's Listening?" Research Division Report no. 31, National Endowment for the Arts (Carson, Calif.: Seven Locks Press, 1995); excerpted in Walser, *Keeping Time,* 389–395. This NEA report states that in 1992 people earning more than $50,000 a year were twice as likely to attend jazz shows as those earning less than $25,000. African Americans (who constitute about 11 percent of the U.S. population) made up between 16 and 20 percent of the jazz audience.

57. Burton Peretti, *Jazz in American Culture* (Chicago: Ivan R. Dee, 1997), 166–168.

58. Jazz at Lincoln Center press release, June 27, 2000.

59. Wynton Marsalis, letter to the editor, *New York Times Book Review,* December 19, 1993, 31.

60. Andre Craddock-Willis, "Jazz People: Wynton Marsalis vs. James Lincoln Collier," *Transition* 65 (1995): 142.

61. Craddock-Willis, "Jazz People," 144–145. My analysis of the debate is derived from this transcript.

62. Ibid., 143.

63. Ibid., 147, 152, 154.

64. Ibid., 161, 163, 167.

65. Ibid., 162–164, 166, 169.

66. Boynton, "The Professor of Connection," 101.

67. Rose, *Black Noise,* 21.

68. Gates, *Thirteen Ways of Looking at a Black Man,* 34.

69. Albert Murray, *The Blue Devils of Nada: A Contemporary American Approach to Aesthetic Statement* (New York: Random House, 1996), 86.

70. Stanley Crouch, "Simone at the Gate: Loving Me Isn't Enough," *Village Voice,* March 12, 1979, 63–64.

71. See, for example, Greg Robinson, "Crouch and the Ellison Legacy," *Against the Current,* January/February 1997, 46–48.

72. Marable, *Race, Reform, and Rebellion,* 221.

73. Ibid., 190.

74. Rose, *Black Noise,* 130.

75. Kelley, *Race Rebels,* 187; Rose, *Black Noise,* 104. This view, as Rose and Kelley suggest, also elides the sexual and violent imagery that exists in the blues idiom.

76. Playthell Benjamin, "Miles of Heart," *Village Voice,* November 6, 1990, 91–92.

77. Pawel Brodowski, "Coolin' It with Wynton Marsalis," *Jazz Forum* 121 (June 1989): 30.

78. Wynton Marsalis, liner notes for *The Majesty of the Blues,* Columbia 45091; Greg Tate, "Blow on This," *Village Voice,* July 25, 1989, 81.

79. Marsalis adds to the quality of the recorded performance and the album's function as an exploration of the jazz past by expanding his sextet to include musicians who have been mainstays of New Orleans jazz performance. Joining

Marsalis are venerable banjo player and author Danny Barker, trumpeter Teddy Riley, trombonist Freddie Lonzo, and clarinetist Dr. Michael White.

80. Stanley Crouch, "Premature Autopsies," liner notes for *The Majesty of the Blues.*

81. Ibid.

82. Stanley Crouch, "In the Sweet Embrace of Life," liner notes for *In This House, On This Morning,* Columbia 53220, 4–5.

83. Ibid., 6, 9–10.

84. For comments on this composition, see Stanley Crouch, "Whose Blood, Whose Fields?" liner notes for *Blood on the Fields,* Columbia CXK 57694; Larry Birnbaum, "Blood on the Fields," *Down Beat,* September 1997, 45; Zan Stewart, "Blood Brothers," *Down Beat,* May 1997, 26–28.

85. This perspective is also evident in Murray's recent writings on Ellington; see *The Blue Devils of Nada,* 73–113.

86. Wynton Marsalis and Robert G. O'Meally, "Duke Ellington: 'Music Like a Big Hot Pot of Good Gumbo,'" in O'Meally, *The Jazz Cadence of American Culture,* 143–153.

87. Stewart, "Blood Brothers," 26–28; Theodore Rosengarten, "Songs of Slavery Lifted by a Chorus of Horns," *New York Times,* February 23, 1997, 1, 40.

88. Crouch, liner notes for *Blood on the Fields,* 8.

# Index

| | |
|---|---|
| DESIGNER | Nola Burger |
| COMPOSITOR | Integrated Composition Systems |
| TEXT | 11/13.75 Adobe Garamond |
| DISPLAY | Franklin Gothic Book and Demi |
| PRINTER AND BINDER | Edwards Brothers, Inc. |